Forever Orange

(Above) The Hall of Languages (1873) and Holden Observatory (1887) were the first two buildings constructed on the Syracuse University campus, formerly farmland owned by George Comstock. Syracuse University Photograph Collection, University Archives, Special Collections Research Center, Syracuse University Libraries (hereafter referred to as University Archives).

(Facing page) The Hall of Languages on a spring day. © Syracuse University. Photo by Stephen Sartori.

(Following 2 spreads)

The Carrier Dome has hosted the largest on-campus crowds in the history of college basketball. © Syracuse University. Photo by Charles Wainwright.

Syracuse alumna Eileen Collins displays her school pride while piloting the space shuttle Discovery in 1995. Courtesy of NASA.

FOREVER
Orange

THE STORY OF

Syracuse University

SCOTT PITONIAK AND **RICK BURTON**
FOREWORD BY EILEEN M. COLLINS   AFTERWORD BY FLOYD LITTLE

SYRACUSE UNIVERSITY PRESS

Syracuse University Press
Syracuse, New York 13244-5290

First Edition 2019

19 20 21 22 23 24   6 5 4 3 2 1

∞ The paper used in this publication meets the minimum requirements
of the American National Standard for Information Sciences—Permanence
of Paper for Printed Library Materials, ANSI Z39.48-1992.

For a listing of books published and distributed by Syracuse University Press,
visit https://press.syr.edu.

ISBN: 978-0-8156-1144-8 (hardcover)

Library of Congress Cataloging-in-Publication Data
Available from publisher upon request.

Manufactured in Canada

TRIBUTE

The authors wish to acknowledge with respect
the Onondaga Nation, firekeepers of the
Haudenosaunee, the indigenous people on whose
ancestral lands Syracuse University now stands.

*To my beloved family—Andrew, Edna, Beth, Amy,
Christopher, Camryn, and Peyton—and to all the
people at Syracuse University who helped this ink-
stained wretch realize his dreams.*

—S. P.

*To Barb, Hal, Ethel, and all Burtons, Werners,
Moldans, and Webers near and far. For Jumpin',
JB, Coz, Lebeau, Larry, DJB, Roosevelt, Ho, MoS,
Ski, Spider, Shack, and the much-loved Lorraine
Branham. And to the 'Cuse Nation. Keep on rockin'.*

—R. B.

Syracuse University Alma Mater

Where the vale of Onondaga
Meets the eastern sky
Proudly stands our Alma Mater
On her hilltop high.
Flag we love! Orange! Float for aye,
Old Syracuse, o'er thee,
Loyal be thy sons and daughters
To thy memory

—Written in 1893 by Junius Stevens (lyrics revised 1986)

The SU Marching Band performing at an Orange home football game.
© Syracuse University. Photo by Kevin Tomczak.

Slogans on mortar boards are an SU tradition at commencements. © Syracuse University. Photo by Stephen Sartori.

Contents

Foreword

Eileen Collins. Courtesy of NASA.

I had fantasized about becoming a pilot since the time I was a seven-year-old watching gliders soar high above Harris Hill in my hometown of Elmira, New York. And shortly after I started my final semester at Syracuse University in 1978, it appeared that dream was about to come true.

That January, Colonel Vernon Hagan called me into the Reserve Officer Training Corps (ROTC) offices at old Archbold Gymnasium. He had some good news. He told me he had just submitted an application on my behalf to participate in a US Air Force pilots training program that recently had begun accepting women. I was thrilled, though, true to my ROTC training, I kept my emotions in check. He said the first thing I would need to do was take an eye exam at nearby Hancock Field.

I did as instructed, but the test results were not what I expected. It was revealed that I had 20/25 vision in my left eye, and that meant I was disqualified because pilots are required to have 20/20 vision.

I was devastated.

But Colonel Hagan told me not to panic. He said I should retake the eye exam in two weeks. In the meantime, he suggested I get plenty of rest and cut back on my reading. Not only did I follow his orders, you might say I went above and beyond. From the time I was a little girl, my parents had told me to eat my carrots because they're good for your eyes. I didn't know if that was true or not, but I was going to do everything humanly possible to make sure I passed that exam the second time around. During those two weeks, I ate more carrots than Bugs Bunny. I swear on a stack of Bibles, I ate so many carrots my fingertips actually turned orange, which was apropos, given that was SU's official color.

Well, when I retook the exam, my vision wound up being 20/20 in both eyes. Four months later, I was one of eight female college graduates nationwide accepted into the training program. To this day, I still wonder if it was the carrots or if Colonel Hagan had picked up the phone on my behalf and said: "Give this person a break and you won't be disappointed."

I wouldn't be surprised if he had, because even before I arrived on the Syracuse campus from Corning Community College two years prior, people had greeted me with open arms and seemed intent on helping me realize my dreams and aspirations. The lessons I learned at SU—of discipline, personal responsibility, sacrifice, teamwork, and leadership—have served me well throughout my career and life. That is why when I became the first woman to pilot a space shuttle for NASA in 1995, I unfurled an orange Syracuse University pennant in the cockpit for all the world to see. It was my subtle way of saying thank you for all that my alma mater had done for me.

In retrospect, I have so much appreciation for SU—and so many fond memories. I couldn't have asked for better professors, particularly in my Air Force ROTC program, where I studied under Colonel Hagan, Captain Gene Freid, Major Mike Lythgoe, and Captain Jim O'Rourke. They were impressive people with disparate personalities and approaches. That I still remember their names and the courses they taught is a testament to their lasting impact.

Like many students who leave home for the first time, I struggled at first. The academics were rigorous. I was majoring in mathematics and economics, taking nineteen credit hours per semester, which included some out-of-class ROTC obligations. I remember taking the bus back home to Elmira on the weekends my first month at SU. But I got over any homesickness I might have had, and as I adjusted to my new environment, it wasn't long before Syracuse felt like home.

I'll never forget the girls I lived with on the eighth floor of Lawrinson Hall my first semester. The majority of them were art majors. I think there might have been only three of us who weren't—myself, a psych major, and a gal from India who was an engineering student. That we were from different places, pursuing different things was intriguing. It was a fun bunch, and a welcoming bunch. I remember how the door to our resident advisor's room was always open. It seemed like every time I walked by, she'd be saying, "Come in, Eileen, and hang out with us."

Despite my demanding schedule, I managed to have fun. I was a huge sports nut growing up, and I loved attending basketball games in rowdy Manley Field House and football games in old Archbold Stadium. Our football team wasn't great at the time, and the weather could be bitter cold and wet, but we didn't care. I usually stayed right till the end. There were other social events, too. I recall one time dancing the night away to Beatles music. It was all good, clean fun.

I remember eating slices of pizza at the Varsity and Whoppers at the old Burger King on M Street. I even "piloted" a bed on wheels with my ROTC classmates on the Quad one spring. It was part of an annual "bed race" that SU students staged to raise money for the Muscular Dystrophy Association.

During my senior year, I would have another "piloting" experience that would leave an indelible impression when I flew a C-130 four-engine turboprop military transport plane from Hancock to Patrick Air Force Base on the east coast of Florida. I vividly remember swimming in the ocean at night with my ROTC classmates during that trip. While splashing about, it wasn't lost on me that Patrick was next door to Cape Canaveral and the Kennedy Space Center, where the NASA rocket launches took place. I had this feeling that I was inching closer to my dream of becoming not only a pilot but also an astronaut.

I've been able to return to campus numerous times through the years, and it always conjures warm memories. Each time I'm back, I try to stop by Lawrinson and the old ROTC offices—though I'll have to go to the new ROTC offices next time because the old ones were razed to make way for the new Arch where Archbold Gymnasium once stood. I've never been comfortable calling attention to myself, but I was flattered beyond belief when my alma mater presented me with an Arents Award and an honorary degree.

I was back several years ago to present a student with one of NASA's Astronaut Scholarships. I am proud to be a part of SU's strong connection with the space program—a connection that includes alums such as fellow astronaut F. Story Musgrave, who preceded me on shuttle missions, and former NASA Administrator Sean O'Keefe, who chose me to command the 2005 mission, which launched just two years after the Columbia tragedy. Each time I speak with Sean, we reminisce about our alma mater. Our bonds with SU are strong.

When it was time for my children to choose the college they were going to attend, I told them it would be one of the most important decisions they would ever make because you'll always be associated with your school. It will always be on your resume. Your grades won't. But your school will.

I'll always be associated with Syracuse University, and I couldn't be more proud of that. In retrospect, my dreams truly did take flight there.

As you turn these pages and read about the extraordinary people, events, programs, and places that have made SU an internationally respected university, I think you'll gain a greater understanding and appreciation for why many of us are Forever Orange.

EILEEN M. COLLINS
Class of 1978

Preface

Chancellor Kent Syverud and wife Dr. Ruth Chen are surrounded by SU students during a university event. © Syracuse University. Photo by Stephen Sartori.

Thousands of amazing stories make up the 150 years of Syracuse University history. I am grateful that this sesquicentennial volume captures so many of the stories that make our university wonderful and unique. I thank authors Scott Pitoniak and Rick Burton, the many contributors, and Syracuse University Press for celebrating our milestone anniversary with this book.

As you will see in the pages that follow, Syracuse University and the Syracuse community—in our home city, in our region, and around the world—have grown together. Our university and community nourish and interact and change each other every day, almost always to our mutual benefit. After 150 years of symbiosis between our university and community, few can doubt that in the future we will need to thrive together.

The values of Syracuse University are interlaced through all the stories in this book. We are a university that has not always lived up to its values, but has sure worked to be a distinct leader almost all of the time, and has inspired much more often than it has fallen short.

For 150 years, being Orange has meant being inclusive, competing hard and aiming high, and frequently taking a chance on scrappy people who in turn make the most of an incredible array of academic, athletic, social, and service opportunities. Our people come from everywhere, go everywhere, and seem to do almost everything worthwhile.

I am so proud they are Orange.

Sincerely,
KENT SYVERUD
Twelfth Chancellor and President

A Word from the Authors

Authors Scott Pitoniak and Rick Burton with fellow Newhouse alum Mike Tirico (center). © Syracuse University. Photo by Stephen Sartori.

Perhaps subconsciously we were inspired by artist Ben Shahn's enormous mosaic of Sacco and Vanzetti on the exterior wall of Huntington Beard Crouse Hall, just north of the Quad on Syracuse University's main campus. We hoped that by piecing together thousands of compelling stories and images we could convey a broader perspective of an amazing place that continues to shape and form us decades after our undergraduate days at SU.

So this is our mosaic, if you will.

A vast array held together by mortar and memories.

Our fervent hope is that when you absorb the words and images on these pages, the bigger picture will come into focus and you'll better understand and appreciate the people, events, and buildings that have made this university on a hill internationally renowned; you'll see how Syracuse has molded those who have studied, taught, and played there.

Being *Forever Orange* is more than a title of a book or some catchy marketing slogan. It truly is a state of mind, a tie that binds.

It is studying under revered professors such as Michael Sawyer, Sarah Short, Charles Willie, and Marvin Druger.

It is slices of pizza at the Varsity, toasted honey buns at Cosmos, beers on the M Street Beach, and graffiti-scrawled messages and poems on the walls of Hungry Charley's.

It is momentous research that helped prove Einstein's theories, resulted in the first artificial heart, and created literacy programs that taught the world how to read.

It is the spooky-looking Hall of Languages, majestic Crouse College standing sentinel on the Hill, little Holden Observatory gazing at the heavens, boxy Bird Library, the modernistic Newhouse School complex, twenty-one-story Lawrinson Hall, and the UFO-like Carrier Dome.

It is the chimes ringing out from the Crouse bell tower, the Pride of the Orange marching band playing the "Down the Field" fight song, and Bruce Springsteen, the Rolling Stones, and Drake concerts in the Dome.

It is being true to the founding father's vision of welcoming all people, and building on the tradition of being one of the first universities in the nation to admit women and confer degrees on African Americans, international students, and Native Americans.

It is coming together in Archbold Stadium, Manley Field House, and the Dome to cheer on national championship teams in football, basketball, lacrosse, and field hockey.

It is being one of the best colleges in America for veterans of the armed forces, another long-standing tradition dating back to World War I.

It is reaching-for-the-stars alumni, such as astronauts Eileen Collins and F. Story Musgrave.

It is being captivated by the written words of George Saunders, Joyce Carol Oates, Mike McAlary, and Julia Alvarez—and the spoken words of Frank Langella, Taye Diggs, Peter Falk, and Vanessa Williams.

It is seeing US presidents Franklin Delano Roosevelt, Harry Truman, John F. Kennedy, and Bill Clinton visit campus.

It is trudging across the snowy, icy Quad while the wind painfully pierces several layers of protective clothing. And it is tossing Frisbees and footballs in shorts and bare feet on the emerald green Quad on those early fall and late spring days when the sun makes brilliant, spirit-boosting appearances.

It is Vita the Goat, the Saltine Warrior, and current mascot Otto the Orange.

It is listening to civil rights leader Martin Luther King Jr. "trying out" two of his most famous speeches, and President Lyndon Baines Johnson delivering his infamous Gulf of Tonkin address that led to the escalation of the Vietnam War.

It is hearing sportscasters Marty Glickman, Bob Costas, Mike Tirico, and Beth Mowins describe the action.

It is knowing that US vice president Joe Biden went to law school here.

It is reading the *Daily Orange* and listening to news and sports on WAER and jazz on WJPZ.

It is Belva Lockwood becoming the first woman to argue cases before the Supreme Court, Ernie Davis becoming the first African American to win college football's coveted Heisman Trophy, and Vanessa Williams becoming the first black woman to be crowned Miss America.

It is all of this—and so much more.

When we broached the idea for this project three years ago, we did so enthusiastically, but also with some trepidation. We knew this book would be a labor of love, but also an impossible mission.

Our lives, like thousands of others, were profoundly changed for the better at SU. So this endeavor would be, on many levels, personal. But as historians, we were equally intent on telling a truthful story. Which means you will read about and see the warts and imperfections, and how the university reacted to them—not always in a timely or just manner. Many of the people we've featured have flaws, which we've noted. In other words, they are human.

The mission was impossible because, quite frankly, this private university that began with classes in rented office space in downtown Syracuse in 1871 has produced a disproportionate number of compelling, and, in some cases, world-changing people. Space and time constraints prevented us from including every relevant story and image. We tried our best, knowing full well there probably would be deserving people and moments that aren't in the book, but should have been. We apologize in advance and take sole responsibility for any errors of omission or fact.

Again, the goal was to create a mosaic. Each tile in Shahn's twelve-by-sixty-foot masterpiece—which many of us have walked past thousands of times—conveys the level of detail involved. And when you stand back and observe the entire mural, you notice how they work in harmony to tell the powerful story of Nicola Sacco and Bartolomeo Vanzetti, two Italian American immigrants who were executed for a crime many believed they did not commit.

We write about that work of art in this book, and how the mural was inspired by one of the most politically charged cases in the history of American jurisprudence. It is merely one tile, one tale, among hundreds that we offer.

We hope these stories and images help you understand and appreciate what a remarkable and continually evolving place this is—and what it means to be *Forever Orange*.

Cheers,
SCOTT PITONIAK AND RICK BURTON

Forever Orange

1

"Where the Vale of Onondaga..."

Syracuse University founding father, Bishop Jesse Truesdell Peck. Syracuse University Portrait Collection, University Archives.

A fresh blanket of snow greeted the clergymen and parishioners from Methodist churches throughout New York State as they filed into Shakespeare Hall in downtown Syracuse on February 22, 1870. There, in an auditorium named after the Bard, the conventioneers would determine whether Syracuse University was to be or not to be.

They desired to launch "a great Methodist University" and originally had hoped Genesee College in Lima, New York, just south of Rochester, would relocate to a more populous, on-the-beaten-path upstate city, with train stops such as Syracuse, Buffalo, Rome, and Utica all receiving consideration. But that grand plan was in limbo after angry Lima residents were granted a court injunction blocking the departure of their financially struggling college.

Church leaders decided to move on, and Syracusans were more than willing to accommodate them. The Salt City had much to offer, including a burgeoning manufacturing economy, a booming population, and the three tenets of modern real estate: location, location, location. Situated in the center of upstate New York on fertile and sacred land where Hiawatha, the chief of the Iroquois Confederacy, once trod, Syracuse had prospered enormously from the westward migration of immigrants and businesses ignited by the construction of the Erie Canal and the proliferation of railroads, which had dramatically reduced the time it took to transport people and goods.

Lobbying in the packed hall would prove unnecessary. When it came time to address what the agenda listed as "the college problem," convention-goers overwhelmingly passed the resolution to build a university in Syracuse. City officials offered to kick in $100,000 of seed money. The delegates would have to come up with an additional $400,000 to fund the endowment.

Bishop Jesse Truesdell Peck was eager to strike while the iron was hot. Blessed with a stentorian voice capable of filling a room in those pre-public-address-system days, the minister stepped to the podium and decided the fundraising should commence then and there.

"Talk will not build a college," boomed Peck. "But money will."

Putting his cash where his mouth was, he offered up his and his wife's life savings of $25,000. This kick-started a funding frenzy, and before long enough money was raised to give birth to a university that over time would become world-renowned. Syracuse residents were ecstatic. One of the city's finer cigar makers even made a special stogie and called it the "University."

Peck would be chosen the first president of the board of trustees, and more than anyone would deserve the title of "founding father."

On March 24, 1870—just five years after the end of the Civil War—Syracuse University was officially chartered as a private, coeducational institution of higher learning, offering programs in the physical sciences, modern languages, and Christian studies. Tuition was established at twenty dollars per term, forty dollars per year.

The university's DNA can be traced to the same year DNA was discovered—a year in which Ulysses S. Grant was president of the United States; railway cars traveled coast to coast for the first time; Frederick August Otto Schwarz opened a famous toy store in New York City; novelist Mark Twain worked as a newspaper editor and columnist in Buffalo; the Brooklyn Atlantics snapped the Cincinnati Red Stockings's ninety-two-game professional baseball win streak; and the Fifteenth Amendment to the Constitution was ratified, ensuring the voting rights of all adult males, including many African Americans who just a few years earlier had been slaves.

Against this backdrop of dramatic change, Peck suggested the purchase of fifty acres of farmland from Judge George Comstock on a bluff that became known as Piety Hill in southeastern Syracuse. At his inauguration, Peck seemed inspired by the women's suffragist movement, which had its roots in nearby Seneca Falls, and the abolition of slavery brought about by the War between the States. Peck

Mary Lydia Huntley, Syracuse University's first female graduate. Syracuse University Portrait Collection, University Archives.

stressed the importance of diversity and inclusion, though he didn't use those twenty-first-century buzzwords. He said there would be no discrimination toward women or "persons of any nation or color. The conditions of admission shall be equal to all persons. There shall be no invidious discrimination here . . . brains and heart shall have a fair chance."

As a result of his vision, SU became the first coeducational college in New York State. And it would confer undergraduate, graduate, and medical degrees on African Americans and international students within its first few decades of existence.

WHEN CLASSES BEGAN at SU's temporary campus on the upper floors of the Myers Block building on the corner of Montgomery and East Genesee Streets in downtown Syracuse on September 17, 1871, seven of the forty-one students were women. One of the members of its pioneering classes—Mary Lydia Huntley—would become the first woman to earn undergraduate and graduate degrees from SU, and go on to enjoy a long teaching career. Huntley's classmate Belva Lockwood earned her master's degree in 1872. A contemporary of suffragists Susan B. Anthony and Elizabeth Cady Stanton, Lockwood would become the first woman to run a full campaign for the presidency of the United States and receive votes. She also would become the first woman to argue a case before the US Supreme Court.

A year after Lockwood graduated from SU, Alexander Winchell, a noted geologist who boasted that all the rocks in Michigan knew him, left the Wolverine state to become SU's first chancellor.

The Myers Block Building in downtown Syracuse was SU's first home. Syracuse University Photograph Collection, University Archives.

An early-twentieth-century postcard of Syracuse University's "old row" of buildings. Syracuse University Postcard Collection, University Archives.

Around this time, the university adopted the Latin academic motto *Suos cultores scientia coronat*—which translates as "knowledge crowns those who seek her." It is not known whose idea it was, but it soon became a part of SU's official laurel-wreath seal and continues to be used today.

The university's ambitious early curriculum included the nation's first degree-conferring college of fine arts, as well as one of the first architectural programs and a medical school, which had relocated from nearby Geneva. In 1876, Sarah Loguen Fraser became the first woman and African American to receive a medical degree from SU, and is believed to be the fourth black woman in US history licensed to practice medicine.

Greek life would become part of the student experience in 1871 as the local chapter of the Mystical Seven evolved into the school's first fraternity, Delta Kappa Epsilon. The next year, the first sorority—Alpha Phi—would open on University Avenue. Initially, sororities were called "women's fraternities." The word *sorority* was introduced into the English language in 1874 by Frank Smalley, an advisor to SU's newly born Gamma Phi Beta Society. He felt the word *fraternity* was unbecoming to young ladies, so he suggested using *sorority*, whose root, *soror*, was Latin for sister.

Around this time, SU's first student newspaper, the *University Herald*, began publication. It would be one of five forerunners to the *Daily Orange*, which printed its first issue on September 15, 1903, and continues to be the main student paper today, with both print and digital editions.

IN 1873, the Hall of Languages became the first building on the new campus. Constructed from Onondaga limestone for $136,000, it would stand alone for fourteen years, surrounded by hay fields, whose modest crop was used to defray some of SU's expenses.

Today, the Hall of Languages is one of more than a dozen buildings on campus listed on the National Register of Historic Places. But there was a time not long after its opening when some wondered if it would become a symbol of failure rather than success.

Despite promising beginnings, the university found itself in dire straits just eleven years after its founding. Winchell reportedly was too busy with science to worry about finances. His successor, Erastus O. Haven, resigned after six years with an unfinished building program, unpaid debts, and no endowment. Before leaving office, Haven gloomily advised successor Charles Sims: "You cannot save the university. It must go."

Fortunately for the millions of students who wound up matriculating at SU in the ensuing decades, Sims opted not to heed his advice. Instead, he rolled up his sleeves and devoted his entire being to fundraising. By the time he left in 1894, the university was on firmer financial ground and had grown to 955 students, sixty faculty members, and five buildings, including two iconic edifices: Holden Observatory, constructed in 1887, and Crouse College, erected in

SU's third chancellor, Charles Sims. Syracuse University Portrait Collection, University Archives.

Crouse College. *SU Alumni News*. Syracuse University Alumni Reference Collection, University Archives.

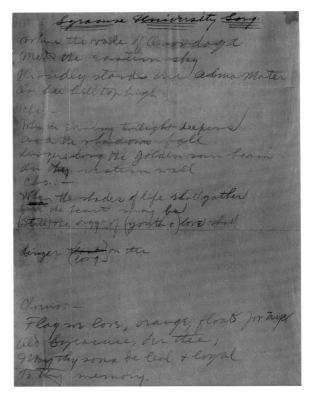

The original text for Syracuse University's alma mater. Syracuse University Student Activities Music Collection, University Archives.

1889. Benefactor John Crouse also would donate chimes for the bell tower of the building bearing his name, and a musical tradition began where students known as Chimesmasters climb ladders and play everything from the alma mater to contemporary tunes for all the university to hear. It's a tradition that continues today.

On March 15, 1893, another tradition began when the Glee and Banjo Club performed the "Song of Syracuse" at a downtown opera house. Written by junior Junius Stevens, it immediately struck a chord with students and eventually became the university's official alma mater. Stevens said the opening lines—"Where the vale of Onondaga meets the eastern sky, proudly stands our alma mater, on a hilltop high"—came to him one day while he was walking back to campus from downtown Syracuse. "I had often noticed how the setting sun lighted up the walls of Crouse College long after dusk had fallen over the city and valley," he recalled. "As I walked through the empty streets, the words of a song took shape in my mind. By the time I reached home, the song was finished."

The year 1893 also would witness the initiation of a dress code in which all freshmen were required to wear an orange or green beanie for their first semester to distinguish them from upperclassmen. They were required to tip those lids if asked to by a sophomore, junior, or senior. Though the "Tip it, Frosh!" ritual could be demeaning at times, it did help freshmen identify with each other and build class camaraderie. A group of students known as the Goon Squad enforced the wearing of the beanies, with frequent violators often publicly humiliated at the annual Penn State football game pep rally. By the end of the 1960s, the beanie tradition had gone the way of the *Tyrannosaurus rex*. Goon Squad members went from being punishers to greeters, helping freshmen move into their dorm rooms when they first arrived on campus.

SYRACUSE FIELDED its first football team four years before the first beanie fashion statement was made. The gridders got off to an ignominious start with a 36-0 thrashing at the hands of the University of Rochester. Things would get better the next season, as they hired their first coach—Bobby Winston—and avenged the loss to their upstate rivals while compiling a 7-4 won-lost record. The Old Oval, located on the site of the present-day Quad, would serve as the school's first athletic field, hosting everything from baseball and football games to track-and-field events.

The Old Oval, present-day site of the Quad. Syracuse University Photograph Collection, University Archives.

Syracuse University's first football team in front of the Hall of Languages. Athletics Department, Syracuse University, used by permission.

An illustration of a nineteenth-century Syracuse football player. Athletics Department, Syracuse University, used by permission.

Another tradition would begin that same year, as orange was adopted as the school's official color after students grew tired of being ridiculed for their teams' "pink and pea green" athletic uniforms. Future generations of SU fans would be spared from chanting, "Let's Go Pink!" Over time, their sports teams became known as the Orangemen, a nickname that would stick until it was shortened officially to the gender-neutral Orange in 2004.

Student activism—a recurring theme throughout SU's history—would lead to the construction of a modern gymnasium in 1891 on the site where Hendricks Chapel now stands. The original gym was a crammed, converted storehouse behind the Hall of Languages. After several years of unsuccessfully lobbying the administration for a new home for physical education, thirteen students took matters into their own hands by burning down the transformed storehouse. The arsonists were temporarily suspended, but they had made their point, and the administration scrounged up funds to make the new gym a reality.

In the spring before the gymnasium's opening, a pint-sized catcher named Stephen Crane arrived on campus, more interested in wielding a baseball bat than a pen. Obsessed with America's burgeoning national pastime rather than his classes, Crane would spend just one semester at SU, but his experiences there may have provided

A graduating class from 1876. Syracuse University Photograph Collection, University Archives.

Stephen Crane and the 1891 Syracuse University baseball team. Stephen Crane Collection Photographs, Special Collections Research Center, Syracuse University Libraries.

fodder for *The Red Badge of Courage*, the seminal novel about the inhumanities of the Civil War that he wrote three years later. Crane would be the first in a long line of creative writers to attend Syracuse, with literary luminaries Joyce Carol Oates, Shirley Jackson, Alice Sebold, George Saunders, William Safire, Mike McAlary, Julia Alvarez, and Nana Kwame Adjei-Brenyah among those following his lead.

THE UNIVERSITY'S financial fortunes would take a turn for the better when Reverend James Roscoe Day was hired as chancellor in 1893. The six-foot-three, 250-pound Day was an imposing presence and a mesmerizing orator. When he spoke, people listened. "I see in my mind's eye a great university on the Hill," he said in one of his inimitable chapel talks. "Instead of three colleges, I see a dozen colleges. Instead of several buildings, I see a score of buildings. Instead of a student body of eight hundred, I see a student body of eight thousand, and this University as the center of the educational system of the state of New York."

Most of what he envisioned came true, as SU experienced unprecedented growth during Day's twenty-eight years on the job—expanding from five to twenty-four buildings, with enrollment increasing more than sevenfold to 6,422 students. His building blitz would include construction of the first dormitories—the all-female Winchell and Haven Halls—and the opening of the College of Law in 1895 and the teachers college (now the School of Education) in 1906. Day's commitment to diversity was further underscored in 1903 when William Herbert Johnson became the first African American and Bessie Seeley became the first woman to receive law degrees from SU.

Eight years before Day's inauguration, Professor Charles Wesley Bennett convinced the university to purchase the voluminous library of world-famous German historian Leopold von Ranke. It was a tremendous "get," greatly enhancing SU's stature as one of the nation's top institutions of higher learning. The massive collection originally was housed in the present-day Tolley Humanities Building between the Hall of Languages and Crouse College. But the building quickly became too small to accommodate von Ranke's library and the thousands of books that were being added annually. The space constraints prompted Day to court philanthropist Andrew Carnegie, who donated $150,000 for the construction of a new library that was completed in 1907. It would be the university's primary book repository until Bird Library opened sixty-five years later.

Reverend James Roscoe Day, SU's fourth chancellor. Syracuse University Portrait Collection, University Archives.

Major donor John D. Archbold overlooking the newly opened Archbold Stadium.
Syracuse University Portrait Collection, University Archives.

During Day's tenure, the school on the Hill would make a dramatic transformation from a small liberal arts college into a major comprehensive university, as more resources were devoted not only to bricks and mortar but also to expanding curriculum, especially in engineering and the sciences.

None of it would have been possible without the generosity of several deep-pocketed benefactors, most notably Day's good friend, John Dustin Archbold. A confidant of the Rockefeller family, Archbold would go on to run Standard Oil Company, at the time one of the richest business enterprises in the world.

Though he did not attend SU, it became a special place for Archbold because of the Christian connection. He began donating money to the school as early as 1871, when he contributed to the construction of the Hall of Languages, which would be one of several buildings on campus to bear his name. (To this day, you can see the words "John Dustin Archbold College of Liberal Arts" carved into the limestone above the main entrance to the building.) Day had been pastor of the Methodist church that Archbold regularly attended in New York City, and the two men formed a close friendship. When the chancellor's position became available in 1893, Archbold hinted to SU's trustees that he would become even more generous if they hired Day.

Archbold became best known for contributing $600,000—at the time the largest individual gift ever made to a university—for the construction of Archbold Stadium, a concrete bowl, which not long after its completion in 1907 was being called "the greatest athletic arena in America." But his reach extended well beyond the stadium, which was designed to resemble the amphitheaters of ancient Greece and the Roman Colosseum. He wrote checks to keep the university afloat during turbulent financial times and later funded the building of Peck, Sims, and Steele Halls and Archbold Gymnasium. He also paid for the acquisition of the Walnut Avenue residence where nine chancellors, including current chancellor Kent Syverud, have resided. If Peck is regarded as the father of Syracuse University and Day its visionary, then Archbold might very well be considered its savior.

Archbold Stadium as depicted on an early postcard. Syracuse University Photograph Collection, University Archives.

Halley's Comet as photographed from Holden Observatory in 1910. Syracuse University Photograph Collection, University Archives.

ATHLETICS WOULD FLOURISH during this era. In 1898, the first season of women's basketball would tip off with games between juniors and seniors as well as city teams and other colleges, including Cornell University, Elmira, and Barnard. The following year, the SU men would field their first hoops team. The Orangemen started inauspiciously with losses in the two games they played that year, but they would experience their first of several golden eras after hiring Eddie Dollard as their first full-time coach in 1911. Dollard would lead the Orangemen to a 132-34 record and their first national championship during his eleven seasons.

Under future College Football Hall of Fame coach Frank O'Neill, Syracuse went 9-1-2 on the gridiron in 1915 and received an invitation to play in the Rose Bowl in Pasadena, California—a big deal because, unlike today when there are nearly fifty postseason football games, back then there was only one. Unfortunately,

the SU athletic budget had been depleted by a West Coast train trip that included an upset of Nebraska, and Day declined the invite.

Two years later, SU forestry professor Laurie Cox would start the school's lacrosse program, leading the Orangemen to their first national title in 1920. The success he enjoyed would prompt sportswriters and historians to refer to him as the father of college lacrosse. The crew team—known as the Syracuse Navy under James Ten Eyck—also would capture national championships while rowing on nearby Onondaga Lake, which wound up hosting numerous intercollegiate regattas.

OVER TIME, SU's Methodist roots began to restrict its growth as the Carnegie Foundation and the New York State legislature became increasingly reluctant to give money to a church-affiliated institution. While seeking funds for the construction of a state forestry school and scholarship aid at SU, Louis Marshall (for whom Marshall Street is named) argued that the Methodist Church had little influence over the college. He pointed to himself as living proof of that, citing his Jewish heritage and position on the board of trustees. Marshall also emphasized that the faculty and student body included people of several religions. In 1920, SU's board voted to change its charter, weakening its ties to Methodism, which opened the way for increased state aid.

Day also would guide the university through two wars—the Spanish-American conflict in 1898 and World War I (1917-19). Like other institutions of higher learning, SU gave the male students who had been drafted a rousing send-off. On campus, roughly one thousand men, including future chancellor William Pearson Tolley, received training as members of the Student Army Training Corps (SATC). The program would be the start of a long-standing relationship between SU and the armed forces, which remains strong today through the recently constructed National Veterans

1895 SU women's basketball team. Onondagans Reference Collection, University Archives.

Vita the Goat was one of Syracuse's earliest mascots. Syracuse University Photograph Collection, University Archives.

Smith Hall, longtime home of the College of Engineering. Syracuse University Photograph Collection, University Archives.

Resource Center on the block between the Newhouse School of Public Communications and Marshall Street. Eighty-one students and alumni died in World War I, including thirteen SATC members who fell victim to the flu epidemic of 1918-19.

One of the war's heroes was SU alumnus William Shemin, who risked his own life rescuing three wounded comrades during a skirmish in northern France. The explosion of a German grenade embedded shrapnel in his back, perilously close to his spine. And a stray bullet grazed his helmet and caused him to go deaf in one ear. In 2015, the extent of his heroism was finally recognized when he was awarded the Medal of Honor posthumously by President Barack Obama.

Following the World War I armistice in November 1918, SU became the first school to institute an on-campus Reserve Officer Training Corps (ROTC). The program, which prepares officers for the Army and Air Force, remains one of the most respected in the nation.

Sergeant William Shemin
MEDAL OF HONOR
WORLD WAR I

World War I Medal of Honor winner William Shemin. Institute for Veterans and Military Families, Syracuse University, used by permission.

THE QUALITY OF STUDENT LIFE changed dramatically under Day, with the number of fraternities and sororities skyrocketing from ten to twenty-five during his chancellorship. There were times when he feared students were straying too far from the school's core values and he attempted to curb what he described as the "passions of youth" by enforcing stricter rush rules and curfews. By most accounts, he was only mildly successful. In 1921, he actually banned dancing for the final weeks of the semester, informing students: "We are close upon examinations and have no time to dance."

That same year, the campus would be rocked by a bizarre tragedy when J. Herman Wharton, the dean of the business school, was shot nine times and killed by Professor Holmes Beckwith, whom Wharton had recently fired. Beckwith would subsequently kill himself.

Day would retire the following year, leaving successor Charles Wesley Flint to guide SU through the peaks of the Roaring Twenties and the depths of the Great Depression. A former president of Cornell College in Iowa, Flint inherited a university that had expanded beyond its wildest expectations, but also one that was operating at a deficit because it had grown too fast. He deftly managed to get the college's finances back in the black by increasing enrollment and adding several academic programs—no small feat, considering the formidable challenges wrought by Wall Street's infamous crash in 1929. The effects of the Depression would be felt, as faculty members agreed to a 10 percent salary reduction and the College of Agriculture closed.

Under Flint's leadership, SU opened a journalism school, which was housed in the now-defunct Yates Castle; the Maxwell School of Citizenship and Public Affairs, thanks to a $500,000 gift from 1888 alumnus George Maxwell; and the school of forestry,

SU's Boar's Head Dramatic Society operated from 1904 to 1972, producing more than two hundred plays. J. Herman Wharton Papers, University Archives.

Orange sprinter Marty Glickman hands the baton to Ohio State's Jesse Owens during warmups for the 1936 Summer Olympic Games in Berlin. PA Images Archive / Getty Images.

which came to be after Marshall's successful lobbying yielded a large grant from New York governor Franklin Delano Roosevelt. FDR had developed close ties with the university, speaking at SU's commencement in 1930, and returning six years later as president of the United States to lay the cornerstone for a building that would house the medical school.

Flint also ensured the completion of Hendricks Chapel on June 8, 1930. A decade earlier, late Syracuse mayor and New York State senator Francis J. Hendricks bequeathed a half million dollars for a chapel to be constructed on campus in memory of his late wife, Eliza Jane. Matching money was hard to come by, and construction on the distinctive 1,450-seat chapel didn't begin until 1929.

Radio's popularity was beginning to soar during this era, and thanks to Professor Kenneth Bartlett, Syracuse would become a pioneering university in the field of broadcasting, airing programs as early as 1931. Years later, this would result in the start of student radio station WAER—whose call letters stood for Always Excellent Radio. It would become a breeding ground for nationally known broadcasters, including Dick Clark, Ted Koppel, Bob Costas, and Steve Kroft.

Initially, the radio major was part of the School of Public Speech and Dramatic Art, which also oversaw the nationally respected Tambourine and Bones musical group and the Boar's Head Dramatic Society. Legendary professor Sawyer Falk was a driving force behind both programs. He also helped form Syracuse Stage, enhancing a drama department that would launch the careers of iconic performers Sheldon Leonard, Peter Falk, Jerry Stiller, Frank Langella, Vanessa Williams, and Taye Diggs.

THE UNIVERSITY was still dealing with the Great Depression and growing concerns about the expansion of Nazi power in Germany and beyond when William Pratt Graham became the first alumnus to be named chancellor in 1936. He had received his liberal arts degree forty-seven years earlier and would lead the university until 1942.

President Franklin D. Roosevelt lays the cornerstone for Syracuse University's medical school in 1936. To his left is acting Chancellor William Graham. Syracuse University Photograph Collection, University Archives.

The year Graham took office, Orange sprinter Marty Glickman sailed across the Atlantic to Berlin for the Summer Olympics. A contemporary of four-time gold medalist Jesse Owens, Glickman was scheduled to run a leg on the US 4-by-100-yard relay team. But just before the race, officials from the US Olympic Committee kowtowed to anti-Semitic demands by German chancellor Adolf Hitler that Glickman, a Jew, not compete. Infuriated and devastated by the loss of an opportunity that almost certainly would have resulted in a gold medal, Glickman returned to Syracuse, where he would continue to stand out as a sprinter and football player. By accident, his gridiron heroics led to his own campus radio show, launching a brilliant broadcasting career that would inspire the likes of Marv Albert, Dick Stockton, Beth Mowins, Sean McDonough, Mike Tirico, Bob Costas, and scores of others to attend SU and help forge its reputation as "Sportscaster U."

Glickman and his football teammates would experience firsthand the fervor of Syracuse's bitter rivalry with nearby Colgate University—a rivalry that included a "Hoodoo" hex purportedly placed on the Orange by Red Raiders fans, and plenty of hijinks between students of both schools. The night before one of the games, three Syracusans rented a plane and flew over the Colgate campus

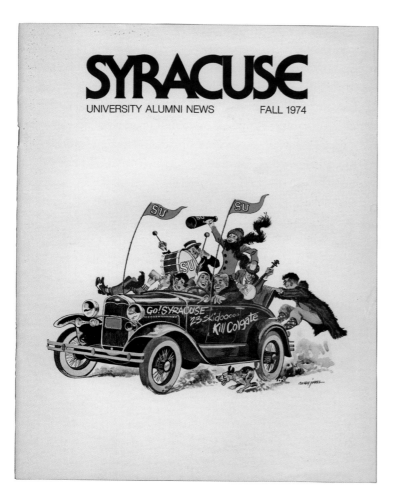

One of Syracuse's fiercest athletic rivalries was the football series against Colgate. *SU Alumni News*. Syracuse University Alumni Reference Collection, University Archives.

dropping pamphlets forecasting an SU victory and pouring bags of orange dye into Taylor Lake. At virtually the same time, a group of Colgate students scaled the gate at Archbold Stadium and, using gasoline, burned a huge C near the middle of the field.

One of the most memorable games in the rivalry occurred in 1938, when Phil Allen scored on an end around for the only touchdown in a victory that snapped Colgate's thirteen-game unbeaten streak. When the final gun sounded, the chimes of Crouse College could be heard miles away as thousands of delirious SU fans tore down the goal posts before forming a conga line and dancing down the Hill to downtown Syracuse bars.

A SECOND SU ALUMNUS, William Pearson Tolley, became chancellor in 1942, arriving just six months after the Japanese attack on Pearl Harbor thrust the United States into World War II. Despite the unsettled times, Tolley expressed optimism, saying, "It is not the business of a university to limit its vision to immediate goals." Thanks to his vision, particularly during and after the war, SU would experience another building blitz and the rapid transformation from a relatively small liberal arts college into a large research institution.

Spurred by patriotism and practicality during a period of dramatic declines in male enrollment because of the draft, Tolley established the War Service College. Working with the US armed forces, Syracuse created training programs that brought nearly eight thousand cadets, sailors, and airmen to campus. The government paid a fee for the soldiers' attendance, which helped keep SU afloat. "I knew we could not survive without students," Tolley explained years later. "And that meant (recruiting) men in uniform."

While those men—and women—in uniform prepared to ship out to the Atlantic and Pacific theaters, other students got behind the cause on campus, raising thousands of dollars in war bonds. The need for nurses on foreign fronts prompted the opening of the School of Nursing in 1943, under the deft leadership of Edith H. Smith. Austerity measures were put in place throughout campus, with the *Daily Orange*—featuring an all-female staff—cutting back publication from five days a week to four, and sports programs suspended for the duration of the war.

Despite Tolley's above-and-beyond commitment to the war effort, his patriotism would be called into question after he agreed to accept sixty-five Japanese American students from Roosevelt-ordered internment camps, which had been set up in remote desert regions of the West out of concerns that Americans of Japanese ancestry would be loyal to their native land and might sabotage the United States from within. The hysteria resulted in more than one hundred thousand people being resettled into what amounted to prison camps. Tolley believed the fears were motivated in part by racism. His critics thought otherwise, and after the new students arrived he was viciously attacked in the editorial pages of the Syracuse newspapers, by local veterans groups, and by some university board members and benefactors.

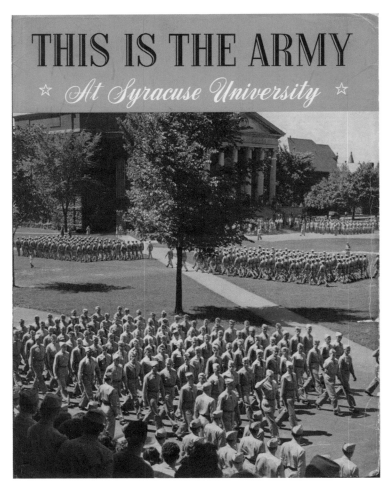

THIS IS THE ARMY
☆ At Syracuse University ☆

World War II cadets marching on SU's Quad. Syracuse University Photograph Collection, University Archives.

Some of Tolley's detractors were momentarily quieted by the actions of a Japanese American student named Frank Watanabe, who won a campus-wide contest for his design of a patriotic poster. Tolley chose the university's ROTC cadet review ceremony to make the presentation of the one hundred dollar award. At first, the cadets appeared aghast that a Japanese American would be receiving such an honor, but Watanabe quickly defused the situation by announcing he would donate the money to the American Red Cross. That prompted the cadets to rise from their seats and give him a standing ovation. While history would show Tolley had done the right and courageous thing by accepting those students, many of the city's conservative leaders never forgave him for allowing "the enemy" to matriculate on the Hill.

Roughly eighteen thousand SU alumni, students, and faculty would serve their country during this time. Of those, 195 were killed and another fifty-one were listed as missing in action. Among the casualties was Wilmeth Sidat-Singh, a premed graduate who had been an Orange basketball star and one of the first African American quarterbacks in college football history. Sidat-Singh died during a training flight with the famed Tuskegee Airmen in 1942. Sixty-three years later, a historical oversight finally would be righted

when his Number 19 basketball jersey was retired in a pregame ceremony in the Carrier Dome.

THE SERVICEMEN'S READJUSTMENT ACT of 1944 would prove to be one of the most significant pieces of legislation ever passed by Congress. And nowhere would its impact be felt more than at Syracuse University. Commonly referred to as the GI Bill, it offered millions of returning veterans a college education. Truth be told, many institutions of higher learning were not interested in fully participating in the program because it meant the influx of what some considered "inferior students," including many who were not able to finish high school because of the war. But Tolley decided to give vets the "orange" carpet treatment, creating educational opportunities for servicemen and servicewomen who were able to pass entrance exams. "When World War II ended, New York governor Thomas E. Dewey called the state's college presidents together and announced that there was a national emergency," Tolley recalled. "Thousands of returning GIs would need an education. He asked the universities to take all they could under the GI Bill. Some universities were not receptive and were unwilling to increase their size.

"In effect, these administrations were saying, 'We don't give a damn for the welfare of the nation, and we don't care what problems these human beings face. We come first, and we're not going to be impaired by this glut of returning veterans.' I felt our attitude should be just the opposite. We had always been in the business of public service. We had trained teachers and preachers by the thousands. We may not have trained as many millionaires as the Ivy League schools had, but thousands of our alumni had gone on to become useful, productive citizens. What most impressed me was Dewey's statement that this was an emergency. I realized that if a veteran

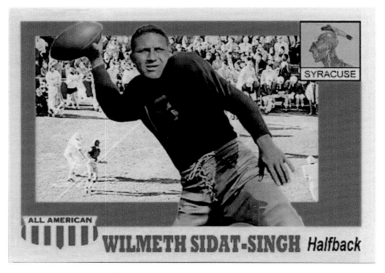

Syracuse football star Wilmeth Sidat-Singh was one of the first African American college football players known for his passing skills. Courtesy of Mary Ann Lemke.

Chancellor William Pearson Tolley. Syracuse University Portrait Collection, University Archives.

From: SYRACUSE UNIVERSITY
To: RETURNED WAR VETERANS
Subject: YOUR FUTURE

A Personal Word

THE purpose of this folder is to tell you briefly of the arrangements that we of Syracuse University have made to enable men and women discharged from the Armed Services to resume their education and prepare themselves for their future work and their return to civilian life.

These arrangements have been planned to accommodate as wide a range of needs and requirements as possible.

As an individual you may fit into one of the following groups:

(1) Men and women who have already done some college work and want to complete their requirements for a degree.

(2) High school graduates who want to get started on their college course.

(3) Men and women who are not in a position to undertake a full college course but wish to prepare for a particular job or for work in a specific field in the shortest time possible.

(4) Those men and women who entered the Armed Forces before completing their high school course and are still undecided about future educational training.

In our Veterans Educational Program, outlined in the following pages, we have aimed to meet all such requirements to the best of our ability and to provide the type of training needed, whether it be a four-year degree program or a vocational course on the college level that can be completed in eight months. If yours is a special case, we shall welcome an opportunity to discuss it with you and to arrange a program suited to your individual needs. If you need help in making your decisions for the future, our staff of experts in guidance is available to you.

If you have questions that are not answered here, or if there are points on which you would like to have further information, please write to Dr. Ernest Reed, Director Veterans Educational Program, Syracuse University, Syracuse 10, N. Y.

William P. Tolley
CHANCELLOR, SYRACUSE UNIVERSITY

SYRACUSE UNIVERSITY
ARCHIVES

Chancellor William Pearson Tolley's historic letter inviting US Veterans to attend Syracuse University after World War II. Syracuse University World Wars and the Military Reference Collection, University Archives.

didn't go to college as soon as he came back, he'd never have another chance.

"It was now or never. Now was not the time to shut the doors. Our doors opened wide in 1946."

Did they ever. Like floodgates.

SU admitted 9,464 freshmen, nearly quadrupling the previous incoming class. Between the academic years of 1945-46 and 1948-49, the so-called GI Bulge would prompt a meteoric surge in enrollment from 5,716 to 19,698 students. The size of the faculty tripled during this time, and grad school enrollment expanded almost sevenfold.

As one might imagine, the explosive expansion created all sorts of stresses and strains. To accommodate the huge influx of veterans, Tolley created Utica College and Triple Cities College (now Binghamton University)—branch campuses where students could earn SU degrees. In the Salt City, University College also was started, and it, along with extension schools in several other upstate New York cities, provided essential educational opportunities for veterans who held full-time jobs and could only attend classes in the evening.

The university arranged the purchase of about three hundred prefab buildings from the US War Department, with two-thirds of

them used for housing and one-third for classrooms and laboratories. Many of these so-called Quonset huts were shoehorned onto the present-day quadrangle.

"My classes were filled to overflowing with former corporals and sergeants, captains and colonels," recounted William Fleming, a professor of fine arts. "The seats, aisles, and floors were wall-to-wall students right up to the place where I was standing. I had to spell out the names of artists and composers because I could not get to the blackboard to write them down."

Until the new housing was ready, many students were forced to live all over the greater Syracuse area. One vet remembered sharing a room with ten people in a former nitric acid plant in Baldwinsville, a forty-five-minute bus ride from the main campus. He was lucky compared to another vet, who recalled sharing living quarters with ninety-two ex-GIs in the drafty, chilly cow barn at the New York State Fairgrounds, about five miles from campus. Nearly two hundred trailers for married students were set up at the Drumlins apple orchard on South Campus, a place that became known derisively as "mud hollow" after a particularly soggy spring.

Though many veterans engaged in common student activities, many others did not feel a part of campus life for a variety of reasons. A large number lived off campus, worked full-time jobs, and were

The influx of thousands of returning veterans from World War II resulted in a crowded campus. Syracuse University Photograph Collection, University Archives.

married and raising young families, so they tended to socialize with other veteran families and even formed their own organizations. They differed from traditional students in another way, too. "We were in a hurry," explained Frank Funk, a 1949 graduate and future dean of SU's Continuing Education program at University College. "If there hadn't been a war, we would have been out of school by that time and established in our careers. We wanted to get out and get on with our lives. The main demand we made of the university was to give us as many courses as possible."

Despite its enormous challenges, the GI Bill proved a godsend for hundreds of thousands of veterans and for Syracuse University—a win-win for a place Tolley had labeled "Victory University."

The rapid velocity of change would continue throughout the 1950s and into the early 1960s. By the end of the decade, Syracuse would rank twelfth nationally in sponsored research, as Tolley's vision continued to be realized. Innovations would include a pioneering special education program that applied progressive views to teaching people with various disabilities. The emphasis on "special ed" would continue under deans Burton Blatt and Douglas Biklen, who became nationally respected for their creative approaches and inclusivity. Increased interest in technology prompted SU to open a 120-acre engineering campus at the former naval war plant on Thompson Road. Nicknamed T-Road by students, it attracted thirty new faculty members and helped quadruple enrollment in the Lyman C. Smith College of Applied Sciences.

For nearly a half century, women at SU had limited access to Archbold Gymnasium. In 1953, thanks to the tireless efforts of physical education professor Katherine Sibley, the Women's Building opened. It rapidly became the hub of not only women's intercollegiate and intramural athletics but also organizations such as Women's Student Government and the Panhellenic Association.

Tolley boosted SU's academic reputation by hiring world-class teachers. This included the recruitment of biology professor Arthur Phillips from MIT. At Syracuse, Phillips would start the first pathogen-free animal research laboratory. Another impressive hire was Ivan Mestrovic, a Croatian artist who was considered the greatest sculptor of religious statues since the Renaissance. Critics called him a modern day Michelangelo.

Construction would become as big a part of Tolley's legacy as instruction, as he oversaw the spending of nearly $86 million on the erection or purchase of buildings. During the Tolley era, SU averaged two new buildings per year. Many of the new edifices were dormitories, including Flint and Day Halls on the campus's highest hill—Mount Olympus.

Athletics also would flourish under Tolley. In 1949, SU signed little-known coach Ben Schwartzwalder to revive its moribund football program. Alumni were underwhelmed by the hire, but Schwartzwalder won them over, taking a team that had gone 1-8 the year before to a national championship ten years later. During Ol' Ben's twenty-five-year reign, the Orangemen would post 153 wins, ninety-one losses, and three ties, and would make seven bowl appearances while becoming an Eastern and national football power.

Of all the All-Americans Schwartzwalder recruited, none would have a greater impact than Jim Brown, who arrived on campus in 1953. Winner of eleven varsity letters at Manhasset High School on Long Island, Brown sought jersey Number 33 when he reported for his first practice on the Hill. Told it was already taken, he "settled" for 44, which would wind up becoming the most significant

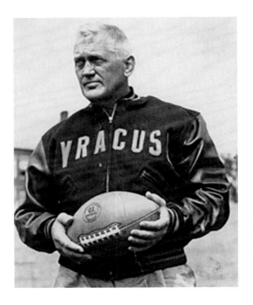

Ben Schwartzwalder during 1952 season. Athletics Department, Syracuse University, used by permission.

Jim Brown was the first of SU's famous 44s. Athletics Department, Syracuse University, used by permission.

President John F. Kennedy met with Syracuse's Ernie Davis (left) shortly after Davis was awarded the 1961 Heisman Trophy. Cecil Stoughton. White House Photographs. John F. Kennedy Presidential Library and Museum, Boston.

number in Syracuse sports history. Not only would Brown earn All-American football honors wearing those digits, he also would prompt Ernie Davis and Floyd Little to wear the same number with similar storied distinction after he had left SU to play in the National Football League. The number eventually was retired and would become a permanent part of the university's zip code (13244) and phone exchange (443).

At Brown's commencement at Archbold Stadium in June 1957, he and his fellow graduates were treated to an address by a charismatic political up-and-comer, a US senator from Massachusetts named John F. Kennedy. Called "an apostle of political courage" upon receiving his honorary degree, the future president spoke of politics but also encouraged graduates to be concerned about the contributions they could make to society and the world. It would foreshadow his memorable inaugural address four years later, when he challenged Americans to "ask not what your country can do for you—ask what you can do for your country."

Two years after Brown's graduation, Davis donned the famed 44, and he and a punishing group of linemen known as the Sizeable Seven would lead the Orangemen to an 11-0 record and the national college football championship. They were so dominant and deep in talent that College and Pro Football Hall of Famer Red Grange opined: "If Syracuse's first team is the number one team in the country, then their second team must be number two."

Another seminal Syracuse moment would occur in 1961. In the same year that JFK became the youngest president in US history and launched his New Frontier, Davis blazed his own trail by becoming the first African American to win the Heisman Trophy, college football's most prestigious award. Sadly, the promise of

both men would end tragically two years later, when Davis died of leukemia at age twenty-three and Kennedy was assassinated at age forty-six.

NINETEEN SIXTY-ONE also would be the year that civil rights movement leader Martin Luther King Jr. made the first of two campus visits, at the request of Charles V. Willie, one of SU's first African American professors and administrators. In his first speech in Syracuse, given at Sims Hall, King tried out many of the powerful phrases and messages that would appear in his famous "I Have a Dream" address delivered from the steps of the Lincoln Memorial in front of a quarter of a million people in 1963.

Tolley's construction boom continued with the 1962 completion of Manley Field House—named for SU graduate and trustee George Leroy Manley. Built primarily to give Schwartzwalder's football team a place to practice during inclement weather, the arena became a multipurpose facility, most notably home to the Orangemen's basketball team. Manley's cozy confines and raucous student cheer section, aptly named the Zoo, contributed to a distinct home-court advantage that saw the Syracuse hoopsters reel off a 190-28 record in eighteen seasons, including a fifty-seven-game win streak.

The arena's completion coincided with the arrival of two freshmen who would change the course of SU basketball history. Highly

The *Daily Orange* covered Martin Luther King Jr.'s visit to Syracuse in July 1965. *Daily Orange*. Syracuse University Student Publications Reference Collection, University Archives.

President Lyndon B. Johnson dedicating the opening of the S.I. Newhouse School of Public Communications in 1964. *Newhouse Network*, Syracuse University, used by permission.

recruited guard Dave Bing from Washington, DC, would become a consensus All-American and establish school scoring records that still stand, while helping a team that lost twenty-seven consecutive games before his arrival reach the Elite Eight of the NCAA basketball tournament for the first time.

His classmate and backcourt mate, Jim Boeheim, also would be part of the hoops program's transformation. Boeheim was a good player, but his greatest contributions would come as a coach. The 2019-20 season marked his forty-fourth year heading the program. Along the way he had become the second-winningest coach in the history of men's college basketball, guiding the Orange to forty-two postseason appearances, highlighted by an NCAA national championship in 2003. Two years after summiting the Mount Everest of college hoops, Boeheim joined Bing as an inductee in the Naismith

Memorial Basketball Hall of Fame in Springfield, Massachusetts. They are the only former college roommates to be enshrined.

IN THE FALL OF 1964, Tolley cut the ribbon on another building that would further enhance SU's global reputation and reach. Thanks to a $1 million gift from publishing mogul Samuel Irving Newhouse Jr., a new edifice to house the university's communications and journalism school became a reality. President Lyndon B. Johnson was on hand for the dedication of Newhouse I, which was designed by famed architect I. M. Pei and received national recognition for its modernistic design. The ceremony was made all the more memorable when LBJ became the first sitting US president to receive

Jim Boeheim and Dave Bing arrived on campus in the summer of 1962, changing the fortunes of SU basketball. Athletics Department, Syracuse University, used by permission.

Anti-ROTC demonstrations in May 1964 prompted Chancellor Tolley to strike a Syracuse student protester. *Daily Orange*. Syracuse University Student Publications Reference Collection, University Archives.

Students at Syracuse protest the Kent State shootings in May 1970. Syracuse University Photograph Collection, University Archives.

an honorary degree from Syracuse, and used his remarks that day to deliver his historic Gulf of Tonkin speech, resolving to escalate America's participation in the Vietnam War. It was a decision that would divide the country and convince LBJ not to run for reelection.

Tolley's triumphant opening of Newhouse would be followed by a nationally embarrassing moment both for him and for the university. Angered by an antiwar demonstration during an ROTC ceremony, the chancellor called a protestor a "bum" and struck him in the arm with his cane. A United Press International photograph captured the moment for posterity, and the picture appeared in newspapers throughout the United States and the world.

The times, as singer/poet Bob Dylan noted, were "a changin'," especially on college campuses such as Syracuse, where student activism in favor of civil rights here and against the war in Southeast Asia was gaining steam.

AFTER HAVING OVERSEEN the biggest growth spurt in university history, Tolley stepped down in 1969 and was replaced by John E. Corbally, a former provost and vice president of Ohio State University. Corbally arrived during a tumultuous time and would serve just eighteen months, the shortest tenure of any Syracuse chancellor.

SU turned one hundred years old in 1970, but the centennial was remembered more for protests than celebrations. The killing of four Kent State University students by Ohio National Guard troops on May 4, 1970, during a protest against the American invasion of Cambodia, ignited a nationwide movement by college students that shut down more than four hundred educational institutions, including Syracuse. Decades later, noted filmmaker Oliver Stone's movie *Born on the Fourth of July* would depict a major riot on the SU campus following the Kent State shootings, but the portrayal was fictional. Students actually sat peacefully on the Quad, listening

Antiwar student protestors wanted SU's administration to close campus for the rest of the semester in the spring of 1970. Syracuse University Photograph Collection, University Archives.

to impassioned strike protestors speak from the steps of Hendricks Chapel.

Afterward, hundreds of them staged a sit-in in the Administration Building and barricaded all the entrances to campus with wire and wood. Not everyone behaved peacefully. The SU bookstore was firebombed, and shattered glass was strewn about campus after students hurled rocks through more than seventy windows. The protestor who spray-painted the words "Shut it down" on the Hall of Languages would get his wish, as Corbally canceled the final six weeks of classes.

Later that year, student activism would grab the Syracuse football program by the facemask as nine African American players petitioned for better medical care, academic support, unbiased assignment of starting positions, and racial integration of the coaching staff. When their demands were not satisfied, the student-athletes boycotted the season, ending both their collegiate sports careers and their chances to play professionally because National Football League teams viewed them as "troublemakers." A twelve-member investigating committee later found evidence of racism in the SU football program and concluded there was "substance" to the athletes' allegations. In 2006, the university issued an official apology to each member of the Syracuse Eight (media reports failed to account for a ninth player), and they were awarded letterman jackets and Chancellor's Medals by Nancy Cantor before an SU football game in the Carrier Dome.

IN SEARCH OF A BRIDGE over troubled waters, the SU trustees named Melvin A. Eggers to replace Corbally in 1971. Eggers had come to the university as an economics professor in 1950 and earned the respect of his peers, eventually ascending to the positions of department head, vice chancellor, and provost. His timing would prove better than his predecessor's, as the antiwar movement resulted in an end to the United States' involvement in Vietnam in 1973 and gentler times at SU and other campuses.

Eggers was forced to put his economics background to full use, having inherited a university that was more than $1 million in debt. Despite the challenges, he would oversee another construction boom, spending more than $200 million during his tenure, as student enrollment and the number of faculty reached new highs.

Ernest Stevenson Bird (class of 1916) donated money for the building of a six-story library that bore his name and opened in 1972. Nicknamed Big Bird after the Sesame Street television character, it quintupled the space of Carnegie Library, providing seating for 2,500. A year later, the Hall of Languages celebrated its centennial by being added to the National Register of Historic Places, making it eligible for federal preservation funds, which were used, along with more than one thousand alumni donations, to completely renovate the "Dowager Queen" of campus.

Eggers also followed through on the completion of Link Hall—the second of a two-building engineering complex—the opening of the William B. Heroy Geology Laboratory, and major renovations of Steele Hall and Crouse College. The early 1970s also saw the construction of 101 two-bedroom apartments at Skytop on South Campus.

By this time, Syracuse's journalism program had established itself among the nation's best, prompting Samuel Newhouse to build Newhouse II across the plaza from Newhouse I. The second of what would become a three-building communications complex opened in 1974 and provided state-of-the-art equipment and studios for SU's television-radio majors.

The Newhouse Complex. Photo by Scott Pitoniak.

Student housing was added at Skytop on South Campus during the early 1970s to accommodate increased enrollment. © Syracuse University. Photo by Stephen Sartori.

Few things galvanize a campus more than a successful sports program, and in 1975 students, faculty, and administrators came together to celebrate a glorious run by the men's overachieving basketball team. Led by head coach Roy Danforth and star players Rudy Hackett and Jimmy Lee, the Orangemen scored two overtime victories and upset NCAA East Region favorite North Carolina on their way to SU's first appearance in the tournament's Final Four. "I think it all started to come together when we found out the Final Four was going to be in San Diego," joked Bob Parker, a backup center. "We were all sick of the Syracuse winter." The Orangemen lost in the semifinals, but that didn't matter. Their improbable journey did wonders for school spirit and laid the foundation for future NCAA tournament runs under Boeheim, who would succeed the departing Danforth as coach in 1976.

SU's men's basketball team made an improbable run to the 1975 NCAA Final Four. It was the Orangemen's first trip to college basketball's showcase event. Athletics Department, Syracuse University, used by permission.

SU GRID
SYRACUSE
vs.
NAVY

Est. Price .93
Taxes .07
$1.00

Archbold Stadium
November 11, 1978

After seventy-one years as home to Syracuse athletics, Archbold Stadium was officially closed November 11, 1978, with SU's football team defeating Navy. Athletics Department, Syracuse University, used by permission.

Speaking of school spirit, undergraduates had advocated for a student center almost since SU's inception, but it wasn't until 1985 that it became a reality. Funded by a generous gift from trustee Renée Schine Crown (class of 1950), the Schine Student Center opened, replete with spacious social and dining areas, a 1,500-seat auditorium, and a modern bookstore. It quickly became a favorite gathering place.

OF ALL THE BUILDINGS erected during Eggers's time as chancellor, none became more iconic or nationally recognizable than the Carrier Dome. By the late 1960s, Archbold Stadium had devolved into a dilapidated eyesore. The concrete bowl had fallen into such disrepair that SU coaches avoided showing recruits the stadium unless they asked to see it. "We must give up Archbold, or give up football," Eggers told the school's board of trustees. "It is as simple as that."

The board agreed, and Eggers and new athletics director Jake Crouthamel began looking for alternative sites to build a new stadium. They ultimately opted to construct it on the site of Archbold, which meant the Orangemen would have to play their entire 1979 schedule on the road.

The Carrier Dome opened on September 20, 1980, with Syracuse defeating Miami of Ohio in front of a still-record crowd of 50,564. Athletics Department, Syracuse University, used by permission.

With $10 million in state aid and a $2.75 million naming rights gift from the Carrier Corporation, the Carrier Dome opened in 1980. The 49,500-seat, roofed stadium would transform not only the university's skyline but also its sports programs. Under new football coach Dick MacPherson and his successor Paul Pasqualoni, Syracuse football would experience a renaissance that would see the Orangemen make twelve bowl appearances in fifteen years. The peak of that run would come in 1987, when quarterback Don McPherson, a Heisman Trophy runner-up, led SU to an 11-0-1 record, its first unbeaten mark since its national championship season.

In hopes of realizing a slight spike in basketball attendance, the men's hoops team moved to the Dome from Manley Field House in 1980, despite vehement protests from Boeheim, who understandably wanted to retain the home-court advantage he had forged in the much smaller arena. But the venue change would help the Orange

blossom into a national program, as on-campus record crowds in excess of thirty thousand regularly packed the Dome to watch the likes of Dwayne "Pearl" Washington, Derrick Coleman, Billy Owens, Carmelo Anthony, and Gerry McNamara perform their basketball magic. SU would go on to lead the nation in attendance thirteen times and finish among the top four draws every year since moving into the arena. The men's and women's lacrosse teams and female hoopsters also would benefit greatly from playing beneath the Teflon-coated, air-supported roof.

The Loud House's impact would be felt beyond sports. Starting with Frank Sinatra in 1980, the Dome would host some of the biggest musical acts of all time, including Bruce Springsteen, the Rolling Stones, Paul McCartney, The Who, Billy Joel, Elton John, Prince, 50 Cent, Dolly Parton, U2, Pink Floyd, Drake, and Eric Clapton. The versatile building also would be home to high school games, a National Football League exhibition, monster truck competitions, an attendance-record-setting minor league hockey game, Billy Graham crusades, a Dalai Lama conversation, an Ice Capades featuring Olympic skater Nancy Kerrigan, New York State Field Band Conference championships, and annual commencements. "Name any other building that's had more of an impact on the university or the city of Syracuse," said former Dome managing director Pat Campbell. "What the Dome did was make us Major League."

Chancellor Melvin Eggers has some fun kicking a football held by SU varsity kicker Dave Jacobs on the Quad.

Rock star Bruce Springsteen performs in the Carrier Dome in 1985. © Syracuse University. Photo by Steve Parker.

In 1978, the headdress-wearing Saltine Warrior Indian mascot was dropped because it was insensitive to Native Americans. © Syracuse University. Photo by Stephen Sartori.

A YEAR BEFORE Archbold was razed, another familiar SU symbol disappeared when Eggers decided to permanently retire the Indian headdress-wearing Saltine Warrior as the school's mascot because it was demeaning to members of the Onondaga Nation, upon whose ancestral lands the university resides. The announcement was controversial, with debate raging on the pages of the local newspapers for months. Some alumni claimed in letters to the editor that SU had overreacted, but Eggers said the decision was the right one and irreversible.

The Saltine Warrior was born out of a hoax published in the October 1931 issue of the *Syracuse Orange Peel*, a campus magazine. The fictitious Native American character became so popular that its likeness was used on university letterhead and its costume worn at football and basketball games by members of Lambda Chi Alpha fraternity. After the headdress and buckskins were placed in

mothballs, SU began searching for a new mascot. But it wasn't until 1995 that Otto the Orange was officially named by Chancellor Kenneth "Buzz" Shaw, after the fuzzy character beat out a wolf, a gladiator, and a lion for the right to represent Syracuse. Over time, Otto would become beloved by students and alumni and emerge as one of the most recognizable mascots in all of sports.

In 1984, SU would attract national attention when sophomore Vanessa Williams became the first African American to be voted Miss America. Her reign would be immensely popular, but short, as she was forced to relinquish her crown after nude modeling photographs were published without her permission in *Penthouse* magazine. Many thought Williams's dreams of a singing and acting career were over, but she persevered and wound up becoming an international entertainment star, producing platinum-selling albums and winning prestigious acting awards for her work on stage and in films and television series.

Not long after Williams was crowned, Elliott Portnoy became SU's first Rhodes Scholar, and Maxwell educator Ralph Ketcham was named national Professor of the Year by the Council for Advancement and Support of Education. While at Oxford University, Portnoy founded a nonprofit organization that provided sports opportunities to children with profound and severe disabilities. It's still

In 1984, Syracuse sophomore Vanessa Williams became the first African American crowned Miss America. Associated Press. © 2019 The Associated Press.

Otto the Orange became the university's official mascot in 1995. Syracuse University Photograph Collection, University Archives.

In 1984, Elliott Portnoy became SU's first Rhodes Scholar. Syracuse University Portrait Collection, University Archives.

On December 21, 1988, a terrorist bombing of Pan Am Flight 103 over Lockerbie, Scotland, took the lives of 270 people, including thirty-five SU Abroad students. ROY LETKEY / AFP / Getty Images.

going strong today, with programs in the United States and United Kingdom. Portnoy would go on to become the global chief executive officer of Dentons—the world's largest law firm.

Ketcham, meanwhile, became an immensely popular and innovative teacher, and a respected scholar of the Founding Fathers, especially US president James Madison. With the exception of a few years teaching at the University of Chicago and Yale, Ketcham would spend nearly sixty years teaching at SU, starting in 1951 while he was earning his PhD from Maxwell, which during his time became the nation's top-ranked graduate school for public affairs—a distinction it's held for more than three decades.

SU would enjoy one of its finest sports seasons ever in 1987, with the men's basketball team reaching the NCAA championship game and the football team finishing unbeaten and ranked fourth in the final national polls. In a cruel twist, each team would experience deflating endings in the same building—the Louisiana Superdome in New Orleans—as the Orange hoopsters lost in the final seconds on a jump shot by Indiana University's Keith Smart and the football

Football coach Dick MacPherson celebrates during SU's 1984 upset of top-ranked Nebraska. Athletics Department, Syracuse University, used by permission.

team wound up being tied on a field goal by Auburn as time ran out in the Sugar Bowl.

The decade would wind down on a tragic note with the bombing of Pan Am Flight 103 over Lockerbie, Scotland, on December 21, 1988. The terrorist attack took the lives of 270 people, including thirty-five Syracuse University Abroad students who were returning home after a semester of study in London. The tragedy jolted the SU campus, its impact still felt more than three decades later. A memorial service was held in the Carrier Dome upon the students' return three weeks later. But Eggers wanted to do more to honor the deceased, whom he referred to as "the best and the brightest."

During the ceremony, he made a commitment to the families of the victims that Syracuse University would always remember their loved ones. This led to the construction of the Place of Remembrance memorial in front of the walkway leading up to the Hall of Languages. It also resulted in the establishment of Remembrance Scholarships, presented annually to thirty-five SU seniors in memory of the deceased students, and Lockerbie Scholarships, which bring two students from the Scottish community to study for a year at SU.

EGGERS'S MEMORABLE RUN as chancellor would conclude in 1991, shortly after the dedication of the Center for Science and Technology and the opening of the Shaffer Art Building. He would be succeeded by Buzz Shaw, who had spent time as president of the University of Wisconsin System and chancellor of the Southern Illinois University System.

Shaw inherited a $38 million deficit, forcing him to take tough measures immediately. These included reducing the faculty by 15 percent and trimming the budgets of many schools, departments, and programs. But along with making the university smaller, he made it stronger. After getting the budget under control, Shaw

Astronaut F. Story Musgrave. Courtesy of NASA.

launched a $300 million "Commitment to Learning" fundraising campaign to help fulfill his vision for Syracuse as the nation's leading student-centered research university; this successful campaign ultimately raised over $370 million.

Under Shaw, the university continued to expand its use of new technology. A large grant from Apple Corporation allowed for the increased use of computers in the classroom. Funding also led to the enhancement of the university's pace-setting Biomolecular

Research Institute and a growing relationship with the National Aeronautics and Space Administration (NASA). The work with NASA was a great fit, considering SU's tradition of producing astronauts, including F. Story Musgrave, who oversaw the outer-space repair of the Hubble Space Telescope, and Eileen Collins, the first woman to pilot and command a space shuttle.

The university's long-standing commitment to community service and charities was underscored once more in 1992, when students, faculty and staff participated in the Muscular Dystrophy Association Dance Marathon for the twentieth consecutive year, continuing a tradition that had raised more than $1 million.

Along with a financial crisis, Shaw inherited an athletic program facing charges of impropriety. The men's basketball program would be the hardest hit by the NCAA Infractions Committee, which docked the Orangemen several scholarships and banished them from the 1993 postseason. The program would rebound, and three years later would ride the play of future National Basketball Association first-round draft pick John Wallace to the national championship game, which it lost to Kentucky.

To honor his predecessor, Shaw oversaw the construction and opening of Eggers Hall, a new wing connected to the Maxwell School that featured seminar rooms honoring the Seneca Falls Women's Movement and the Onondaga Nation. In order to make room for the new building, the 320-ton Holden Observatory was placed on 20 hydraulic dollies and moved 190 feet to the southwest, its current location, just behind Crouse College.

In 1995, SU celebrated its 125th anniversary, bringing back to campus scores of prominent alumni for a gala dinner in the Carrier Dome. Among the returnees was 1951 graduate Dick Clark, who served as master of ceremonies. The festivities included the first

NCAA CHAMPIONS

Sports Illustrated

SWEET VICTORY

Orangemen: Unranked to No.1

Freshman Carmelo Anthony driving on Kansas

Forward Carmelo Anthony and Coach Jim Boeheim helped lead the Syracuse men's basketball team to its first NCAA national championship in 2003. Cover image: John Biever / SI Cover / Sports Illustrated / Getty Images; image of Boeheim: Athletics Department, Syracuse University, used by permission.

National Orange Day on March 24, kicking off an annual tradition in which SU alumni are encouraged to commemorate their alma mater's founding by devoting time to community service.

After the terrorist attacks of September 11, 2001, students gathered in Hendricks Chapel and residence halls to support one another and try to make sense of the tragedy. To help people work through their grief and anger, the Student Association placed "Sheets of Expression" on the Quad. Students, faculty, and staff wrote down their thoughts, fears, and prayers, and drew symbols of peace, hope, and patriotism on the sheets laid out on the grass. A vigil was held to memorialize the nearly forty people with SU ties who were killed in that tragedy, including two dozen who had worked in the World Trade Center's Twin Towers.

Two years later, the campus community would gather again, this time for a celebration, after Syracuse University's basketball team avenged previous close calls in the NCAA basketball tournament, and finally won it all. Youth would not be wasted on the young this time around, as precocious freshmen Carmelo Anthony and Gerry McNamara helped Boeheim's Orangemen defeat Kansas in the title game in the Louisiana Superdome—the same court where, sixteen years earlier, they had lost a championship game to Indiana. After the team returned home, a celebration was held in the Dome. Twenty-five thousand people showed up.

Buzz Shaw retired following that high note, and the university hired Nancy Cantor as its first female chancellor in 2004. She had formerly served as chancellor of the University of Illinois at Urbana-Champaign and as provost at the University of Michigan. In a quest to explore the "Soul of Syracuse," she convened members of the university and Central New York community for discussions on how they could better work together. Those conversations led to the establishment of programs such as Say Yes to Education Syracuse and the Connective Corridor, which physically linked more than thirty arts, cultural, and education venues.

Just before Cantor's inauguration, SU and Iroquois representatives jointly announced the Haudenosaunee Promise program, which offered full scholarships to qualified students from the Six Nations. The initiative was meant to honor and further expand the historical and cultural relationship between the university and Native Americans, particularly the Onondaga Nation.

Cantor strove to make the university more diverse, increasing overall undergraduate enrollment by about 22 percent, with an emphasis on accepting ethnically, socioeconomically, and geographically diverse students. Her passion for inclusion resulted in an increase in the representation of undergraduate students of color from 17 to 31 percent. She also hired several African Americans for high-profile administrative positions, including Dean Lorraine

The Carrier Dome was nicknamed the Loud House. Athletics Department, Syracuse University, used by permission.

Branham, who oversaw the opening of Newhouse III, and Athletics Director Daryl Gross, who dramatically upgraded women's sports and the so-called Olympic sports at SU, resulting in national championships in women's field hockey and men's cross-country, and a first-time trip to the NCAA championship game by the women's basketball team.

Gross also would be charged with guiding Orange athletics through a time of great flux in college sports as many schools began switching league affiliations. SU had enjoyed enormous success as a member of the Big East Conference since the early 1980s, but the sports landscape was changing dramatically and rapidly, prompting Gross to move Syracuse to the Atlantic Coast Conference. Fellow Big East members Boston College and Pittsburgh followed suit, as SU became part of a league that featured peer academic institutions, such as Duke, North Carolina, and Miami. Longtime intense rivalries like those with Georgetown and Connecticut in basketball would be replaced by new ones. Basketball games with Duke, in particular, would stoke passions and lead to on-campus attendance records of 35,446 in the Dome when the Blue Devils and Orange clashed in nationally televised matchups in 2014 and 2015.

S. I. Newhouse's dream of a three-building communications complex came true in 2007, when Newhouse III was dedicated to the west of Newhouse I and II. The new edifice featured a collaborative media room, a 350-seat auditorium funded by alumna Joyce Hergenhan, and a café, as SU became a leader in teaching and researching digital journalism. US Supreme Court Chief Justice John Roberts delivered the dedication address in front of the "Liberty Wrap," which featured the words of the First Amendment etched in six-foot-high letters on the building's glass façade. A few years later, the new Dick Clark Television Studios would open in Newhouse II, with Oprah Winfrey as the keynote speaker at the dedication.

The same year Newhouse III opened, Hollywood came to campus for the filming of *The Express*, a Universal Studios biopic about Ernie Davis. The film, starring Dennis Quaid as former Orange football coach Ben Schwartzwalder, staged its world premiere in Syracuse in 2008. The nationwide release of *The Express* coincided with the unveiling of a statue of Davis and the opening of a new dormitory in his memory.

The celebration of one of Syracuse's famed "forty-fours" and the first African American to win the Heisman would coincide with the election of the first African American president of the United States, who just so happened to be the forty-fourth commander in chief. And Barack Obama's historic victory would be aided by a man with Orange ties. Obama chose Joe Biden as his running mate, and the Syracuse College of Law alumnus would twice help him secure the necessary working-class votes to reach the Oval Office. Obama would call Biden the greatest vice president in history and reward

(Top) In the 2007 movie, *The Express*, actor Rob Brown (portraying Ernie Davis) is hoisted onto the shoulders of his Syracuse teammates. ©2008 Universal Pictures. Courtesy of Universal Studios Licensing LLC.

(Bottom) Some of the filming took place on campus. © Syracuse University. Photo by Stephen Sartori.

The third building in the Newhouse communications complex opened in 2007. © Syracuse University. Photo by Stephen Sartori.

Vice President Joe Biden served President Barack Obama during his two terms in the White House. Courtesy of the White House. Photo by Pete Souza.

him with the Presidential Medal of Freedom, the nation's highest civilian honor, just before the two men completed their second term in January 2017.

NANCY CANTOR'S successful billion-dollar fundraising initiative would lead to the construction of the Life Sciences Complex, a five-story, L-shaped building that featured a research wing and brought the biology, chemistry, and biochemistry departments under one roof for the first time. The College of Engineering and Computer Science also would receive a boost when an addition to Link Hall—known as Link+—was completed.

Drawing upon its long-standing relationship with the military and veterans, Syracuse established the Institute for Veterans and Military Families, a first in higher education. The institute, which opened in 2011, offered education and employment-focused programs, collaborating with businesses, government and the veterans community.

To leverage its strong alumni ties to the entertainment industry, SU established a Los Angeles center, where students could spend a semester studying under prominent graduates such as Academy Award- and Emmy Award-winning screenwriter Aaron Sorkin.

SU's international studies programs, which date back to 1919, when students first went to Chungking, China, continued to expand. In addition to the Florence and London centers, the university opened branch campuses in Hong Kong, Istanbul, Madrid, Santiago (Chile), Strasbourg (France), and Beijing.

The men's and women's hoops programs would benefit from the 2009 opening of the 54,000-square-foot Carmelo K. Anthony Basketball Center, adjacent to Manley Field House. The state-of-the-art facility was jump-started by a $3 million donation from the former basketball star for whom the building is named.

Cantor's time as chancellor was not without controversy. Her efforts to serve the greater community, though laudable, plunged the university's budget into the red. Her perceived authoritarian style of leadership resulted in strained relationships with many faculty members and administrators, who claimed her programs, and the velocity at which she attempted to enact them, hurt SU's academic reputation. Some blamed her focus on off-campus initiatives, along with her decision to withdraw from the prestigious Association of American Universities, for SU's dramatic drop in the *U.S. News & World Report*'s college rankings from the low forties in the mid-1990s to number sixty-two by the time she left in 2013.

On November 7, 2011—just weeks after the Jerry Sandusky child sex abuse scandal rocked the Penn State football program and the sports world—ESPN reported that longtime SU assistant basketball coach Bernie Fine had molested a former ball boy. Fine denied the allegations, and SU officials said they had conducted an investigation when the accusations were first brought to their attention in 2005 and could not find anyone to corroborate the claims. Cantor fired Fine shortly after ESPN's report aired. After nearly a year of scouring more than one hundred thousand pages of seized documents and interviewing 130 witnesses, the federal investigation concluded without Fine or anyone else being charged.

CANTOR'S LARGE MONETARY COMMITMENT to the community-at-large, coupled with the Great Recession of 2008, put the university in a tough spot by the end of her tenure. "Whoever comes in is going to face the same problems that [previous chancellor] Buzz Shaw had," Maxwell School professor emeritus Jeffrey Stonecash said in a 2013 *Daily Orange* interview. "Bite the bullet, start finding things to reallocate. It's going to take a serious rearrangement of priorities."

That difficult challenge would fall to Kent Syverud, a noted legal scholar and educator who formally took office as Syracuse University's twelfth chancellor and president on January 13, 2014. A native of Irondequoit, New York—a Rochester suburb just ninety miles west of campus—Syverud came to SU after serving as law school dean at Washington University in St. Louis and Vanderbilt University.

Syverud's impressive credentials included clerking for Justice Sandra Day O'Connor shortly after she became the first woman named to the Supreme Court in 1981. O'Connor was effusive in

Chancellor Kent Syverud and Supreme Court Justice Sandra Day O'Connor at Syverud's inauguration. © Syracuse University. Photo by Stephen Sartori.

A rendering of SU's new Institute for Veterans and Military Families. Institute for Veterans and Military Families, Syracuse University, used by permission.

her praise of her former clerk during his inauguration in Hendricks Chapel. "I have watched Kent throughout his career, and I want you to know that the important things about him have not changed in those years," she said from the Hendricks pulpit. "He is very intelligent. He has wonderful values. He cares about people, and he can write and speak exceedingly well. He is going to serve you well and make you proud."

During those ceremonies, Syverud outlined key priorities he believed would help Syracuse continue to flourish as a global research university. They included providing an outstanding undergraduate experience, empowering research excellence, fostering and supporting change and innovation, and positioning SU as the best university in the world for veterans.

"Each of us, including me, is called upon to do our part for this great place, and for its mission," he said in his acceptance speech. "Each of us, especially me, is a steward for the accumulated good works of the last 144 years. I will never forget, and I hope none of us ever forgets, that our efforts, while so important, add only one more layer, really a thin veneer, to the great accumulated work that is this university."

To get a true sense of student life, Syverud and his wife—Dr. Ruth Chen—spent several weeks living in an apartment in the Brewster, Boland, and Brockway dormitory complex overlooking Route 81. During the first year of his chancellorship, he also scheduled dinners, lunches, or coffee get-togethers with as many university employees as possible. The goal was to understand SU at its core.

As Professor Stonecash had predicted, Syverud inherited a school dealing with an onerous budget deficit. In addition to rearranging the priorities of his predecessor, the new chancellor was forced to reduce the number of SU employees through buyouts and layoffs. It was a painful process, but it enabled Syverud to get the university's budget back into the black within a few years.

He also deftly maneuvered through a thorny NCAA investigation of the men's basketball program stemming from improprieties

that occurred several years before he arrived at SU. Sanctions would include a reduction of three men's basketball scholarships for each of the next four seasons, the vacation of 101 wins, and a nine-game suspension for Coach Jim Boeheim.

In April 2018—about three weeks before the end of the spring semester—Syverud was confronted with another crisis that attracted national attention, after videos were released showing members of the Theta Tau engineering fraternity using racial and ethnic slurs and miming the sexual assault of a person with disabilities. After a student conduct review, it was recommended that the fraternity be permanently expelled from SU, and Syverud addressed students and alumni about the decision. A new code of conduct for Greek life on campus was enacted. On June 8, 2018, fifteen students connected to the Theta Tau video were suspended. Several of them filed lawsuits seeking reinstatement and restitution for damages.

DESPITE THE CHALLENGES, Syracuse continued to thrive under Syverud. A $20 million gift from 1968 alumnus Daniel D'Aniello and his wife, Gayle, brought the chancellor's vision of making SU the best university for veterans closer to fruition. The donation was used to construct the National Veterans Resource Center on the block bordering Newhouse III, the Varsity, and Marshall Street. With completion set for the fall of 2020, the center is expected to serve tens of thousands of veterans and their families, as well as student veterans, in the coming years.

Syverud also wanted to bolster the reputation of SU's College of Law, and that goal received a huge boost with the opening of Dineen Hall in the autumn of 2014. Named in memory of two law school alumni—Robert Emmet Dineen (class of 1924) and Carolyn Bareham Dineen (class of 1932)—the five-story, two-hundred-thousand-square-foot facility across the street from the Carrier

Dome brought law students and faculty under one roof for the first time in decades. The project was made possible by a large donation from the Dineens' three children.

Syverud also began following through on his framework to physically transform the main campus. The most dramatic evidence of this was closing the heavily trafficked University Place and replacing it with the Einhorn Family Walk, a pedestrian mall funded by alumni Steven and Sherry Einhorn. The brick walk became a hit with students by eliminating vehicular travel along that stretch. It helped open up the campus, making it seem even more spacious. Student life also would be enhanced by the construction of the Arch, a health and wellness center funded by alumnus Stephen Barnes on the site of old Archbold Gymnasium, as well as major upgrades to the Schine Student Center.

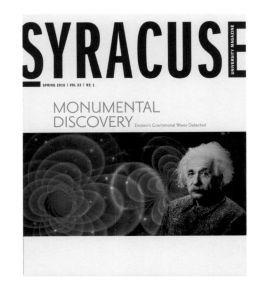

SU professors and students helped prove Einstein's prediction that gravitational waves exist. *Syracuse University Magazine.* Syracuse University News and Public Affairs Reference Collection, University Archives.

Panoramic view of the SU campus. © Syracuse University. Photo by Stephen Sartori.

For several years, administrators debated over what to do with the aging Carrier Dome. After an exhaustive committee study, the board of trustees decided to renovate the stadium rather than build a new one. The last step in a multiyear makeover involved replacing the air-supported Teflon-coated roof with a hard-shell, permanent one.

Syracuse's reputation as an international research university was enhanced in 2015, when the Laser Interferometer Gravitational-Wave Observatory (LIGO) detected two black holes colliding. Physics department researchers Peter Saulson, Duncan Brown, and Stefan Ballmer had been leading members of the one-thousand-person, worldwide Scientific Collaboration for decades, giving SU the honor of being one of the key institutions that made LIGO's discoveries possible. Two years later, they observed the universe creating gold and platinum when two neutron stars collided. Their discoveries marked the culmination of more than four decades of research into gravitational waves. "It opened up a new window onto the universe," Saulson said.

SU would receive more global acclaim in October 2017, when Orange alumnus and English professor George Saunders received the Man Booker Prize, one of the world's most distinguished literary awards, for his first novel, *Lincoln in the Bardo*. The book had debuted seven months earlier atop the *New York Times* bestseller list. Not long after the novel's publication, Saunders received another prestigious honor when he was elected to the American Academy of Arts and Letters. "Only two other Americans, Mark Twain and Kurt Vonnegut, make it look so easy," Academy member Jonathan Franzen said at the awards ceremony. "Saunders is their hugely gifted heir."

In the summer of 2018, SU's board of trustees voted to extend Syverud's contract through 2025. A few months later, their faith in him was further vindicated when Syracuse improved dramatically in the *U.S. News & World Report* rankings, climbing nine spots to number fifty-three.

As SU prepared to celebrate its sesquicentennial in 2020, it was time for reflection. The seed had been planted on that wintry late-February day in 1870 by a bunch of visionaries in a downtown Syracuse hall named for Shakespeare. To paraphrase the Bard, that meeting wound up being much ado about *something*. Yes, there would be daunting obstacles along the way, including occasions when it appeared SU might not survive. But over time, the idea sown by those Methodist convention-goers would blossom into a world-class research university featuring thirteen colleges, more than 270 majors and 150 minors, with fifteen thousand undergraduates, six thousand graduate students, and more than a quarter of a million alumni from all fifty states and more than 170 countries.

A disproportionate number of those alumni would go on to change the world in ways big and small.

And Syracuse would become, as Chancellor James Roscoe Day envisioned, a great university on the Hill.

Syracuse University's Confusing Origins

The words "Genesee College Founded 1851" and "Syracuse University Founded 1871" are chiseled into the granite façade above the four columns in front of Carnegie Library on the south end of the Quad.

Genesee College, which was located in Lima, New York, about eighty-five miles east of SU, was supposed to be relocated to Syracuse by the Methodist Episcopal Church. But that plan fell through when angry residents of Lima sought and received a court injunction.

Church officials, with financial backing from Syracuse city officials, decided to go ahead with their plans to build a university in the Salt City. Many of Genesee's students and faculty members wound up transferring to Syracuse when the new university began classes in 1871. Genesee never recovered from the dramatic decline in enrollment and eventually folded.

"To help resolve hard feelings after the college's closing, SU's board of trustees allowed Genesee College alumni to consider SU their alma mater," said Syracuse University archivist Meg Mason, who, with former archivists Edward Galvin and Mary O'Brien, coauthored a 128-page photo history book about SU in 2013. "I'm always comfortable making it clear that they aren't true alumni."

Interestingly, SU's Office of Alumni Engagement continues to list as Syracuse alumni several Genesee alumni who never studied in the Salt City. Despite what it says in granite at Carnegie, 1870 is acknowledged as the year of SU's official founding, even though classes didn't begin until 1871.

Carnegie Library. © Syracuse University. Photo by Stephen Sartori.

2 Bricks, Mortar, and Teflon

We shape our buildings; thereafter they shape us.
—Winston Churchill

The Einhorn Family Walk and the steps leading up to the Hall of Languages.
© Syracuse University. Photo by Stephen Sartori.

Students take advantage of Crouse College's hill and Syracuse's wintry weather for a little sledding at night. © Syracuse University. Photo by Stephen Sartori.

After the first members of Syracuse University's faculty were inaugurated on August 31, 1871, in the rented downtown office space that served as the college's first home, Bishop Jesse Truesdell Peck led a procession of five to six thousand enthusiastic Salt City residents up the hill to a barren hayfield. There, on rural land provided by George Comstock, the first chair of the university's board of trustees laid the cornerstone for the Hall of Languages.

Designed by architect Horatio Nelson White and constructed of Onondaga limestone for $136,000, the iconic edifice would open two years later and a new campus would begin to take shape.

Peck envisioned a mix of buildings lined up side-by-side in the old row style popularized by Yale University in the 1790s. Although a national bank panic prevented his vision from being realized immediately, Peck's dream eventually came true.

To stroll on campus today is to journey through an architectural smorgasbord that undoubtedly has gone beyond the wildest expectations of SU's founding father. From the eerie-looking Hall of Languages, to the Romanesque Crouse College standing majestically on the Hill, to the twenty-one-story Lawrinson Hall, to the Greek columns at Maxwell, to the familiar billowy white roof of the Carrier Dome, there's a little something for every taste. A bountiful mix of classic and contemporary architecture on a hill offering a panoramic view of the city, countryside, and Onondaga Lake.

Clearly, many of the buildings have stood the test of time, with the Hall of Languages, Crouse College, Hendricks Chapel, and tiny Holden Observatory among fourteen SU edifices listed on the National Register of Historic Places. Through the decades, the university has experienced several building spurts, and that has included the disappearance of historic places, such as Archbold Stadium and Yates Castle, which were razed to make way for new structures.

Progress has its downsides. Some critics believed there were times when the university grew too fast, and not enough attention was paid to architectural harmony, historical significance, and congestion issues. They decried the hodgepodge, seemingly rhyme-without-reason evolution of the campus.

Despite all the construction, destruction, and reconstruction, SU managed to maintain many of its green spaces, particularly the Quad, an open expanse of lawn and walkways in the heart of campus that's a favorite student gathering place. There's another enormous stretch of grass, trees, and flowers in front of the Hall of Languages and the other original buildings lined up in linear fashion along SU's version of the old row. In essence, this is the university's front yard. For many years, it was bordered on the north by University Place, a heavily trafficked road used by cars and trucks. As part of a new master plan, the road was closed to all vehicular traffic and replaced by the brick-lined Einhorn Family Walk.

SU's architectural diversity is on full display along the walk, with modernistic structures such as Newhouse I, II, and III, the Schine Student Center, and Bird Library, as well as the Goldstein Alumni and Faculty Center, a three-story colonial mansion that once was the Deke fraternity house.

The campus is enhanced by numerous outdoor statues, including a pensive Abraham Lincoln seated between the Tolley Humanities Building and Maxwell, the Saltine Warrior firing an arrow skyward in front of Carnegie Library on the south end of the Quad, and an agonized Job outside Bowne Hall.

Perhaps the most hallowed and reflective place on campus is the Flight 103 Memorial, a granite semicircle just beyond the opening arches leading up to the Hall of Languages. Chiseled there are the names of the thirty-five SU students who were killed in a terrorist bombing while flying over Lockerbie, Scotland, in December 1988 on their return from a semester abroad in London.

On the east exterior wall of Huntington Beard Crouse Hall is another work of art that evokes emotion—a huge, colorful, tile

SU's original buildings form the campus's "old row." Syracuse University Photograph Collection, University Archives.

Inside the Hall of Languages. © Syracuse University. Photo by Stephen Sartori.

Donor John Archbold's impact on the building of Syracuse University can still be seen on the entrance to the Hall of Languages. © Syracuse University. Photo by Stephen Sartori.

and several hundred feet of covered stairways that provide students protection from wintry weather while hoofing to and from classes.

South Campus, about a five-minute bus ride away, is known as Skytop and features housing for about 2,500 students. It was first utilized following World War II, when student enrollment tripled during the GI Bulge.

South Campus also is home to a massive athletic complex, featuring numerous playing fields for a variety of intercollegiate, club, and intramural sports. At the west end of the complex sits the Carmelo K. Anthony Basketball Center, and on the east edge is the Ensley Athletic Center, a rectangular indoor field house featuring a 120-yard football field. In the middle are coaches' offices, study rooms, and Manley Field House, which once was home to SU basketball, but now is used mostly as a practice facility.

SU also owns or leases several buildings in the Armory Square section of downtown Syracuse, just blocks from where the university held its first classes. These include the Nancy Cantor Warehouse, a renovated furniture repository that houses several design programs and a gallery.

A few blocks north of campus sits Syracuse Stage, which features two stages, including the Storch Theater, named after long-time SU drama professor and director Arthur Storch and used for student-produced plays and musicals.

Although it's not technically on campus, Marshall Street, known fondly as M Street, has long been the main street of Syracuse University. An eclectic mix of bars, novelty shops, and restaurants, this block has been a favorite gathering place for students since the opening of Varsity pizza, across the street on South Crouse Avenue, in 1926. M Street can become quite congested, especially before and after Orange football and basketball games. But it's not as heavily trafficked as the nearby hospital zone, which features three hospitals as well as the Syracuse VA Medical Center and serves as a main entrance road to the university.

The SU campus extends far beyond Central New York. The Lubin House in New York City and the Greenberg House in Washington, DC, are hubs for alumni events in those metropolitan areas. The university's strong Hollywood ties resulted in the Los Angeles center, where students can spend a semester studying under prominent alumni. And since 1919, SU has provided students with opportunities to study abroad, with satellite campuses in places as distant as Beijing and London.

The epicenter, though, remains a sprawling, 721-acre urban campus that once was a hayfield.

"Stylistic eclecticism" was the architectural goal cited in one of the university's early master plans.

That vision was realized—not always in perfect harmony—with a diverse collection of old and new buildings that have helped shape tens of thousands of impressionable minds through the decades.

mosaic dedicated to Nicola Sacco and Bartolomeo Vanzetti, Italian immigrants who many historians and legal scholars believe were wrongly sentenced to death after being accused of murder.

The campus also is adorned with numerous benches that were gifts of alumni, including the famous granite-slabbed Kissing Bench near the west side of the Hall of Languages. Legend has it that if two SU undergrads kiss while seated there, they will wind up getting married.

The university's expansion has entailed land, along with buildings. The largest tract remains the main or North Campus, which houses not only a majority of the academic and administration buildings but also all twenty-one residence halls, as well as the Sheraton Syracuse University Hotel & Conference Center (which SU owns) and the Dome. A two-dorm complex called Mount Olympus because of its high elevation overlooks the Teflon-roofed stadium to the west and the massive Oakwood Cemetery to the south. The Mount features a steep, curvy access road

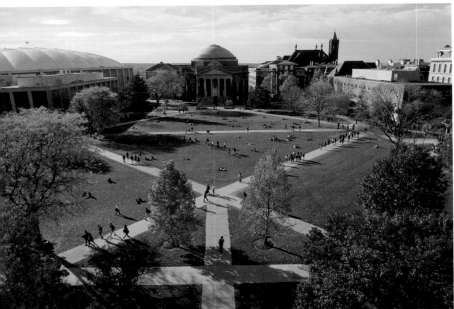

(Above) The green space of the Shaw Quadrangle—best known as the Quad—is located at the heart of SU's main campus. © Syracuse University. Photo by Stephen Sartori.

(Left) The Quad. © Syracuse University. Photo by Stephen Sartori.

(Below) The Quad can be tough to negotiate on fierce winter days. © Syracuse University. Photo by Stephen Sartori.

SU trustee and local coal merchant Erastus Holden funded the construction of Holden Observatory in 1887 in memory of his son, Charles Demarest Holden, an early Syracuse graduate. © Syracuse University. Photo by Stephen Sartori.

The Ernest S. Bird Library, which opened in 1972, is the busiest academic space on campus. © Syracuse University. Photo by Stephen Sartori.

In 1991, the 320-ton Holden Observatory was moved 190 feet to the southwest and 60 feet to the south to make room for the Melvin Eggers Hall addition to the Maxwell School. Syracuse University Photograph Collection, University Archives.

Architectural Kings

Founded by Archimedes Russell in 1868, King + King Architects is the oldest continuously operating architectural firm in New York State and the third oldest in the nation. It also is the firm that has had the greatest influence on the buildings of Syracuse University. Starting with the construction of Holden Observatory in 1887, King + King has been involved in thirty-nine campus projects. In addition to Holden, the firm designed such iconic SU structures as Crouse College, the von Ranke Library (now the Tolley Humanities Building), Manley Field House, Newhouse I, Lawrinson Hall, Bird Library, and the Carmelo K. Anthony Basketball Center. "The story of the King + King family is interwoven with the story of Syracuse University and the School of Architecture," said the school's dean, Michael Speaks. "Indeed, you cannot tell one without the other."

Numerous members of the King family graduated from SU with degrees in architecture. They include Harry King (1924), who studied under Russell when he was a Syracuse professor; F. Curtis King (1924); Russell King (1952); Peter King (1977); James King (1977); and Alex King (2011). The firm's current CEO/managing partner, Kirk Narburgh, has a master's degree in architecture from SU and teaches there as an adjunct. And Peter King serves on the architecture school's advisory board.

Sacco and Vanzetti Mural

On October 10, 1967, noted artist Ben Shahn's new mosaic, *The Passion of Sacco and Vanzetti*, was unveiled on the exterior east wall of Huntington Beard Crouse Hall.

"This event has special significance far beyond the history it depicts for us," said Frank Piskor, Syracuse vice president for academic affairs. "It is an appeal to conscience by a man of integrity and deep social sympathies. Its concern is the never-ending quest of human beings not only for the good, the true and the beautiful, but for the just."

Shahn's massive twelve-by-sixty-foot marble and enamel artwork focused attention on one of the most politically charged murder cases in American history. In August 1927, two Italian American immigrants, Nicola Sacco and Bartolomeo Vanzetti, men with anarchist connections, were executed in Massachusetts for a crime many believed they did not commit.

An artist who was a social realist, Shahn saw the two men as modern day martyrs, dying for their political beliefs amid an atmosphere of fear, hatred, and intolerance. To make a point, in the mural's right corner, standing before the presiding judge, are the members of the Lowell Commission who approved the court proceeding. They are portrayed as representatives of that era's legal, political, and moral institutions while standing over the coffins of the executed men.

Artist Ben Shahn's *The Passion of Sacco and Vanzetti* mosaic on the east wall of Huntington Beard Crouse Hall is arguably the most recognizable work of art on campus. © Syracuse University. Photo by Stephen Sartori.

Some believe the spooky-looking Hall of Languages was the inspiration for the opening graphic of the haunted mansion in the popular *Addams Family* television sitcom. © Syracuse University. Photo by Stephen Sartori.

Sacco and Vanzetti's greatest legacy may lie in the numerous decisions made by the US Supreme Court that now extend due process to anyone charged with a crime and thus try to protect American civil rights.

Shahn, who was born in Lithuania, had created an illustration of Dr. Martin Luther King Jr. for the cover of *Time* in 1965. By early 1966, he was in discussions with the dean of SU's art school, Laurence Schmeckebier, to create what instantly became one of the most recognizable pieces of artwork on SU's sprawling campus.

The idea of using university buildings and grounds as settings for works of art started in 1957 with the acquisition of Rico Lebrun's mural *Crucifixion*, which was placed in Heroy Geology Laboratory. This work inspired a plan to place original mural-sized paintings around campus. The high point of this creative effort was the installation of Shahn's monumental mosaic on the façade of Huntington Beard Crouse.

The Sacco and Vanzetti mural is dedicated to Richard Evans III, a former Syracuse student and US Army veteran who died in a motorcycle accident in July 1965. It underwent an extensive restoration in 2011.

It's Creepy and It's Spooky

No one seems to know for sure how and when the urban legend began that the Hall of Languages was the model for the morbid mansion seen in *The Addams Family* television sitcom. But at some point fiction was accepted as fact, and the tale continues to be passed down from one generation of Syracuse students to the next.

It's easy to see why people would come to this conclusion because the spooky-looking Addams family house at 0001 Cemetery Lane does bear a striking resemblance to Syracuse's "haunted" hall. Still, there is no proof that SU's oldest edifice inspired cartoonist Charles Addams, whose drawings of Gomez, Morticia, Thing, and Cousin Itt for the *New Yorker*, starting in 1938, were brought to life in the mid-1960s television series and subsequent movies. Addams did attend nearby Colgate University for two years before transferring to the University of Pennsylvania, but there's no record of him setting foot on the SU campus. And there has been talk that a house in his hometown of Westfield, New Jersey, or Penn's College Hall may have been the true inspiration for the Victorian Gothic mansion that housed the Addams family. Addams denied these suppositions but never elaborated.

There also were rumors that an SU graduate working on the show used the Hall of Languages to create the eerie illustration of the mansion's exterior that was seen in the opening of each episode. So the source remains a mystery. A mystery that's become part of SU lore.

(Above) An aerial view of Archbold Stadium's prominence on the Syracuse campus. Syracuse University Photograph Collection, University Archives.

(Left) The entrance castle towers were Archbold Stadium's most distinctive feature. Athletics Department, Syracuse University, used by permission.

(Above) Archbold Gymnasium was almost destroyed by fire in January 1947. The quickly spreading blaze caused the roof to collapse, and extra firefighters were needed to save nearby Carnegie Library. Reconstruction of the gym wasn't completed until 1952. Syracuse University Photograph Collection, University Archives.

(Right) Designed in the 1850s and purchased by SU in 1906, Yates Castle housed the new Teacher's College and later the School of Journalism. It was sold to the State of New York in 1950 and was demolished in 1954. Syracuse University Photograph Collection, University Archives.

(Left) The Carrier Dome took on the appearance of a giant spaceship that had landed on campus. Athletics Department, Syracuse University, used by permission.

(Below) A construction worker tests the sturdiness of one of the thick, Teflon-coated, cable-supported roof panels during the construction of the Carrier Dome in the spring of 1980. Syracuse University Photograph Collection, University Archives.

(Above) Major renovations to the Dome are expected to include a permanent, girder-supported roof to replace the current air-supported ceiling. Courtesy of Syracuse University.

(Below) Constructed at first to provide the football team with a place to practice during inclement weather, Manley Field House quickly became better known as home to Syracuse University basketball. Athletics Department, Syracuse University, used by permission.

The Maxwell School of Citizenship and Public Affairs opened in 1937 and was expanded upon in 1994. Its graduate program for public administration has been ranked nationally for several decades. © Syracuse University. Photo by Stephen Sartori.

The statue of a seated Abraham Lincoln on the courtyard between the Maxwell School and the Tolley Humanities Building was sculpted by James Earle Fraser, who may be best known for designing the Buffalo nickel. It was set in its current place in 1968. Fraser also sculpted a statue of a young Lincoln on the SUNY College of Environmental Science and Forestry campus, just south of the Carrier Dome. © Syracuse University. Photo by Stephen Sartori.

A replica of Jean-Antoine Houdon's life-size statue of George Washington stands in front of the inscription of the Athenian oath of citizenship in the Maxwell School's antechamber. © Syracuse University. Photo by Stephen Sartori.

(Above) Students gather for a spirit session in the Flint Hall courtyard on Mount Olympus during orientation week. © Syracuse University. Photo by Stephen Sartori.

(Left) Opened in 1965 as an all-male dorm overlooking Archbold Stadium, Lawrinson Hall remains the tallest building on campus—twenty-two stories high. © Syracuse University. Photo by Stephen Sartori.

(Right) In 1964, Haven Hall became the second women's dormitory named for SU Chancellor Erastus O. Haven. (The first was torn down to make room for the Newhouse complex.) Its interesting architecture led students to refer to it affectionately as the "toilet bowl." Syracuse University Photograph Collection, University Archives.

Newhouse II features state-of-the-art television studios.
© Syracuse University. Photo by Stephen Sartori.

In 2007, S. I. Newhouse's original vision of a three-building communications complex was finalized with the opening of Newhouse III.
© Syracuse University. Photo by Stephen Sartori.

(Left) The Lyman C. Smith College of Applied Science opened in 1902 and was SU's first engineering school. Syracuse University Photograph Collection, University Archives.

(Right) Initially called the Esther Baker Steele Hall of Physics after the benefactor and trustee who donated money for its construction in 1898, Steele Hall provided much-needed space for the science department. Later, the building would become home to many of the university's administrative offices, including the Office of Student Affairs and the registrar. Syracuse University Photograph Collection, University Archives.

(Left) A Syracuse student takes advantage of a quiet study area in the Schine Student Center, with the Hall of Languages evident in the distance. © Syracuse University. Photo by Stephen Sartori.

(Above) At the corner of College Place, Psi Upsilon was the first structure on campus to be built specifically as a fraternity house. The mansion, which was designed by SU School of Architecture alumnus Wellington Taber, is one of several campus buildings on the National Register of Historic Places. © Syracuse University. Photo by Stephen Sartori.

(Right) Fashion students gather on a sidewalk outside the Lubin House in Manhattan's fashionable Upper East Side. The brownstone was gifted to SU by philanthropist Joseph Lubin and has long been the focal point for Orange activities in the Big Apple. © Syracuse University. Photo by Stephen Sartori.

(Above) The bronze statue of the Greek archer Herakles was created by French artist Emile Antoine Bourdelle and was the gift of S. I. Newhouse and his wife. Like many statues on the SU campus, it has been moved several times and now resides on the northeast Quad near Hinds Hall. © Syracuse University. Photo by Stephen Sartori.

(Right) Sculptures of Job and Moses are prominently displayed in Mestrovic's Garden on the southeast side of the Quad. They are the works of Ivan Mestrovic, a world-famous sculptor who taught at SU for eight years. © Syracuse University. Photo by Stephen Sartori.

(Below) A student has fun with the Elemental Man statue, next to Falk College. © Syracuse University. Photo by Stephen Sartori.

(Above) A gift of philanthropist Andrew Carnegie, the Carnegie Library on the south side of the Quad opened its doors in 1907. It is counted among the original Carnegie libraries still in use on college campuses. © Syracuse University. Photo by Stephen Sartori.

(Left) The William B. Heroy Geology Laboratory features a large illuminated globe hanging from the ceiling that can be seen through the lobby's three-story glass windows. © Syracuse University. Photo by Stephen Sartori.

(Above) The Einhorn Family Walk turned a street once heavily trafficked by motor vehicles into a popular pedestrian-only mall. The brick walk was funded by alumni Steven and Sherry Einhorn. © Syracuse University. Photo by Stephen Sartori.

(Right) The steps leading up to Crouse College provide an interesting perspective on just how steep SU's main hill is. © Syracuse University. Photo by Stephen Sartori.

3 It's Academic

A student takes advantage of the nice weather to study outside the Hall of Languages. © Syracuse University. Photo by Stephen Sartori.

Suos.
Cultores.
Scientia.
Coronat.

Latin for "knowledge crowns those who seek her," this brilliantly simple and simply brilliant academic motto began appearing on Syracuse University's laurel-wreath seal a few years after the school's 1870 incorporation as an institution of higher education. And although it's not known who suggested its adoption, the words continue to be a guiding force 150 years later at a university that has fulfilled its founding father's vision and achieved national and international acclaim.

On any given school day, you'll find more than twenty-two thousand SU students seeking knowledge. And they do so in a vast variety of subjects, while pursuing degrees in more than two hundred majors and one hundred minors in the university's thirteen schools and colleges. They are supported by more than five thousand faculty members and staff, and many of the professors and deans are world-respected experts in their fields. Nearly one-third of the roughly fifteen thousand undergraduate students are based in the College of Arts and Sciences, where they focus on the physical sciences, math, humanities, and social sciences.

Through the decades, an Orange trinity of administrators, teachers, and students has consistently delivered a wide range of academic accomplishments, encompassing breakthroughs in literature, journalism, architecture, law, business, engineering, data management, the sciences, nursing, social work, public service, and military training.

Research has long been a top priority, with Syracuse recognized as one of only 120 R1 Carnegie-classified universities in the world. Exploration and curiosity are emphasized, and SU students, representing all fifty states and more than 120 countries, have collaborated with faculty on scores of world-changing discoveries, including the proving of Albert Einstein's gravitational

A student conducting an experiment in the biology lab. © Syracuse University. Photo by Stephen Sartori.

waves theory and the development of artificial hearts and literacy programs.

At the graduate and doctoral level, Syracuse features more than seven thousand full- and part-time enrollees involved with degree work or quantitative and qualitative research in numerous fields. Further, SU's University College is a recognized leader in nontraditional education, covering online courses, certificates of advanced study, and noncredit courses designed to accelerate professional careers.

Not all Syracuse students take their classes in upstate New York. Many study at the SU in LA campus in southern California, at New York City's Fisher Center, or via online courses from distant settings. In fact, SU provides learning opportunities in more than sixty countries and features centers in Strasbourg, France; Florence, Italy; London, England; Hong Kong; Santiago, Chile; and Madrid, Spain.

Many of its departments and programs are nationally ranked and thus help showcase SU as one of America's top fifty universities. Faculty and students from Maxwell, Newhouse, Visual and Performing Arts, Architecture, Whitman, Falk, the iSchool, the Institute for Veterans and Military Families, creative writing, sport management/sport analytics, and numerous other schools and programs make an Orange education all the more desirable.

Its academic support facilities also are top-notch, including Syracuse University Libraries, which contain the Special Collections Research Center and feature more than 4.6 million physical items (books, microforms, journals, periodicals, maps, audio recordings, photographs, manuscripts, etc.) and millions of online titles/electronic books.

SU Libraries began with the purchase of the massive von Ranke book collection from Germany in 1887 and the subsequent construction of what is now the Tolley Humanities Building in 1888 to house it. When the von Ranke Library could no longer contain

A Newhouse professor instructs a student how to operate a studio television camera. © Syracuse University. Photo by Stephen Sartori.

Professors and students conduct a lava flow experiment on the Quad. © Syracuse University. Photo by Stephen Sartori.

Reputation

its celebrated collection and frequent new inclusions, Carnegie Library was opened in 1907. Bird Library followed in 1972 and kept SU Libraries at the academic heart of what has long been a major research university.

Open twenty-four hours a day during the semester, Bird is a vibrant, inclusive hub for students, with interior centers dedicated to innovation and entrepreneurship, tutoring, undergraduate research, and digital scholarship. It also provides collaborative and contemplative study spaces and is the busiest academic space on campus, with 1.3 million visitors a year.

Other institutional highlights include cutting-edge labs in the Life Sciences Complex, renovated classrooms in the historic Hall of Languages, a NASA-quality flight simulator in Link Hall, and dynamic creative spaces in the iSchool. All are part of a rich heritage of academic innovation, experimentation, and productivity.

Syracuse University's Schools and Colleges

School of Architecture

The fourth oldest architecture school in the country, it offers a professional curriculum that stresses creativity, research, and problem-solving. The five-year program leads to a Bachelor of Architecture degree. Founded: 1873. Enrollment (2018-19 academic year): 658.

College of Arts and Sciences

SU's founding college remains at the center of undergraduate learning. It is divided into the natural sciences and mathematics, the humanities, and the social sciences, with the latter offered in partnership with the Maxwell School. Founded: 1870. Enrollment: 5,946.

School of Education

A national leader in enhancing educational practice and a pioneer in the inclusion movement, the School of Education continues that tradition through its work to improve urban education. Founded: 1906. Enrollment: 1,108.

College of Engineering and Computer Science

Future engineers and computer scientists learn to create new knowledge and technologies through ten undergraduate majors. Students have access to nationally regarded research centers, state-of-the-art lab spaces, and challenging internships. Founded: 1901. Enrollment: 2,624.

David B. Falk College of Sport and Human Dynamics

Social justice principles are at the foundation of programs in child and family studies, food studies, marriage and family therapy, public

Architecture students examine the base of their wooden design. © Syracuse University. Photo by Stephen Sartori.

health, nutrition, social work, and sport management. Academics, service learning projects, internships, research opportunities, and clubs connected to Falk majors prepare students for their careers. Founded: School of Home Economics, 1917; College of Nursing, 1943; School of Social Work, 1946; College of Human Development, 1971. Enrollment: 1,568.

School of Information Studies

The nation's "original information school," the iSchool is a leader in preparing students for a fast-paced digital future by teaching the technological, communication, management, and design skills necessary to develop solutions for any industry or startup. Founded: 1896. Enrollment: 1,755.

College of Law

With the law school's emphasis on small classes, students study and argue cases in Dineen Hall, which opened in 2014 and is listed by Best Choice Schools among the fifty most impressive law school buildings in the world. Founded: 1895. Enrollment: 572.

Martin J. Whitman School of Management

Whitman develops entrepreneurial leaders for an increasingly competitive global market. Programs are built around today's major driving forces in business: entrepreneurial management, globalization, technology, and leadership. Founded: 1919. Enrollment: 2,909.

Maxwell School of Citizenship and Public Affairs

Maxwell serves as SU's home for innovative, interdisciplinary teaching and research in the social sciences, public policy, public administration, and international relations. It includes America's top-ranked graduate program in public affairs, offering highly regarded professional degrees alongside advanced scholarly degrees in the social sciences. Founded: 1924. Enrollment: 589.

S.I. Newhouse School of Public Communications

Long recognized as one of the elite mass communications schools, Newhouse embraces virtually every known form of information dissemination. Programs are rooted in the liberal arts, and students learn to manage and produce for the mass media and other areas of public communications. Founded: 1934 (originally as the School of Journalism). Enrollment: 2,027.

College of Visual and Performing Arts (VPA)

VPA is divided into six areas: the School of Art; the Department of Communication and Rhetorical Studies; the School of Design; the Department of Drama; the Rose, Jules R. and Stanford S. Setnor School of Music; and the Department of Transmedia. Founded: 1873. Enrollment: 2,017.

University College

Almost all Syracuse degrees can be completed part time, with day, evening, online, weekend, and accelerated or condensed class options. University College also offers two part-time Bachelor of Professional Studies (BPS) degrees and certificate programs, which can be completed fully online or in a blended format of online and on-campus classes. Founded: 1918. Enrollment: 594.

Graduate School

The Graduate School oversees SU's academic policy, graduate degree and certificate program modification and development, and professional development programs for graduate study. Founded: 1912. Enrollment: 7,433.

Some Professors of Note throughout SU's History

David Bennett

At the end of each semester, it was not uncommon for David Bennett's students to rise from their seats in Maxwell Auditorium and give the American history professor a standing ovation. That he would receive a response befitting a great stage performance was apropos because Bennett's lectures were filled with drama. And that drama did more than entertain; it also informed in a way that made potentially boring material comprehensible and real. "Professor Bennett's anecdotes break up what could have been a monotonous history class," former student Abraham Reisch said in a *Daily Orange* interview. "His stories help me remember the material much more than complicated, confusing notes ever would."

John Judson, another former student of Bennett's, concurred.

David Bennett. © Syracuse University. Photo by Stephen Sartori.

"Professor Bennett's lectures really made you feel the material," he said. "You can tell he's lecturing about something he really loves. He makes it really personal."

Bennett modeled his narrative style of lecturing after two teachers he had during his undergraduate days at SU: English professor David Owen and T. V. Smith, a professor of citizenship. "They were so good at what they did," Bennett said. "I knew it could be done that way."

Like an actor taking the stage or an athlete taking the field, Bennett said he "would really get up for a lecture. It's very involving." His riveting stories grabbed his students' attention, made history relatable. "I want my students to have a sense of the drama of history, and the way history shapes our lives and the world in which we live," he said in a *Syracuse University Magazine* interview. "I want my students to look back on my classes and have them make sense in some way."

A Syracuse native, Bennett attended his hometown university with designs on becoming a journalist. While at SU, he served as editorial page editor of the *DO*, stirring things up with a series of stories advocating a student union on campus. In his junior year, he switched majors, and he graduated with a degree in American studies from Maxwell in 1956. After earning graduate degrees from the University of Chicago, he returned to SU in 1961 to teach, and continues to work as an emeritus history professor nearly six decades later.

Along the way, he became a respected expert on political extremism in America, winning the Myers Prize in 1988 for his book *The Party of Fear: From Nativist Movements to the New Right in American History*. The recipient of numerous honors from SU, including a 1991 Chancellor's Citation for Exceptional Academic Achievement, Bennett also chaired the university's athletic policy board, headed the search committee that hired Jim Boeheim as men's basketball coach in 1976, and worked with former athletics director Jake Crouthamel to get the Carrier Dome built on the site of old Archbold Stadium.

But to thousands of students who took his history courses, he's best remembered as the professor who delivered lectures worthy of a standing ovation.

Burton Blatt

Burton Blatt was a professor at Boston University in 1966 when he published his seminal work, *Christmas in Purgatory*. The book was a photographic exposé of the horrifying conditions that existed at state institutions for individuals with cognitive and developmental disabilities.

Two important things happened soon afterward. First, Lyndon Johnson personally contacted him about leveraging the book's depiction of abusive treatment of individuals with disabilities to inform the work of the President's Committee on Mental Retardation.

Then, in 1969, Syracuse University hired him as a professor and director of the Division of Special Education and Rehabilitation. The following year, he was named a Centennial Professor in recognition of his highly influential national leadership of the deinstitutionalization movement.

By 1976, Blatt was dean of SU's School of Education, had founded the Center on Human Policy, and had been selected as president of the American Association on Mental Deficiency. During the remainder of his career at Syracuse, Blatt would win numerous awards for his tireless, impassioned support of disability rights while publishing numerous books, scholarly papers, and journalistic columns on public policy, special education, and institutional care.

Blatt died suddenly in 1985 at age fifty-seven, but twenty years later SU created the Burton Blatt Institute to "advance the empowered participation of people with disabilities." The institute's offices in Syracuse, Washington, DC, New York City, Atlanta, and Lexington, Kentucky, foster policy research and public-private discussion of key societal issues. In 2017, the American Bar Association launched a first-of-its-kind nationwide study, conducted by the Burton Blatt Institute (in conjunction with SU's College of Law), to identify biases encountered by LGBTQ and/or disabled lawyers in the legal profession and thus help develop and implement strategies to address them.

Tom Brutsaert

When exercise science professor Tom Brutsaert began teaching at Syracuse University in the autumn of 2009, he knew his high-altitude research on humans would benefit from continued work in the Andes with the Quechua populations in Peru and Aymara communities in Bolivia. These were places where the Cornell-educated biological anthropologist had long studied human response to higher altitudes, including genetic, developmental, and physiological modes of adaptation.

But he also knew that Mount Everest, the world's tallest mountain (at 29,029 feet), was the one place he really wanted to

As part of Professor Tom Brutsaert's exercise science course, SU Abroad students traverse a bridge near Mount Everest. Courtesy of Andrew Burton.

Marvin Druger. © Syracuse University. Photo by Stephen Sartori.

take SU students. To make that vision a reality, Brutsaert joined a May 2017 Canadian expedition there. A year later, he took SU undergraduate and graduate students to Nepal's breathtaking Himalayan mountain range as part of a dynamic twenty-three-day adventure that included long hours of trekking and altitude acclimatization.

Basing out of Kathmandu, Nepal, Brutsaert took fifteen Orange students as high as Kalapatthar, a serrated ridge set at 18,500 feet looking down onto Everest Base Camp and up toward the famous windswept peak known to the Nepalese as Sagarmāthā and to the Tibetans as Chomolungma.

"It took a lot of planning," said Brutsaert upon returning from Everest. "We wanted to give Syracuse Study Abroad students a real chance to see field research, as opposed to our Altitude Simulation Lab on campus, and connect their understanding of concepts like hypoxia, high-altitude edema, the reduction or saturation of oxygen content in blood, and heart rate reaction. And, we wanted to do so with actual climbers."

Brutsaert's willingness to give SU students a firsthand look at real-world science while exposing them to the cultural benefits of places like the infamous airstrip at Lukla, the monastery at Tengboche, the Hillary School in Khumjung, and the Hillary Foundation Hospital in Khunde (where Sherpas and the world's best climbers congregate) was significant.

Interestingly, Brutsaert's expedition, expertly coordinated by Nima Sherpa, reached Everest Base Camp during the early afternoon of May 29—the sixty-fifth anniversary of Sir Edmund Hillary and Sherpa Tenzing Norgay's first summiting Everest in 1953.

Marvin Druger

Today, he's probably best known as a cardboard cutout (complete with outstretched arms) perpetually welcoming shoppers to the SU bookstore's textbook section. But for five decades, he was one of Syracuse's most energetic and enthusiastic professors. Colorful and cool. Crazy but supercommitted to his students.

Those are just some of the ways that Orange students would describe Syracuse biology professor Marvin Druger.

Other descriptions apply, too: loving husband, Orange philanthropist, author, magazine columnist, radio host (*Druger's Zoo* on WAER-FM), whimsical scientist, and president of the National Science Teachers Association (the world's largest science education organization), the Society for College Science Teachers, and the Association for the Education of Teachers in Science.

For Druger, a Laura J. and L. Douglas Meredith Professor (a select honor given for teaching excellence), each semester offered countless ways to inspire BIO 121 and 123 students to have fun and creatively acquire scientific knowledge.

"The most important question a teacher has to ask is 'If I were a student sitting in that classroom, what would I want to know about the subject and why?'" he once said. "Then, as a teacher, I must answer that. I'm trying to reach inside each person and make him or her sit up and take notice. Once I've grabbed the spark of interest, the rest is easy."

As medical school student Amanda Swank recalled in 2008: "He made science fun and interesting. You could relate it to your everyday life. If I had taken this intro class and the professor had been miserable and dull, then I probably wouldn't have been inspired to go on with science."

Armed with a doctoral degree in zoology from Columbia (1961), Druger arrived at Syracuse in 1962 and never left. His impact was evident in the more than forty thousand students he taught and is commemorated on a bench near Huntington Beard Crouse Hall, with an Orange Grove brick, and in the 2015 restoration of

Holden Observatory, which houses the Patricia Meyers Druger Astronomy Learning Center.

Sawyer Falk and Arthur Storch

If Syracuse University's drama department and its many graduates (Peter Falk, Jerry Stiller, Vanessa Williams, Aaron Sorkin, to name a few) are internationally recognized, and Syracuse Stage is nationally revered, it is due largely to the efforts of two amazing professors who shaped the university's performing arts major between 1927 and 1992.

Floridian Sawyer Falk, who chaired the department from 1927 until his sudden death in 1961, and Brooklynite Arthur Storch, who stalked the Syracuse boards from 1973 to 1992, left huge marks on Central New York's theater scene. In fact, at Storch's passing in 2013, the *New York Times* noted that as a regional theater company, Syracuse Stage was "considered one of the most successful in the country."

After arriving at Syracuse as a professor of drama and chair of the department, Falk quickly emerged as a Broadway "play doctor," capable of stepping in to direct a major show while running an academic department. Over the next three decades, he inspired the creation of the Boar's Head Dramatic Society and moved his troupes from the all-purpose Crouse College auditorium to the eight-hundred-seat Regent Theater Complex and, eventually, the year-round New Playhouse. Falk's charges responded by consistently securing roles on Broadway, on television, and in Hollywood films.

Falk also convinced famous actors to come to Syracuse, and he once got the great Helen Hayes to star in SU's production of *Harriet*. When Falk ultimately brought the play to the Great White Way, *Harriet* became the first-ever college-produced play on Broadway.

Where Falk primarily focused his energies on directing in the classroom (and often took students abroad for his summer courses in England at Stratford-on-Avon), Storch came to Syracuse as a highly successful actor who wasn't sure he wanted the job. Already a noted Broadway player with roles in works such as *The Owl and the Pussycat* and *Look Homeward Angel*, Storch had just wrapped production as the overwhelmed psychiatrist in 1973's horror hit *The Exorcist* when Syracuse's drama department came calling.

He took the job, but not without friends debating his decision to leave a "thriving career in Manhattan for the uncertainty and provincial atmosphere of Syracuse."

Storch, the founding artistic director of Syracuse Stage and chief instigator in the facility's 1980 remodel, was famous for his goading candor with students, often telling them that happiness on the stage was fleeting and there would always be "fierce competition and constant pressure to earn profits for investors." That led him to dryly note, "If there is anything else you can do, you should do it."

That didn't deter a legion of theater majors from selecting Syracuse. They yearned to study under Falk and Storch. The two professors left sizable legacies at the corner of East Genesee Street and Irving Avenue, where the Archbold Theater and the Arthur Storch Theater now sit prominently in the Syracuse Stage/Drama Theater Complex.

Sol Gordon and Joe Fanelli

If there is one class that nearly every Syracuse student took or discussed over the last fifty years, it is probably Human Sexuality, taught first by Sol Gordon and then by Joe Fanelli.

Gordon, a professor of child and family studies and the director of SU's Institute for Family Research and Education, taught at SU from 1970 to 1985. During that time, he gained fame through a series of comic books (some banned) that he created to facilitate sex education. While some educators gasped, Gordon reportedly sold millions of twenty-five-cent copies featuring Captain Veedee-O and Ms. Wanda Lust, with titles like "VD Claptrap" and "Ten Heavy Facts About Sex." He told the *New York Times* he used "humor to reduce the anxiety of teen-agers. Besides, comic books are the only things that a huge number of adolescents willingly read."

Besides being a brilliant teacher, Gordon was an author (*Sex and the Family: A Guide for Parents and Children*) and TV host, filming more than fifty episodes of a Canadian series called *This Program Is about Sex*.

When Gordon left SU in 1985, he was replaced by the hugely likable Fanelli, who started at Syracuse as an adjunct faculty member in 1984. Fanelli would go on to famously teach CFS 388 (Human Sexuality) and CFS 425 (Lust, Love and Relationships), amazing his students with his ability to discuss intimate topics with humor and compassion.

"The real goal of psychosexual development is not to enhance our capacity to orgasm, but rather to enhance our capacity to love," said Fanelli, who retired in May 2018 after thirty-three years. "That is what human sexuality's real gift is."

Ralph Ketcham

Perhaps the secret to Ralph Ketcham's teaching success was that he always viewed his students as teachers. From the moment he arrived at Syracuse University in 1951 as an instructor and PhD candidate till the last class he taught as a Maxwell School emeritus professor a year before his death in 2017, he imparted knowledge to them, and they to him. And he never allowed his reputation as an internationally recognized scholar, author, and teacher to get in the way or create a wall.

"What stood out about Ralph is that his mind connected directly with yours in a kind of two-way dialogue in which he expects to learn as much from you as you expect to learn from him," said

Ralph Ketchum. Syracuse University Portrait Collection, University Archives.

Bill Polf, who studied under Ketcham and earned his doctorate from Maxwell in 1973.

Kevin Gottlieb, a 1970 PhD Maxwell alumnus, seconded those emotions.

"In 1964, when I walked into Ralph's office, he saw what I was, but instead focused on what I could become," Gottlieb said. "I owe him forever."

That Ketcham would wind up at Syracuse isn't surprising, given his family's Orange lineage. Not only did his parents meet there as undergrads, but six of their siblings also attended SU.

After earning his PhD in American studies from Maxwell in 1956, Ketcham taught at the University of Chicago and Yale before returning to SU seven years later. Maxwell afforded him the creative latitude to teach a variety of courses, including political science, public affairs, citizenship, and American history. A prolific writer, Ketcham authored a dozen books, including seminal tomes on James Madison and Benjamin Franklin. He also spent semesters in Japan, India, and the Netherlands, lecturing as a Fulbright Scholar.

In 1987, he reached the top of his profession when he was named national Professor of the Year by the Council for Advancement and Support of Education—the first and only SU professor to be so honored. A dozen years later, Ketcham's alma mater awarded him an honorary doctorate of humane letters and created a Maxwell School scholarship in his name. In 2003, Syracuse presented him with an Arents Award. But his greatest rewards came from seeing his students' success. During his work as a Fulbright Scholar in Japan in 1965, he established a scholarship program allowing students to study at SU.

"His contributions to the education of young people in Japan and around the world are immeasurable," said Masako Iino, a student who took advantage of the program.

Kermit Lee Jr.

A pioneer, an encouraging mentor, an accomplished professor of architecture.

Those were ways of describing Kermit Lee Jr., the first African American graduate of SU's School of Architecture. Lee graduated magna cum laude from SU in 1957 and won every prize awarded by the school, including the Henry Adams Prize and an American Institute of Architects Medal, the Alpha Rho Chi Medal, the Luther Gifford Prize in Design, and the New York Society of Architects Medal.

Following graduate study as a Fulbright Fellow at Technische Hochschule in Braunschweig, Germany, Lee enlisted in the Air Force and served as the civilian chief of architecture for the US Seventh Air Force before returning to Syracuse in 1966 to begin a nearly three-decade career teaching at his alma mater.

From then until his retirement in 1995, Lee consistently worked to "lift up" students after they received traditionally difficult critiques for their undergraduate architecture projects. So often, he was there for his students during their times of crisis.

His notable legacy, however, wasn't restricted to SU's classrooms.

While at Syracuse, Lee chaired the New York State Board of Architecture and was selected as a charter member of Governor Mario Cuomo's Cultural Advisory Committee for Times Square and Forty-Second Street. The Springfield, Massachusetts, native also won a prestigious National Endowment for the Arts Design Award, and received the lifetime designation of Fellow in the American Institute of Architects, the highest honor the institute confers on members.

In recognition of his service to Syracuse, the School of Architecture created the Kermit J. Lee Jr. Scholarship Fund in 1996 to provide promising students with resources to complete their degrees. The Lee Scholarship recognizes academic achievement, leadership, and professional promise, and is awarded annually to students nearing degree completion.

Mary Marshall

Want to discuss an "honorable" teacher? Then let's start with Mary Marshall, the first woman to hold a full-time professorship in English at Syracuse and the founder of the university's long-standing Honors Program.

Marshall was a fixture on campus for teaching the works of William Shakespeare, as well as Middle Ages and Renaissance drama, for more than forty years. But for her brightest students, it was Marshall's 1963 creation (and enthusiastic direction) of SU's Honors Program in the College of Arts and Sciences that stood out.

"Mary understood that a modern inquiring mind should be a contrarian mind," then director of the program Steve Kuusisto said in 2014. "She was a great teacher, and always looking to improve

Mary Marshall. Syracuse University Portrait Collection, University Archives.

not only the study and scholarship of students, but of the university she served." Edward Menkin, a former graduate student of Marshall's, recalled her strong advice. "She said to me, 'Don't take courses, take people.'"

Marshall earned her PhD in English from Yale University in 1932 and was encouraged by her home department to seek a full-time faculty appointment. Yale's board of trustees, however, reportedly rejected that plan because Yale didn't hire women. Yale's loss was ultimately SU's gain. Following a Guggenheim Fellowship from 1945 to 1947, Marshall began teaching at Syracuse in 1948.

Nearly a decade later, Marshall received the *Syracuse Post-Standard*'s 1957 Library Award for "outstanding service to the Syracuse University library" for her work on the Arents Rare Book Room at Carnegie Library. Additionally, as chair of the University Senate's library committee, she played a significant role in Bird Library's construction.

Marshall formally retired in 1970 but continued to teach as the Jesse T. Peck Professor Emeritus of English Literature at University College. Today, Marshall's legacy lives on in two distinct places: a Hall of Languages lecture hall, whose refurbishment was made possible by an anonymous $100,000 naming gift, and the Mary Marshall Capstone Library in Bowne Hall, dedicated during the Honors Program's fiftieth anniversary celebration.

That honor seems only fitting.

Ivan Mestrovic

Syracuse University chancellor William Pearson Tolley was visiting the office of Artur Nikoloric in New York City one day in 1946

when he overheard the Yugoslav lawyer discussing the plight of his friend Ivan Mestrovic. During World War II, Mestrovic, the most famous religious sculptor since Michelangelo, had been imprisoned for several months by the Nazis. He eventually was granted asylum in Sweden, then Rome. After the war, the Croatian native refused to return to Yugoslavia, which had fallen under Communist rule.

Nikoloric had been unsuccessful in finding an institution to bring Mestrovic to the United States. But upon hearing the story, Tolley didn't hesitate. He invited Mestrovic to start a sculpting program at SU while serving as the school's sculptor-in-residence.

The artist without a country jumped at the offer, and, although the former student of legendary French sculptor Auguste Rodin spent just seven years on the Hill, that would be long enough to leave an impression that continues to this day. Two years into Mestrovic's SU residency, the Metropolitan Museum of Art in New York City sponsored a one-man show of his works, the first time in its then seventy-five-year history that a living artist had been so honored.

Nicknamed Maestro for his ability to orchestrate a hunk of wood or stone, Mestrovic continued to produce great works of art while teaching students at a former carriage house barn on Marshall Street that served as a studio and classroom. Several of his statues remain on display in the Mestrovic Sculpture Court between the Shaffer Art Building and Bowne Hall on the northeast side of the Quad. They include *Supplicant Persephone*, a bronze statue of the daughter of the Greek god Zeus, and *Moses*, which originally was intended to be the centerpiece of a New York City memorial for Holocaust victims but wound up finding a permanent home at SU after financial problems and political squabbles doomed the Big Apple project.

Statues would not be all that Mestrovic molded at SU. Many of his students would go on to prominent careers—among them Jim

Ivan Mestrovic. Ivan Meštrović Collection, University Archives.

Ridlon, an Orange football All-American and former NFL defensive back who returned to his alma mater as an art professor.

"Being in (Mestrovic's) class was probably the greatest break I ever had as an artist," Ridlon said. "He was amazing to watch work, and he worked at breakneck speed, pumping out a piece of work almost weekly. He was doing clay models and wood and stone carving. It was really something to see him carve. He was built like an interior football lineman; massive arms and legs. He'd hit a piece of marble, and in two or three swipes there would be a huge pile of chips on the floor. The man was incredible."

Daniel Patrick Moynihan

At a towering six foot five, Daniel Patrick Moynihan may have been the biggest and most famous professor ever to stride the marbled hallways of SU's Maxwell School of Citizenship and Public Affairs. Moynihan taught at Syracuse twice—as a junior faculty member from 1959 to 1961, and four decades later, after twenty-five years as a Democratic senator from New York (1977-2001), as a University Professor from 2001 until his death in 2003.

"Senator Moynihan is the country's number one public intellectual and a national treasure," said Maxwell dean John Palmer, welcoming Moynihan to the SU faculty in January 2001. Palmer cemented Moynihan's long-standing relationship with SU by establishing Maxwell's Moynihan Prize for Outstanding Junior Faculty in 1986.

Having grown up poor in New York's Hell's Kitchen neighborhood, Moynihan was a political wunderkind.

A Navy veteran and former longshoreman who emerged as a member of John F. Kennedy's delegate pool in 1960, Moynihan served as an assistant to the labor secretary (1961-63), counselor to President Richard Nixon (1969-70), ambassador to India

Daniel Patrick Moynihan taught at Maxwell before and after he served as a US senator from New York. Syracuse University Portrait Collection, University Archives.

(1973-75) and the United Nations (1975-76), and chair of the Senate's Environment Committee (1992-93) and Finance Committee (1993-95). In addition, he found time to write nineteen books, causing journalist friend George Will of the *Washington Post* to dryly note Moynihan "wrote more books than most senators have read."

His political bravery was legendary. When Moynihan left the Senate for his professorship at Syracuse, Will suggested that few politicians had ever been as adventurous or as warmly humorous. "Who will do what he has done for the intellectual nutritiousness of public life?" asked Will. "The nation is not apt to see his like again, never having seen it before."

Said one political scientist about Moynihan: "Pat is the finest thinker among politicians since Abraham Lincoln and the finest politician among thinkers since Thomas Jefferson." A Republican aide to President Reagan offered similar praise, noting Moynihan was "distinctly bipartisan in an era of partisan bickering, and a statesman-intellectual at a time of blow-dried politicians. He [called] attention to matters no one else was doing."

In 2018, Moynihan was the subject of a powerful documentary titled simply *Moynihan*. Had he lived to meet with the filmmakers, he might have reuttered one of his most famous quotes: "The central conservative truth is that culture, not politics, determines the success of a society. The central liberal truth is that politics can change a culture and save it from itself."

Moynihan's importance to the American political landscape was celebrated on several occasions, including August 9, 2000, when he received the Presidential Medal of Freedom from President Bill Clinton. In December 2000, the twenty-seven-floor Daniel Patrick Moynihan United States Courthouse (home to the US District Court for the Southern District of New York) was rededicated in recognition of Moynihan's congressional efforts with numerous New York City mayors. The Maxwell School was not far behind, renaming a center as the Moynihan Institute of Global Affairs in 2005.

Moynihan's supreme mastery of complex policy issues (including laying the groundwork for major antipoverty legislation) and his love of Syracuse provided a towering benefit to Syracuse's Maxwell students.

Michael O. Sawyer

"If I'd ask someone whether they knew Mike Sawyer, their faces would light up. People would break into a smile."

So said Keith Bybee, Michael O. Sawyer Professor of Constitutional Law and Politics, after he left Harvard's faculty for Syracuse to become the Sawyer Chair in 2002.

Sawyer had retired from Syracuse in 1990 (giving a historic late-April final lecture to an overflow crowd), but not before completing forty-two years of fabled teaching at the Maxwell School.

"Mike was one of the most beloved teachers in the history of Maxwell," said Dean John Palmer, after presenting him with a plaque bearing the original brass handles of the college's auditorium doors and an inscription that confirmed Sawyer was "a part of the place forever." "I have more alumni speak to me about Mike, how he touched their lives and made more of a difference to them than anyone else."

Michael Sawyer was like that.

He arrived at Syracuse in the late 1930s and never really left. Along the way, he picked up undergraduate (1941), master's (1947), and doctoral degrees (1957). He earned a law degree from George Washington University (1962) and reached the rank of full Syracuse professor in 1965. Twenty-one years later, he won SU's highest alumni award, the George Arents Pioneer Medal, and was named Outstanding Professor of Syracuse University (an award voted on by students).

Upon Sawyer's death on Christmas Eve in 2002, Maxwell associates were effusive in describing his greatness and legacy. "He was so serious and wise about the craft of teaching," said Professor Emeritus Ralph Ketcham. "His student following was the greatest of anyone I know."

"I have never known and will surely never know a teacher with a greater love for students and a greater impact on their lives," said Senior Associate Dean Robert McClure. "Mike will rank forever as a Maxwell and Syracuse legend. [He was] the college teacher everyone dreams of having."

Sawyer's Orange course load included constitutional law, jurisprudence, administrative law, and party politics. He also found time to produce numerous publications and hold visiting lectureships at such universities as Notre Dame, North Carolina, and Oregon. But Syracuse was the place he loved. During the 1970s and 1980s, Sawyer took on a range of administrative roles, serving as interim vice chancellor for student programs (1972-73), special assistant to Chancellor Melvin A. Eggers (1973-75), vice chancellor for university relations (1975-79), and vice chancellor and executive assistant to the chancellor (1979-87).

The *New York Times*, which covered Sawyer's last lecture, noted that he offered "a ready tongue, a sharp wit and a wicked jab (usually aimed at the state of New Jersey). His blending of humor with lectures made students remember his lessons. He was accessible, his door always open and [he held] sincere concern for their problems, scholastic and personal."

Sarah Short

She'd paint psychedelic images on her legs and show them off under black lights. She got a motorcycle license in order to ride a thundering chrome bike into her classes.

Overnight, she became one of Syracuse University's most famous professors (ever), and during more than five decades of stellar

Sarah Short. Photograph by Anestis Diakopoulos. Syracuse University Portrait Collection, University Archives.

instruction, Sarah Short taught some 45,000 nutrition students, many in standing-room-only settings. The *New York Times* featured her in 1975 with long blond hair astride her Honda and noted, "If popping out of a cake or riding on a motorcycle will rivet her students to their seats, Dr. Short does it."

A year later, *People* magazine called her Psychedelic Sally and spoke of her ahead-of-the-curve multimedia skills. TV shows like *Good Morning America* and *Today* wanted her as well.

"I've often thought, 'Gee, what am I doing horsing around like this?'" Short told one reporter. "I'm sure some people think I'm stark raving insane. But I've got that class with me from the first day."

That creativity meant she was beloved by students, with her courses closing out early to majors and nonmajors alike. There was always mystery as to what Short might do next. One time, the SU marching band followed her into class. On other occasions, students found themselves sniffing incense and rocking out to contemporary tunes while gazing "at patterns beamed onto walls from flickering strobes and projectors."

Short's commitment to her students was TED-Talk-style excellence. And her unorthodox methods meant SU students mastered food chemistry, dietetics, and nutrition.

Robert Thompson

Syracuse professor Robert Thompson sometimes does seventy media interviews a day. That statistic may seem outrageous, but those short discussions probably make the S.I. Newhouse School Trustee Professor the most quoted academic in the United States. Possibly the world.

Helping journalists create and finish stories is simply a daily obligation for Thompson, the founding director of SU's Bleier Center for Television and Popular Culture. He's America's pop culture guru, famous for providing short, compelling soundbites. In other words, the media's go-to interview when it comes to examining a TV show or explaining a major TV event's relevance.

"Unlike many people in his position," Associated Press television writer David Bauder (class of 1981) said in 2007, "he always finds an angle or perspective that I hadn't thought about." That doesn't mean the media always loves him. Jossip.com once suggested he should be known as Mr. Soundbite. Others have called him a "quote whore." Still, those quotes pile up, bringing Syracuse University massive visibility.

Of a certain cartoon character, Thompson told the *Washington Times* in 2000, "Homer Simpson is one of the great creations in the history of Western drama. He's an Everyloser, a totally democratic doofus. If life will simply give him a doughnut every now and again, he's willing to accept horrors which compete with the Old Testament challenges of Job."

Asked about religious movies of the 1950s, Thompson noted, "The Bible is very cinematic. It's filled with audiovisual stuff like crazy. You've got burning bushes, seas parting, locust plagues."

How did this historian, critic, author, and publicity machine get to Syracuse? Back in 1990, Newhouse dean David Rubin convinced a young Northwestern University doctoral student to join the Syracuse faculty. By 1997, Thompson would open a center that fully encompassed the history of television. Rubin's directive to Thompson was clear: "This center will study television entertainment programs with the same care and passion as musicologists study Mozart and Ellington, or professors of English study Melville and Pynchon."

That's what Bob Thompson does. Every day.

Charles V. Willie

Upon receiving the Chancellor's Citation Lifetime Achievement Award on April 25, 2017, Charles V. Willie stepped to the Hendricks Chapel podium and deadpanned: "You live long enough, and something good's going to happen."

The audience burst into laughter.

Charles Willie. Syracuse University Portrait Collection, University Archives.

The charismatic eighty-nine-year-old then began reflecting warmly on his quarter century as a student, professor, and administrator at Syracuse University.

"This is where I made thousands of friends and learned hundreds of lessons about reform and rebellion, redemption and reconciliation," he said.

It was a place where, as his wife, Mary Sue, later said, "he really feels that he grew up."

The grandson of slaves, Willie was raised in Texas during a time of harsh Jim Crow segregation. He decided early in life that education held the key for him and other African Americans to overcome the hatred they encountered daily. He also decided early on to become active in the civil rights movement in hopes of breaking down the barriers imposed by bigotry.

Willie wound up at Morehouse College in Atlanta in 1944, arriving, as luck would have it, at the same time as Martin Luther King Jr. The classmates shared a passion for social justice and developed a friendship that would last a lifetime.

A year after graduating, Willie came to SU as a teaching assistant. He would earn his PhD in sociology from the Maxwell School in 1957 and be hired as one of Syracuse's first African American professors. He later would head the sociology department and become vice president for student affairs. Along the way, he would convince his old friend Dr. King to come to campus to speak on two separate occasions.

Willie also would hear the concerns of the Syracuse Eight, a group of African American football players who accused coach Ben Schwartzwalder and his staff of discrimination. After anti-Vietnam War student protestors took control of the Administration Building in May 1970, Willie and Syracuse police chief Thomas Sardino talked to them for several hours, helping defuse the situation without violence.

By this time, Willie had established himself as a nationally renowned expert on family and race relations and the urban community. That reputation would be enhanced after he left SU to teach at

Harvard University, where he continued a writing career that saw him author more than thirty books.

He was in his glory each time he returned to Syracuse to speak, often at events honoring his late friend Dr. King.

After Willie's 2017 speech at Hendricks, he was approached by Cameron MacPherson, a football player who had been honored for his academic achievements with a postgraduate scholarship.

"This is a better place because of you," he said, shaking Willie's hand.

The old man thanked him for his kindness before wiping away a tear.

Roosevelt "Rick" Wright Jr.

For generations of S.I. Newhouse School of Public Communications students, hearing the booming baritone of television, radio, and film professor Rick Wright was a sure sign they would soon get "schooled" in the fine art of broadcasting and performance. And in a Rick Wright classroom, there was no escaping his smiling, Southern "boom."

Wright came to Newhouse as a PhD student in 1970 after serving as a US Navy captain and earning an undergraduate degree from Elizabeth City State University and a master's from North Carolina Central. An educator at heart, Wright is the informal historian of Syracuse radio. He has written about broadcasting for national publications (*Jet*, *Ebony*, *Broadcasting Magazine*, and *Billboard*), and he never wavers in his commitment to radio or his belief in its power to shape communities.

That's because Wright is the rare individual who previously worked as a general manager, program director, account executive, DJ, chief engineer, and local sales manager for any number of radio stations, as well as faculty manager for SU's WAER-FM and faculty advisor/licensee for WJPZ-FM, SU's student-owned and student-operated station.

Roosevelt "Rick" Wright. © Syracuse University. Photo by Stephen Sartori.

Winner of the 2014 Community Service Award from 100 Black Men of Syracuse, Wright moved to emeritus status in 2014. He was long one of the few African American professors at SU. In fact, "the galloping ghost from coast to coast" was the first black faculty member at Newhouse and was instrumental in bringing black programming and the "black radio style" he'd helped pioneer in the South to Syracuse. Not surprisingly, he served as an inspiration to numerous students of color—among them future broadcasters Mike Roberts and Verna Smith.

Many legends have taught at Syracuse University, but there are few whose voice (and command of the broadcast studio) was instantly recognizable and engagingly discussed long after he'd left the room.

Some Programs of Note

Haudenosaunee Promise Scholarships

It came to life during a personal visit from the chancellor of the university that rests upon the Onondaga Nation's ancestral lands.

"When Chancellor [Nancy] Cantor sat with the chiefs in the longhouse and told us about the Haudenosaunee Promise, we were beyond surprised," said Chief Oren Lyons. "It was much more than just a promise—it is a door held open."

That open portal, one of Syracuse University's most significant scholarship opportunities, was created in August 2005 by a promise to the people of the Onondaga Nation and the Haudenosaunee nations beyond Central New York. The Haudenosaunee Promise stated that SU's educational opportunities would be made available to admitted, qualified, first-year and transfer Haudenosaunee students beginning in the fall semester of 2006.

Chancellor Nancy Cantor (*seated, right*) initiated the Haudenosaunee Promise program, which provided scholarships to Native American students from the Six Nations. Onondaga Nation Faithkeeper Oren Lyons (*left*) and Tadodaho Sid Hill (*podium*) took part in Cantor's inauguration. © Syracuse University. Photo by Stephen Sartori.

The promise expresses "SU's gratitude and appreciation for the historical, political, and cultural legacies of the Haudenosaunee, and is designed to continue building relationships between the university and the historic Haudenosaunee nations of the Mohawk, Oneida, Onondaga, Cayuga, Seneca, and Tuscarora."

Those six nation territories include the Akwesasne Mohawk, Allegany Seneca, Cattaraugus Seneca, Cayuga, Ganienke Mohawk, Kahnawake Mohawk, Kanatsiohareke Mohawk, Kanesatake Mohawk, Niagara Falls Seneca, Oil Spring Seneca, Oneida of the Thames (Ontario), Onondaga Six Nations (Canada), Tonawanda Seneca, Tuscarora, Tyendinaga Mohawk, and Oneida (Wisconsin) communities.

Selected students would receive significant financial assistance plus access to Native American Orange alumni who could help with the admissions process, campus tours, frequently asked questions, and high school visits.

At the time of the announcement, Robert Odawi Porter, a Seneca from the Allegany Territory and director of the SU College of Law's Center for Indigenous Law, Governance and Citizenship, said: "No other university has made this kind of commitment to neighboring aboriginal peoples. For too long, we have struggled to resist Western efforts to de-culture our people through education. Now, through Chancellor Cantor's leadership, SU is creating an opportunity for us to achieve a Haudenosaunee intellectual renaissance."

In 2010, the first four scholars (Joie Lynn Hill, Lisa Parker, Brittany Jock, and Shanelle Mohawk) from the inaugural promise graduated in the Carrier Dome. They were among a group of thirty-five initial recipients of aid from Syracuse University (which does not limit the number of Haudenosaunee Promise scholarships awarded annually).

That pioneering quartet added to the legacies left by Lyons, who, in 1958, became SU's first Native American graduate; Stephanie Waterman, the first Onondaga to earn a PhD (2004); and Amber Hill, the first known Native American woman to play in an NCAA tournament, who graduated in 2009.

The Write Stuff

When Stephen Crane began writing short stories and novellas like *Maggie: A Girl of the Streets* in his Delta Upsilon bedroom, he couldn't have known that in addition to masterpieces, he was creating a legacy. Indeed, the university has attracted its share of literati since the novella's 1893 publication. Many of them owe their success to the top-ranked MFA Creative Writing Program.

Since its inception in the early 1960s, the three-year program has launched the careers of authors, poets, scholars, and teachers. Hundreds of applicants from around the world—about 500 fiction writers and 150 poets—vie each year for a mere dozen openings. Part of the allure is the blue-chip faculty, many of whom come to

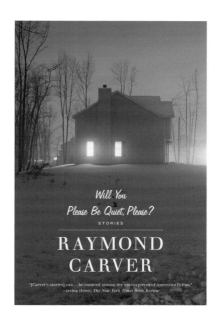

Will You Please Be Quiet, Please? Courtesy of Penguin Random House LLC.

Syracuse before hitting it big. "We get Raymond Carver *before* he becomes Raymond Carver, Toby Wolff *before* he's Toby Wolff, George Saunders *before* he's George Saunders," says director Christopher Kennedy, who received his graduate degree in 1988.

Some professors are program alumni, notably Saunders (1988) and Brooks Haxton (1981). Other star faculty have included W. D. Snodgrass, Hayden Carruth, Heather McHugh, Tess Gallagher, Donald Justice, Delmore Schwartz (who mentored musician Lou Reed), Junot Díaz, and Mary Gaitskill.

If success is measured by turning out one notable writer a decade (a metric used by Iowa, Stanford, and other peer institutions), Syracuse exceeds expectations. Professor Mary Karr attributes the program's success to selectivity and personalized attention. "We attract good writers because we invest in them," she says. "Unlike students at other MFA programs, each one at Syracuse comes with funding. We also have a strong intellectual and critical component to our curriculum, culminating with an MFA thesis. These are big differentiators."

A glance at the list of MFA alumni reveals such luminaries as Stephen Dunn, Jay McInerney, Tom Perrotta, Cheryl Strayed, and Nana Kwame Adjei-Brenyah. Undergraduates who have helped shape the program (or were influenced by it) include Michael Herr, Shirley Jackson, Joyce Carol Oates, William Safire, Alice Sebold, and Koren Zailckas.

Carver, who taught creative writing at SU in the early 1980s, became legendary in the minds of many critics as a "blue-collar minimalist" or, like his friend Tobias Wolff, a purveyor of "dirty realism." Carver's short stories and poetry were widely praised, and author John Updike selected the Oregon native's *Where I'm Calling From* for *The Best American Short Stories of the Century*.

"Ray's stories took place in a world that he knew," said Wolff. "They were stories of social observation, without being preachy."

In honor of Carver's influence, SU's Creative Writing Program established the Raymond Carver Reading Series, which brings twelve to fourteen writers and poets to campus each year. That seems only fitting, since Carver won five O. Henry Awards and was nominated for the Pulitzer Prize for Fiction and the National Book Award for his 1983 collection *Cathedral* (which includes *Where I'm Calling From*).

Helping Prove Einstein's Theories

Syracuse helped make science history in 2015, when researchers in the physics department detected two black holes colliding, thus proving Albert Einstein's theory of relativity. Then, in 2017, history was made a second time when the research team saw the universe create gold and platinum as two neutron stars collided. These discoveries were made by observing gravitational waves when the stars collided.

The waves came from the collision of two black holes more than a billion years ago. By the time the signal reached detectors on Earth, it was a thousand times smaller than an atomic nucleus—a curious chirp destined to become one of science's great soundbites.

Peter Saulson, the Martin A. Pomerantz '37 Professor of Physics, says the Nobel Prize-winning discovery marked the culmination of more than four decades of research. "It opened up a new window onto the universe."

Saulson, Duncan Brown, and Stefan Ballmer co-led SU's Gravitational-Wave Research Group, which is part of the Laser Interferometer Gravitational-Wave Observatory (LIGO) Scientific Collaboration, an international team of more than one thousand scientists. Saulson noted the discovery of gravitational waves fulfilled a key prediction by Einstein.

"He saw gravity not as a force, but as a warping, or curvature, of space and time," said Saulson.

Syracuse helped LIGO detect gravitational waves a half-dozen times. One event, in 2017, involved a 130-million-year-old collision of two neutron stars. The impact created a bright afterglow, inside of which were distinct chemical signatures of gold, silver, and platinum.

"It was like watching space alchemy," observed Brown, the Charles Brightman Endowed Professor of Physics.

Ballmer, who helped design and build LIGO's instrumentation in Louisiana and Washington state, saw to LIGO's very specific tuning. "The slightest whiff of background noise can drown out a gravitational-wave signal," said Ballmer. "We work hard to keep any conceivable noise away from the detector. The mirrors of LIGO's interferometers are literally the quietest place on Earth."

The LIGO interferometers might have been quiet, but they led to some notable celebrating by dedicated Syracuse scientists after each discovery.

Studying Abroad

Mention DIPA (the Division of International Programs Abroad) or Syracuse University Abroad to a current or former Syracuse student, and there's a good chance the topic will resonate. The reason? Syracuse has been one of the most active American universities in channeling its students toward international experiences.

The first significant faculty-led excursion at Syracuse University occurred in 1922, when an Orange medical team organized the Chungking Hospital under the leadership of Gordon Hoople. Syracuse-in-China (as it was called) was a "three-fold program" of medicine, evangelism, and education, with SU working in conjunction with the Board of Foreign Missions of the Methodist Episcopal Church. Syracuse-in-China began occupying a building that had been built by the Methodist Church but was largely unused. At the same time, the program took over management of a high school in Chungking to further its educational mission. Both were intended to serve as models for the rest of China. Over the next few years, Syracuse-in-China added the Bishop Lewis Memorial Institutional Church, church reading rooms, a pharmacy, a nursing school, and a health clinic.

Syracuse-in-China's campus was disrupted multiple times by major fires, Chiang Kai-shek's Northern Expedition of 1926-28, and heavy Japanese bombing from 1938 to 1943. Mao Zedong's Communist Party of China captured Chungking in 1949, and as a result, Syracuse-in-China moved to Bangkok in 1951 and was renamed Syracuse-in-Thailand in 1952. In 1953 it was renamed again—this time, Syracuse-in-Asia—before its eventual incorporation into SU Abroad.

In 1959, the university saw its first group of students attend a semester abroad at an SU center established in Florence, Italy. It was a new model for Syracuse that eliminated a language prerequisite and featured classes taught in both English and Italian, while also incorporating lengthy in-country homestays to facilitate language and cultural adoption.

SU Abroad students take a selfie in front of the British landmark Stonehenge. Syracuse Abroad, Syracuse University, used by permission.

SU Abroad students visit the Roman Coliseum. Syracuse Abroad, Syracuse University, used by permission.

SU's first foray into Africa would take place in 1974, when Maxwell professor Jim Newman began taking student groups to Kenya and East Africa. Just under twenty years later, in 1993, Horace Campbell helped establish SU's first semester-long program in Harare, Zimbabwe.

Along the way, Syracuse centers opened in seven other locations (London, Beijing, Istanbul, Hong Kong, Santiago, Strasbourg, and Madrid), and a theme-based program that extensively explores Central Europe was added. These centers—with the exception of the Istanbul Center, which closed in 2016, and the Beijing Center, scheduled to suspend operations in Fall 2019—coexist with more than sixty World Partner schools and more than thirty summer programs, including ones in Nepal (a trip to Mount Everest Base Camp), Morocco, Australia, and South Africa.

From a numbers standpoint, SU Abroad is more popular than ever, with nearly 45 percent of all SU students (roughly two thousand per year) studying internationally. It makes clear what SU students have enjoyed discovering for the last one hundred years: There's an interesting world out there waiting for them.

Collecting Greatness

Whether it's fifteenth-century handwritten letters from Mary Queen of Scots, the photo collection of pioneering photojournalist Margaret Bourke-White, the rare first-edition books of authors Rudyard Kipling and L. Frank Baum (of *Wizard of Oz* fame), the research papers of Nobel Prize-winning physician Albert Schweitzer, or the artwork of Picasso, Rembrandt, and Norman Rockwell, there's a little something for everyone in Syracuse University's voluminous Special Collections Research Center. It's a true treasure trove for scholars of art, history, literature, and pop culture.

Tucked among the roughly fifty thousand two- and three-dimensional objects, you'll find not only the artist's work but also the artist's tools of the trade. Like the boxy camera and tripod Bourke-White used to photograph Gandhi at his spinning wheel.

Or the typewriter Kipling used to write *The Jungle Book*, *The Man Who Would Be King*, and the poem "Gunga Din."

Over time, SU's leaders realized the importance of collecting books, letters, artifacts, audio and video recordings, and works of art—objects that not only enhance the university's academic and cultural experience, but serve as magnets to researchers and aficionados of art, literature, and history.

So, if you want to learn more about the women's suffrage or abolitionist movements of the nineteenth century, you can delve into the voluminous papers of Gerrit Smith, an upstate New York reformer who seemed connected to everyone. Or you can listen to Robert Frost read poetry, or to Mike Wallace interview celebrities and politicians at the university's Belfer Audio Laboratory and Archive. Or you can ask to view an original Andy Warhol print or original Native American folk art. You can even ask to hold the Oscar won by Miklós Rózsa in 1959 for the score of the movie *Ben-Hur*.

A huge chunk of the university's eclectic collection is housed in the research center on the sixth floor of Bird Library. But, due to space constraints, the majority is stored elsewhere, including galleries across campus.

The collection also contains many items relating to SU history—everything from the original Otto the Orange mascot costume, to a baseball signed by SU alum and author Stephen Crane, to a recording of a famous speech delivered on campus by Martin Luther King Jr.

Rudyard Kipling's typewriter. Rudyard Kipling Collection, Special Collections Research Center, Syracuse University Libraries.

A fifteenth-century book. Special Collections Research Center, Syracuse University Libraries.

Margaret Bourke-White's famous "Bread Line" photograph. Margaret Bourke-White / Time Life Pictures / Getty Images.

Margaret Bourke-White donated her remarkable photography collection to Syracuse University Special Collections Research Center. Among her most famous photographs is this one of Gandhi. Margaret Bourke-White / Time & Life Pictures / Getty Images.

Margaret Bourke-White would go just about any place, including out on a gargoyle of New York's Chrysler Building to get just the right shot. Oscar Graubner / Time Life Pictures / The LIFE Images Collection / Getty Images.

Syracuse University Memorabilia Collection, University Archives.

4 Traditions and Student Life

Color Us Orange

Had Frank Marion and his Syracuse University classmates not raised a stink about the school's colors in 1890, generations of Orange fans might have been chanting "Let's Go Pink!" and the title of this book might have been "Forever Pink." According to research by the university's archivists, the school's original colors were—they're not making this up—pink and pea green. In 1873, the colors were changed to rose pink and azure blue. Orange wasn't adopted until seventeen years later, the result of embarrassment and frustration experienced by Marion and his classmates on the train ride back from a track meet at Hamilton College.

During his fiftieth reunion in 1940, Marion, a motion picture pioneer, described how the switch came about:

> A number of us went along to cheer our team. We wore high collars, right up to our chins—cutaway coats, baggy trousers, and rolled brim derby hats. On our canes we had ribbons of the college colors, pink and blue. Much to our surprise, we won the meet, and on the train coming home from Utica we tried to "whoop it up." What kind of "whoopee" can be made with pink and blue, the pale kind you use on babies' what-do-you-call-thems? It just couldn't be done!
>
> So on Monday morning a lot of us went to see the chancellor in his office and told him our tale of woe. Chancellor [Charles] Sims was a kindly old gentleman, a real father to us all, and he was sympathetic. He agreed that pink and blue were not very suitable colors.
>
> Professor J. Scott Clark was named chairman of a committee to find new colors. I recall that we seniors had a sneaking idea that we might put over the class colors, orange and olive green. Professor Clark consulted *Baird's Manual*, then the authority on college matters, to see what combinations of orange had already been taken. Orange and blue were the most popular, but orange alone apparently was not claimed by any school and was

Syracuse's for the taking. It was adopted unanimously by the committee, the faculty, the Alumni Association, and finally the trustees.

Not long after the color's adoption, people began referring to the school's teams as the Orangemen, and the nickname started appearing in newspaper headlines and stories. Over time, blue became an unofficial secondary color. In recent years, gray has joined the lineup. The nickname Orangemen stuck until the school shortened it to Orange in the 1990s, making it gender neutral.

Orange has been Syracuse University's official color since 1890. *SU Alumni News.* Syracuse University, used by permission.

The Bells of Crouse College

Three times a day—morning, lunchtime, and evening—a member of the secret student society known as the Chimesmasters climbs the ladder inside Crouse College's seventy-foot bell tower and begins manipulating pulleys and levers. Huge tin clappers pound against the ten enormous copper Crouse Chimes, and the musical notes can be heard throughout the Syracuse campus and beyond. Everything from the alma mater to the latest pop music chart-topper is played, and the Chimesmaster—usually a music major—gets quite the workout pushing and pulling the levers that ring 10,500 pounds worth of bells.

With each song, a tradition continues—one dating back to June 3, 1889.

The bells of Crouse College have been tolling on campus since 1889. © Syracuse University. Photo by Stephen Sartori.

"The chimes are part of the culture of Syracuse," Professor Patrick M. Jones said in a 2014 *Syracuse University Magazine* interview. "They create an aura."

They also create a sonorous soundtrack for anyone who's spent time on the Hill.

"Whether the chimes ring in times of joy or sadness, generations of students and alumni will forever remember them as part of their Syracuse University experience," said Ann Clarke, dean emerita of the College of Visual and Performing Arts.

The bells toll because of the vision and generosity of John Crouse, the building's benefactor and a former university trustee, who purchased the first nine chimes—ranging in weight from 375 to 3,000 pounds. Though he never saw the building finished, he was able to hear the bells ring for the first time when the original chime musicians played "Carol Sweetly Carol" in the summer of 1889, just twenty-four days before his death. A local newspaper described the inauguration with this florid prose: "Last night, as twilight began to fall and the heavens to shake out their sable ropes of night, here pealed forth upon the air from the college on University Hill the sweet, harmonious tones of the first chime of bells that ever greeted the ear of Syracuse."

For decades, the brothers of Delta Kappa Epsilon were responsible for the ringing of the chimes, except during World War II, when Alpha Phi sorority took on the duty. In their 130-year history, the Crouse Chimes have rarely been silent. They stopped ringing in 1981-82, while being repaired, and again in 1985, when Delta Kappa Epsilon was suspended for hazing. Four years later, energized by music education major Dan Beich, the Chimesmasters group was founded, and its members have handled bell-ringing chores ever since.

They do so in relative anonymity, and that leads many listeners to believe the bell ringing is automated. "It's interesting," said Alex

Manipulating the Crouse College chime levers is a mental and physical exercise. © Syracuse University. Photo by Stephen Sartori.

Ganes, who chaired the society before graduating in 2015. "It's like, 'Who's ringing the bells?' That's the mystery of it."

Marshall Street

Never mind that the street signs read "Marshall Street" and "Louis Marshall Way." To generations of Syracuse students, faculty members, townies, and visitors, it will always be known by its abbreviated version, M Street. And although it technically isn't on university property, running instead adjacent to the campus's northern border, it long has been regarded as SU's Main Street.

South Crouse Avenue and the back alley that ran parallel to M Street also have been considered part of this University Hill neighborhood—an eclectic mix of bars, fast-food joints, and novelty shops where students have gathered for decades to grab slices of pizza, celebrate Orange sports victories, commiserate over break-ups with girlfriends and boyfriends, purchase T-shirts, sweatshirts, records, and tattoos, and even get naked.

Like the university itself, the neighborhood is constantly evolving, with stores, bars, and restaurants coming and going. And that change has continued with the 2018 opening of a six-story building of upscale lofts known as the Marshall, and the scheduled 2020 dedication of the National Veterans Resource Center bordering Marshall Street and Crouse and Waverly Avenues.

The one constant in the area has been the Varsity, the popular pizza place founded by Greek immigrant Jerry Dellas in 1926. It remains the hub of the neighborhood. A few years after Dellas served his first customer, the street across from his business was renamed in memory of Louis Marshall, a former university trustee who was instrumental in founding the forestry school. Marshall was a respected constitutional lawyer and Jewish American community leader who worked tirelessly to secure religious, political, and cultural freedom for all minority groups.

It wasn't long before Dellas had company and competition, as a number of bars, restaurants, clothing shops, and record and book stores sprang up next door to the rapidly growing university. There was money to be made as students and faculty members sought food and libation, as well as apparel advertising their school pride. In 1947, Manny's opened and provided patrons with a wide array of orange and blue T-shirts, sweatshirts, and baseball caps featuring Syracuse's familiar block S logo. Several decades later, just a few doors away, former SU placekicker Dave Jacobs would open a similar store. One of the most popular items would be a series of orange T-shirts with blue lettering touting that Real Men, Real Women, Real—you name it—Wear Orange.

Marshall Street. Photograph by Anestis Diakopoulos. Syracuse University Photograph Collection, University Archives.

Although it technically isn't on campus, Marshall Street has long been a part of SU students' and faculty members' lives. Syracuse University Photograph Collection, University Archives.

While it no longer exists, the M Street "Beach" was a popular place for students to relax when the weather warmed up in the spring, summer, or fall. Syracuse University Photograph Collection, University Archives.

A strip of grass at the corner of Marshall and Crouse known as the Beach became a favorite student hangout, especially on rare sunny days in the fall and spring. It wasn't uncommon during the 1960s and 1970s for some of the "beachgoers" to smoke pot there, inspired perhaps by the Down Under Leather head shop just across the street, which featured Grateful Dead logos and tie-dyed shirts in its window displays. Street musicians occasionally performed on the Beach, and legend has it that Harry Chapin once staged an impromptu concert there.

Other popular eateries included Faegan's Café & Pub, which also was owned by the Dellas family and located down the block from the Varsity; Cosmos, a pizza and sandwich restaurant founded in 1963 by George Cannelos and Demo Stathis Sr. that became popular not only for its pizza but also for its toasted honey buns and the Cosmo State Fair Special (a Philly cheesesteak); Funk

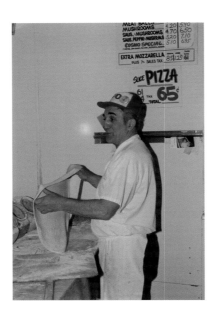

George Cannellos helped found Cosmos in 1963 and made pizza for generations of Syracuse students until his death in January 2013. Syracuse University Photograph Collection, University Archives.

'n' Waffles, a place with a coffeehouse vibe that was opened by SU alumni Adam Gold and Kyle Corea; Acropolis pizza (yes, there was a Greek theme going on here, because several of the owners were Greek immigrants); and King David's, which opened in 1974 and specialized in Middle Eastern cuisine, baklava, and Turkish coffee. By the 2000s, businesses such as Insomnia Cookies and Starbucks had joined the M Street lineup to fulfill students' changing desires.

Many of the M Street-area bars became legendary watering holes where students would go to dance the night away on sticky, beer-coated floors while listening to bands or disc jockeys spinning tunes. Few of the establishments still exist.

In 1997, *Sports Illustrated* named 44's Tavern one of its five must-visit campus sports bars. Three years later, the bar was renamed Konrad's, after Miami Dolphins fullback Rob Konrad, the last football player to wear Syracuse's famed Number 44 jersey. The establishment was shut down by the State Liquor Authority in 2004 and became a Verizon store.

The closing of bars in the area for violations of laws forbidding the sale of alcohol to minors was a recurring theme. The same thing that happened to Konrad's happened to Maggie's Tavern, which authorities called "a bad news bar," and Sutter's Mill and Mining Company, which became so infamous that the block behind M Street was nicknamed Sutter's Alley. Hungry Charley's was located in that alley, and became a favorite destination of students and local bands looking for gigs. The dive bar's walls were covered with graffiti, as patrons were allowed to sign their names and express themselves, sometimes in profane ways.

Hungry Charley's begat Sutter's, which begat Chuck's Café, which became one of the few cheap beer bars that survived the police stings and raids closing other establishments. The new Chuck's met its demise when the space was acquired for the Marshall lofts.

In the 1950s, 1960s, and 1970s, the Orange on South Crouse Avenue was one of the most popular bars near campus. It eventually became Buggsy's Back Alley Bar, which featured a dunk tank used by fraternities and sororities for fundraisers, and later changed to Lucy's Retired Surfer Bar and the current Orange Crate Brewing Co.

In the 1990s and 2000s, Gertis McDowell became well known for calling every passerby either "big poppa" or "pretty lady" as he shook his tin can of change outside Starbucks. Regarded as the "mayor of Marshall Street," the beloved panhandler died in 2015.

The area became a magnet for overflowing crowds following major Syracuse sports victories. Fans of the Orangemen's basketball championship in 2003 recall the raucous M Street celebration featuring a naked man in a tree. He wasn't the first person to appear on M Street sans clothes. In 1974, Lady Godiva, wearing nothing but a blonde wig and boots, rode a horse down the road as a fundraiser for the Muscular Dystrophy Foundation. The mood wasn't nearly

Hungry Charley's (later renamed Hungry Chuck's) was known for many things, including its funky logo. *Daily Orange*, Syracuse University, used by permission.

727 S. Crouse Ave.
Syracuse, NY

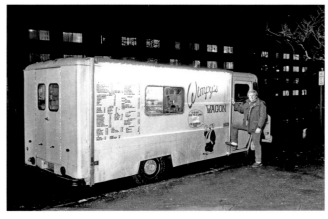

Before coaching the Orange lacrosse team to five national championships, John Desko helped pay for his Syracuse tuition by operating the Wimpy Wagon food truck on campus. Courtesy of the *Daily Orange*.

Sutter's was one of M Street's most popular watering holes. Courtesy of *Syracuse New Times*.

The Varsity

Like many immigrants, Greece native Jerry Dellas arrived in America in 1923 with not much more than the clothes on his back and a dream. His was to own a restaurant. And after three years of selling popcorn and candy from a cart near the Syracuse campus, he had saved enough money to make that dream come true.

Dellas purchased a house across the street from where he'd been a vendor and converted it into a restaurant and coffee shop called the Varsity. In time, the popular pizza joint on South Crouse Avenue, three long blocks down the hill from the Carrier Dome, became an integral part of the Orange experience. Now owned and operated by Jerry Dellas's grandsons, the Varsity remains a must-stop destination for students and alumni, especially on SU football and basketball game days.

It's a place where they serve up slices of pizza—and history. The side walls above the booths are festooned with enormous black-and-white photographs of great moments in SU sports—with some

as playful after the SU men's hoops team suffered a last-second loss to Indiana in the 1987 NCAA championship game. In fact, it was riotous, as a mob of angry fans smashed the window of an ice cream shop and twenty-nine people (including fifteen students) were arrested, mostly for disorderly conduct.

The M Street area continues to evolve and change. It will be interesting to see the impact of the new residential buildings and veterans center. It also will be interesting to see if the Dellas family follows through on plans for a high-rise development on South Crouse Avenue. The venerable Varsity is expected to be part of the new building, whose modern upgrades won't change the pizza parlor's old charm.

Kathy Sampalia, who has worked for John and Jerry Dellas for more than thirty years, expressed hope that M Street developers would continue to follow the lead of the restaurant's third-generation owners by retaining the "tried and true nostalgic atmosphere while moving forward with the times."

"I'm hoping," she said in a 2017 *Syracuse Post-Standard* interview, "we can have the best of both worlds."

The Varsity has been a hub of student activity since 1926. Photo by Scott Pitoniak.

signed by Orange sports legends Dick MacPherson, Floyd Little, and Tim Green. On the back wall, just above the main cafeteria-like serving area, hang rectangular banners of each of SU's football opponents. During the 1959 season, a tradition was started: After a victory, an Orangeman would show up, climb a ladder, and turn the banner upside down as the patrons went wild. That year, they turned every banner upside down, as the Orange went 11-0 to win the national championship.

That tradition continues today, and a new tradition recently began where the banners of basketball opponents are turned upside down. For many years, members of the SU football team worked part time at the Varsity, baking pizzas, bussing tables, pouring sodas. Among those who played for the varsity and worked at the Varsity was Little, a three-time football All-American.

The restaurant has undergone numerous renovations and menu changes in the past nine decades to keep up with students' changing demands. But in many respects the place remains the same. Like the Hall of Languages and Crouse College, it's an enduring symbol of tradition and stability on the Hill.

After founding the Varsity, Jerry Dellas noticed that as the university grew, so too did his business. All four of his sons—Speros, Ted, John, and Nick—ran the pizza shop with him and lived in the area their entire lives. Ted Dellas served in World War II, and returned home shortly before his father's death in 1952. That's when the business made its first generation-to-generation ownership transfer. As the business continued to flourish, several grandsons decided to forgo their original career plans and join the family business.

"John (the grandson) was thinking about law school and I was looking into dental school," said Jerry Dellas, who was named after the Varsity's founder. "We had always talked about owning a restaurant like my dad, then one day John called me about it and we just decided to open a restaurant near the Varsity."

In 1978, they launched Faegan's Café & Pub, just a few doors away, which offered a menu far more extensive than other

Otto the Orange performing at an SU basketball game in the Carrier Dome. © Syracuse University. Photo by Michael Okoniewski.

Jerry Dellas was part of four generations from his family who owned and operated the Varsity. Syracuse University Photograph Collection, University Archives.

restaurants in the Marshall Street area. Faegan's flourished, as did the Varsity, and in 2001, Ted Dellas handed the reins of the older restaurant to John and Jerry. Their acquisition of the Varsity coincided with the renovation of the streets near the university, and that boosted business.

"Basically, what you see is what's been here since 1926," said John Dellas, a 1977 SU graduate. "The only thing that's different is that all of the houses are gone. It's just businesses now."

And the granddaddy of those businesses remains the Varsity, whose roots can be traced to an immigrant's dream.

Otto, the Saltine Warrior, and Other Mascots

Just about everyone associated with Syracuse University is familiar with Otto, the lovable mascot who has received almost as much national television airtime through the years as Hall of Fame basketball coach Jim Boeheim. But even the most diehard Orange follower probably has never heard of Eric Heath. A former SU cheerleader who dropped out of school to join the Ringling Brothers Clown College, Heath claims to be the brains behind Otto. In 1982, four years after SU permanently retired the headdress-wearing Saltine Warrior as the school's mascot because it was offensive to Native Americans, Heath sent sketches of a fuzzy orange character with a blue baseball cap and blue arms and legs to school officials, who eventually accepted the idea.

"The Orange's first appearance was at the opening home football game of 1982, SU vs. Temple," Heath said in an interview with the *Syracuse Post-Standard*. "We built a large box, piece by piece, and then the sides fell away, revealing the new mascot."

The 29,574 spectators, many of whom were still angry about the university's controversial decision to retire the Saltine Warrior, appeared underwhelmed. But at least they didn't boo him off the field the way they did an orange-clad Roman gladiator school mascot-wannabe at Archbold Stadium during a 1978 football game.

By the mid-1980s, SU fans still hadn't settled on one mascot. The fuzzy Orange found itself in competition with a parade of other unofficial candidates, including the Dome Ranger, who dressed in an orange cowboy outfit and blue mask; a penguin wearing a huge orange scarf; Dome Eddie, who donned an orange wig and gaudy, oversized Elton John glasses; the Beast of the East, who resembled a green monster; and the Abominable Orangeman, a huge, scary-looking, orange-colored snowman that fans found as abominable as one of Syracuse's infamous lake effect blizzards.

Slowly but surely the competition dropped by the wayside, and the Orange began to grow on people. During the summer of 1990, the mascot accompanied the SU cheerleaders to a camp in Tennessee, and the students chosen to suit up in the costume narrowed the Orange's name down to two: Opie and Otto. They concluded that the name Opie would lead to the inevitable rhyme with "dopey," so they settled on Otto. Later, word got out that the cheerleaders were calling the mascot Otto, and fans and alumni picked up on it.

In February 1995, Chancellor Kenneth Shaw sought to resolve the issue of an official mascot once and for all. He appointed an eighteen-member committee of students, faculty, and staff to recommend a logo and mascot. They narrowed the candidates to a wolf, a lion, and an orange. Lobbying efforts by the students who acted as Otto convinced Shaw to stick with the orange, and that December it became the school's official mascot. Thanks in large part to comedic appearances on ESPN commercials, Otto has become an adored figure among alumni and students, who, several years ago, renamed their cheering section Otto's Army.

The history of SU mascots goes back more than one hundred years. Early-twentieth-century team photos of SU football teams show a dog wearing a leather football helmet. In the 1920s, the four-legged theme continued with Vita the Goat. According to Syracuse

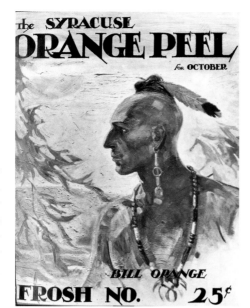

The introduction of the Saltine Warrior mascot can be traced to a fictitious story in the October 1931 issue of the *Syracuse Orange Peel*. Syracuse University Photograph Collection, University Archives.

University archivists, he was "held in leash by freshman guardians" during the games and often showed up wearing signage such as "Beat Colgate."

Vita eventually gave way to the Saltine Warrior, which was born out of a hoax published in the October 1931 issue of the *Syracuse Orange Peel*, a campus magazine. The story claimed that the remains of a sixteenth-century Onondaga chief had been found in the excavations near Steele Hall three years earlier. Though the story was fictitious, it took on a life of its own, and the legend of the Saltine Warrior, also known as Big Chief Bill Orange, was born.

In 1951, the senior class commissioned a statue of the Saltine Warrior to be placed near the "discovery" site. Winning sculptor Luise Kaish arranged for a member of the Onondaga Nation to pose for her statue, which depicts a Native American shooting an arrow skyward. The bronze statue has been moved several times, and now resides on the southeast corner of the Quad near Carnegie Library.

In the mid-1950s, the father of a Lambda Chi Alpha fraternity brother designed a Saltine Warrior costume for his son to wear at football games, thus beginning a long tradition of Lambda Chi members serving as mascots. In 1976, Native American students at SU and members of the Onondaga Nation, just seven miles south of campus, began voicing concerns over the Saltine Warrior. Oren Lyons, an Onondaga chief and former SU All-American lacrosse goalie, said the mascot lacked dignity and authenticity. "The thing that offended me when I was there was that guy was running around like a nut," Lyons said. "That's derogatory." Chancellor Melvin Eggers agreed, and in 1978 he decided to remove the Saltine Warrior as SU's official mascot.

The announcement was controversial, and debate filled the student and local newspapers for weeks. Many alumni believed the university had overreacted, but Eggers said the decision was the right one and was irreversible. Today, SU offers a Native American Studies minor and has established the Haudenosaunee

Promise, which offers scholarships to Native Americans who qualify academically.

Lockerbie and Remembrance Scholars

Fergus Barrie was born July 29, 1993, less than five years after the fuselage of Pan Am Flight 103 (known as the Clipper Maid of the Seas) crashed into his hometown of Lockerbie, Scotland, killing all 259 passengers and crew on board, plus eleven residents on the ground. The act of international terrorism would impact him and his village in ways neither ever could have imagined.

"I knew about the Lockerbie tragedy from an early age," Barrie said. "My dad's best friend's grandmother lived in the Sherwood Crescent house where that infamous crater picture was taken. There was nothing ever found from her house. I remember my dad telling me around Christmastime that he had to call the news station to ask them to stop replaying footage of the houses destroyed because it was so distressing."

Years later, his connection to the tragedy would become even more personal when he was awarded one of two annual scholarships that SU presents to Lockerbie students in memory of the thirty-five SU Abroad students killed on Flight 103 as they returned home for the winter holidays.

THE DATE WAS DECEMBER 21, 1988, and twenty-five Syracuse students, plus ten students from nine other universities, were on board

A Remembrance Quilt honors the SU students who perished in the Flight 103 tragedy in 1988. Remembrance Quilt Collection, Pan Am Flight 103/Lockerbie Air Disaster Archives, Syracuse University Libraries.

the Boeing 747 headed home from Florence and London to New York City. They included sophomores, juniors, seniors, and graduate students. They were single and married. Their lives lay in front of them.

What they didn't know was that terrorists, reportedly working under the orders of Libya's Colonel Muammar Mohammed Gaddafi, had planted a Semtex plastic explosive bomb inside an unaccompanied bag placed into Flight 103's baggage hold in Frankfurt, Germany.

The time of the in-flight explosion was just after 7 p.m. locally, but in Syracuse, five time zones behind, it was only 2:03 in the afternoon. The majority of SU students had finished their finals and were departing campus for home. At New York's JFK International Airport, parents and friends were gathered, eagerly anticipating the 9:30 p.m. arrival of their loved ones.

In Lockerbie, however, residents were already grappling with the reality of dead bodies scattered throughout their small village. And the absence of noise. Nearly 290 tons of wreckage lay burning in fields, on houses, and in Lockerbie's streets. As the *Guardian* reported in February 2000, "For several terrible moments, there had been a long and unnatural silence. Almost all the electricity, gas, water and telephone lines had been cut. For a while, there was only sound and light where houses were burning."

IT WOULD TAKE YEARS for any kind of healing to begin, but following exhaustive FBI and British investigations, perpetrators of the attack were pursued, and Libyan intelligence officer Abdelbaset al-Megrahi was found guilty and sentenced to life in prison.

Verdicts in terrorism cases rarely satisfy those grieving, but Syracuse University chancellor Melvin Eggers made a point of assuring the victims' loved ones that SU would never forget those who perished. A granite semicircle Place of Remembrance memorial bearing the carved names of the victims was constructed just beyond the front gate leading up to the Hall of Languages, and during the 1989 spring semester, Syracuse began selecting thirty-five seniors-to-be to receive one-year scholarships to remember the students whose lives were lost.

Competition for these scholarships was rigorous, with selection committee members drawn from staff, faculty and, as the years went by, existing scholarship winners. During interviews, undergraduate candidates are asked what the university should do to commemorate the victims and how to address the broader concept of terrorism.

As of May 2019, 1,050 Remembrance Scholars had been selected, with an additional sixty Lockerbie Scholars chosen from the village of Lockerbie.

"There is now a network of Lockerbie and Remembrance scholars," former Lockerbie and Remembrance Scholar Erin McLaughlin told a gathering at the Dryfesdale Parish Church on the twenty-fifth anniversary of the tragedy. "They have gone on to

(Above Left) A student becomes emotional during a ceremony at SU's Place of Remembrance. © Syracuse University. Photo by Stephen Sartori.

(Above Right) A Remembrance Scholar places a rose during a ceremony at the Place of Remembrance on the SU campus. © Syracuse University. Photo by Stephen Sartori.

(Below) Syracuse University formed an enduring relationship with members of the Lockerbie community following the Flight 103 tragedy, which occurred over that Scottish village. Courtesy of Lawrence Mason Jr.

Eleven Lockerbie residents died during the Pan Am 103 tragedy. Courtesy of Lawrence Mason Jr.

The Thirty-Five SU Students Who Perished on Flight 103

Steven Russell Berrell
Kenneth J. Bissett
Stephen J. Boland
Nicole Elise Boulanger
Timothy M. Cardwell
Theodora Cohen
Eric M. Coker
Jason M. Coker
Gary L. Colasanti
Scott Marsh Cory
Gretchen Joyce Dater
Shannon Davis
Turhan Michael Ergin
John P. Flynn
Pamela Elaine Herbert
Karen Lee Hunt
Christopher Andrew Jones
Julianne F. Kelly

Wendy A. Lincoln
Alexander Lowenstein
Suzanne Marie Miazga
Richard Paul Monetti
Anne Lindsey Otenasek
Peter R. Peirce
Sarah S.B. Philipps
Frederick "Sandy" Phillips
Louise "Luann" Rogers
Thomas Britton Schultz
Amy Elizabeth Shapiro
Cynthia J. Smith
Mark Lawrence Tobin
Alexia Kathryn Tsairis
Nicholas Andreas Vrenios
Kesha Weedon
Miriam Luby Wolfe

Plaques of two SU Abroad students killed in the Flight 103 tragedy. Courtesy of Lawrence Mason Jr.

become global advocates, educators, activists, government officials, scientists, entrepreneurs, and entertainers, all while embodying the spirit of those lost on Pan Am 103. It's clear that from disaster sprung a beautiful relationship that shaped a number of scholars' lives in many ways."

Collectively, the Syracuse and Scottish scholars have focused their senior year at Syracuse on keeping remembrance alive. This commitment to "Look Back, Act Forward" includes placing folding chairs on the Kenneth A. Shaw Quadrangle (representing where the thirty-five students were seated on Pan Am 103), a rose-laying ceremony at the Place of Remembrance, and a celebratory service in Hendricks Chapel. The scholars also participate in educational and community service projects, in which they educate their peers about the history of Flight 103 and promote regional awareness.

Separate from the work of SU's student scholars has been the development of the Pan Am Flight 103/Lockerbie Air Disaster Archives at SU's Bird Library, featuring more than three hundred linear feet of materials.

For the thirtieth anniversary in 2018, SU Libraries staged a major exhibition exploring the many ways in which the 270 victims were remembered. Additionally, Chancellor Kent Syverud appointed Lawrence "Doc" Mason Jr., a longtime Newhouse School photography professor (and author of the book *Looking for Lockerbie*), to serve as Syracuse University's Remembrance and Lockerbie Ambassador.

For Fergus Barrie, the journey to Syracuse, like that of Erin McLaughlin, started with a one-year residency at the university. From there, Barrie found a way (with support from SU soccer coach Ian McIntyre and the Falk College) to stay at Syracuse for the next eight

years—first as a full-time sport management undergraduate student and manager of the Syracuse men's soccer team, and then as a graduate student and communications coordinator for the athletics department. He was also selected as a Remembrance Scholar and accompanied Syverud and his wife, Dr. Ruth Chen, to Lockerbie during a historic visit in May 2017.

"Studying at Syracuse wasn't a once-in-a-lifetime experience," Barrie said. "It was much rarer. When I arrived at Syracuse, I immediately fell in love with the university, the campus and culture. I felt right at home and developed a desire to stay here. Although I'm 3,000-plus miles from home, I was part of a community that shares a special connection with my hometown. SU's commitment to the Lockerbie Scholarship is an amazing tribute to each of the students lost in 1988. Although nothing can make up for what happened, things like the scholarship and other initiatives help create positive outcomes from such a terrible event.

"To graduate as a Remembrance Scholar is an honor which I never dreamt I could receive. I was lucky enough to know the Remembrance Scholars for four years straight. Each of them brought something different to the table, but all were uniquely brilliant in their own right. To be considered a member of that group is an honor not only for me, but for the people of Lockerbie. It's great seeing more than thirty years on, Syracuse still remembers not only their own students, but all who were lost in the Pan Am 103 tragedy."

Goon Squad

(Above & Top Right) A group of students known as the Goon Squad was originally formed to ensure that freshmen wore their beanies and tipped them to upperclassmen per tradition. But when SU students no longer were required to wear beanies (starting in the mid-1960s), the Goon squad became collaborators rather than punishers, helping incoming students move into their dorm rooms. © Syracuse University. Photos by Stephen Sartori.

Pride of the Orange

Ablaze in their orange band uniforms with the blue sashes and feathered hats, they march down the field, their trumpets blaring and their drums pounding, rousing spectators from their Carrier Dome seats. There are few things that connect students and alumni to their alma mater on the Hill like the sights and sounds of the SU marching band. Pride of the Orange, indeed.

Formed in 1901, it is one of the oldest marching bands in the country. And with nearly two hundred members and twelve different types of instruments in its ensemble, the band continues to provide a soundtrack for Orange experiences. Known originally as the University Band, it performed at athletic, social, and religious events, including parades on campus and in the city of Syracuse. In 1925, the band, then directed by Marvin A. Fairbanks, began an official partnership with the SU athletics department. Before long, the Pride

Before home football games, the SU marching band entertains fans on the steps of Hendricks Chapel. © Syracuse University. Photo by Stephen Sartori.

Known as the Orange Girl, SU baton twirler Dottie Grover was featured on the cover of *Life* magazine in 1953. Syracuse University Portrait Collection, University Archives.

of the Orange was playing at every home football game and at least one away game each season.

Through the years, the band has tried a variety of novel ideas to enhance its shows, including a short-lived experiment that put some musicians on horseback. In 1947, a baton-twirling "Orange Girl" joined the then all-male band, and her performances were choreographed to the music. Dorothy "Dottie" Grover (class of 1953) became the most famous of the twirlers. She was pictured on the cover of *Life* magazine and was asked to perform at the inauguration of President Dwight D. Eisenhower. She capped her career with the band—then known as One Hundred Men and a Girl—at SU's first-ever football bowl game, the 1953 Orange Bowl in Miami, Florida. The tradition of the Orange Girl continues, but the misogynistic tradition of excluding female musicians ended in the early 1970s.

Perhaps the proudest moment for the Pride of the Orange came in February 2014, when the band was asked to perform at the Super Bowl at MetLife Stadium in New Jersey. Because the game was being played at the home of the New York Giants and New York Jets, the National Football League and Super Bowl host committee wanted a New York-themed show. SU was branding itself as "New York's college team" at the time, and that swayed the Super Bowl host committee. The SU marching band played a five-song medley during the pregame show that included two anthems from two Jersey natives—Bruce Springsteen's "Born to Run" and Frank Sinatra's "New York, New York."

Another band highlight was the opening of the Carrier Dome on September 20, 1980. No longer would the marching musicians have to brave the dank weather that often assaulted them at Archbold. But the indoor stadium sans air conditioning presented a temperature challenge of a different kind on opening night. "It had to be 100 degrees-plus on the field, and we were in those wool uniforms, but we knew we were making history," said class of 1981 band member Deb Lombard. "It was absolutely thrilling to march onto that field for the first time."

And members are still marching onto that field, four decades later, rousing fans to their feet and connecting students and alumni to their alma mater.

Down, Down the Field

It may not be in the same league as "Three Cheers for Ol' Notre Dame," or "On Wisconsin," or "Fight on USC," or Michigan's "Hail to the Victors," but Syracuse's "Down the Field" is still a pretty catchy, foot-stomping, hand-clapping fight song.

It's great to hum, but can be tough to sing because the words, quite frankly, don't exactly mesh well with the music. And the reality is that the majority of students and alumni don't know any of the lyrics, other than "Down, down the field goes old Syracuse." SU actually had two fight songs before this one, but this one stuck. The rousing tune was composed by Syracuse student C. Harold Lewis in 1914. Another student, Ralph Murphy, penned the following words to accompany the music:

Out upon the gridiron stands old Syracuse,
Warriors clad in orange and in blue,
Fighting for the fame of Alma Mater.
Soon those Crouse chimes will be ringing,
Soon you'll hear those fellows singing.
Onondaga's braves are out to win today,
The sons of Syracuse are ready for the fray,
The line holds like a wall and now the Orange has the ball,
So ready for that old long yell. Rah! Rah! Rah!

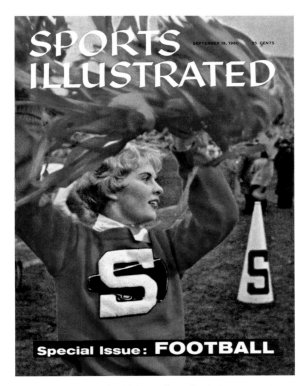

In its September 19, 1960, college football preview issue, *Sports Illustrated* honored SU's national championship by featuring an Orange cheerleader on the cover. Marvin E. Newman / Sports Illustrated / Getty Images.

(Chorus)
Down, Down the field goes old Syracuse,
Just see those backs hit the line and go thro';
Down, down the field they go marching,
Fighting for the Orange staunch and true.
Rah! Rah! Rah!
Vict'ry's in sight for old Syr-a-cuse,
Each loyal son knows she ne'er more will lose,
For we'll fight, yes, we'll fight, and with all our might
For the glory of old Syracuse.

Beanie Babies

Beginning in 1893, all first-year Syracuse students made a fashion statement when they were required to wear green or orange beanies or lids during their first semester to distinguish them from upperclassmen. When told by a sophomore, junior, or senior to "Tip It, Frosh," the first-year student was expected to follow orders as a sign of respect for their elders. The tradition eventually found its way into the freshman section of the university's official student handbook.

Though it could be demeaning at times, the beanies did allow freshmen to identify with their classmates and helped them develop camaraderie among their peers.

A group of students known as the Goon Squad was responsible for enforcing the wearing of the sacred beanies. Those caught not wearing or tipping them were punished through public humiliation at the annual Penn State football game pep rally.

The wearing of beanies became a requirement of Syracuse's freshmen students in 1893, and the tradition continued into the mid-1960s. Syracuse University Photograph Collection, University Archives.

An SU freshman beanie. Syracuse University Memorabilia Collection, University Archives.

Many returning military veterans refused to take part in the tradition when they became SU students under the GI Bill following World War II. The freshmen class began burning their beanies at the end of 1964, and the tradition fell away by end of the decade.

An "Ivy" Tower

In the spring of 1873, a silver shovel was plunged into the earth in front of the Hall of Languages, and several graduates from that year's class placed a sprig of ivy into the ground. With that simple act, a plant—and a commencement tradition—would take root.

"We plant here what will cling like our memories to these old walls, always beautifying them, and clinging closer as storm or time would weaken their grip," said an unnamed orator, according to an 1873 article in the *University Herald*. "It further will be a memory of us long after we move off the stage."

Unfortunately, the original plant did not survive the harsh Syracuse winter that followed. Undaunted, members from the next year's class used the same trowel to plant another sprig. This one was hearty enough to endure the Hill's infamous snow and cold, and for the next seven decades the planting of ivy near the exterior walls

Planting sprigs of ivy outside the Hall of Languages was SU's first tradition. © Syracuse University. Photo by Stephen Sartori.

of the Hall of Languages was a commencement tradition. After each planting, a member of the senior class would give a speech, known as an ivy oration, and the shovel would be presented to a member of the junior class. It's not known when the tradition ended. A 1940 photograph of four students gathered around a small piece of ivy is the last reference to it, according to University Archives.

Diana and Her Dog

The twelve-foot-high bronze statue of Diana and her dog greets visitors in the front lobby of Carnegie Library, but few stop to take notice. Created by sculptor Anna Hyatt Huntington, it was modeled after Diana, a mythological Roman huntress. In Huntington's depiction, Diana has just released an arrow into flight, and the goddess and her dog are watching its ascent. The statue was donated to the

Goddess Diana and her dog greet visitors in the Carnegie Library lobby. © Syracuse University. Photo by Stephen Sartori.

university in 1932, and through the decades has had several homes, including Bird Library.

According to legend, if a student rubs the dog's paw and says a brief prayer, he or she will be ensured success in any quiz or examination. Over time, several layers of the dog's paw have worn off. A small metal ring now surrounds the statue to dissuade students from touching it. The protective ring might not be necessary, though, because students haven't participated in the ritual for years.

Hoya Paranoia and Other Cursed Sports Rivalries

Georgetown was just another basketball team on the schedule and John Thompson was just another faceless coach until the night of February 12, 1980. That evening, a Hoyas upset that snapped second-ranked Syracuse's fifty-seven-game win streak in the Manley Field House finale and some salt-in-the-wounds words delivered by Thompson ignited a rivalry that became one of the most passionate in SU and college sports history. Moments after spoiling the Orangemen's Manley farewell party, the hulking six-foot-ten Thompson grinned broadly and told reporters: "Manley Field House is officially closed."

Neither the Georgetown rivalry nor the fledgling Big East Conference would ever be the same. Thompson had gone from being an anonymous coach to public enemy number one in Syracuse. "It was almost like fighting words, like 'Remember the Alamo,' or Pearl Harbor—like casting bad remarks at your mother or something," said longtime SU sports information director Larry Kimball.

Over the next three decades, the Hoyas and the Orangemen would play some of the most memorable games in Big East annals—often in front of thirty-thousand-plus crowds in the Carrier Dome or packed houses at New York's Madison Square Garden for the annual conference tournament. There was no shortage of star power in the series, as the Hoyas relied on big men like Patrick Ewing, Dikembe Mutombo, and Alonzo Mourning, while SU often rode the clutch performances of guards such as Pearl Washington, Sherman Douglas, and Gerry McNamara. At the focal point were the coaches, Jim Boeheim and Thompson, who started out as fierce enemies and became close friends. And Big John relished playing the role of the villain in Syracuse. "I always had a love-hate thing with Syracuse because of the atmosphere," he said. "It was competitive dislike, but I respected the fans."

Long before "Hoya Paranoia," there was the "Hoodoo," a bastardization of the word *voodoo*. The Hoodoo purportedly was a hex placed on SU by fans of the Colgate University football team, which resulted in the Red Raiders going 31-15-5 against the Orange during the first half of the twentieth century. This included a stretch from 1925 through 1937, when legendary Colgate coach Andy Kerr's teams went 11-0-2 in the series. Just how the myth originated isn't clear, but the most creative theory claims that a student buried a Colgate letterman's sweater into the concrete during the construction of Archbold Stadium, and that "a wraith-like spectre of the Hoodoo slipped out of its resting place and joined 11 Colgate men on the football field," helping the Raiders win, 6-0, in the first game between the schools in 1908. Not long after that a tradition began, where the Colgate student section would begin chanting "Hoodoo! Hoodoo!" before and during games. Eventually, the SU student section began chanting "We do! We do!" in response. The proximity of the schools—they are about forty miles apart—clearly fueled the passion of students and alumni. In addition to the requisite bonfires, pep rallies, and creative fraternity and sorority house displays, the hijinks would include the dumping of orange dye into Taylor Lake on the Colgate campus, and the painting of the word "Gate" on SU academic buildings.

Eventually, Syracuse began dominating the series. In 1956, Jim Brown scored 43 points in a 61-7 annihilation of the Raiders. Three years later, during SU's national championship season, the Orangemen won, 71-0. After 46-6 and 51-8 Syracuse victories the next two seasons, the series was discontinued, though the teams have played each other a handful of times since.

The other passionate sports rivalry of note was the SU-Penn State football series. It began with a 0-0 tie in 1922, and over the next fifty years the game often decided who reigned supreme in Eastern football. Over time, the Nittany Lions, behind the coaching of Joe Paterno, would hold the upper hand. Penn State wound up winning sixteen consecutive games in the rivalry. That streak finally ended in 1987, when SU's All-American quarterback Don McPherson and his teammates clobbered the Nittany Lions, 48-21, in the Carrier Dome. The schools stopped playing each other annually after Syracuse joined the Big East Conference and Penn State joined the Big Ten.

The symbolic burying of "John R. Calculus" was an early SU tradition. Syracuse University Scrapbook Collection, University Archives.

Calculated Risks

Starting in 1873, SU's liberal arts sophomores were required to take calculus, a course most of them loathed. This led to a tradition where, upon successful completion of the course, they would gather to ceremonially "dispose" of the character John R. Calculus and his wife, Anna Lytics, who were members of the "evil" Matthew Mattics family. "Disposal" would take on many forms. Housed in a coffin, the characters might be buried on Science Hill (now Crouse College Hill), sent off in a hot air balloon, or tossed into watery graves in Onondaga, Oneida, Skaneateles, and Cazenovia Lakes. Programs were printed in advance of the lightheartedly macabre ceremonies, which often featured picnics, fireworks, songs, and dances.

Here's a verse from one of the burial songs:

He was a man of horrid fame, of horrid fame was he,
To torture Sophs, to scare the Frosh was John R.'s perfect glee.

Georgetown basketball coach John Thompson's incendiary words helped incite one of SU's fiercest sports rivalries. Athletics Department, Syracuse University, used by permission.

In 1920, Syracuse University celebrated its fiftieth anniversary with a five-day celebration known as the Golden Jubilee. On the Old Oval (present-day Quad), there was a huge birthday cake with candles as well as parades and speeches. Homage was paid to those who had served in World War I. Syracuse University Photograph Collection, University Archives.

The tradition is believed to have ended during the World War II era.

Rushes to Judgment

Competitions between freshman and sophomore classes were common for decades at SU. And some of the more fierce ones eventually got out of hand and were banished. The tradition of the "rushes" emerged in the 1880s, when sophomores began pelting freshmen with salt and even rubbing it into their hair. Eventually, the second-year students went from tossing handfuls of salt to entire bags. This then developed into sophomores defending Crouse College Hill against the charging frosh, who attempted to reach the summit. A variety of new rushes would emerge, with flour, snow, canes, and oranges as weapons. World War I put the tradition on hold, and by the World War II era rushes died out completely, their demise precipitated in large part by a 1941 rush in which a sophomore was seriously injured.

Ceremonial Mace Bearers

The ritual of mace bearers at Syracuse University began in June 1949, when registrar Keith Kennedy held up an ornamental wooden staff while leading graduates into old Archbold Stadium for commencement.

Though it was a first for SU, Kennedy was merely carrying on a tradition that could be traced at least as far back as 1180 AD and the reign of King Richard I, the English monarch who became better known as Richard the Lionheart. Original mace bearers were actually bodyguards, who used the wooden or metal staffs to protect the king. Over time, the maces became obsolete as soldiers stopped

wearing armor. But monarchs liked what they symbolized and continued to employ them at royal ceremonies. The ritual eventually made its way across the Atlantic Ocean as mace bearers became leadoff hitters at academic ceremonies, whose cap-and-gown processions clearly have royal and religious roots.

SU's first mace was rather nondescript and was replaced in 1959 by the one currently in use—a sterling silver staff with precious stones that was given to the university as a gift by former mace bearer Gordon Hoople.

Through the years, esteemed professors, deans, administrators, and students have assumed the honorary role.

In 2004, Nancy Weatherly Sharp, a longtime journalism professor at the Newhouse School, became the first woman to carry the mace at SU. She continued to do so until her retirement following the new student convocation in August 2017. Student Association president James Franco and Graduate Student Organization president Jack Wilson then became the first students to be mace bearers, and they were succeeded by John Palmer, a longtime Maxwell School professor and dean.

"Traditions like the mace bearer help us point to the past and take stock of the present," said Hendricks Chapel dean Brian Konkol, adding that sometimes "it's very powerful" when a physical object symbolizes the university's identity.

A Kiss Isn't Just a Kiss on This Bench

The tradition of graduating classes leaving memorial gifts to the university began when the class of 1912 raised money for the placement of a smooth granite bench beneath a tree between the Hall of Languages and the present-day Tolley Humanities Building. The thought was that such gifts would enhance the beauty of the campus. But over time, this particular gift would become better known for another tradition: kissing. It's unknown exactly when SU students

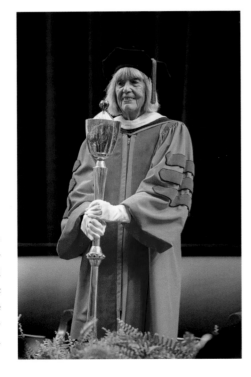

For thirteen years, Newhouse professor Nancy Weatherly Sharp carried SU's mace at academic ceremonies. © Syracuse University. Photo by Stephen Sartori.

The Kissing Bench was presented to the university by the class of 1912. © Syracuse University. Photo by Stephen Sartori.

Passionate members of "Otto's Army" during a basketball game at the Carrier Dome in 2016. © Syracuse University. Photo by Stephen Sartori.

started referring to it as the Kissing Bench, but by the 1950s it was believed that a coed who was kissed on the bench would not become a spinster. The tradition eventually evolved to its present-day belief that if two people kiss while sitting on the stone slab, they will wind up getting married.

Otto's Army, the Manley Zoo, and Other Cheering Sections

Duke may have its Cameron Crazies, Texas A&M its 12th Man, and Clemson its Death Valley, but if you believe *Princeton Review* magazine's school spirit rankings, none of those student cheering sections can beat Otto's Army. Named for Syracuse University's cuddly, fuzzy mascot, the army boasts more than five thousand members who form an intimidating sea of orange in the first and upper decks during basketball and football games at the Carrier

An SU student showing his true (school) colors. © Syracuse University. Photo by Stephen Sartori.

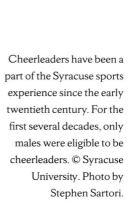

Cheerleaders have been a part of the Syracuse sports experience since the early twentieth century. For the first several decades, only males were eligible to be cheerleaders. © Syracuse University. Photo by Stephen Sartori.

Dome. Otto's Army's membership is four times the size of Duke's student section and is one of the reasons the magazine ranked SU number one among 382 schools across the country in the "Students Pack the Stadium" category from 2015 to 2018.

The group was founded in the days leading up to Gerry McNamara's final home basketball game on March 5, 2006, which attracted an on-campus record crowd (since broken) of 33,633 to the Dome. Before the G-Mac finale, student leaders devised a list system to organize the process of students claiming their seats and help keep them safe by preventing the mad dash that usually occurred before most games. The system worked so well for that game that Otto's Army became SU's official student section.

Like its unofficial predecessor—the Manley Zoo—the army has a number of standard chants, which include "Let's Go Orange!" as well as the "Who's He? So What? Big Sh-t!" greetings when the opposition's starting five are announced at basketball games. The signs fans generate for each game can be quite creative and occasionally profane. Students often will hoist Big Head cardboard images of Jim Boeheim, Dino Babers, and some of the players. Each member of the army must wear orange, and some enhance their wardrobes with orange wigs, helmets, caps, and face paint.

Rowdy cheering sections at SU sporting events have been a tradition since the early twentieth century. For many years, Archbold Stadium had placard sections at football games, where students would hold up colored squares spelling out messages like "Beat Colgate" or "Hi Mom." For nearly a half century, male and female students were required to sit in separate sections.

Through the years, no SU student section was more raucous than the Zoo in Manley Field House. Although the Dome has hosted basketball crowds nearly four times the size of Manley's biggest crowd (roughly 9,500), coaches, players, and referees say the

Fan participation at old Archbold Stadium included the use of placards like these. Syracuse University Photograph Collection, University Archives.

Student-run radio station WAER-FM has launched scores of broadcasting careers. Syracuse University Photograph Collection, University Archives.

smaller venue was vastly more intimidating. "There's no comparison," said former NCAA basketball referee Gene Monje. "Manley was ten times tougher to work than the Dome. At Manley, people were close enough they could touch you if they wanted to." And verbal barbs weren't the only things fans tossed at the opposition. "There were games you had to dodge oranges, and there was this one game when my assistant, Billy Kalbaugh, got plunked with a softball on the shoulder," said former St. Bonaventure head basketball coach and longtime SU radio analyst Jim Satalin. "We laugh about it now, but it wasn't so funny then. That could be a tough crowd. They could take your mind off the game."

The Zoo gave the Orange a distinct home-court advantage. In eighteen seasons there, Syracuse went 190-28, which included a fifty-seven-game win streak. From 1971 until a loss to Georgetown in the Manley finale in 1980, the Orange lost only five of 126 games.

National Orange Day

One of the newer Syracuse traditions was begun on March 24, 1994, to commemorate the day the university was officially chartered in 1870. Designated National Orange Day, the anniversary is intended not only to celebrate the school's founding but also to encourage students and alumni to participate in community service-oriented activities throughout the country and the world.

WAER

"It was a pretty grungy place. It was an old Quonset hut left over from World War II," said Ted Koppel about the studios and facilities of WAER-FM radio in 1959. "But there were these throngs of people coming in and out, putting programs on the air all day long."

Koppel was student program director at WAER during his time as an undergraduate at the university. He is one of thousands of students who have worked at the station over its seventy-year history.

WAER launched on April 12, 1947, as part of a joint experiment by the SU communications program and General Electric, which sought to expand its business of radio transmitter and broadcast electronics production at major US colleges. The station's success was immediate, as more than one hundred students showed up to audition for the inaugural broadcasts. It has operated as an FM radio station, with only one multiday disruption, ever since.

WAER's programming has shifted dramatically over the years—from theater programming, to progressive rock and soul, to live concert music, and eventually to a jazz and National Public Radio format. It also has perennially served as broadcast home to SU sports, providing a distinctive learning experience for its sports broadcasting students.

Throughout its history, WAER has been a training ground for generations of elite sports, news, and entertainment broadcasters. Among its alumni are Koppel, Dick Clark, Lou Reed, Marv Albert, Bob Costas, Steve Kroft, Mike Tirico, Sean McDonough, Beth Mowins, Len Berman, Ian Eagle, and Bob Dotson. Its alumni include scores of major market and network sports and news voices, many of whom first opened a microphone inside WAER studios. "WAER was in an old facility," Dotson said. "But that's ok, because if you don't have all the new bells and whistles, you find ways to make do with what you have."

The radio station has faced struggles along the way—including ones over format, funding for equipment, and a takeover of station management by the university. In its first thirty-six years, WAER was chiefly managed by students. Faculty and university oversight were nominal. That included a vibrant week for the station in May

1970, when WAER served as a beacon of news during a large student protest that shuttered campus.

In October 1978, a school administrator authored a memo to a university vice chancellor detailing plans to have SU assume management and control of WAER. It read: "The present system (at the radio station) is a waste of University-funded resources." In a separate memo, a university administrator said, "The University needs its own voice and has it, but for some invisible reason simply won't use it."

In April 1983, after a years-long tug-of-war between the school and the station's students, a newly hired professional manager pulled WAER off the air. He removed several student leaders from the station and discarded its music library, including vinyl records from musicians like Joe Jackson and the Clash. He executed a shift to a public radio format. The changeover triggered campus protests and media coverage.

"I think that left a bad taste in students' mouths," said Kenny Dees, a WAER staffer prior to the 1983 shift. "The (students) were thinking that their creativity and their efforts were just being thrown out the window."

Though the switch was controversial, the public radio format introduced in 1983 has proven resilient. WAER remains a National Public Radio affiliate and continues to draw more than one hundred student broadcasters each year, including another two generations of elite sportscasters and newscasters.

The radio station outgrew its small, run-down World War II-era facility near Carnegie Library in 1973, moving to a new suite in Newhouse II. At the turn of the century, it moved into the renovated Haft Hall complex, where it now houses modern digital studios, a large news and sports hub, and studio spaces for live audio, podcasts, and production.

The passion, friendships, and dedication of students that launched WAER to immediate success have continued without interruption. "That simply has not changed," said station general manager Joe Lee.

"All of us recall the WAER days," said Costas during his induction into the WAER Hall of Fame in 2015. "Not just because it gave us a chance to hone our craft, but for the sense of camaraderie."

The Daily Orange

It took Irving Templeton twenty-five hours to handset the first edition of the *Daily Orange*.

On Sept. 15, 1903, he delivered five hundred copies of the first edition of what turned into the paper of record of Syracuse University and a breeding ground for some of the world's top journalists.

"Today students are given the first issue of a daily college paper devoted to their interest and to the growth of Syracuse," the opening editorial read.

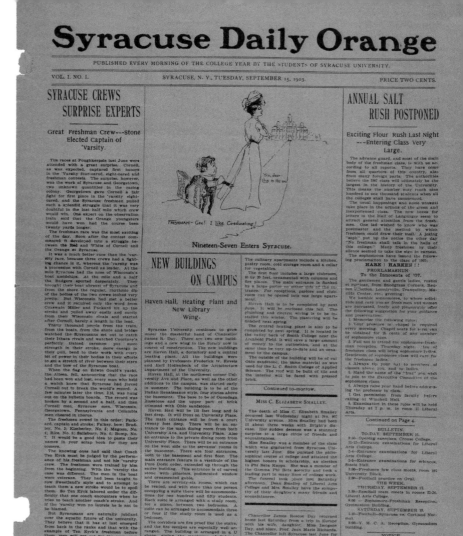

(Above) The *Daily Orange* has been SU's student newspaper since publishing its first edition on September 15, 1903. Syracuse University Student Publications Reference Collection, University Archives.

(Right) A student catches up on the news of the day. © Syracuse University. Photo by Stephen Sartori.

Some Prominent
Daily Orange Alumni

- Mike McAlary, former reporter and columnist at the *New York Daily News* who won a Pulitzer Prize for exposing police brutality
- Sy Montgomery, author of more than twenty books, including a finalist for the 2015 National Book Award for Nonfiction
- Jim Naughton, former *New York Times* and *Washington Post* reporter.
- Larry Kramer, former president and publisher of *USA Today* and founder of CBS Marketwatch.com
- Eli Saslow, *Washington Post* and *ESPN the Magazine* writer who won a Pulitzer Prize for a series on food stamps in the United States
- Jim Morin, editorial cartoonist at the *Miami Herald* who has won two Pulitzer Prizes
- Harry Rosenfeld, former *Washington Post* editor who oversaw the newspaper's coverage of Watergate
- Jayson Stark, baseball reporter at the *Athletic*, formerly with ESPN
- Meredith Goldstein, advice columnist at the *Boston Globe*
- Rose Ciotta, former *Philadelphia Inquirer* editor who won a Pulitzer Prize for a series on school violence
- Brad Anderson, creator of the Marmaduke comic strip
- Robb Armstrong, creator of the Jump Start comic strip

The first edition was small, having just four pages, but it came with the first cartoon to run in a college newspaper. The paper was inexpensive, with students forking over $2.50 (about $65 in today's market) for a year-long subscription to the Tuesday-Saturday editions.

The paper did well in its first few years, opening one of the first student-owned and student-operated print shops in the United States and building a two-story facility opposite the steps of Archbold Stadium. But ten years after the *DO*'s inception, the building's cost and a lagging subscriber base almost forced its closure. The Athletic Governing Board, realizing the importance of the paper's athletics coverage, saved it from folding, but only temporarily. It continued to lose money and closed its doors in 1921.

That lasted one week.

A vote to levy a $2.50 subscription tax on students passed, and the *DO* reopened its doors. It's been publishing ever since. While its award-winning stories, photos, and cartoons have remained a constant, the place it calls home has not. It has worked out of the building near Archbold, the Yates Castle grounds, and now a small house on Ostrom Avenue, among other locations.

The major turning point in the *DO*'s history came in 1971, when it declared independence from the university. The paper's support of the 1970 student strike upset SU's administration, leading officials to suspend its summer editions and not support it when it was sued for libel. The administration elected its own editor-in-chief, while the paper countered, electing somebody else. A mediation board picked the paper's choice. The following fall, the Student Association consolidated the three campus newspapers to save money. So in 1971, an independent *DO* was born. Two decades later, the paper became financially independent of the university, no longer relying on student fees to fund its operation.

After more than one hundred years of publication, the *DO* continues to evolve. Its presence is no longer just in print; it now has an intense online focus to serve a changing readership.

The newspaper's legacy is—and always will be—its dedication to covering Syracuse University. It has had its financial troubles, with dwindling advertising dollars, but its commitment to quality coverage of all things on the Hill and serving as a learning laboratory for future journalists remains paramount. That commitment has been recognized by the Society of Professional Journalists, which named the *DO* Best All-Around Daily Student Newspaper for 2017.

Coming Back Together and Our Time Has Come

For many African American and Latino students attending Syracuse University during the 1950s and 1960s, the truth was obvious: There were few students of color, and fewer still who understood the challenges of attending a school as a distinct minority.

But in 1983, thanks to the efforts of basketball legend and entrepreneur Dave Bing and university leaders Robert Hill and Evelyn Walker, the Coming Back Together (CBT) reunion was organized to create a stronger bond between SU and minority alumni and students. CBT was the first reunion of its kind in the United States.

Four years later, the Our Time Has Come (OTHC) Scholarship was created to serve as a launch pad for African American and Latino career success. The goal was for like-minded alumni to fund scholarships that promoted a diverse student body.

"Many of us received financial aid during our years at Syracuse, so we can appreciate the importance of scholarships," said Bing, the first chair of the OTHC fundraising campaign. "Now that we are in the position to do so, I felt it was important to give back and help students of promise succeed."

Bing's leadership generated more than $1 million, and a second campaign led by program development vice president Larry Martin generated another $3 million in gifts from individuals and groups such as the Syracuse Eight, Martin Whitman, and the Black Celestial Choral Ensemble. By 2017, CBT had become a major tradition at SU, with famous speakers such as network journalist Soledad O'Brien headlining its festivities.

Alumni of color celebrate the triennial Coming Back Together reunion. © Syracuse University. Photo by Stephen Sartori.

"Coming Back Together reunions and the OTHC Scholarship Fund are of really significant importance to Syracuse University," said Barry L. Wells, special assistant to the chancellor and former senior vice president and dean of student affairs. "That's because students past and present are critical partners in the growth and development of SU's ongoing commitment to diversity and inclusive excellence. For students of color, alumni engagement is vitally important both because of the OTHC Fund and because they can share knowledge, experiences, networking tips, and potentially help with job placements."

Jam Time

SU's Juice Jam music festival (the big concert event of the fall semester) and the Spring Block Party/Mayfest have consistently delivered some of the biggest names in music (Drake, Kendrick Lamar, Childish Gambino) to the Carrier Dome or SU's Skytop Field.

Starting in 2007, University Union (UU) began bringing acts to campus in September like Third Eye Blind (2007), Ra Ra Riot (2008), Gambino (2012), Lamar (2013), Big Sean (2015), and A$AP Ferg and Playboi Carti (2018). Those events allowed students to gather loudly when upstate New York's weather was still spectacular and pressures from studying and tests were still a ways off.

Often, the act selected by UU organizers is on its way up the charts, as was the case in 2010 when Drake played the Dome for Block Party. Following on the success of his 2009 hit single "So Far Gone," the Canadian rapper's debut album/CD, *Thank Me Later*, hit number one on the *Billboard* 200 the same year he played the Dome.

On rare occasions, the weather (particularly for Mayfest) has been miserable, or the star act has failed to appear. One memorable case took place in 2016, when rapper Fetty Wap famously missed his flight the day of the Juice Jam concert and UU organizers found themselves scrambling to keep a restless crowd entertained.

For many students, serving on UU (one of SU's largest student-run clubs) is the entrée to careers in the entertainment industry. UU committee positions help students get real-life experience staging concerts, special cinema offerings, and live performances. Students also work in social media, data collection, technology research, marketing, public relations, design, production, and collaborations. UU was established in 1962 as the official programming board of SU.

Greek Life

The headline of the October 1, 2018, *Daily Orange* read: "Students divided over SU Greek Life." It was a familiar sentiment because ever since 1871, when Delta Kappa Epsilon, Syracuse's first fraternity, began a colonization process on SU's campus, students and administrators have been divided over what Greek life stands for and whether it enhances the university.

According to the *DO* story, in a survey that generated nearly four thousand responses, 97 percent of the Greek respondents believed their fraternal organizations helped them "interact with other students." But 40 percent of non-Greek students said they felt fraternities and sororities did not socialize with students outside the Panhellenic system.

That sense of elitism is probably wrapped up in the historical roots of fraternal organizations and traces back to 1776, when Phi Beta Kappa was founded at the College of William and Mary. Almost immediately, fraternities leveraged secrecy, ritual oaths, initiations, mysterious handshakes, and requirements of fidelity to the brotherhood of members. Less than a century later, Syracuse would emulate Ivy League schools by adding frats or even secret senior men's groups similar to Yale's Skull and Bones, which was started in 1832 when three debating societies at the New Haven,

Delta Delta Delta—better known as Tri-Delt—is one of several Greek houses on Walnut Avenue. © Syracuse University. Photo by Stephen Sartori.

Connecticut, university reportedly began arguing over Phi Beta Kappa awards.

Exposure to the Greek system is often bothersome, especially to those who see or hear about raunchy movies like 1978's *Animal House*, 2003's *Old School*, 2008's *House Bunny*, or 2016's *Neighbors 2: Sorority Rising*. Those films feature now-familiar tropes (excessive partying, sexual debauchery, academic dishonesty, drug use, unwanted sexual advances) and do a great deal to offset the positive attributes actively promoted by the Greek system: the creation of deep friendships, egalitarianism, legendary social engagements, philanthropy, and the commitment to higher ideals.

Those platitudes have rung hollow, however, when Syracuse fraternities or sororities were suspended or expelled because of conduct violations. One of the most infamous cases at Syracuse occurred in the spring of 2018, when the Theta Tau engineering fraternity conducted a private meeting in which the brothers horrifically and offensively created an oath that mocked numerous races, creeds, sexual orientations, and women.

Not surprisingly, when a video of the Theta Tau incident went viral via the internet, the SU campus erupted in outrage, with protests setting off a firestorm of complaints about the need for fraternities and sororities at Syracuse.

Defenders of Greek life have frequently noted that while excessively rowdy behavior can emanate from chapter houses (just as it can from residence halls or off-campus houses), the large majority of pledges and members highly value their experience in a Greek house.

Of special note, the oldest surviving fraternity house at SU, that belonging to the Pi Chapter of Psi Upsilon (101 College Place), was placed on the National Register of Historic Places in 1985. With its location next to the Life Sciences Complex and its diagonal proximity to Bird Library, it stands, like many dignified houses in the Walnut Park Historic District, as a representation of Greek life at Syracuse since the early 1900s.

Like fraternities, the sorority system at SU features a rich history, which includes the establishment of three national sororities at Syracuse: Alpha Phi (1872), Gamma Phi Beta (1874), and Alpha Gamma Delta (1904).

Jabberwocky

Of all the coffee houses or clubs at Syracuse (such as Two Below, SUCH, and People's Place in Hendricks Chapel), the Jabberwocky was probably the wildest. Nestled beneath Kimmel Dining Hall, the "Jab" was legendary to multiple generations of SU students for its raw musical vibe.

The club draws its name from the fierce character appearing in Lewis Carroll's unusual novel *Through the Looking Glass*. The character first appears in a poem with these oft-repeated stanzas:

Until its closing in 1985 after sixteen years, the Jabberwocky hosted scores of wild concerts on campus. Photograph by Anestis Diakopoulos. Syracuse University Photograph Collection, University Archives.

'Twas brillig, and the slithy toves
Did gyre and gimble in the wabe:
All mimsy were the borogoves,
And the mome raths outgrabe.

"Beware the Jabberwock, my son!
The jaws that bite, the claws that catch!
Beware the Jubjub bird, and shun
The frumious Bandersnatch!"

That kind of hazy language fit the era of the late 1960s perfectly, and since Syracuse had no student union, the University Union board pressured the administration to open a student club in a dank, vacant cellar (as an indication that a larger meeting place would ultimately be built).

The SU administrators never could have envisioned that, from opening night in 1969 until the final week of concerts sixteen years later, a smoke-filled rectangle of 2,800 square feet would consistently unite music lovers from all over the East Coast. Yet by the time the club closed on May 4, 1985, Jabberwocky, with its famed Alice-in-Wonderland murals, was possibly the "greatest live venue in the history of Central New York."

Acts like Junior Wells, James Taylor, James Brown, Buddy Guy, Jackson Browne, Bonnie Raitt, the Talking Heads, and Southside Johnny and the Asbury Jukes roared under the club's low ceiling and all over the beer-stained floor and walls.

The Jab's small, slightly elevated stage stood in front of the always-crowded bar, and the narrow nature of the room—with three annoying, vision-blocking support pillars—ensured every performer was intimately connected to students and locals in front of and behind them. Additionally, many concerts were broadcast live on WAER-FM to help drive nightly attendance.

"WAER was a [noted] tastemaker," said David Rezak, retired founding director of the Bandier Program, about the early 1970s. "There were times when artists played at Jab because they wanted to get 'broken' on WAER."

The 1980s brought numerous changes that would lead to the Jab's demise, including the raising of the national minimum drinking age to twenty-one, the ending of WAER's status as a student-run station, and the opening of the Schine Student Center.

The claustrophobic music venue's last week of concerts would wind up being memorable. On that Monday night, Wells, who opened Jabberwocky in 1969, drank himself nearly blind before telling the crowd, "I opened this [expletive] house and I'm gonna close this [expletive] house." The next night, it was former Byrd's guitarist Roger McGuinn followed by Jorma Kaukonen (Jefferson Airplane, Hot Tuna). The Godfather of Soul (Brown) "blew up the house" on Thursday night, giving the packed Jab one of its most epic concerts ever.

The final Friday belonged to John Cale, who had formed the Velvet Underground with SU's Lou Reed and was then touring with members of Funkadelic under the stage name Bernie Worrel and Friends. With funk in their hearts, "they shut the Jab down."

As Joe Bronowich, Jabberwocky's last student manager responsible for booking acts, told Syracuse.com in 2015, "The great, unique and wonderful thing about Jab was unlike almost every other club in the world, we were not required to make a profit. And we sure didn't. We could book whoever we wanted for whatever reason we wanted. The music always came first."

The old Jabberwocky site is now a technology-focused workspace known as MakerSpace.

5 Famous Visitors

Throughout its history, Syracuse University has been a magnet, attracting not only notable students and faculty, but also some of the world's most famous people.

This is a place where Dr. Martin Luther King Jr. and Lyndon Baines Johnson delivered historically significant speeches.

A place where Babe Ruth hit long home runs, Michael Jordan hit long jump shots, and Jim Thorpe hit the pay dirt of the end zone after a long touchdown run.

A place where figures as diverse as the Dalai Lama, Jane Goodall, Walter Cronkite, Kurt Vonnegut, Oprah Winfrey, Robert Frost, Jesse Jackson, Billy Graham, Spike Lee, Charles Lindbergh, and Elie Wiesel imparted words of wisdom.

A place where Frank Sinatra, Paul McCartney, Bruce Springsteen, Dolly Parton, Drake, and the Rolling Stones sang classics.

A place where Hollywood came to film movies, such as *The Express*.

A magnet, indeed.

The Speech Heard 'Round the World

Lyndon Baines Johnson looked worn and weary when he showed up on campus the morning of August 5, 1964, to receive an honorary doctor of laws degree and preside over the dedication of Newhouse I. That the thirty-sixth president of the United States appeared to be bearing the weight of the world was understandable because much of the previous day had been spent huddling with generals, admirals, advisors, and congressmen plotting a response to an attack on a US Navy destroyer by North Vietnam. And that chaotic day would be capped by a hastily scheduled, twelve-minute live television address to the nation just before midnight.

The trip to Syracuse University had been scheduled weeks earlier, and despite the gravity of the situation in Southeast Asia, LBJ decided to honor his commitment. His spirits would be temporarily boosted when he stepped to the dais on the Newhouse plaza that morning and looked out on an enthusiastic throng of more than twenty thousand spectators on the lawn that stretched up the Hill

On August 5, 1964, President Lyndon Baines Johnson delivered his historic Gulf of Tonkin speech at the dedication of Newhouse I. Syracuse University Photograph Collection, University Archives.

to Crouse College and the Hall of Languages. The Vietnam conflict had not yet escalated. And in the nine months following the assassination of John F. Kennedy, Johnson had ridden a huge wave of popularity that enabled him to shepherd some of his predecessor's legislation through Congress, most notably the Civil Rights Act. Johnson was expected to win in a landslide over Republican challenger Barry Goldwater in 1964 and then continue passing legislation to create what he had termed a "Great Society."

But LBJ's plans would unravel over the next four years as the United States became mired in the Vietnam War. And some historians trace the beginning of the end to his presidency to the infamous "Gulf of Tonkin" speech Johnson delivered in cap and gown that August morning just minutes before cutting the ribbon to officially open Newhouse I.

In his speech, the man who had promised a peaceful solution to the growing conflict in Vietnam picked up where he had left off the night before. This time, though, he said he was speaking not only to the American public, but "to people of all nations—so that they may understand without mistake our purpose in the action that we've been required to take."

He mentioned two attacks against the USS *Maddox* in the Gulf of Tonkin by hostile vessels of the government of North Vietnam.

"The attacks were deliberate," he said. "The attacks were unprovoked. The attacks have been answered."

The "answer"—given during the previous night and even as Johnson spoke at SU—was retaliatory bombing attacks by the US Navy's Seventh Fleet in and around the waters off the coast of the Communist-controlled country.

"I say this: There is no threat to any peaceful power from the United States of America," he continued during his speech at Newhouse. "But there can be no peace by aggression and no immunity from reply. That is what is meant by the actions that we took yesterday."

Several times during his remarks, Johnson was interrupted by rousing applause. And when he was finished, the crowd gave him a standing ovation. After being presented with his honorary degree—making him the first sitting president to be so honored by SU—Johnson and his wife Lady Bird were given a pair of large golden scissors, and they, along with Chancellor William Pearson Tolley and benefactors Samuel and Mitzi Newhouse, cut the ribbons near the building's front door.

Orange alumnus and longtime *Syracuse Herald-Journal* columnist Dick Case was one of the 277 accredited media members covering the ceremonies that day. Seated next to CBS newsman Dan Rather, Case was approached by a city policeman before Johnson's speech. He told Case the president needed a typewriter. "I gave him my Royal office model—and never saw it again," Case said in a 2014 *Syracuse University Magazine* interview. Whether Johnson himself used the typewriter is unknown, and its whereabouts remains a mystery.

More than twenty thousand people showed up for President Lyndon Johnson's appearance at SU in 1964. Syracuse University Photograph Collection, University Archives.

Two days after Johnson's visit to Central New York, he presented both houses of Congress with a resolution asking for sweeping authorization to wage war in Southeast Asia, primarily in Vietnam. On August 7, the Tonkin Gulf Resolution passed the House unanimously, 416-0, and the Senate, 88-2, with ten senators not voting.

Over time, the war would become extremely unpopular, dividing the country and resulting in the deaths of nearly sixty thousand American soldiers. By 1968, the rousing ovation Johnson received on the Syracuse campus seemed a distant memory. Protestors were burning him in effigy, and in March of that year he announced he would not seek reelection for a second term.

Hail to the Chiefs

Lyndon Baines Johnson was one of six US presidents to speak on SU's campus.

Franklin Delano Roosevelt was the first commander in chief to visit, and he did so twice. In 1930, as governor of New York State, he delivered the commencement address. Six years later he returned to lay the cornerstone for the university's new College of Medicine building. "I congratulate you with great assurance on the added usefulness to humanity which this building provides and which you will give the future generations of America," he said during his dedication speech.

A year later, FDR's White House predecessor, Herbert Hoover, was on hand for the dedication of Maxwell Hall.

In 1957, John F. Kennedy, a young, up-and-coming US senator from Massachusetts, delivered the commencement speech at Archbold Stadium. His remarks served as a precursor to the famous "Ask not what America can do for you" speech he would give at his presidential inauguration four years later.

Future president John F. Kennedy delivered the SU commencement address at Archbold Stadium in 1957. Syracuse University Photograph Collection, University Archives.

In the spring of 1960, Harry S. Truman spoke to more than one thousand high school students and teachers as part of a citizenship conference in packed Hendricks Chapel. After finishing his remarks, the man who had been the thirty-third president of the United States was told there were about a thousand people out on the Quad who were unable to get into Hendricks and hear his talk. Truman asked if they could quickly set up a microphone and speaker outside, and he wound up delivering his speech a second time.

Bill Clinton was the only other president to make an appearance. He actually gave a campaign speech on the steps of Hendricks in April 1992 before winning the election against George H. W. Bush that November. Eleven years later, Clinton returned to deliver the commencement address, which included him replacing his mortarboard with a baseball cap celebrating the SU men's 2003 NCAA basketball championship.

Although there is no record of him appearing on campus, Grover Cleveland—the only man to serve nonconsecutive terms as president—was a member of SU's board of trustees. The University College building is named for him.

Former president Harry Truman spoke on campus— twice on the same day—in 1960. Syracuse University Portrait Collection, University Archives.

Ronald Reagan never appeared at SU, but his wife, Nancy, did as part of a 1980 Republican Party fundraiser in the Carrier Dome. Frank Sinatra and Wayne Newton performed at that gala, making them the first musical acts to entertain spectators in the Dome.

Dwight D. Eisenhower spoke at a Republican fundraiser at the Onondaga War Memorial in 1962. Jimmy Carter was part of a Democratic Party presidential primary debate in downtown Syracuse in 1976. Gerald Ford also was downtown in the 1990s for a Republican fundraiser. But none of the three ever made their way from downtown to the Hill.

Neither did Richard Nixon during a Syracuse appearance in 1970. The antiwar movement was in full swing by that time. Two hundred student protestors ventured to the Onondaga War Memorial and attempted unsuccessfully to drown out Nixon by singing "The Sounds of Silence," a popular Simon and Garfunkel song that had become an anthem for antiwar activists.

Former president Bill Clinton donned a baseball cap denoting SU's national basketball championship while posing with Chancellor Buzz Shaw before commencement in 2003. © Syracuse University. Photo by Stephen Sartori.

In 1961, two years before Dr. Martin Luther King Jr. gave his historic "I Have a Dream" speech in Washington, DC, he "auditioned" several passages in an address at Syracuse University. Agence France Presse / Getty Images.

Martin Luther King Jr. Spoke of His American Dream at SU

Years before revealing he had been to the mountaintop, Martin Luther King Jr. visited the Hill. Twice, in fact, as favors to Charles V. Willie, the pioneering African American Syracuse University graduate student, professor, and administrator whom King had befriended during their undergraduate days at Morehouse College in Atlanta.

Willie was certain the famed civil rights leader and orator would deliver memorable speeches to SU students and faculty members, and he wasn't disappointed. In fact, King's first oratory before an overflow crowd at Sadler Hall on July 13, 1961, would be spellbinding as he provided a sneak preview of the monumental "I Have

a Dream" address he would give two years later from the steps of the Lincoln Memorial in front of a quarter of a million people.

Greeted with a *Daily Orange* headline blaring, "South's 'Gandhi' Speaks Here Tonight," King arrived at Sadler primed to talk about how his nonviolent approach to the civil rights movement was modeled after the strategy pacifist Mahatma Gandhi had employed years earlier during India's struggle for independence from British rule. King said the courage of the Freedom Riders had helped integrate municipal buses in Montgomery, Alabama, and the "lunch-counter sit-down strike" had forced southern restaurants to allow African Americans to sit next to white patrons.

But King also stressed how much work remained to be done. And, while doing so, the famed orator boomed out several indelible phrases that would be repeated in future speeches.

SU professor and administrator Charles Willie convinced former college classmate and longtime friend Dr. Martin Luther King Jr. to speak at the university twice. Courtesy of Sarah Willie-LeBreton.

"The problem that we confront in the world and in our own nation is that of unity," King said. "We must learn to live together as brothers or we will perish as fools." That this speech was a precursor to his most famous oratory was further underscored when he concluded with the following words:

> So with this faith in the future, we will be able to adjourn the councils of despair, rise from the fatigue of darkness to the buoyancy of hope, and we will be able to bring into being this new society, and realize the American Dream. This will be the day when all of God's children, black men and white men, Jews and Gentiles, Protestants and Catholics will be able to join hands and sing in the words of the old Negro spiritual:
>
> Free at last, free at last
> Thank God almighty
> We are free at last!

King's remarks were greeted with a standing ovation. Many of those in Sadler undoubtedly would remember his powerful message when they heard King speak two years later in Washington, DC.

At Willie's request, King returned to SU on July 15, 1965—this time at Sims Hall. This speech was even more anticipated than the one he delivered four years earlier, with the one thousand tickets selling out rapidly, prompting the Summer Series banquet organizers to set up speakers in Gifford Auditorium so even more people could hear his speech. This address, entitled "The Role of Education in the Civil Rights Movement," would be a continuation of points he had made in his award-winning book, *Why We Can't Wait*.

In his introduction, Willie praised King as a "suffering servant" and described him as a "marked man." King shook hands with his friend, then took a moment to thank the ministers from Syracuse who had joined him and others in their protest march from Selma to Montgomery, Alabama, which would result in the passage of the landmark Voting Rights Act that August in the Oval Office at

a signing ceremony in which King stood next to President Lyndon Johnson.

Whereas his 1961 SU speech would be a precursor to his famed "Dream" speech, this address appeared to foreshadow his equally unforgettable "I've Been to the Mountaintop" speech. Riveted audiences in Sims and Gifford listened raptly as King said: "There are some things so dear, some things so precious, some things so eternally true that they're worth dying for. And if a man has not discovered something that he will die for, he isn't fit to live." He finished, as he had at SU in 1961 and at the National Mall in Washington two years later, with his "free at last" lines, and the audience responded with thunderous applause.

Less than three years later, King was assassinated in Memphis, his premonition of martyrdom sadly coming true.

A half century later, his connection to Syracuse University continues to be celebrated. In 1971, the Martin Luther King Jr. Memorial Library was established in Sims Hall as an extension of the university's Department of African American Studies. Each year since 1985, an event commemorating King's life is held on campus, with keynote speakers. Appropriately, in 2017, Willie returned to take part in the ceremonies. In memory of the fiftieth anniversary of King's death, a plaque celebrating his 1965 speech at SU was unveiled near the site where he spoke.

"My great hope is because of this plaque generations of students and visitors to Syracuse University will have the curiosity to read and think about what Dr. King actually said here—and act on it," Chancellor Kent Syverud said at the unveiling.

Commencement Speakers

Stewart L. Woodford's internet biographies tell you that he was a Columbia University graduate, a colonel in the Union Army during the Civil War, a prominent New York City attorney, and a US

English primatologist and anthropologist Jane Goodall delivered the commencement address in 2005. © Syracuse University. Photo by Stephen Sartori.

Legendary CBS news anchor Walter Cronkite was Syracuse's commencement speaker in 1968. Syracuse University Photograph Collection, University Archives.

Rock star Billy Joel led the students in song at Syracuse's 2006 commencement. © Syracuse University. Photo by Stephen Sartori.

congressman, who, after one term, was appointed ambassador to Spain by President William McKinley.

What they don't tell you is that Woodford also delivered the first commencement address at Syracuse University in 1893.

Since that time, more than 150 people, including presidents (Franklin Roosevelt, John F. Kennedy, and Bill Clinton), captains of industry, nationally known journalists (Walter Cronkite and Tom Brokaw), best-selling authors (Kurt Vonnegut and Frank McCourt), renowned scientists (Jane Goodall), popular entertainers (Billy Joel and Pearl Bailey), and world-changing activists (Vernon Jordan and Kathrine Switzer) have continued the pomp-and-circumstance tradition begun by Woodford. Because of Syracuse's Methodist roots, commencement speeches were dominated by Christian clergymen for several decades. A woman wasn't afforded the honor until 1937, when syndicated newspaper columnist and SU alumna Dorothy Thompson spoke to graduates. The first African American commencement speaker at Syracuse is believed to be former US senator and civil rights activist Julian Bond in 1970.

There have been several academic years in which there were multiple commencements, with as many as three per year during World War II, when degree programs were accelerated to aid the war effort. This trend would continue in the postwar years, as SU dealt with the tripling of enrollment caused by the thousands of returning veterans during what was known as the GI Bulge. Chancellor William Pearson Tolley filled the role of commencement speaker at several of the additional graduation ceremonies. That explains why he is the all-time leader at SU, with five commencement addresses. The only others to deliver keynote oratories at more than one commencement were prominent journalists and Syracuse alumni Ted Koppel (1982 and 2000) and William Safire (1978 and 1990).

One of the more powerful speeches was delivered by Cronkite, the famed CBS news anchor, at the height of the civil rights and antiwar movement on June 2, 1968, just three days before presidential candidate Robert F. Kennedy was assassinated. "There are a lot of things wrong with this world we've made," Cronkite told the audience of several thousand in Archbold Stadium.

> Poverty, ugliness, corruption, intolerance, waste of our resources, pollution of our air and water, urban sprawl, inefficient transportation, outmoded concepts of national sovereignty, the secret society of the establishment elite, the power of the military-industrial complex, the atomic arms race, the population explosion, war.
>
> The mere fact that the species has survived so far seems hardly adequate cause for self-applause, nor can we indulge in self-congratulations for our civilization's considerable material and cultural development that has failed to guarantee survival or nurture the bodies and the spirit of all humankind.
>
> If we are to survive and wipe out not only the symptoms but the causes of injustice and decay, there must be change. There is going to be change. This is inevitable. The question that the future asks is: What kind of change—for the good or for the bad, coming rapidly or more slowly, by radical excitement of the old, by amputation and transplant . . . or by mutation.

Cronkite ended his speech on an upbeat note, calling on the newly minted graduates to be a part of a positive revolution.

> This country has not lost its ability to respond to challenge, and while the challenges of today seem frightening in their complexity, there is no reason for despair. The more and the greater the challenges, the greater the heroism of thought, deed and courage to surmount them—and the more exciting the prospect of the combat, and the sweeter the taste of victory.

In Concert with the Dome

On October 22, 1980, Frank Sinatra and Wayne Newton became the first recording artists to perform in the Carrier Dome. Their concert was part of a Republican fundraiser that attracted 11,350 spectators, including special guest Nancy Reagan, who would become the First Lady after her husband, Ronald Reagan, won the presidential election two weeks later.

Sinatra and Newton kicked off a tradition of Dome concerts that continues to this day. Through 2018, eighty-three concerts had been held under the Teflon big top, and they've included some of the biggest musical acts of all time. Here is a look at the artists who have performed the most times in the Dome:

Billy Joel: 7	Pink Floyd: 2
The Rolling Stones: 6	Elton John: 2
Genesis: 4	Garth Brooks: 2
Bruce Springsteen: 3	Neil Diamond: 2
Grateful Dead: 3	The Police: 2
Kenny Rogers: 3	

Billy Joel holds the Carrier Dome record for most concerts, with seven. Actually, he's performed there eight times if you include the song he sang at SU's commencement in 2006. © Syracuse University. Photo by Steve Parker.

Memorable, too, was the oration of Oscar and Emmy Award-winning screenwriter and producer Aaron Sorkin. The Syracuse alumnus told the class of 2012:

> Don't ever forget that you're a citizen of this world, and there are things you can do to lift the human spirit, things that are easy, things that are free, things that you can do every day. Civility, respect, kindness, character. You're too good for schadenfreude. You're too good for gossip and snark. You're too good for intolerance—and since you're walking into the middle of a presidential election, it's worth mentioning that you're too good to think people who disagree with you are your enemy.

Jumping Back into the Music Business

While managing the Carrier Dome, Pete Sala has overseen the booking and production of nearly one hundred concerts. None was more memorable than two mega-band tour stops that took place six days apart in 1987. On October 3 that year, Pink Floyd performed in front of 34,710 spectators. But Sala and his crew didn't have much time to savor that performance because they immediately had to coordinate breakdown and setup for an October 9 event featuring U2, which drew a crowd of 39,248 as part of the famed *Joshua Tree* tour.

"Those two were unbelievably special for the Dome staff because of the back story," said Sala, SU's vice president and chief campus facilities officer. "The Dome had previously hosted Prince on March 30, 1985, and drawn 30,715. But in the days following the Prince concert, the city and university engaged in a tax dispute that resulted in Syracuse University not hosting concerts for upwards of eighteen months."

For a venue that prided itself on hosting major music acts like the Rolling Stones and Bruce Springsteen, not having shows for the students and community was a huge disappointment.

"Once an agreement was in place, we were back in business with the two shows mentioned above," he said. "Pink Floyd and U2 in one building in one week. It was an incredible way to jump back into the concert business and, without a doubt, two of the best shows the Dome ever hosted."

Of all the SU commencement speeches, perhaps none was more unusual than the one spoken and sung by Billy Joel in 2006. The rock-and-roll star finished his brief remarks with a ditty he composed on his way to SU from Long Island. Many in the Carrier Dome crowd of nearly twenty thousand applauded Joel's creative efforts, though several said afterword they would rather have heard him perform one of his numerous chart-topping hits.

Honorary Degrees

Syracuse University has been quite generous in conferring honorary degrees through the years, with more than one thousand such diplomas awarded. The peak occurred in 1920 when forty-two people were so honored. In recent decades the practice has become much more selective, with the average dropping to four to five per year.

The tradition began at SU in 1872 when James Harman Hoose received a doctor of philosophy degree. At the time, Hoose was the principal of the Normal College in Cortland, New York, roughly forty miles south of Syracuse. He later would teach at the University of Southern California in Los Angeles.

Like most universities at the time, SU did not offer graduate school programs but often awarded higher degrees based on

(Above) Sir Paul McCartney put on a rousing three-hour concert in the Carrier Dome on September 23, 2017. Temperatures inside the arena that night climbed into the low eighties, but the 36,200 spectators didn't seem to mind as they sung along with the former Beatle, who performed a number of the group's old classics, such as "Hey Jude," "Lady Madonna," and "Sgt. Pepper's Lonely Hearts Club Band." Photo by Rocco Carbone.

(Below) Mick Jagger and the Rolling Stones performed back-to-back Dome concerts on November 27 and 28 in 1981, attracting 85,812 concertgoers in two nights. They clearly enjoyed rocking the Loud House, coming back four more times. © Syracuse University. Photo by Steve Parker.

(Above) Frontman Bono performed with an injured arm during U2's 1987 concert in the Carrier Dome. Athletics Department, Syracuse University, used by permission.

(Below) Dolly Parton was part of a Dome concert with Kenny Rogers and the Oak Ridge Boys on November 26, 1988, drawing a crowd of 13,414. © Syracuse University. Photo by Steve Parker.

Baseball legend Babe Ruth appeared on campus several times, including August 19, 1924, when he smacked an unforgettable home run over the press box roof at Archbold Stadium. Bettmann / Getty Images.

professional experience or in honorary recognition of one's services to the college, the Methodist Church, New York State, or the nation. SU officials also adopted a resolution giving special consideration to alumni from Genesee College, the Lima, New York, school Methodist officials originally had hoped to relocate to Syracuse. Hoose had graduated from Genesee in 1861.

In 1876, Ellen Sargent became the first female to receive an honorary degree from SU when she was awarded a master of arts.

Numerous SU alumni have been recipients of honorary doctorates, including astronauts Eileen Collins and F. Story Musgrave, author Joyce Carol Oates, US vice president Joe Biden, journalists Bob Costas, William Safire, and Ted Koppel, and athletes Floyd Little and Dave Bing.

Four presidents—Franklin Roosevelt, John F. Kennedy, Lyndon Johnson, and Bill Clinton—also were feted by SU, along with

US Supreme Court justices Thurgood Marshall, Earl Warren, and Clarence Thomas. Other honorary degree recipients include poet Robert Frost, General John Pershing, Admiral Chester Nimitz, consumer activist Ralph Nader, Baseball Hall of Famer Dave Winfield, Russian author/activist Aleksandr Solzhenitsyn, news anchor Walter Cronkite, singers Pearl Bailey and Billy Joel, and anthropologist Jane Goodall.

The Babe Goes Deep in Syracuse

Before a New York Yankees exhibition baseball game against the Syracuse Stars at Archbold Stadium on August 19, 1924, Babe Ruth decided to do what he did best—put on a show. The legendary Yankees slugger grabbed his forty-two-ounce wooden club and stepped to the plate for some batting practice.

Archbold Stadium was the longtime home of Orange baseball and hosted several Major League Baseball exhibition games during the 1910s and 1920s. Athletics Department, Syracuse University, used by permission.

As ten thousand fans oohed and aahed at the concrete football bowl that doubled for many years as the home to Orange baseball, the Sultan of Swat smacked ball after ball deep into the outfield stands. One swat in particular would stand out among the rest. In baseball parlance, he would "get all of that one," launching the pitch over the top of the press box roof in right field and completely out of the stadium. Several longtime fans called it the longest ball ever hit at Archbold, a true Ruthian blast.

The Bambino singled twice in four at bats during the game that day as the Stars knocked off the Yankees, 12-8. But nobody in attendance was talking about those singles. It was the pregame smash that exited the entire stadium that had made an indelible impact.

Ruth would return to Archbold on October 14, 1928, with his famous teammate Lou Gehrig. The two sluggers were in town to play in a barnstorming game between the Bustin' Babes and the Larrupin' Lous at Star Park in downtown Syracuse. But the game was rained out, so the dynamic duo took in a Syracuse football game. As the two Bronx Bombers looked on from the press box, the Orangemen clobbered Johns Hopkins University, 58-0.

Tom Brady Wasn't So Terrific versus Orange

Tom Brady showed few signs that day of the greatness to come. In fact, the man now regarded by many as the finest quarterback of all time looked mediocre. His Michigan Wolverines would defeat the Orange, 18-13, in front of 49,249 spectators in the Carrier Dome during that September 18, 1999, game. And they'd do so, really, in spite of Brady, who wound up completing five-of-ten passes for twenty-six yards while splitting time with Drew Henson. Though Henson wasn't much better, he did lead Michigan to its four offensive scores—a touchdown and three field goals.

The year before, at Michigan's "Big House," Brady was even worse. His first drive resulted in an interception, and after Donovan McNabb quarterbacked the Orange to a 17-0 lead, Brady left the field to a chorus of boos. He would be replaced by Henson as Syracuse extended its lead to 31 points on its way to a 38-28 win.

Brady wound up lasting until the sixth round of the 2000 draft, finally being selected by the New England Patriots. He obviously was a late bloomer, because over the next two decades he led the Patriots to six Super Bowl championships while establishing numerous NFL passing records.

No one who ever saw him play against Syracuse could ever have envisioned he would blossom into arguably the greatest signal-caller of all time.

Michael Jordan's Memorable Moments at SU

The world-famous basketball player known as Air Jordan experienced several to-the-rafter moments in the Carrier Dome. And one really deflating one, too.

Of the four games Michael Jordan played there, the most satisfying had to be the December 11, 1983, contest in which he scored 19 points in North Carolina's 23-point annihilation of a Syracuse team led by Pearl Washington in front of 32,235 stunned fans. "I was surprised that we beat them as badly as we did," he said after he and guard Kenny Smith limited Washington to 8 points on 3-of-11 shooting. "We really wanted to take the crowd out of the game and we were able to do that."

Just eight months earlier, the man regarded as the best basketball player of all time suffered the most humiliating defeat of his collegiate career in the Dome—but not at the hands of the Orange. Playing in the NCAA East Region Finals against Georgia, Jordan scored 26 points, but it wasn't enough, as North Carolina was upset and denied a trip to the Final Four.

Basketball icon Michael Jordan visited the Carrier Dome several times, including a 1983 matchup with Orange star Pearl Washington. Jerry Wachter / Sports Illustrated / Getty Images.

He would return to the Dome in 1992 for a National Basketball Association exhibition game against a New Jersey Nets team featuring former Syracuse All-American Derrick Coleman. Jordan wound up scoring 17 points in twenty-four minutes, four of them coming after he sank a thirty-five-foot jump shot while being fouled. "You guys are great basketball fans," he told the crowd after the game. "Believe me when I say that. The Carrier Dome is great. I can't promise anything, but I'll try to come back some day."

He would return, twenty-two years later, as a spectator, watching with pride at SU's commencement as his daughter Jasmine graduated with a degree from the school named for David Falk, the super-agent who had helped Jordan land several lucrative endorsement deals, including the mega-million-dollar one with sporting goods giant NIKE.

And Jordan's loose Syracuse connection would become even tighter when Jasmine announced her engagement to former Orange center Rakeem Christmas in 2018.

Jim Thorpe's SU Experiences Were Upsetting and Euphoric

The autumn before Jim Thorpe panned Olympic gold in Stockholm, Sweden, he found himself stuck in the mud in Syracuse, New York. Most had expected the Native American track-and-field star and undisputed best player in college football to come to Archbold Stadium on November 18, 1911, and have a field day against the overmatched Orangemen.

But thanks in large part to torrential rains that turned Archie into a quagmire, Thorpe's speed was somewhat negated, and underdog Syracuse scored one of the most monumental upsets in its storied history, edging the undefeated Carlisle Indians, 12-11.

Despite the nasty conditions, Thorpe still managed to score two touchdowns, but he missed an extra point, and that would wind up being the difference. "Jim was inconsolable after the game," Syracuse alumnus Robert Wheeler wrote in his book, *Jim Thorpe: World's Greatest Athlete*. "He had kept them in the game, but he blamed himself for the defeat because his celebrated toe failed to convert one of the extra points."

Carlisle would go on to win its next two games and finish 11-1. The Indians outscored their opponents by a combined total of 298-49 that season as Thorpe was selected first-team All-American.

The next year, he added to his legend, winning gold medals in both the decathlon and pentathlon at the Summer Olympics, prompting Swedish King Gustav to dub him "the world's greatest athlete." On October 12, 1912, Thorpe returned to Archbold and atoned for the previous season's loss by scoring three touchdowns in Carlisle's 33-0 rout of Syracuse.

He would go on to play professional football for the Canton Bulldogs and help launch the National Football League. In a 1950 poll of the nation's sportswriters, Thorpe was voted the greatest athlete of the first half of the century, edging luminaries such as Babe Ruth, Jesse Owens, Jack Dempsey, and Joe Louis. A year later, a full-length movie about his life, starring Burt Lancaster, was released nationwide.

The Orange scored one of its biggest football upsets ever when it defeated the Jim Thorpe-led Carlisle Indians at Archbold Stadium in 1911. Hulton Archive / Getty Images.

(Above) The Dalai Lama visited the Syracuse University campus on October 7 and 8, 2012, as part of the Common Ground for Peace. The spiritual leader of Tibet participated in two panel discussions on campus before taking center stage at the Carrier Dome. He sent the crowd of about 24,000 into a joyful frenzy when he stepped to the podium, removed an orange-and-blue visor from his robe, and put it on his head. He wore it throughout his fifty-minute speech. © Syracuse University. Photo by Steve Parker.

(Below) Oprah Winfrey was on hand for the dedication of the Dick Clark Studios and the Alan Gerry Center for Media Innovation at Newhouse in 2014. Dubbed the "queen of media" by Newhouse Dean Lorraine Branham, Winfrey told students: "Allow the passion in your heart to lead you to do good, and do great work." © Syracuse University. Photo by Stephen Sartori.

6 Forty-Four Alumni of Note

Julia Alvarez. Syracuse University Portrait Collection, University Archives.

Julia Alvarez

Author

In an age when governmental forces seem to push against the concepts of inclusion and diversity, there may be no more powerful literary voice speaking to the issue of immigration, disconnection, and democracy than that of 1975 Syracuse graduate Julia Alvarez.

Considered by many to be one of the most significant Latina writers of the modern era, the author of *How the Garcia Girls Lost Their Accents*, *In the Time of the Butterflies*, and *Before We Were Free* has received hundreds of honors, but perhaps none more significant than the 2013 National Medal of Arts medal bestowed on her by President Barack Obama in a ceremony at the White House.

Recognized alongside filmmaker and Syracuse alumnus Albert Maysles, as well as Hollywood legend Jeffrey Katzenberg, Alvarez's citation recognized the Dominican American "novelist, poet, and essayist for her extraordinary storytelling. In poetry and in prose, Ms. Alvarez explores themes of identity, family, and cultural divides. She illustrates the complexity of navigating two worlds and reveals the human capacity for strength in the face of oppression."

Born in New York City, Alvarez's family moved to the Dominican Republic when she was three months old. She spent the next ten years there before her father became involved with an attempt to remove Rafael Trujillo, the island's feared military dictator. That forced the family to escape back to the United States, an experience captured graphically in her poem "Exile."

> The night we fled the country, Papi,
> you told me we were going to the beach,
> hurried me to get dressed along with the others,
> while posted at a window, you looked out.

Later, the struggling young girl of the poem describes a "hurried bag, allowing one toy a piece" to partially explain the heartache of leaving her treasured belongings and homeland behind.

Her American assimilation, while difficult, ultimately took place through literature. She considered New York's Forty-Second Street Public Library a "cathedral for books," and all the more unbelievable because she would be trusted to take home anything she wanted.

"I fell in love with books . . . which I didn't have at all growing up," she once noted. "In the Dominican Republic, I was a nonreader and hated books."

It was less that the self-described tomboy "preferred physical activity to reading" and more that owning books was dangerous during Trujillo's brutal regime. People who read to enhance their intelligence were identified as troublemakers and threats to the government.

Moving to America opened up new opportunities for the relocated ten-year-old.

"Not understanding the [English] language, I had to pay close attention to each word—great training to a writer," said Alvarez, who grew up with her island's strong oral tradition. "My family was full of great storytellers. My father was always telling stories when I was growing up. It was how we all learned about the past and how we planned for the future."

Unfortunately for Alvarez, it wasn't long before the young woman who loved storytelling was facing discrimination and racial indignities from her new Catholic school classmates. This immigrant experience and youthful alienation drove her deeper into literature, creating a "portable homeland" shaping the many writing forms she would explore for years to come.

Since then, Alvarez has utilized her various personal experiences to create novels, children's books, poetry collections, essays, and even young adult novels like *Before We Were Free*. Works such as *How the Garcia Girls Lost Their Accents* in 1991 (her first novel and one that was published at age forty-one) or 1994's *In the Time of the Butterflies* cogently describe the development of a young girl's identity while facing governmental oppression. They also cemented her position as one of the most influential Latina writers. As she explained in a 2015 interview:

> I feel like more accurately I'm an all-American author, with all the Americas (North and South) inside me, sort of speaking my Spanish and my English. The rhythms, the syntax, word choices are affected by the fact my first language was Spanish. These phrases that we use to identify where you came from and what you're bringing to the circle, they're fine. They're part of tracing a root system. But if you stop at that and get into a racial bunker and it's us against them, then it really doesn't work for me.
>
> If there's one thing literature teaches us, it's that this is a table set for all. To write a book, anybody can read it and become the characters in that book. It could be written by a woman. By someone from the upper class. It could be written by a kid that

started out as a street kid. That's what I love about stories. It's a huge democracy. It's the grand democracy.

Alvarez, who has long lived in Vermont while teaching at Middlebury College, attended Syracuse University for two years beginning in 1973 (while living in a tiny attic apartment on Comstock Avenue) before graduating with a master's degree in creative writing. During her time on campus, she won the Academy of American Poetry Prize in 1974. After departing Syracuse, she would live in fifteen different settings, continuing her comfort with those who are displaced or whose voices often remain unheard.

"I felt like the [Walt] Whitman poem where he travels throughout the country and now will do nothing but listen," she told *Publishers Weekly*. "I was listening. I was seeing the inside of so many places and so many people, from the Mennonites of Southern Kentucky to the people of Appalachia. I was a migrant poet."

Joe Biden

US Senator and Vice President

This love affair between Syracuse and the man who would become the forty-seventh vice president of the United States can be traced to a spring break trip Joe Biden and some of his University of Delaware classmates took to the Bahamas in 1964. Biden arrived in the Caribbean thinking tan, not Orange, but those thoughts changed the instant he laid eyes on a former Syracuse University homecoming queen named Neilia Hunter in a hotel lobby.

"She was stunningly beautiful, inside and out," he said. "And I fell head over heels in love."

She was smitten, too, and Biden soon began making weekend trips from Delaware to Syracuse, where Neilia was teaching at a city elementary school. Biden intended to attend Cornell Law School, but during one of his Syracuse visits Neilia suggested he tour the SU campus and law school. He did, liked what he saw, applied, and was accepted.

Biden described those three years in Syracuse as "magical." He and Neilia got married in 1966 and immersed themselves in their city neighborhood. When not in class or the law library, Biden could be found playing touch football with the neighborhood kids, or walking the couple's German shepherd—prophetically named Senator—at a nearby reservoir. Biden wound up graduating from SU's College of Law with much more than a degree. The friendships he formed and the resilience he learned in Syracuse would serve him well through the times of triumph and tragedy that followed.

The Bidens left Syracuse in 1968 and returned to Joe's home in Delaware, where he began practicing law. Intrigued with public service ever since hearing John F. Kennedy's inspiring "what you can do for your country" inauguration speech in 1961, Biden ran for

Joe Biden. © Syracuse University. Photo by Stephen Sartori.

office as a city councilman in 1970 and won. Then, two years later, he pulled off a major election upset, beating a Republican incumbent to become the fifth youngest US senator in history. But two weeks before Biden took office, Neilia and the couple's eighteen-month-old daughter were killed in an automobile accident while returning home with the family Christmas tree. Sons Beau and Hunter also were critically injured in the crash but survived.

A devastated Biden arranged to take his Senate oath at the hospital where his sons were still convalescing. Grief overwhelmed him as he adjusted to life as a single dad and senator. Years later, he wrote about how he briefly contemplated ending it all. "I began to understand how despair led people to just cash in; how suicide wasn't just an option, but a rational option," he said. "I felt God had played a horrible trick on me, and I was angry."

Somehow he mustered the strength to carry on. To keep his young sons' lives as normal as possible, he continued to live in Wilmington, Delaware, commuting daily to and from Washington, DC—a practice he continued throughout his six terms as senator.

Biden recalls how people from his Syracuse days, particularly law school professors and classmates, were there for him during the painful weeks and months following his wife's death.

And they would be there for him during a political crisis in 1987, when his first presidential campaign was short-circuited by allegations that he had stolen passages for some of his speeches. His problems were compounded when someone leaked an old school paper from SU in which Biden had failed to footnote excerpts from an article. Amid the controversy, which made Biden the butt of late night talk show jokes, SU invited him back to campus to speak. Many of his old professors and classmates showed up to shake his hand. Biden never forgot that show of loyalty and support.

His SU friends—and his second wife, Jill, whom he married in 1977—would be there for him again a year later, when Biden began experiencing memory loss and headaches and was diagnosed with two life-threatening brain aneurysms that required surgery and seven months of recuperation.

The self-described "scrappy kid from hardscrabble Scranton, Pennsylvania" is nothing if not resilient. He credits his father, who repaired furnaces and sold cars, and his mom for instilling toughness and perseverance. Through the years, Biden has repeatedly told people how his father loved to tell him: "Champ, the measure of a man is not how often he is knocked down, but how quickly he gets up."

Biden would become known on the Senate floor and as vice president as someone not afraid to speak his mind. That was in stark contrast to his shyness as a youth. Plagued by a speech impediment, he often was ridiculed and bullied by neighborhood kids, who referred to him as Joe Impedimenta. Biden's feisty mother encouraged him not to take any guff. "Bloody their nose so you can walk down the street the next day!" she implored. He overcame his stuttering problem by memorizing poetry and reciting it out loud in front of a mirror.

Years later, while living in Syracuse, Biden castigated several neighborhood kids for bullying a young boy who stuttered. The boy went on to become a successful businessman and never forgot how Biden had changed his life by speaking up for him.

During his career as a senator, Biden continued sticking up for people while becoming a leading voice on foreign policy, civil liberties, and crime prevention. As chair of the Judiciary Committee he spearheaded passage of landmark domestic violence legislation, and as chair of the Committee on Foreign Relations he advocated strategic arms limitations with the Soviet Union and expanded NATO to include former Soviet bloc nations.

Biden made another presidential run in 2008 but dropped out early in the campaign. After Barack Obama secured the Democratic nomination, he asked Biden to be his vice presidential candidate, and the man with the working-class roots helped the campaign communicate its message of economic recovery to blue-collar voters in crucial swing states like Ohio and Pennsylvania. A strong advocate of civil rights throughout his legislative career, Biden was ecstatic to play a role in the election of the first African American president. "This is a historic moment," he said after Obama's victory. "It's a new America. It's the reflection of a new America, and I couldn't be more excited."

Biden became a trusted confidant and advisor during the eight years he served the president. Before leaving office, Obama surprised his vice president by awarding him the Presidential Medal of Freedom with Distinction, the nation's highest civilian honor. He called Biden "the best vice president America's ever had" and "a lion of American history."

Biden announced on April 25, 2019, that he was running for president a third time. Many wished he had run three years earlier, but he opted not to because he was still grieving over the death of his son Beau from brain cancer in 2015. The tie between father and son had been strong, and it included a powerful Orange thread. Beau graduated from SU's College of Law in 1994—an event all the more special because his dad delivered the commencement speech that day. A recipient of a Bronze Star for his National Guard service in Iraq, the younger Biden pursued a political career, rising to the position of state attorney general in Delaware.

In 2011, Beau followed in his father's footsteps again, returning to his alma mater to deliver a commencement address to the law school's graduates. Afterward, he spoke lovingly about his dad and Syracuse. "Families can get torn apart and never recover or they grow even closer," he told the *Syracuse Post-Standard*. "My dad set about rebuilding his family."

It was all part of a remarkable and circuitous journey that included an unexpected detour to a place that will be forever special to Joe Biden.

Dave Bing

Basketball Player, Entrepreneur, Politician

When Dave Bing began classes at Syracuse in the summer of 1962, football was king of the Hill. The Orangemen were still basking in the glow of winning the national championship three years earlier and were just a year removed from Ernie Davis becoming the first African American to win the Heisman Trophy. Football was a source of pride on campus. Basketball, meanwhile, was a source of ridicule—something students and the local populace followed with lukewarm interest, if at all.

"We didn't get any respect," recalled Jim Boeheim, Bing's teammate and roommate. "They had just built Manley Field House so the football team would have a place to prepare for bowl games. We were merely an afterthought. They had a dirt floor in Manley, and they placed the basketball court off to the side so we wouldn't

Dave Bing. © Syracuse University. Photo by Stephen Sartori.

get in the way of the football team. They would come in while we were practicing in December, and kick up all this dust. We'd have to stop our practice several times and get dust mops to clean the court off."

While the football team was making annual bowl appearances, the basketball team was getting bowled over. Two years before Bing joined the varsity, Syracuse lost twenty-seven consecutive games—at the time the longest losing streak in major college basketball.

But that would change dramatically, thanks to Bing. He would do for Syracuse hoops what Arnold Palmer had done for golf. The hotshot recruit from Washington, DC, would popularize basketball on campus and help the sport gain equal status with football. "The success we continue to enjoy more than a half century later can be traced directly back to Dave Bing," said Boeheim, the Orange head coach since 1976. "He's the guy who turned things around here. He raised this program from the ashes."

And the dirt and dust from that raised wooden court at Manley.

How's this for a hoops resurrection? After joining the varsity for the 1963-64 season, Bing led a team that had lost forty-one of forty-seven games prior to his arrival to a 52-24 record and two postseason tournaments in three varsity seasons. (Freshmen weren't eligible to play varsity sports back then.) Along the way, he established school scoring records that still stand. Bing saved his best for last, averaging 28.4 points and 10.8 rebounds per game his senior season, becoming Syracuse's first consensus basketball All-American since Vic Hanson in 1927. That 1965-66 Orange squad averaged a nation-leading 99 points per game, posted a 22-6 record, and reached the finals of NCAA East Regional, where they lost to Duke in the Elite Eight.

The opportunity to be the guy who elevated a team that had fallen on hard times appealed to Bing, who spurned scholarship offers from two hundred other schools, including the UCLA powerhouse coached by John Wooden. "Syracuse Coach Fred Lewis convinced me that the program had bottomed out and that I could be the catalyst in turning things around," he said. "I welcomed that challenge."

Lewis shrewdly scheduled Bing's recruiting visit during May rather than the heart of winter. "I had no idea about the way it snows and snows and snows in Syracuse," Bing joked. "I'm up there on a sunny, spring day and the students are all over the place, wearing shorts and having a good, old time, and I'm thinking to myself, 'Wow, it must be like this year-round.' Nobody told me how bad the winters were."

But the thing that may have sealed the deal was Davis, who served as Bing's chaperone during his campus visit.

> I was clearly awestruck being in Ernie's presence. I had a chance to speak to him at length. . . . He was honest and frank. He told me about the good experiences and the bad experiences he had at SU. I walked away thinking, "What an impressive human being." And I thought that if SU could help develop a human being like Ernie Davis, then I wanted to go there and try to follow in his footsteps. The way he handled himself on and off the field with such dignity, set a standard, I believe, for everyone at Syracuse to follow. I remember when I was getting ready to leave campus that weekend he told me I had an opportunity to be the "Ernie Davis of basketball." That was the clincher for me.

Bing lived up to those lofty standards—on and off the court. Following his SU career, he was drafted second overall by the Detroit Pistons and played twelve years in the National Basketball Association, earning all-star honors seven times and being named one of the fifty greatest players in professional basketball history.

His post-playing achievements were equally impressive. After his playing career, he founded Bing Steel, a processing company that was so successful Bing received the National Minority Small Business Person of the Year Award in 1984 from President Ronald Reagan. Thanks to Bing's acumen, the business soon grew into a multimillion-dollar Detroit-based conglomerate—the Bing Group—which became one of Michigan's largest steel companies.

Detroit had fallen on hard economic times by the late 1990s and early 2000s, and although he was comfortably retired, the philanthropic Bing felt compelled to help the Motor City. He was elected mayor of Detroit and spent parts of two terms trying to revive a city that had been decimated by the collapse of the auto industry there.

Bing has returned to his alma mater numerous times through the years. During a December 19, 1981, ceremony in the Dome, his Number 22 was retired along with Hanson's Number 8, making them the first athletes in school history to have their jersey numbers taken out of circulation. Nine years later, Bing received another prestigious honor when he was inducted into the Naismith Memorial Basketball Hall of Fame in Springfield, Massachusetts.

Jim Boeheim

Basketball Coach

In the spring of 1962, toward the end of Jim Boeheim's senior year of high school, he climbed into the family's black Ford station wagon—the same one he used to pick up flowers for the family-owned funeral home—and made the forty-five-minute drive from Lyons, New York, to the Syracuse University campus. The teenager from the little town wound up getting lost in the "big" city, but after asking several people for directions, he finally made his way to South Campus, where he toured the recently constructed Manley Field House.

Although it was still just a shell with a dirt floor, it might as well have been Madison Square Garden as far as Boeheim was concerned. The arena was cavernous enough to house several high school gymnasiums.

The awestruck teenager then met with Orange basketball coach Fred Lewis and was immediately captivated. "There was just something about Fred's enthusiasm that appealed to me right away," Boeheim recalled. "He said he wanted to build a national program from the ashes and I believed he could do it. He's the best recruiter I've ever known."

Lewis told Boeheim he didn't have any more scholarships to offer but said Boeheim could try out for the team as a walk-on, and if he produced he would earn free tuition and room and board by his sophomore year. That deal was fine with Jim but not so fine with his father, who believed his son was taking a huge gamble and that Colgate and Cornell offered better opportunities to play. Jim's high school coach, Dick Blackwell, agreed with the elder Boeheim but kept his mouth shut when the teenager told him of his plans. "I was leery, too, about him going to Syracuse because I didn't know if he could play at that level," Blackwell said in a 1996 interview. "But I never told him that because I didn't want to discourage him."

Boeheim's father had already mailed a nonrefundable one hundred dollar deposit check to Colgate. But he might as well have taken a match to the money because the younger Boeheim, over his dad's vehement objections, had made his mind up to attend Syracuse. And when his mind was made up, you could forget about it, because he could be as stubborn as the mule that tugged that Erie Canal boat that brought his German-born ancestors to upstate New York in 1853.

Like one of his early sports idols, Jim Brown, Boeheim was dead set on becoming an Orange man. So he showed up on the SU campus that September, and more than a half century later he's still there. With more than 1,500 victories under his belt as a player, assistant, and head coach, he's still stubbornly churning out twenty-win seasons and NCAA tournament appearances. "When I think of Syracuse basketball, two words come immediately to mind: Jimmy Boeheim," said longtime ESPN college basketball analyst Dick Vitale. "The 'Cuse and Boeheim are inseparable. They go together perfectly, like spaghetti and meatballs."

(Above) Jim Boeheim. Athletics Department, Syracuse University, used by permission.

(Below) A magnet was handed out to fans when Syracuse named its basketball floor Jim Boeheim Court. Athletics Department, Syracuse University, used by permission.

Through the years, Ohio State and a few NBA teams courted him with financial offers that dwarfed what he was making at Syracuse. Though flattered, he never seriously considered leaving. By staying put—by deciding, in the words of one of his former assistants "to be become a nester rather than a nomad"—Boeheim was able to build a hoops juggernaut in his own backyard.

Along the way, he has racked up the second most wins in men's college basketball history and has become to Syracuse what Nick Saban is to Alabama, John Wooden was to UCLA, and Mike Krzyzewski is to Duke—a legend in his adopted hometown, the face of not only a program but a university. And it could be argued quite cogently that Boeheim's ties to his school run even deeper than those other iconic coaches because he played at SU, too. Which means that through the 2018-19 season, he had been around for 57 of the 120 years they've been dribbling, passing, and shooting basketballs on Piety Hill.

"I guess I've always viewed things a little differently from most people," Boeheim said, when asked about his longevity at his school. "Most people believe the grass is greener on the other side. But I guess I was fortunate enough early on to appreciate the greenness of grass on my side of the fence."

The funny thing is that few expected Boeheim to last a semester, let alone six decades. Lewis had his doubts about the scrawny, bespectacled, physically underwhelming kid, which is why Boeheim arrived on campus sans scholarship. He eventually won over Lewis and his teammates with his toughness, smarts, and scoring ability. Not only would he receive his scholarship, he would receive Lewis's undying appreciation for teaming with All-American Dave Bing to help revive a moribund program.

"If you play the game, you know sometimes you go against somebody who doesn't look like they can do it," Lewis said of Boeheim, who converted 57 percent of his shots and averaged 14.6 points per game his senior year. "You think, 'This will be an easy game. I'll kill this guy.' And by the end of the game, he's beaten your brains in. That was Jim. He had a tremendous advantage. People looked at him and thought every step would be his last, but that last step never came."

Boeheim tried out for the NBA, but after being one of the final players cut by the Chicago Bulls at their training camp in 1966, he returned to Syracuse to work on his master's degree, which he earned in 1967. Though he continued playing professionally on weekends for Scranton in the old Eastern League, he began his coaching career at his alma mater, first as a graduate assistant and then as a full-time assistant. Under head coach Roy Danforth, Boeheim helped the 1974-75 Orangemen make the school's first trip to the Final Four.

When Danforth left after the following season, Boeheim applied for the head coaching vacancy. He had been true to his school as both a player and assistant coach, so he figured it was a slam dunk he would be promoted. But when Syracuse athletics director Les Dye announced he would conduct a national coaching search, Boeheim became livid. He decided to interview for a similar position at the University of Rochester and was offered the job. On his drive back from Rochester, he intended to force the issue with the Syracuse search committee. "Give me the job now, or I'm moving to Rochester," would be his ultimatum. Committee members already had consulted several Syracuse players and liked what they heard about Boeheim, so they called off the search and offered him the job. They would not regret their decision.

Thanks to the recruitment of center Roosevelt Bouie and forward Louis Orr, the Orangemen got off to a fast start, going 26-4 in Boeheim's first season. The "Louie and Bouie Show" went 100-16 with four consecutive NCAA tournament appearances. "Those two launched the ship," Boeheim said. "They laid the foundation for all the success we've enjoyed since."

The excellence of the program over such a long stretch may be unparalleled in college basketball. Boeheim has never experienced a losing season, and only three times have the Orangemen failed to win at least twenty games. During this era, they've made thirty-three NCAA tournament appearances and have reached the Final Four five times, including 2003, when they won it all.

Boeheim's reputation also has been burnished by his work in the Olympics, where, as an assistant, he helped the United States win gold medals at the Summer Games in 2008, 2012, and 2016. The only blemishes on his resume have been NCAA violations on two different occasions, one which resulted in the vacation of 101 wins.

Boeheim's philanthropy has been as impressive as his coaching achievements. Through the Jim and Juli Boeheim Foundation, which he established with his wife, he has raised millions of dollars to aid charitable causes throughout Syracuse and Central New York.

In 2018, the Boeheim connection to SU extended to the next generation when Jim's son Buddy joined the Orange hoops team. Buddy asked to wear Number 35, the same number his father wore at SU.

On September 9, 2005, Boeheim was inducted into the Naismith Memorial Basketball Hall of Fame in Springfield, Massachusetts. His presenter at the ceremony was Bing, who had been inducted fifteen years earlier.

"He's created a program that year-in, year-out demands excellence, and that's not easy to sustain in the dog-eat-dog world of college basketball," said former Georgetown University coach John Thompson of his longtime nemesis and friend. "Most programs hit a rut at some point, and it's tough for them to get out of it. Jim's program has never been in a rut for any prolonged period of time, and that's a tribute to him."

Jim Brown

Football Player, Actor, Social Activist

Jim Brown forged his legacy as a football player, actor, entrepreneur, and social activist by refusing to back down. Didn't matter if the opponent was a football team stacking eleven players against him at the line of scrimmage or a Hollywood filmmaker who didn't believe Brown worthy of a leading role because he was African American. Somehow, some way, the man who would become known as "the black John Wayne" always sought a way to run past, through, or over obstacles.

But there was a time during his sophomore year at Syracuse University when he suffered a crisis of confidence that threatened to stop him well short of the goal line. In Brown's estimation, head football coach Ben Schwartzwalder was keeping him buried down the depth chart for no good reason.

"The first thing my football coach attacked was my talent," Brown recalled in a 1996 *Syracuse University Magazine* interview. "He said I couldn't run the ball and that I wasn't any good. I would fight it every day, but finally I thought, 'Maybe he's right; maybe I can't run.'"

The indestructible running back decided to quit.

When word got back to Brown's Long Island hometown of Manhasset, judge Kenneth Malloy—an SU alumnus who helped pay

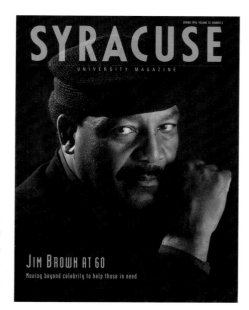

Jim Brown. *Syracuse University Magazine.* Syracuse University News and Public Affairs Reference Collection, University Archives.

On June 4, 1967, Jim Brown convened a meeting of top African American athletes at the Cleveland offices of his Negro and Economic Union to show support for boxer Muhammad Ali, who had refused to fight in the Vietnam War. *Front row, left to right:* Bill Russell, Ali, Brown, and Lew Alcindor (Kareem Abdul-Jabbar). *Back row:* attorney Carl Stokes, Walter Beach, Bobby Mitchell, Sid Williams, Curtis McClinton, Willie Davis, Jim Shorter, and John Wooten. Two weeks later, Ali was found guilty of draft evasion. Robert Abbott Sengstacke / Getty Images.

Jim's tuition his freshman year—contacted Raymond Collins, the superintendent of schools in Manhasset, who immediately drove up to Syracuse. After a long heart-to-heart with Collins, Brown had a change of heart. His decision to stay would be life altering.

"Because of the love of this man, because of the wisdom of this man, he convinced me not to walk away from Syracuse University," Brown said of Collins while accepting a George Arents Award from his college alma mater in 2016. "It was the greatest thing that ever happened to me. One moment, I was going to give it up. The next moment, with his esprit de corps, I was ready to accept the challenges."

The two running backs ahead of Brown wound up suffering injuries, and the sophomore was inserted into the lineup. He seized the opportunity. By his senior year, there was no stopping him. In a game at Archbold Stadium on November 17, 1956, Brown scored a college football record 43 points in a 61-7 rout of Colgate. As good as that performance was, his effort against Texas Christian University in the Cotton Bowl six weeks later may have been even more impressive. Though the Horned Frogs won, 28-27, Brown rushed for 132 yards and scored 21 points. "The headlines should have read, 'TCU 28, Jim Brown U. 27,'" said Ron Luciano, a former All-American offensive lineman at SU, who went on to become one of the most famous umpires in baseball history. "Jim was a one-man wrecking crew that day. The rest of us were just along for the ride."

A chiseled six-foot-two, 212-pound Adonis with sprinter's speed, Brown went on to become arguably the greatest running back—and football player—of all time, earning three National Football League Most Valuable Player awards, while leading the league in rushing a record eight times in nine seasons. At Syracuse, he would start the legend of 44, not only by wearing that number with distinction, but also by convincing future Orange 44s—Ernie Davis and Floyd Little—to follow in his footsteps.

As great as he was in football, Brown might have been even better in lacrosse, where he earned All-American honors his senior year after scoring forty-three goals for the 10-0 Orangemen. Brown also was superb in basketball, lettering twice and averaging 11.3 points per game his junior year. Some have surmised that if Brown had played hoops his senior year, SU might have upset North Carolina and faced Kansas and its seven-foot-one superstar center, Wilt Chamberlain, in the national championship game.

Brown also lettered in track and field, placing fifth in the college decathlon championships. He once competed in two varsity sports in the same day at Archbold. He finished first in the high jump and discus and second in the javelin to account for 13 points in a track-and-field victory against Colgate in the morning. Then he put on his lacrosse gear and scored the winning goals against Army. "That was just Jim," said Roy Simmons Jr., a teammate of Brown's who went on to coach SU to six national lacrosse championships. "He was just a natural at anything he did."

Brown also excelled in the classroom. A B+ student, he routinely made the dean's list, was named a class marshal, and rose to the rank of second lieutenant in the US Army ROTC.

"I'm very happy that I went to Syracuse, and I'm very grateful I've been able to contribute something to Syracuse because Syracuse has contributed a lot to me," he said during his Arents acceptance speech. "So, it's a real story. It wasn't always the greatest relationship, but it turned out to be a great relationship."

The only person who wound up stopping Brown in the NFL was Brown himself. While still in the prime of his career, he announced his retirement from professional football at age thirty so he could concentrate on acting full time. "I probably had a good five to six seasons left in me, but I had accomplished everything I set out to and had so many other things I wanted to accomplish," he said.

He enjoyed a successful movie career, acting in more than forty films and numerous television dramas while establishing himself as Hollywood's first black action hero. "Even if he had never put on a pair of athletic shoes, he would have made his mark as an actor," said SU professor Robert Thompson, one of the nation's foremost experts on pop culture. "He was in a number of really good movies, and he has a serious body of work. But beyond that, he opened doors for many African American actors who followed."

His lifelong role as social activist would be his most significant. During the civil rights movement, Brown joined the fight to uplift the black community, befriending activists like Malcolm X at a time when such associations were unpopular with much of white America. "My fight was and is to get racism and inequality off the backs of others," he said. "If you are a healthy country you can't accept racism, lack of opportunity, and the status quo. You have to speak out and fight against it in every way you can."

Brown stressed education and economic empowerment. In 1966, he helped establish the Black Economic Union. Bolstered by a $1 million grant from the Ford Foundation, the organization used the moral and financial support of professional athletes like Muhammad Ali and Kareem Abdul-Jabbar as well as young African American MBAs to assist more than four hundred minority-run companies. Two decades later, he founded Amer-I-Can, a nationally recognized organization that addresses the problems of troubled youth. The program seeks to develop personal skills and is geared to helping former gang members, ex-convicts, inmates, and recovering drug addicts, while working with law enforcement agencies. "Amer-I-Can deals with human beings," he said. "No one is perfect, but everyone can achieve success."

Brown's complex life has not been without controversy. He has been accused several times of domestic violence and has denied all the allegations. In 1999, he was charged with a misdemeanor for vandalizing his wife's car, and he served several weeks in jail after refusing to participate in domestic violence counseling, community service, and probation programs. In 2018, two SU alumnae called for Brown's statue near Manley Field House to be removed and for his Arents Award to be rescinded.

"I think Big Jim is a complicated individual, as we all are, with some good and some bad," said the late Roy Simmons Sr., one of Brown's SU coaches and mentors. "He's a fiercely proud individual with strong beliefs. He isn't going to back down. That's part of what made him a great athlete. He ran the football with conviction. He shot the lacrosse ball with conviction. I always got along with the guy. I think he respected the fact that I tried to understand what he was going through [as a black man and as someone raised without a father]. I think he's done much more good than bad in his life."

Dick Clark

Cultural Icon

During his senior year at A. B. Davis High School in Mount Vernon, New York, Dick Clark was elected class president and "the person most likely to sell the Brooklyn Bridge."

To the best of anyone's knowledge, Clark never sold any bridges, but as the host and brains behind the iconic television song-and-dance fest known as *American Bandstand*, he sold a lot of records and did as much as anyone to advance the influence of teenagers and rock and roll on American culture.

As 1950s and 1960s recording artist Paul Anka said: "At a time when there was no youth culture, he created it."

The perpetually youthful-looking Clark would become known as "the world's oldest teenager" and would help launch or boost the careers of scores of recording artists during the show's incredible run from 1957 through 1989. He'd also play an important role in bridging racial divides.

"The list of well-known performers who were seen on [*Bandstand*], many of them lip-synching their recently recorded hits, spanned generations," wrote the *New York Times* at the time of Clark's death at age eighty-two in 2012. "From Ritchie Valens to Luther Vandross; from the Monkees to Madonna; from Little Anthony and the Imperials to Los Lobos; from Dusty Springfield to Buffalo Springfield, Mr. Clark was around for it all."

Legitimizing rock and roll at a time when many American adults regarded it as the work of the devil.

"With the exception of Elvis Presley, Clark was considered to be the person most responsible for the bonfire spread of rock 'n' roll across the country in the late 1950s," wrote a music critic for the *Los Angeles Times*. "It made him a household name." As well known

Dick Clark on the set of the popular weekly television show *American Bandstand*. ABC Photo Archives / © ABC / Getty Images.

Ryan Seacrest and Dick Clark during a *Rockin' New Year's Eve* telecast. Theo Wargo / DCNYRE2010 / Getty Images.

as President Dwight D. Eisenhower, and perhaps even more popular at the time.

If Clark had done nothing more than *Bandstand*, he would have left an indelible mark. But that famous show was merely one facet of a multifaceted career that saw the 1951 Syracuse University graduate earn induction into the television, radio, and rock and roll halls of fame, as well as a place on *Forbes* magazine's list of wealthiest people on the planet. Clark would not only introduce Americans to new recording artists and a wide array of music genres, but he'd also help them ring in the New Year, laugh at TV bloopers, and play along while watching game shows.

"With the boyish good looks of a bound-for-success junior executive and a ubiquitous on-camera presence, Mr. Clark was among the most recognizable faces in the world, even if what he was most famous for—spinning records and jabbering with teenagers—was on the insubstantial side," the *Times* continued in its obituary. "In addition to *American Bandstand* and *New Year's Rockin' Eve*, he hosted innumerable awards shows, comedy specials, series based on TV outtakes and the game show *$10,000 Pyramid* (which lasted long enough to see the stakes ratcheted up to $100,000)."

That he became a legendary showman and entrepreneur didn't surprise those who remember his early years. At age five, Clark began publishing a neighborhood gossip tip sheet, selling it for two cents a copy. A year later, he opened a sidewalk restaurant featuring peanut butter sandwiches and staged a backyard carnival where he hawked gum and old *Life* magazines.

His father, Richard Augustus Clark—also an SU alumnus (class of 1918)—was a salesman at a cosmetics company before becoming the manager of a radio station. The younger Clark often would accompany him to the station and do gofer duties. The boy loved everything about the environment, particularly the access to popular music.

When he was thirteen, Clark viewed his first live radio broadcast—the old *Jimmy Durante Show* with Garry Moore. "I looked at the stars and the actors around them and thought, 'Wouldn't this be a great way to make a living!'" Clark said in a 1989 *Syracuse University Magazine* interview.

Clark began taking speech classes and acted in high school dramas. Shortly before graduating, he worked a weekend on-air job at his father's new radio station, WRUN in Utica, New York. That fall, he enrolled at SU and majored in advertising, with hopes of running a radio station someday. He approached officials at SU student station WAER-FM about management positions, but there weren't any openings, so Clark tried his hand at announcing, serving as a newscaster, actor, and pop and country disc jockey. He also lined up work at Syracuse commercial station WOLF-AM, making one dollar an hour hosting shows like the "Polka Parade."

Syracuse classmates recalled Clark's legendary work ethic but also remembered fun times downing five-cent beers at Nickel Charlies, a popular, off-campus student watering hole. In addition to classes and his radio duties, Clark augmented his income by making beds and scrubbing pots and pans in a frat house, selling brushes door-to-door, and building chicken crates for 52 cents an hour. "I remember the winters," Clark later recalled with a chuckle. "No, my recollections of Syracuse are all very positive." So positive that eighteen members of his family wound up attending SU, including his daughter, Cindy, who graduated in 1986. And so positive that he hosted scores of students at his Los Angeles headquarters and became a major benefactor, donating millions to the university, including a posthumous gift that resulted in the building of the Dick Clark Studios in Newhouse II in 2013.

After graduating, Clark did a short stint as news anchor for WKTV in Utica. In 1952, he joined Philadelphia TV and radio station WFIL, and four years later he became the full-time director of *Bandstand*. Under his leadership, the television dance show took off and in 1957 began airing nationally on ABC, where it would remain a programming staple for parts of four decades. *Bandstand* was the first television show to cash in on the youth market and made Clark one of the most powerful DJs in America. His approval of a record—"It's got a good beat and you can dance to it"—meant almost certain sales success.

Clark was pleased that *Bandstand* was a ratings and advertising bonanza, but the thing that made him most proud was how the show shattered racial barriers. Not only did Clark feature black artists such as Chubby Checker, Sam Cooke, James Brown, Jackie Wilson, Chuck Berry, and the Supremes early in their careers, but he also made sure the dance floor was integrated. "The first time that black and white kids got on the dance floor together on social occasions was on that show," Clark said in an interview with the *Christian Science Monitor*. "It was a very segregated society that we lived in, yet this step was an inevitability. It wasn't anything terribly startling. It had to be done."

Another courageous moment would occur after Clark suffered a stroke in 2004. He returned to host *New Year's Rockin' Eve* the following year, and although his speech at times was difficult to understand, many, including other stroke victims, praised his bravery.

Clark always boasted a keen ear for music that appealed to teenagers. But there was one time his instincts failed him. In the early 1960s, a friend returned from England with a recording he urged Clark to play on *Bandstand*'s "Rate-A-Record" segment. "I listened to it and he showed me a picture of these guys and I said, 'Oh, come on, you're kidding me,'" Clark recalled in a 1988 *Syracuse Herald-Journal* interview. He grudgingly played the song on the show and the kids gave it a mediocre 73 out of 100 rating. Afterward, Clark told his friend: "I don't know about your group. I don't know whether they're going to make it." The song was "She Loves You." The band was the Beatles.

Clark later tried unsuccessfully to book the group.

"Oh, well," he sighed. "Sometimes you swing and miss."

It was a rare strikeout in a career where the hits just kept on coming.

Eileen Collins

Astronaut

Yes, the astronaut who would go where no woman had gone before watched *Star Trek* as a kid. And while Eileen Collins enjoyed the sci-fi series, she enjoyed the telecasts of real-life NASA launches even more. Who needed Captain James T. Kirk when you had Colonel John H. Glenn? When Mission Control would give the countdown—". . . *three, two, one, liftoff!*"—Collins's heart would race as if she were sitting in the pilot's seat atop that massive missile on the launch pad at Cape Canaveral, Florida.

By the fourth grade, the girl who grew up watching sleek gliders soar overhead from Harris Hill in her hometown of Elmira, New

Eileen Collins (*left*) with student in SU's flight simulator in the L. C. Smith College of Engineering during a campus visit in 2013. © Syracuse University. Photo by Stephen Sartori.

York, knew what she wanted to be when she grew up. Never mind that there weren't any female astronauts at the time.

"I don't remember consciously feeling like I couldn't do it because they were all men and I was a young girl," she once wrote. "I remember thinking, I'll just be a woman astronaut. It wasn't until high school that I realized it would be impossible for me to be an astronaut as a woman. I remember very distinctly that I didn't tell anyone I wanted to be an astronaut because I didn't want anyone to tell me, 'You can't do that.' I didn't want to hear it. So I kept it inside."

Her hidden dream would take flight at Syracuse University, which she attended on a US Air Force ROTC scholarship. Six months before graduating with a degree in mathematics and economics in the spring of 1978, Collins learned that the Air Force was going to start training female pilots.

"*Three, two, one, liftoff!*" There would be no stopping her from that point on.

After receiving her SU diploma, Collins became one of just eight female students in a class of three hundred to participate in the military pilot training program at Vance Air Force Base in Enid, Oklahoma. She earned her wings within a year and was so highly regarded as a leader that the Air Force asked her to become an instructor. Over the next decade, she would log thousands of miles while piloting several different types of aircraft; earn master's degrees from Stanford and Webster Universities, and teach at the Air Force Academy, rising to the rank of colonel.

Upon graduating in 1990 as the Air Force's second female test-pilot, Collins received a life-changing phone call from childhood hero John Young, an astronaut who had walked on the moon and landed the first space shuttle. "He said, 'You're going to be a pilot. You will be the first woman pilot of the space shuttle,'" recalled Collins, who was chosen from a field of 178 candidates. "I hung up the phone. I didn't feel like jumping up and down or partying. I felt a huge sense of relief, a huge sense of calmness."

Although she didn't realize it at the time, she was about to become an aviation pioneer, like the women she had read about through the years. Heroines such as Amelia Earhart, the first female to make a solo flight across the Atlantic Ocean; Valentina Tereshkova, a Soviet cosmonaut who, in 1963, became the first woman in space; and Sally Ride, who two decades later became the first American female space traveler.

Not only would Collins become the first female pilot and commander of a space shuttle, she also would help restore faith in the American space program while leading a courageous mission just two years after the Columbia disaster in 2003, when seven astronauts died when the shuttle disintegrated during reentry into the Earth's atmosphere.

She would wind up being inducted into the astronaut and women's halls of fame, receive an honorary degree and George Arents Award from Syracuse University, have her photograph taken by celebrity photographer Annie Leibovitz, and be named to *Encyclopedia Britannica*'s list of three hundred women who changed the world.

"I didn't set out to become a pioneer," Collins said. "I just wanted the opportunity to fly and explore. We, as human beings, are naturally curious. Most humans don't want to stay in the same place all the time. We want to go out and learn and explore and discover."

Her curiosity about flight began at an early age, her interest piqued by the fact she grew up in a city known as "the soaring capital of America." She fondly recalls traveling to Harris Hill, not far from her home, and watching in wonderment as those gliders drifted overhead, rising or dipping depending on the air currents. And she would dream about being up there in the sky, piloting one of those planes over the trees and rolling hills.

Collins grew up in a family of modest means, and it wasn't until the summer between her junior and senior years of college that she raised enough money (by waitressing at a local pizza shop) to take her first flying lessons. She was a natural from the start.

After receiving her associate's degree from Corning Community College, she earned an ROTC scholarship to SU after scoring one of the highest grades in the history of the qualifying test. Syracuse professors and classmates recall her being a "math whiz" and a "natural-born leader." She had a fun side, too, helping "pilot" a "flying bed" in the 1977 Great Bed Race on campus, which raised money for muscular dystrophy research.

SU had a profound impact on her.

"At Syracuse I learned how to think, how to reason, how to set priorities, and I learned how to learn," she said. "Syracuse really broadened my horizons, helped me become more independent."

In 1995, during her historic first mission, she showed her school pride by displaying a Syracuse University pennant in the cockpit of the Discovery. Two years later, she piloted the Atlantis on a docking mission with Mir, the Russian space station. After she returned from that flight, President Bill Clinton invited her to the White House, where he announced that Collins would become the first female commander of a space shuttle in 1999. "Today, we celebrate the falling away of another barrier in America's quest to conquer the frontiers of space," Clinton said in a Rose Garden ceremony that included Ride and other female aviation pioneers. "Her life is a story of challenges set and challenges met."

That historic mission would test her mettle as two of the main engine computers short-circuited on launch. Backups kicked in, but a second breakdown—a liquid hydrogen leak—threatened to force an emergency landing before the Columbia got into orbit. Collins maintained her cool and was able to guide the shuttle into space. Five days after placing the Chandra X-Ray Observatory into orbit, Collins glided the Columbia to a feather-soft landing at the Kennedy Space Center in Florida. "Eileen rocks," said Jeff Ashby, the pilot on that mission.

Her fourth and final shuttle mission occurred in 2005 and proved to be historic as well. Following the Columbia tragedy two years earlier, the space program had been temporarily grounded, its future in doubt. NASA head and fellow SU grad Sean O'Keefe chose Collins to command the all-important "Return to Flight" mission that July 26. His faith in her was rewarded as Collins conducted a successful repair of the shuttle's exterior in space before leading a smooth landing on August 9.

The following year, Collins retired from NASA to spend more time with her husband, son, and daughter. An engaging speaker, Collins makes numerous appearances around the country, extolling the importance of space exploration and the pursuit of dreams. She believes that one day a human being will set foot on Mars. She wishes she could be part of that trip, but she takes pride in the trips she took.

"My daughter just thinks that all moms fly the space shuttle," she said while preparing for her third mission in 1999. "That's a true sign of progress."

Progress made possible by a woman who refused to subject herself to the phrase: "You can't do that."

Ruth Colvin

Literacy Advocate

Ruth Colvin was sitting at the kitchen table of her Syracuse home in the spring of 1961, sipping coffee and leisurely reading the newspaper when she stumbled upon something that disturbed her deeply. In a story about the latest US census figures, the forty-five-year-old mother of two discovered that eleven thousand people in her hometown were functionally illiterate.

"In my city, an educational city," Colvin recalled incredulously in a December 2016 *Syracuse Post-Standard* interview.

Ruth Colvin (center) giving literacy instructions. Syracuse University Photograph Collection, University Archives.

The Syracuse University graduate had been a voracious reader all her life, devouring everything in sight, including most of the literary classics. But nothing she read had ever impacted her the way that newspaper story did. Never mind not being able to enjoy the words of Shakespeare, Dickens, and Austen. She couldn't fathom what it was like not being able to read road signs or menus or Dr. Seuss books to your children. Colvin was shocked by this tale of two cities. She had to do something about it.

She met a person from Church Women United, and before they knew it they were setting up an office in the basement of Colvin's home and recruiting and training volunteers from churches and schools throughout Syracuse. Initially, they didn't have shelves in the makeshift office, so they ingeniously stacked their books and materials in an old, disconnected refrigerator. With the assistance and counsel of some of her reading professors at her alma mater, Colvin wrote the teaching materials used by the volunteers.

A year later, she founded Literacy Volunteers of America, which in 2002 merged with Laubach Literacy to become ProLiteracy, a worldwide organization still based in Syracuse.

In the half century since discovering her calling, Colvin's organization helped teach hundreds of thousands throughout the United States and the world how to read. She personally taught hundreds of people herself and wrote nine instructional books and programs, including *Tutor* and *I Speak English*, which have become the authoritative sources for literacy volunteers.

Colvin's extraordinary and far-reaching work did not go unnoticed. In 1983, Syracuse University awarded her an honorary degree. Four years later, Ronald Reagan presented her with the President's Volunteer Action Award. And she was invited back to the White House in 2006 by George W. Bush to receive the Presidential Medal of Freedom, the highest civilian award in the land.

"It's been incredibly rewarding and gratifying seeing the ripple effect of that pebble we threw in the water so long ago," she said.

Growing up in Chicago during the 1920s, Ruth dreamed of becoming an artist. But those plans changed after her father, Harry Johnson, died when she was twelve. Her uncle took over control of family decisions and the checkbook. Though accepted into the University of Illinois's art program, Ruth was not allowed to attend because her uncle said the college money needed to be saved for the boys of the family.

Ruth was devastated but never blamed her uncle. She was an optimist by nature, and she brushed it off by saying times were different back then. She rationalized that it was the Great Depression and he was just trying to be prudent. She instead wound up studying business at a much more affordable community college in suburban Chicago. While there, she met her future husband, Robert Colvin. They married in 1940, and two years later his work as a salesman for a chemical company brought the couple to Syracuse. Ruth handled his books and raised the couple's two children before completing her studies and earning her bachelor's degree from SU in 1959.

It wasn't until she came across that newspaper story two years after graduation that she discovered her true purpose in life.

Although she literally wrote the book on literacy, her greatest satisfaction was derived from her one-on-one teaching sessions. In the 1970s, she tutored an adult mother who had dropped out of school after tenth grade. Colvin didn't just teach the woman how to read, but also helped her find the resources her children needed whenever they struggled. Each of the woman's four children graduated from high school, and two went onto four-year schools, while another attended community college. There are many other similar stories about kindly "Aunt Ruth" positively changing people's lives by unlocking their abilities to read.

Colvin was still tutoring tutors and students even after turning one hundred on December 16, 2016. Her friends teased that she was a Pollyanna, always looking for silver linings when life took a wrong turn. Neither the nickname nor the perception bothered her because they were spot-on. She was relentlessly positive.

"Out of everything bad, something good comes" were words Colvin always lived by. In 1961, the mother of adult literacy was shocked into action. She began turning something really bad into something really good. By doing so, the woman who loved to read lived a life worth reading about.

Bob Costas

Broadcaster

The most decorated career in the history of sports broadcasting can trace its roots to the dashboard radio of a parked car in a Commack, New York, driveway, just off the Long Island Expressway. It was there, in the family jalopy, that ten-year-old Bob Costas would spend many an evening scanning the dial of America's blowtorch stations in search of scores from games his father had bet on.

"When the rent is riding on whether Whitey Ford can get Al Kaline out, or Wilt Chamberlain can make two free throws—that's a little anxiety provoking," Costas said in a 2016 *Washington Post* interview.

Young Bob would not only report the scores to his gambling-addicted father, but would do so with the flair of a gifted storyteller.

"There was a romance to the airwaves," Costas recalled. "A notion that moving the dial just slightly enabled you to eavesdrop on what people heard in Baltimore—or, a little farther over, Cincinnati, Philadelphia, and on a really clear night, St. Louis."

By listening to all those different calls, Costas would find his calling. A broadcaster would be born. Arguably the most versatile broadcaster of all time.

The Syracuse University alumnus would go on to earn twenty-eight Emmys, be named national sportscaster of the year a record eight times, host twelve Olympics, and earn induction into the broadcasters' wing of the Baseball Hall of Fame in Cooperstown,

Bob Costas during the 2008 Beijing Summer Olympics. Courtesy of Bob Costas and NBC Sports.

New York. Name a major sporting event—the Olympics, World Series, Super Bowl, NBA Finals, US Open, Kentucky Derby—and there's a good chance Costas was the voice of it. And his versatility was not only on display as a studio host or a play-by-play broadcaster or a commentator, but also as an interviewer. In fact, in that genre, he may have no peer.

Although his relationship with his father was often strained, his dad did him a favor by dispatching him to the driveway of their Long Island home. It was there that Costas began his journalism training. His teachers wound up being some of the greatest radio storytellers of all time.

"You pick up a little bit from each and every one [of the broadcasters who influence you]," he said in a 2018 interview after being named the Baseball Hall of Fame's Ford C. Frick winner. "I've always felt you don't copy the people you admire, but you learn from them—whether it's preparation or a turn of a phrase. I don't think I've copied purposely or sound like somebody else, but whatever I am as a broadcaster is a conglomeration of all those influences."

One day, while thumbing through a New York Knicks yearbook, Costas discovered that two of his favorite broadcasters, Marty Glickman and Marv Albert, had attended Syracuse. That's all he needed to know. He would follow in their footsteps, further enhancing SU's reputation as the nation's top producer of sportscasters.

Like many before and since, Costas cut his teeth working for student radio station WAER-FM, but his skills already were so refined by the time he arrived on campus that WSYR, Syracuse's NBC television and radio affiliate, gave him part-time gigs as a weekend sports anchor and as the play-by-play man for the Syracuse Blazers, an Eastern Hockey League team that was one of the inspirations for *Slapshot*, the cult classic comedy film about life in the brawling bush leagues, starring Paul Newman.

Costas has many fond, humorous memories of those days, when the fisticuffs in backwater hockey towns like Johnstown, Pennsylvania, weren't restricted to the players on the ice. There

was one incident—now funny, but then harrowing—in which Costas's career was almost ended by a Blazers bruiser known as Bill "Harpo" Goldthorpe. Costas related the story in a 1992 *Syracuse Post-Standard* interview:

> There were only two things Harpo wanted to do—fight and drink. We're on the bus after a game, and he's upset with a comment I made on a broadcast, and he rips a newspaper out of my hand and tears it in half. I figure I can't back down.
> So, I say, "Don't feel bad, Goldie. I'll teach you how to read." Well, he grabs me and slams me up against the wall of the bus. He reaches up and grabs this hacksaw that players used to shave their sticks. He has this hacksaw up against my neck; he threatens to decapitate me.
> You've got to understand that Goldthorpe—they modeled a *Slapshot* character after Goldie—probably has no intention of using that hacksaw. But buses hit bumps, or swerve. Let us just say that I perceived a level of danger he didn't.

Goldthorpe eventually came to his senses and let Costas go, or else a brilliant broadcasting career might have met a premature ending.

Costas wound up leaving SU in 1974, a few credit hours shy of his degree, to take a job with KMOX, a St. Louis radio station known as a breeding ground for some of the finest sportscasters of all time. In 1980, he began a career with NBC Sports doing NFL and NBA broadcasts. He remained with the peacock network for thirty-eight years.

Of all his assignments, none have garnered bigger audiences or more acclaim than his work as the host of the Olympics. Following in the footsteps of legendary broadcaster Jim McKay, Costas hosted his first Olympic Games in Barcelona in 1992 and his last in Rio de Janeiro in 2016 before handing off the duties to fellow SU alumnus Mike Tirico. His favorite Olympic moment was the 1996 Opening Ceremonies in Atlanta when Muhammad Ali lit the cauldron after receiving the torch from swimmer Janet Evans. No one knew Ali

Bob Costas speaks to a student during a visit to campus in 2017. © Syracuse University. Photo by Stephen Sartori.

would be doing the lighting. "They had staged this in such a way that Ali literally stepped out of the shadows," Costas said. "And when he received that torch from her, even then his arm and body were trembling from Parkinson's. There was a couple of seconds of silence and almost an audible gasp. A sound you almost never heard in a stadium. Until the place erupted in tremendous and sustained applause."

It's no secret that baseball has always been Costas's favorite sport to watch and broadcast. He has long carried a 1958 Mickey Mantle baseball card with him, and in 1995 he delivered a poignant eulogy of the ballplayer who became the favorite of Costas and millions of other baby boomers.

"Because of my love of baseball and because of the other names that [won the Frick Award], this is at the top of my list," he said before receiving his Baseball Hall of Fame honor. "No disrespect to all the other awards, because they all mean a lot to me, but this means the most. In some sense, you're on the same team as Jack Buck, Vin Scully, Ernie Harwell . . . and all the people I worked with and who are my friends, like Tim McCarver and Tony Kubek. There's a sense of belonging to a really exclusive fraternity."

And he was introduced to many members of that fraternity decades ago while scanning the radio dial in the family's jalopy in search of scores for games on which his father had placed bets.

Stephen Crane

Novelist

It would be inaccurate to say that legendary novelist Stephen Crane was a graduate of Syracuse University. He wasn't.

In fact, the New Jersey native attended Syracuse for only one semester in 1891 before dropping out to wholeheartedly pursue a career in journalism and literary fiction. But, oh, what a career he fashioned.

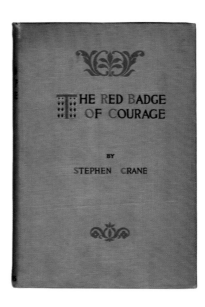

The first edition of Stephen Crane's *Red Badge of Courage*. Special Collections Research Center, Syracuse University Libraries.

By the time he died of tuberculosis at the age of twenty-eight in 1900, Crane had written the definitive American Civil War novel, *The Red Badge of Courage*, and stood squarely alongside Mark Twain, Jack London, Edith Wharton, Joseph Conrad, and H. G. Wells as one of the most influential voices of late-nineteenth and early-twentieth-century literature.

Crane had arrived at SU in January of 1891 intending primarily to play baseball and appease his widowed mother, who had aggressively used her Methodist Church connections to convince Syracuse administrators to admit a young man limping away from an unsuccessful academic stint at Lafayette College in Pennsylvania. But Syracuse gave Crane new life and, arriving in upstate New York, the budding author immediately joined the Delta Upsilon fraternity, enrolled in classes, and signed up for a variety of fraternity activities, including cricket, winter sledding, and eating clubs.

But Crane's first love was baseball, and here he served the Orange as an undersized (five-foot-six, 125-pound) catcher, then the game's most courageous position, before moving to shortstop. He was an average batter (hitting less than .300) but possibly the most competitive member of the young varsity squad. As one teammate noted, Crane played the game "with fiendish glee."

In a November 1895 letter to the editor of *Leslie's Weekly*, Crane wrote, "When I was at school, few of my studies interested me, and as a result I was a bad scholar. They used to say at Syracuse University, where, by the way, I didn't finish the course, that I was cut out to be a professional base-ball player. And the truth of the matter is that I went there more to play base-ball than to study."

A year later, Crane confided to a friend, "I did little work in school but confined my abilities, such as they were, to the diamond. Not that I disliked books, but the cut-and-dried curriculum of the college did not appeal to me. Humanity was a much more interesting study. When I ought to have been at recitations I was studying faces on the streets, and when I ought to have been studying my next day's lessons I was watching the trains roll in and out of the Central Station."

Could SU have shaped the writing of Crane's 1895 masterpiece? Very possibly.

Crane's late-winter view from the top-of-the-hill Delta Upsilon house (at the intersection of what is now Marshall Street and Ostrom Avenue) could have inspired the following passage: "The cold passed reluctantly from the earth, and the retiring fogs revealed an army stretched out on the hills, resting. As the landscape changed from brown to green, the army awakened, and began to tremble with eagerness at the noise of rumors. It cast its eyes upon the roads, which were growing from long troughs of liquid mud to proper thoroughfares."

That imagery is consistent with period photographs of SU and fits the pastoral, albeit muddy, setting of a small but growing Methodist-Episcopalian university sitting on a ridgeline overlooking Onondaga Lake.

A few pages later, in chapter one of *Red Badge*, Crane might have channeled Crouse College's chimes getting rung loudly after Syracuse football games (and at five o'clock each evening) by the Delta Kappa Epsilon brothers: "One night, as he [central character Henry Fleming] lay in bed, the winds had carried to him the clangoring of the church bell as some enthusiast jerked the rope frantically to tell the twisted news of a great battle."

As Fleming prepares to leave his hometown to join the Union forces, Crane delivered a possible farewell to Syracuse by writing: "From his home he had gone to the seminary to bid adieu to many schoolmates. They had thronged about him with wonder and admiration."

But later, Crane's protagonist "runs from battle, deserting his unit in the face of a Confederate counterattack." This theme of desertion is significant in *Red Badge* and may have come from two moments in Crane's baseball career. The first took place during Crane's time at Claverack Military Academy, where he was offered the captaincy of the baseball team but turned down the honor. The second, and possibly more influential, occurred on June 6, 1891, when Crane's Orangemen traveled to Hamilton, New York, to play Colgate.

Crane was Syracuse's shortstop at the time, but for this contest he was forced to play first base when two teammates never materialized. "Syracuse was badly crippled by the fact that only seven of their regular players went to Hamilton," the *Syracuse Sunday Herald* reported the next day.

"The shortstop had to play first base and the manager [Shepherd] had to play center field, one position being vacant." Interestingly, in the June 8, 1891, Syracuse *University News* an unnamed writer reported, "Since we lost our chance for the pennant, the interest in base ball seems to be entirely dead. At Hamilton on Friday, we lost a game to a team far inferior to ours, on account of this woeful lack of enthusiasm."

Crane would leave Syracuse within the month, likely disgusted by two teammates not bothering to show up for a game that determined the regional pennant. But following an initial attempt at fiction in 1893 with *Maggie: A Girl of the Streets* (reportedly written about a woman seen during Crane's forays into downtown Syracuse), he unleashed a pounding commentary on the brutality of war and the reality of cowardice considered. More than one hundred years later, Crane's work is considered to have greatly influenced author Ernest Hemingway and is consistently considered to be among the strongest examples of early American realist or naturalist writing styles.

Ernie Davis

Football Player, Pioneer

There's a scene early in the film *The Express* where Ernie Davis and his uncle are gazing intently through a department store display window at a black-and-white television screen. It is the late 1940s,

an era when racial segregation still reigns in America, and young Ernie is astonished to see a man with mahogany skin as dark as his own wearing a Major League Baseball uniform.

"He plays for the Brooklyn Dodgers?" Ernie asks in disbelief.

"That's right, boy," says the uncle he calls Pops. "That, there, is Jackie Robinson."

We then see young Ernie beaming with pride as he tacks a photograph of the man who broke baseball's color barrier to his bedroom wall.

A decade later, in a nation on the brink of cataclysmic changes, thousands of young boys—black and white—would tack photographs of Ernie Davis to their bedroom walls.

The movie, which debuted in 2008, draws parallels between Robinson and Davis and the courage they mustered to overcome the racial bigotry of the times. In 1961, just fourteen years after Robinson broke the color barrier in baseball, Davis bowled over another barrier by becoming the first African American to win the Heisman Trophy as college football's premier player. And the significance of that feat is not lost on Floyd Little, the College and Pro Football Hall-of-Fame running back who succeeded Davis and Jim Brown in the Syracuse University backfield and donned the same Number 44 jersey they had.

"I really believe Ernie's achievement has been kind of underplayed by history," said Little, who served as a special assistant to the athletics director at his alma mater after a successful business career. "Yes, the movie shed a little light on his remarkable life and the racial discrimination that he overcame with great courage and dignity. But I still don't believe Ernie has gotten his full due as a historical figure. In many ways, he was like Jackie Robinson. He didn't fight back and

Ernie Davis, circa 1962. Gift of the Varsity Club. Syracuse University Art Collection. © The Estate of Lee S. Trimm. Photo by Stephen Sartori.

The *Daily Orange*'s coverage of Ernie Davis's Heisman win. *Daily Orange.* Syracuse University Student Publications Reference Collection, University Archives.

get angry the way most of us would have if we had faced what he did. That wasn't Ernie. Even though that stuff hurt him deeply, he opted to let his actions speak for him. On and off the field."

And those actions spoke loudly, especially during the final, heroic months of a life cut short by leukemia at age twenty-three, just two years after winning the Heisman. "It's hard not to wonder at times how things might have turned out for Ernie," Davis's late mother, Marie Fleming, said in a 2003 interview. "But I'd rather focus on what was rather than on what might have been. He lived more life in 23 years than most people live in 83 years."

A three-sport star at Elmira (New York) Free Academy, Davis burst onto the national scene during his sophomore season at Syracuse in 1959 by guiding the Orangemen to an 11-0 record and the national championship. Despite playing with a severely pulled hamstring, the player known as the Elmira Express put an exclamation point on that season in the Cotton Bowl, rushing for fifty-seven yards on eight carries, catching an eighty-seven-yard touchdown pass, and intercepting a pass in SU's 23-14 victory over second-ranked Texas. "The thing that impressed me and most other people even more than his enormous athletic skills was his character," said Pat Stark, an assistant coach on SU's title team. "Ernie was one of the most modest, kind-hearted, caring individuals I ever met. You couldn't help but love the guy."

Two years later, after concluding a career in which he averaged a school-record 6.6 yards per carry, Davis was awarded the Heisman in New York City. Shortly after he was handed the distinctive bronze trophy, he received word that President John F. Kennedy was in town to make a speech and wanted to meet him. Davis and the trophy were immediately whisked away in a limo for a brief face-to-face with the commander in chief. "Imagine that?" the humble Davis told reporters afterward. "The President of the United

States wanting to meet me. I got to shake hands with him. That was almost as big a thrill as winning the Heisman."

A few months later, Davis received another thrill when he was the first player selected in the NFL draft. The Cleveland Browns traded All-Pro Bobby Mitchell to the Washington Redskins to acquire the rights to the Syracuse All-American. Art Modell, the Browns owner at the time, couldn't wait to pair the strapping six-foot-two, 220-pound Davis in the same backfield with the incomparable Jim Brown. "The world was Ernie's oyster," said John Brown, a teammate of Davis's at Syracuse. "He had everything going for him. Health. Looks. Riches. Youth. Fame. Just about anybody would have traded places with him. His future seemed limitless."

By the end of the summer of 1962, few would have traded places with him.

While preparing for a college all-star game against the defending NFL champion Green Bay Packers that July in Chicago, Davis developed sores in his mouth and lumps in his neck. Thinking maybe he had the mumps, he checked into an Evanston, Illinois, hospital where doctors diagnosed him with acute monocytic leukemia, a fatal blood disorder.

Though his chances for survival were slim, Davis refused to feel sorry for himself. In a gesture reminiscent of Lou Gehrig's "luckiest-man-on-the-face-of-the-earth" speech, Davis penned a piece for the *Saturday Evening Post* titled "I'm Not Unlucky."

At one point, Davis's leukemia went into remission, and there was talk that he might be able to play in a game for Cleveland. But his doctors advised against it. Although he never played a down for the team, Davis did get to suit up so he would be able to experience what it was like to have his name announced and walk onto the field at Cleveland's old Municipal Stadium. It occurred during an exhibition game in the summer of 1962.

"They turned all the lights off, and then they introduced Ernie and they flashed the spotlight on him as he walked through the goal posts," said John Brown, who spent ten seasons as an offensive lineman in the NFL and wound up naming his son after Ernie. "Eighty-four thousand people were screaming and clapping their hands and stomping their feet. It felt like an earthquake." Added Modell: "There wasn't a dry eye in the stadium."

Eight months later, on May 18, 1963, Davis died. His death touched a nation. His story transcended sports.

An estimated ten thousand people viewed his body before he was buried in Elmira's Woodlawn Cemetery not far from the grave of Samuel Clemens, the great American writer better known as Mark Twain. Modell chartered two planes to bring members of his organization to the funeral and announced that the Browns would retire the Number 45 jersey Davis never got to wear in a game.

Almost six decades later, Davis's presence can be felt on the Syracuse campus, where there are two statues of him and a residence hall named in his honor. His Heisman Trophy is on display in the football hall of honor next door to Manley Field House.

But he also lives on in those who knew him, including Little, who made up his mind to attend Syracuse instead of the US Military Academy at West Point the day Davis died. "I've attempted to honor Ernie by living a full life, a dedicated life, a life Ernie didn't get a chance to live," Little said.

Karen DeCrow

Attorney, Author, Activist

Before joining iconic figures such as Susan B. Anthony, Eleanor Roosevelt, and Sandra Day O'Connor as National Women's Hall of Fame inductees in Seneca Falls, New York, Karen DeCrow took a moment to reflect.

"Imagine that," she marveled during that memorable summer weekend in 2009. "I lived to see a world where a little girl could dream of being anything."

Not only had DeCrow lived to see such a world; she had helped create it.

As an activist, attorney, and author, the 1972 Syracuse University College of Law graduate worked tirelessly to tear down barriers and make dreams come true. And along the way, she would become a pioneer herself, carrying on the work begun by nineteenth-century suffragists like Anthony and Elizabeth Cady Stanton.

In 1969, while still a law student, DeCrow became the first woman in New York State to run for mayor, and although she was unsuccessful in her bid to lead the city of Syracuse, she inspired other women to run for political office. One of those women, Stephanie Miner, would become the first female mayor of the Salt City a few weeks after DeCrow's induction into the Hall.

While serving as president of the National Organization for Women (NOW) during the turbulent 1970s, DeCrow pushed for equal pay for equal work, stopped National Collegiate Athletic Association officials in their attempts to torpedo the Title IX legislation that wound up sparking a participation revolution in women's

Karen DeCrow. Syracuse University Portrait Collection, University Archives.

sports, pressured NASA and the major television networks to hire more women, helped convince the service academies and heretofore all-male Ivy League schools to become coeducational, and championed passage of the Equal Rights Amendment. Her flurry of activism resulted in *Time* magazine recognizing her as one of America's Leaders of Tomorrow in 1974.

"I dreamed of a world where the gender of a baby would have little or no relevance to the future pursuits and pleasure of that person—personal, political, economic, social and professional," she said. "And I've dedicated my life to that."

Born Karen Lipschultz, she grew up in Chicago dreaming of becoming a writer and wound up graduating from Northwestern University with a degree in journalism. In 1967, after a brief first marriage, she was living in Syracuse with her second husband, Roger DeCrow, and working for a small publishing company when she and some of her female colleagues discovered they were being paid less than their male counterparts. That prompted her to join the nascent group NOW and form a Syracuse chapter, of which she became president. "I wasn't a feminist," she said in a 1975 *New York Times* interview. "I just wanted more money."

Spurred to action by that injustice and the dearth of writing jobs in Central New York, DeCrow decided to stop taking graduate journalism courses at the Newhouse School and apply to the College of Law. "I thought to myself, 'What do you want to be when you grow up?'" she said in a 2009 *Syracuse University Magazine* interview. "And the idea of law school popped up. The things I like to do best are read, write and talk. I had gotten involved in the feminist movement by then, and I was passionate about that. We were saying in the movement that women can do anything, and being a lawyer was a good fit for me. We were also thinking, 'How can I better the cause?' And I thought this was a great way: bring cases to challenge all the sexist laws and represent women who are being discriminated against."

As the only female student in her law class, she was anything but a traditional student. "I was female, I was married, and I was an ardent feminist," said DeCrow, who also was ten years older than most of her peers. "But I loved it. I'm very grateful to the College of Law for giving me this wonderful profession that I enjoy every day."

College of Law professor emeritus Travis H. D. Lewin called her one of his favorite students of all time. "She was unafraid as a student to raise issues in class, just as she has been fearless on behalf of the equity for women in the workplace, in so-called private organizations, and in many walks of life," he said in 2009 on the eve of DeCrow being presented with a George Arents Award, the university's highest alumni honor. "Karen is the standard-bearer for pro bono lawyering. Her unrelenting lifetime pursuit of justice for those whom justice has been denied is the hallmark of the highest lawyering skill."

Even some feminist supporters thought DeCrow had veered too far away from the most important issues when she took on taverns in

Syracuse and New York City in the 1970s for their refusal to serve women. But DeCrow equated the men-only rules at pubs with white-only policies at lunch counters. And the courts wound up agreeing with her. "The issue was never about whether you could drink," said women's movement historian Georgina Hickey in a 2014 interview with the *Syracuse Post-Standard*. "It was about whether you could function as an autonomous adult in a free society."

Those who knew DeCrow cited not only her fierce determination and crystal clear insight into what needed to be changed, but also her quirky sense of humor. "As I grow older," she wrote in the *New York Times* in 1988, "I become more and more of a Marxist—Groucho that is. When you have lived two-thirds of your life, you know the value of a good joke."

Writing was a passion throughout her life and a powerful platform to bring about change. Through the years, she wrote hundreds of pieces for newspapers and magazines and published several books, including two influential titles in the early 1970s—*The Young Woman's Guide to Liberation* and *Sexist Justice—How Legal Sexism Affects You*.

DeCrow and her contemporaries were forced to confront many of the same challenges that the suffragists faced during the birth of the women's rights movement in Seneca Falls in 1848. "We were ignored to a great extent," DeCrow said. "When they paid attention to us, they were making fun of us. And when they were not making fun of us, they were just hostile. That was what it was like in the beginning. . . . If you are doing something that's changing the culture, that's what you're going to encounter. I felt it was important to me. I felt it was important to the United States. And, immodestly, I felt it was important to the world. So although there were times when I couldn't help but take it personally, I never burned out, and I never thought of stopping."

As a result, she helped create a world where girls could dream of being anything.

"Her tireless work on behalf of women everywhere has left an indelible mark on our country," National Women's Hall of Fame executive director Christine Moulton said about DeCrow, who died in 2014 at age seventy-six. "For decades, she has advocated, debated, spoken out, pushed the envelope, broken barriers, and mentored others to do the same. Her leadership and groundbreaking legal work continue to inspire and empower."

Taye Diggs

Actor

It isn't hard imagining a talented young man named Taye Diggs walking down Syracuse University's sloping hill to Syracuse Stage in late 1989 and hoping that someday he'd light up stages and screens as a successful actor with impressive credits to his name.

Taye Diggs. © Syracuse University. Photo by Stephen Sartori.

Young actors always dream of fame and fortune, but few ultimately achieve those goals.

That was not the case for the young man born Scott Leo Diggs. For Taye, the journey to Broadway and Hollywood moved at hyperspeed. Seemingly overnight, Diggs went from SU student to Hollywood sensation, TV and theater star, and respected author.

Born in Newark, New Jersey, but raised in Rochester, New York, Diggs got an early start by attending a performing arts high school. "I was a large geek," Diggs said in 2000 after his acting career exploded globally. "I had nothing. I was everybody's best friend, but none of the ladies would look at me for a second."

That started changing when he enrolled at Syracuse and began appearing, often vibrantly, in student productions. It was during his senior year, while earning a BFA from the College of Visual and Performing Arts, that Diggs was spotted by a talent scout during a Syracuse showcase.

"I grew socially at Syracuse," Diggs said. "There were a lot of other people that looked like me, spoke like me, behaved like me, which I was not used to. So, it was a place where I felt comfortable, accepted, and was allowed to grow."

Moving immediately to New York City after graduation, Diggs scored an understudy's role in the 1994 Broadway production of *Carousel*. By 1996 (after a brief stop as a dancer at Tokyo Disneyland), Diggs was back in New York's theater district appearing as the original cast's landlord Benny in the Tony and Pulitzer Prize-winning production of *Rent*. That same year, he started grabbing TV roles on dramas like *Law and Order* and *New York Undercover*.

Two years later, Diggs was cast as Angela Bassett's striking love interest in the movie *How Stella Got Her Groove Back*. In less than a decade, Diggs had moved from shy high school student to multitalented sensation and cinematic heartthrob.

The roles didn't stop there. During his second decade in the entertainment industry, Diggs created memorable performances in nearly thirty movies, including *Go, The Best Man, Rent, Brown Sugar, The Wood, Chicago,* and *The Best Man Holiday.* On television, he appeared in multiple episodes of *Guiding Light, Ally McBeal, Private Practice, Will & Grace, Grey's Anatomy, Empire, Murder in the First,* and as Coach Billy Baker in CW's *All American.* He also continued performing on Broadway stages in starring roles such as Fiyero in *Wicked,* Billy Flynn in *Chicago,* and transgender East German rocker Hedwig in *Hedwig and the Angry Inch.*

As if acting wasn't enough, Diggs decided to team up with fellow SU alumnus and noted illustrator Shane Evans to create the 2011 children's book *Chocolate Me!* The pair collaborated again four years later with the book *Mixed Me!*

"I never thought I would be a writer, but I used to just write random poems, and leave them lying around the dorm," Diggs once told *Entertainment Weekly.* "Shane saw one, and, because he was an artist, would take some of my writing and put them to his art. The first thing he put on display was this poem I wrote called 'Chocolate Me!' In its original form, it was more for adults, so he put the poem to some really strong imagery and made a book."

"Taye and I went to the Rochester School of the Arts and Syracuse together," Evans told *Syracuse University Magazine* in 2017. "We were encouraged by many people around us, teachers and family, and our hearts were led by faith. We always found a way to step forward and find a place to put our talents to good work."

That faith and commitment has often led Diggs back to Syracuse or New York's Lubin House. In 2011, the Screen Actors Guild Award winner came back for Orange Central to sign copies of *Chocolate Me!* He was also on campus in 2013 to receive an Arents Award, the university's highest alumni honor. During that visit, he made time to serve as a celebrity bartender on the Quad for an event called 'Cuse Brew and Barbecue, where he poured beers with fellow 1993 alumnus Jay Harrington, who was enjoying his own TV success in shows like *Better Off Ted* and *Hot in Cleveland.* After finishing their bartending chores, Diggs and Harrington reportedly revisited some of their favorite collegiate hangouts, including Chuck's and Harry's.

In 2018, Diggs made his directorial debut with Keenan Scott II's moving play, *Thoughts of a Colored Man on a Day When the Sun Set Too Early.* It's about eight men searching for their identities while coming up against the raw realities of racism, stereotypes, and the resistance commonly faced by men of color. Diggs graciously agreed to present a one-night reading of the show for SU alumni and guests at Lubin House.

The National Association for the Advancement of Colored People (NAACP) presented Diggs with Image Awards for his performances in *Kevin Hill* and *Private Practice,* while the American Black Film Festival honored him for his role in *The Best Man Holiday.*

David Falk

Sports Powerbroker

One can argue that NBA legend Michael Jordan was the greatest athlete and product endorser of the last seventy-five years, maybe ever. One also can argue His Airness wouldn't have ascended to such lofty heights without a huge assist from his agent, Syracuse alumnus David Falk, who steered Jordan toward record-setting contracts, movie deals (*Space Jams, Michael Jordan to the Max*) and the groundbreaking marketing agreements (most notably his shoe contract with NIKE) that changed modern sports marketing.

Falk's status as one of the most influential sports agents of all time is indisputable. You might even call him the Michael Jordan of sports agents.

For twelve straight years from 1990 to 2001, Falk was listed by *The Sporting News* as one of the 100 Most Powerful People in Sports, and in 1995, he was named one of the Top 50 Marketers in the United States by *Advertising Age.* For many years, in the eyes of sports journalists and NBA team general managers, Falk trailed only NBA Commissioner David Stern as the most powerful individual in basketball.

Falk earned these plaudits by consistently revolutionizing the representation of modern American athletes, and by relentlessly driving up the value (and incomes) his stable of stars were able to secure. This did not always make Falk popular with basketball insiders, since they associated Falk (and seemingly Falk alone) with changing the salary profile of the NBA. When Jordan came into the NBA in 1984 and signed with the Chicago Bulls, the average NBA contract was $330,000. By 2001, it was $4.5 million, and many felt Falk was solely responsible for the way in which annual salaries were increasing, despite the fact it was his job to earn as much for his clients as possible.

"There's always something to criticize—I have too much power or too many clients," he once said. "I scoff at that. Think about it: If you lived on a block with $300,000 houses and you sold yours for

David Falk. Courtesy of the *Daily Orange.*

$2.5 million, your neighbors would thank you. But in my business they don't."

And while Jordan may be the name most associated with Falk, players like Alonzo Mourning (who received the NBA's first-ever $100 million contract), Juwan Howard, Kenny Anderson, and Dikembe Mutombo helped Falk generate nearly $400 million in agreements during a stunning six-day negotiating period in 1998.

Player contracts are one thing, but where Falk really excelled was in marketing and matching the strengths of his players with the needs of America's biggest brands. At the pinnacle of this endorsement cavalcade were Falk's efforts on behalf of Jordan. Here, Falk let NIKE build Jordan's brand as an individual and then leveraged Jordan's fame and on-court performance into deals with Coca-Cola, Chevrolet, McDonald's, Gatorade, Wilson, Wheaties, and even Bijan, which designed the Michael Jordan fragrance.

Today, many consider the NIKE ads featuring Jordan to be among the best ever created using a sport celebrity and a branded product (the Air Jordan). Additionally, the Jordan logo, known as Jumpman, is one of the most recognizable brand logos in the world and is the signature motif of NIKE's Jordan brand.

Falk, a 1972 graduate of SU in economics, got his law degree from George Washington University in 1975. But before he'd even graduated, Falk was working for Donald Dell's ProServ agency. Falk's time at ProServ set the table for the creation of his own agency—Falk Associates Management Enterprises, a.k.a. FAME—in 1992. Six years later, Falk sold FAME to SFX Entertainment for a reported $100 million.

"I always knew I didn't want to be an astronaut or a firefighter," Falk has said. "But my classmates said they could see me as a lawyer."

Along the way, Falk found time to represent some of the biggest names in sports, including Boomer Esiason, Danny Ferry, James Worthy, Charles Barkley, Duke basketball coach Mike Krzyzewski, Georgetown coach John Thompson, Allen Iverson, and Desmond Howard. Falk is also an accomplished writer and published his first book, *The Bald Truth*, with Pocket Books in 2009.

He also remained incredibly loyal to SU, with his multimillion dollar gift transforming his alma mater's College of Human Ecology into the David B. Falk College of Sport and Human Dynamics.

As of 2019, he was still active in representing NBA players and entrepreneurial start-ups yet frequently found time to visit Syracuse to guest lecture in sport management classes, where he could be found encouraging the future leaders of the sports industry.

Peter Falk

Actor

Peter Falk would go on to create one of the most beloved and memorable characters in television history—Lieutenant Columbo, the rumpled, cigar-chewing, absent-minded detective who always

Actor Peter Falk as the iconic TV detective *Columbo*. ABC Photo Archives / © ABC / Getty Images.

wound up getting the bad guy or gal after a tortuous cat-and-mouse investigation. Columbo's uncanny ability to solve crime mysteries would be in stark contrast to Falk's real-life inability to decide what he wanted to do with his life while studying for his master's in public administration at the Maxwell School in the early 1950s. The future Emmy Award-winning sleuth had no clue back then.

"I was sure about one thing—I was NOT going to be an actor," he said in a *New York Times* interview. "I was above all that. At least, that's what I told the drama coach, Sawyer Falk (no relation), whenever he brought it up."

The younger Falk was so sure he *wasn't* going to become an actor that he kept showing up for stage productions being directed by the elder Falk.

And it was there, at Syracuse University, that a future star would be born.

"It all started when I couldn't tear myself away from the theater department in Syracuse—where, of course, I had no business being since I was enrolled in Maxwell," Peter Falk recalled. "I ended up spending more time rehearsing than going to classes."

Falk attended enough classes to earn his Maxwell degree in 1953. But he also earned two lead acting roles that wound up being more important to his future success than his diploma. One break occurred when he took over the part of Tyrrel at the last minute in a production of *Richard III*. The other came in an original musical called *White Bucks and Tails*.

"I didn't realize it at the time, but that's when the acting bug really bit me, when I was at Syracuse," he said. "In retrospect, landing those roles excited me more than landing that degree. Looking back, I should have majored in drama. But I was trying to be practical. I was an older student, had already traveled the world with the Merchant Marines, so I guess I was looking for something that would guarantee me a regular paycheck. And I knew acting was a crap-shoot. It was not a profession that guaranteed regular paychecks. Plus, I had a glass eye."

Ah, yes. That's part of the story, too. His right eye was removed when he was diagnosed with a brain tumor at age three. The limited vision didn't prevent him from becoming a star athlete in high school. Falk reveled in telling the story about being called out in a close play during a baseball game. Upset with the ruling, he removed his glass eye, and handed it to the umpire. "You'll do better with this," Falk told the arbiter.

After graduating from Syracuse with an MPA degree, Falk landed a job as an efficiency expert for the budget director in Hartford, Connecticut.

"I was such an efficiency expert that the first morning on the job, I couldn't find the building where I was to report for work," he said in a 1997 interview. "Naturally I was late, which I always was in those days, but, ironically, it was my tendency never to be on time that got me started as a professional actor."

Falk did some acting on the side for a community theater in Hartford, then began taking classes with famous acting coach Eva Le Gallienne in Westport, Connecticut, about a two-hour drive away. He was habitually tardy for class, drawing the ire of his teacher.

"One evening when I arrived late, she looked at me and asked, 'Young man, why are you always late?'" Falk recalled in a 1997 interview with *Cigar Aficionado* magazine. "I said, 'I have to drive down from Hartford.' She looked down her nose and said, 'What do you do in Hartford? There's no theater there. How do you make a living acting?'"

Falk confessed that he had lied his way into her class—that, unlike the other students, he was not a professional actor. Le Gallienne looked at him sternly and said: "Well, you should be." Falk drove back to Hartford that night and quit his job. After a few more months of studying with Le Gallienne, the twenty-nine-year-old moved to Greenwich Village to pursue an acting career.

While rooming with fellow struggling actors Dustin Hoffman and Gene Hackman in 1956, Falk made his professional acting debut in the off-Broadway production of *Don Juan*. His performance was critically acclaimed, and after several other stage roles he played Abe Reles, a violent mob thug in the 1960 film *Murder, Inc.* His portrayal was so compelling that he earned an Academy Award nomination for best supporting actor. He also earned an Emmy nomination for his role in the television series *The Law and Mr. Jones*, making him the first actor ever to earn Oscar and Emmy nominations in the same year, a feat he repeated in 1962 while winning an Emmy for his role in an episode of *The Dick Powell Theater* television series.

His life-changing moment came in 1967, when Bing Crosby and Lee J. Cobb turned down the Columbo role. During the filming of the first television film about the detective, Falk rejected the fashionable attire the costume designers laid out for him, opting instead for shabby clothes, including his signature garment—a tattered raincoat. Falk's disheveled appearance and idiosyncrasies and actorly tics created an underdog character that had everyman appeal.

"He looks like a flood victim," Falk once said. "You feel sorry for him. He appears to be seeing nothing, but he's seeing everything. Columbo has a genuine mistiness about him. It seems to hang in the air . . . and he's capable of being distracted. Columbo is an ass-backwards Sherlock Holmes. Holmes had a long neck. Columbo has no neck. Holmes smoked a pipe. Columbo chews up six cigars a day."

Falk wound up playing the frumpy detective off-and-on for more than twenty years. The unforgettable role earned him a dozen Emmy nominations (he won four times) and the number twenty-one spot on *TV Guide*'s rankings of the top television stars of all time. The show was syndicated all over the world, resulting in the unveiling of a statue of Columbo and his beloved dog in Budapest, Hungary. "It's amazing what a phenomenon it became," Falk said. "I've been to little villages in Africa with maybe one TV set, and little kids will run up to me shouting, 'Columbo! Columbo!'"

Not bad for a guy who insisted he would *not* become an actor while passionately rehearsing to become one many decades ago at Syracuse.

Sarah Loguen Fraser

Medical Pioneer, Civil Rights Activist

Sarah Loguen was standing at a train station in the spring of 1873, preparing to return to Syracuse from Washington, DC, when she was startled by a scream. She jerked her head around and saw that a young boy had been run over by a horse-drawn wagon. She and others ran to the scene, but no one else in the gawking crowd seemed interested in helping out. Loguen frantically searched in vain for a doctor. Eventually, someone carried the crying boy away.

Her shock over the crowd's indifference to the boy's agony and her own sense of helplessness prompted her to make a vow to herself: "I will never, never see a human being in need of aid again and not be able to help."

On that train ride home, she resolved to become a doctor, and by sheer happenstance ran into her family physician, Dr. Michael Benedict. She recounted her horrifying experience and mentioned her new career aspirations. Benedict, the president of the Onondaga County Medical Society, promised to help her any way he could.

Loguen spent the next five months studying diligently under him and was accepted into Syracuse University's College of Medicine. Three years later, this daughter of a slave would become the first female and first African American to graduate from the medical school. Just the fourth black woman to become a licensed physician in US history, Loguen would spend the next fifty years providing medical care to an underserved population while breaking down racial and gender barriers and fighting injustice.

Sarah Loguen Fraser. Portrait by Susan Keeter, 2000. Upstate Portrait Collection, Archives and Special Collections, Upstate Medical University.

She became so beloved at a Philadelphia pediatric hospital that patients and coworkers affectionately referred to her as "Miss Doc." Sarah also became the first female physician in the Dominican Republic—the homeland of her husband, pharmacist Charles Fraser, whom she married in Syracuse in 1882. While living in that Caribbean nation, she offered free medical service to the poor, though by law she was allowed to treat only women and children. She had such an impact in her roughly ten years there that when she died at age eighty-three in 1933, the president of the Dominican Republic ordered a nine-day national mourning period and flags at half-staff.

Sarah was born in Syracuse in 1850, the fifth of eight children of Reverend Jermain Wesley Loguen and his wife, Caroline. A former slave, Reverend Loguen migrated north to the Salt City, where he became a bishop in the African Methodist Episcopal Zion Church and a staunch abolitionist. At the urging of friends Frederick Douglass and Harriet Tubman, Loguen and his wife began providing escaped slaves a refuge on their way to Canada. At least 1,500 people stayed at their "station," also known as a safe house, prompting historians to nickname the elder Loguen the Underground Railroad King. The bishop put himself and his family at great risk because the passage of the Fugitive Slave Act of 1850 criminalized any failure to report the whereabouts of known escaped slaves.

Sarah, like her siblings, would be profoundly influenced by the experience of helping to care for these freedom seekers. "My home and family have always been a beacon to light the way for the poor, oppressed, and hunted of our race," she said. "God knows we need to build strong and healthy bodies. The light that was kindled by Father and Mother must burn on, and I must carry the torch."

After working at hospitals in Philadelphia and Boston, Sarah opened an office for private medical practice in Washington, DC, in 1879, and Douglass, the famed abolitionist, personally nailed up her shingle. She said it was one of the proudest moments of her life.

Her daughter, Gregoria Fraser, was born in 1883 and would later graduate from Syracuse University and launch a successful career as a music teacher. Mother and daughter would remain close, with Gregoria caring for Sarah in the later years of her life.

In 2000—on the sesquicentennial of Sarah's birth—her hometown memorialized her by naming a street in her honor. Upstate Medical University (formerly Syracuse University's College of Medicine) commissioned a portrait of her and also established a scholarship in her name. A life devoted to helping others—a life forever changed by a boy's scream—would not be forgotten.

Marty Glickman

Olympic Athlete, Sportscaster

A day after scoring two touchdowns and intercepting two passes in Syracuse's 1937 upset victory against then college football powerhouse Cornell, Marty Glickman received an offer from a local haberdasher that sounded like a bad fit. Stanley Hyman wanted to capitalize on the young football hero's sudden fame by having him host a weekly radio college sports show.

Though flattered, Glickman told the suburban Syracuse clothier he was ill-suited for the job.

"You don't want me," he said. "I'm nervous. I stutter. I stammer. I've never been on the air before."

"I'll pay you $15 a broadcast," Hyman said.

"I'll take it," replied the cash-strapped student.

And thus began the career of the broadcasting Pied Piper who inspired the likes of Marv Albert, Dick Stockton, and Bob Costas to follow his lead and help SU become "Sportscaster U."

Marty Glickman. Syracuse University Portrait Collection, University Archives.

From that humble radio show on local station WSYR, Glickman would go on to become one of the most influential and versatile sportscasters of all time. The former Orange football star and Olympic sprinter not only started the trend of aspiring sportscasters coming to Syracuse, but also may have been the first famous jock turned broadcaster.

During Glickman's fifty-five-year career behind the microphone he became recognized as the voice of the New York Giants, New York Jets, and New York Knickerbockers. He also did pre- and postgame shows for New York Yankees and Brooklyn Dodgers broadcasts, became HBO's first sports director, and was hired by NBC Sports as a broadcast coach. Throw in his harness racing calls and even a marbles tournament broadcast, and it's estimated he worked more than twenty thousand sporting events.

"So many of us—especially those of us who broadcast basketball—owe a huge debt of gratitude to him," said Albert, who worked as a researcher and statistician for Glickman while still in high school. "Marty painted word pictures. He laid out the geography of the court, helped you see and smell and feel the game on the radio. His broadcasts made it like you were there, sitting in the front row."

A member of the National Sportscasters and Sportswriters Hall of Fame, Glickman is credited with coming up with widely accepted basketball terminology such as swish, top of the key, the lane, and the midcourt stripe.

Long before making his mark at the mic, Glickman made his mark as an athlete. Blessed with incredible speed, he was recruited to run track and play football at Syracuse, earning three varsity letters in each sport. After being named an All-American sprinter for the Orange, he was selected to compete in the 1936 Olympics in Berlin. He was scheduled to run a leg on the 4-by-100-yard relay team, but was scratched at the last minute because he was Jewish, and US officials feared his presence would offend German chancellor Adolf Hitler. Glickman's friend, Jesse Owens, protested the move, even though the benching gave him the opportunity to win a fourth gold medal at the games. The dashed dream would haunt Glickman the rest of his life.

In 1985, he returned to Germany as part of a tribute to Owens and had difficulty suppressing his anger. "As I walked into the stadium, I began to get so angry," he wrote in his 1996 autobiography, *The Fastest Kid on the Block*. "It shocked the hell out of me that this thing of forty-nine years ago could still evoke anger . . . I was cursing. I was really amazed at myself, at this feeling of anger. Not about the German Nazis—that was a given. But the anger at [Olympic officials] Avery Brundage and Dean Cromwell for not allowing an eighteen-year-old kid to compete in the Olympic Games just because he was Jewish. They took my dream away from me."

Demoralized by the anti-Semitic decision, Glickman returned to Syracuse, where he turned his athletic attention to football. His speed served him well on the gridiron. Starting three seasons at running back and end, Glickman helped the Orange rebound from a 1-7 won-lost record in 1936 to 5-2-1 and 5-3 records in succeeding years.

His football heroics led to that life-changing offer to become a broadcaster, but the world-class sprinter would get off to a stumbling start. Glickman spent hours working on his first script. "I typed and retyped and timed it and rehearsed and went over it back and forth for hours at a time," Glickman recalled in a 1998 interview. "I go on the air at 9:15 that night, and my first words out of my mouth are: 'Good afternoon, everybody. Oops! Sorry folks.' And from there, fortunately, I improved."

Interestingly, the first of Syracuse's famous sportscasters did not receive his degree in broadcasting, but rather in political science. Glickman originally enrolled in premed, but switched his major after some early struggles with chemistry.

His fifteen-dollars-per-broadcast salary helped make ends meet during those final days of the Great Depression. So did the generosity of a handful of Jewish alumni from New York City who helped pay for Glickman's tuition. They had been members of the Sammy fraternity, and they sponsored Glickman because they wanted to, in his words, "repay Syracuse for the good things Syracuse did for them" during a time when many colleges either didn't admit Jews or enforced quotas.

That was one of the reasons Glickman developed a lifelong bond with his alma mater, often returning to lecture and always offering to review students' audition tapes.

"Marty was a very giving person," Albert said. "I obviously experienced that first-hand, but I've heard so many similar stories. If you had a Syracuse connection, he felt a kinship with you. But even if you didn't attend SU, he would try to help you. It's just the way he was."

In 1998, sixty-two years after his dream-destroying moment, Glickman received the Douglas MacArthur Award from US Olympic Committee president William J. Hybl. It was the committee's way of officially apologizing for what happened in Germany. Though it didn't make up for the gold medal he almost certainly would have won, Glickman appreciated the gesture.

At his funeral three years later, he was remembered for the way he had bounced back from his Olympic indignity and wound up enjoying an extraordinary career. And he can thank a Syracuse haberdasher for giving him the break that would change his life and the lives of scores of sportscasters who would follow him up the Hill. Glickman and broadcasting were a perfect fit.

Tim Green

Athlete, Author, Lawyer

Two things stood out about Tim Green when he was a student at Syracuse University in the mid-1980s: He had a nose for the football and his nose in a book. Many, many books as it turned out. As a defensive end for the Orange, he ignited a football renaissance on campus while

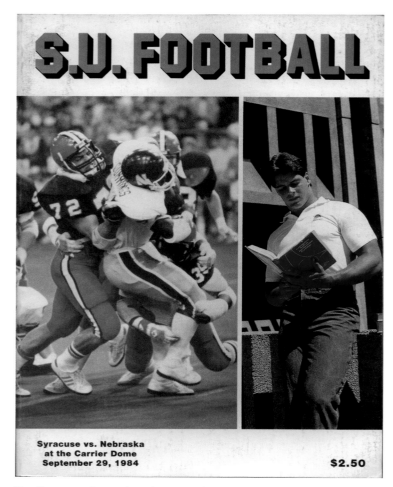

S.U. FOOTBALL

Syracuse vs. Nebraska
at the Carrier Dome
September 29, 1984

$2.50

Tim Green was featured on the cover of the Syracuse football program during his days as a student-athlete. Athletics Department, Syracuse University, used by permission.

establishing a school record for quarterback sacks and twice earning All-American honors. And the English major was just as driven and accomplished in the classroom, becoming a Rhodes Scholar finalist and graduating covaledictorian. That he would realize his childhood dreams of becoming an NFL player and a best-selling author doesn't surprise anyone who knew him back in the day.

While playing for the Atlanta Falcons, Green somehow found the time and energy to attend SU's College of Law. He graduated with honors and became a practicing attorney in 1994. Along the way, he also crafted a successful broadcasting career that saw him work as a football analyst for Fox Sports, cohost the nationally syndicated news show *A Current Affair*, and become a regular contributor to National Public Radio and ABC News.

Oh, and he also became a prolific author of nearly forty books, including fifteen *New York Times* best-sellers. His life's journey took him from sacking quarterbacks to sacking illiteracy. In the mid-2000s, several years after penning revealing best-sellers about the darker side of professional football, Green began writing sports-themed novels for elementary to middle school children in hopes of convincing more young people to read. The fact he had played eight seasons in the NFL gave him instant credibility among his target

audience, and he used that credibility to drive home the importance of reading, education, and kindness.

Green not only wrote compelling books but also started a program called Reading Is Weightlifting for the Brain, visiting close to two thousand schools. His initiative received rave reviews. After a presentation at Orion Junior High in Ogden, Utah, school librarian Amy Hall called Green "a national treasure" and added that "each and every student in America should have the opportunity to hear his message and learn from him." At each stop, Green donated a trunkload of his books.

"It's like everything in my life was pushing me in this direction and I couldn't be happier that it has," he said in a 2016 interview. "This has become my passion, my mission in life. I haven't discovered a cure for cancer or found a solution for peace in the Middle East, but, in some small way, I'd like to think I'm helping make the world a better place."

Famed abolitionist and newspaper editor Frederick Douglass said "once you learn to read, you will forever be free." Those words resonate with Green, who can trace his lifelong love of the written word to the Hardy Boys mystery series he began devouring as a third grader. Like those novels that first hooked him, Green's books are filled with suspenseful plots.

In 2016, he began collaborating on a three-book series with legendary New York Yankees shortstop Derek Jeter. The coauthors made the protagonist a young biracial ballplayer who is subjected to bullying. Green and Jeter said they hoped the story would potentially steer their readers to be kinder and more understanding toward their peers. "I think it affords kids the opportunity to identify with the main character, to admire him and hopefully like that person, and to see that everyone has challenges and obstacles—some of them fair, some unfair," Green told the *Daily Orange* in 2017.

Each of Green's books emphasized the importance of compassion and perseverance. Realizing your dreams is another common theme. He knows that topic well.

A native of Liverpool, just several miles north of SU, Green could have gone anywhere to play college football in the fall of 1982—he was that highly regarded. But he decided to play for his hometown team after Coach Dick MacPherson sold him on the idea of becoming the cornerstone recruit in Syracuse's gridiron resurrection. "I was intrigued with the idea of being on the ground floor of something really special," Green said. "It was an enormous challenge because the program was really down at the time. However, I saw it as an opportunity to make some history."

And so Green attended Syracuse and helped author a chapter that remains special decades later—a chapter that saw him lead the Orangemen in sacks three consecutive years and help engineer a program-changing 17-9 upset of top-ranked Nebraska in the Carrier Dome in 1984. After his senior season, the Falcons drafted him in the first round, and he fashioned a respectable professional football career, recording twenty-four sacks while anchoring a stout defense.

Green has faced numerous challenges along the way—none greater than the one he revealed on November 14, 2018, when he told his Facebook followers that he had been diagnosed with amyotrophic lateral sclerosis, also known as ALS or Lou Gehrig's disease. A rapidly progressive neurodegenerative disorder, ALS affects the cells responsible for controlling voluntary muscles. There is no known cure. Green remained upbeat in his Facebook post, which he ended by writing: "Don't be sorry. Let's beat this." In a poignant, nationally televised *60 Minutes* interview with CBS television journalist and SU alumnus Steve Kroft, he talked about his new Tackle ALS website to boost funding for research.

"As always, I will spend the coming days and years counting the blessings I have instead of pining for the things I don't," he told visitors to his author's page on Facebook. "Today I will work and write, and kiss each of my kids as well as my beautiful wife. That's a great day. As good as it gets." In January 2019, Syracuse University announced it would retire Green's Number 72 football jersey before that September's game against Clemson in the Carrier Dome. His alma mater also presented him with a Chancellor's Medal that April.

Vic Hanson

Athlete, Coach

He was nicknamed the Black Menace for his thick crop of black hair and his ability to torment Syracuse University opponents in three different sports. But a more fitting nickname for Vic Hanson would have been "an Orangeman for all seasons," because that's what he was.

He also was a hometown hero who grew up in Manlius, not far from the Syracuse campus. By spurning offers from Roaring Twenties' college football powerhouses Yale and Michigan and staying put, Hanson went places no Syracuse athlete has gone before or since.

Vic Hanson. Athletics Department, Syracuse University, used by permission.

Not only did he earn a total of nine varsity letters (he might have been awarded twelve had freshmen been eligible back then), he also snagged All-American honors in basketball and football and was a good enough baseball player to sign a minor league contract with the dynastic New York Yankees following his graduation in 1927.

He's believed to be the only athlete in SU history to captain three different sports, and he remains the only athlete to be enshrined in both the Naismith Memorial Basketball Hall of Fame (1960) and the College Football Hall of Fame (1973), and the only athlete selected to Syracuse's All-Century teams in basketball *and* football.

In 1952, famed sportswriter Grantland Rice named Hanson to his All-Time, All-American basketball team, along with George Mikan, John Wooden, Bob Kurland, and Hank Lusetti. Rice called him "the best all-around athlete Syracuse ever had."

As if that wasn't enough, Hanson also was an outstanding and popular student who served as president of his class. "I was the luckiest guy in the world when Vic entered Syracuse," said Lew Andreas, the second-winningest basketball coach in school history and a former SU athletics director.

Hanson guided the Orange hoopsters to a 19-1 record and the national championship his junior year. In his senior season, he was named the top player in college basketball, while establishing scoring records that stood for two decades. As a two-way end in football, he led Syracuse to a 25-5-3 record in three seasons.

Although just five foot ten and 174 pounds, Hanson was exceptionally strong and quick. He became the only sophomore to make the Orange varsity football team, and he made an immediate impact as a punishing tackler on defense and a glue-fingered receiver on offense. He also was like a coach on the field. Formations and positions were different back then. There wasn't a quarterback per se as there is today, and ends often would call out instructions on offense. "He had terrific speed and a great pair of hands," said Andreas, who coached him in both football and basketball. "In this modern passing game he'd be a knockout. He'd make these modern football teams just as he did in his day."

Andreas was even more impressed with Hanson's hardwood prowess. "He was probably the finest basketball player we ever had," said the man who coached the Orange from 1924 to 1950. "He was a wonderful competitor, a very skillful and guileful player, but most of all, a fine team leader."

Hanson was SU's primary scoring threat, and during that era of designated free throw shooters he took nearly all of the Orangemen's foul shots. In perhaps the best game of his career, he scored 25 points in a 30-25 overtime victory at Pennsylvania on December 29, 1925. Hanson scored four of SU's 5 points in overtime and helped the Orangemen hold Penn scoreless in the extra session.

SU's only loss that season came at Penn State, when they had to play without starter Gotch Carr, who was declared academically ineligible, and without Andreas, who was recovering from a severe case of tonsillitis. The loss snapped the Orangemen's fifteen-game win streak, but they avenged it a few weeks later by clobbering the Nittany Lions, 29-12, in Syracuse.

There were no postseason tournaments in those days, and years later the Helms Foundation retroactively decided that SU, which had won nineteen of twenty games and boasted impressive victories over Eastern League champion Penn and Big Ten champ Michigan, was titleworthy. Though he had frequently been double-teamed, Hanson set a school record that season with a 14.2-points-per-game average, the equivalent of about 30 points per game in the modern era.

Although Syracuse slipped to an 11-4 record the next year, Hanson established a new school scoring mark with 14.6 points per game. For the third consecutive season, he earned All-America honors, and Helms named him the national player of the year.

The Yankees had scouted him on the ball diamond and invited him to a tryout, witnessed by sluggers Babe Ruth and Lou Gehrig. He was signed to a minor league contract, but the second baseman's inability to hit the curve ball ended his professional baseball career after just one season. He returned to Syracuse, where he formed a professional basketball team made up of former SU players. The Syracuse All-Americans held their own, beating some of the nation's best teams of the day, including the original Boston Celtics and the New York Renaissance, a superb, All-African American squad known as the Rens.

In 1930, at age twenty-seven, he was named varsity football coach at his alma mater, making him one of the youngest head coaches in America. Hanson did a good job in his seven seasons at the helm, guiding Syracuse to a 33-21-5 record before resigning. His only sin as a coach was that he couldn't beat archrival Colgate, which was a fireable offense in those days.

After leaving SU, he became a prominent insurance salesman, once receiving a national award from his company, Equitable Life Assurance. On December 19, 1981, SU officials retired Hanson's Number 8 and Dave Bing's Number 22—the first jersey retirements in school history.

"I lived a charmed life," Hanson once said. "Sometimes things don't work out when you go to college in your hometown. Too much pressure. But it worked out wonderfully for me."

Robert Jarvik

Medical Revolutionary

The original intent was to become an architect, not a doctor and pioneering medical inventor. And Robert Jarvik might very well have pursued a career designing buildings rather than extending lives had fate not intervened that momentous day during his first semester at Syracuse University in the fall of 1965.

"So, at Syracuse," recalled Jarvik, inventor of the world's first permanent and totally artificial heart, "I began in the School of Architecture and shortly after I arrived, I was studying in Carnegie

Robert Jarvik. Syracuse University Portrait Collection, University Archives.

Library and got paged by someone walking around, calling my name."

The news he received from a fellow student was that Jarvik's father, a surgeon, had suffered a debilitating aortic aneurysm and would require heart surgery in Texas. Jarvik left school to be with his dad and came back tremendously intrigued by lifesaving heart-based science.

Jarvik decided to switch to premed. It was a logical move since he had been observing his father for years and had even "invented a gun-like device that automatically stapled-off blood vessels" while in high school. He called it the Jarvik Suture Machine.

The funny thing, though, was that Jarvik, who loved building model ships as a youngster, wasn't a great premed student. His wide array of interests prompted him to take many classes at Syracuse far removed from the traditional load of biology and chemistry classes.

"I found I became interested in taking a particular course in metalworking and silversmithing in [SU's] School of Art," recalled Jarvik during his 2016 Arents Award acceptance speech. "But I was a premed student in Liberal Arts. That was not allowed. Fortunately, Syracuse had a new computer system that had been running for a couple of years which they used as their method of [class] registration. They had packets of punch cards and these IBM punch cards had a little fallibility."

Convincing an unsuspecting Syracuse art school advisor to give him an envelope of their punch cards, Jarvik took the art school packet, removed the metalworking one he wanted, and mixed it in with his premed classes.

That system weakness allowed the man the *New York Times* would later call "the Dracula of medical technology" to continue learning about mechanical forms, which furthered his interest in machining.

After graduating from Syracuse in 1968 with a degree in zoology but failing to get into any of the roughly fifteen US medical schools he applied to, Jarvik traveled with his wife to Italy, where he enrolled in the University of Bologna medical college. Classes were canceled frequently because of student strikes, and Jarvik lost interest. He decided to return to the states and wound up earning a master's degree from New York University in occupational biomechanics in 1971.

Leaving New York for the University of Utah, Jarvik secured a hundred-dollar-a-week position as a lab assistant to Dr. Willem Kolff, chair of Utah's artificial organs department, and earned his long-desired medical degree there in 1976. He also kept working on the Jarvik-3, an artificial heart designed with layers of smooth elastic similar to the Lycra used in women's girdles.

During those years in Salt Lake City, Jarvik continued refining his designs and testing mechanical hearts in animals. Of note was the Jarvik-5, which kept a calf named Alfred Lord Tennyson alive for a record 268 days.

With the ensuing invention of the Jarvik-7, it was finally time for Jarvik to test his work on a human. Working with lead surgeon William DeVries (the only physician the US Food and Drug Administration would allow to implant a Jarvik-7), the two doctors began surgery on a retired sixty-one-year-old dentist named Barney Clark, who was dying from cardiomyopathy. Clark lived for 112 days with the pyrolytic carbon and titanium heart, and Jarvik became a global sensation.

"It was riveting, but it was terrifying," said Jarvik of the twelve-hour procedure in December 1982. "Especially at the point when the heart was 'in' and there were some tears in the lungs and some problems looked like they could be insurmountable. They had to be fixed right then. I don't think I've had another experience with that kind of fear and that kind of elation when it all worked."

Clark's death resulted in more research and tweaking of the Jarvik-7. Bill Schroeder, the next patient to receive one, lived a record-setting 620 days.

The Jarvik-7 proved artificial hearts could work as a "bridge to transplantation," but the use of compressed air in a prosthetic device caused infections "stemming from the drive lines connecting the heart to the power source." In medical terms, the pericardial membrane surrounding the implanted organ could fail because it provided an inadequate blood supply to fight infections.

Believing the Jarvik-7 would work on a widespread basis was "probably the biggest mistake I ever made," Jarvik told *Syracuse University Magazine*. "I think it's appropriate to recognize the Jarvik-7 heart as a device of limited clinical applicability now, but [it was] a good research device."

Jarvik left the University of Utah and his management of Symbion Inc. in the late 1980s and returned to New York, where he established Jarvik Research and married Marilyn vos Savant, the human with the highest intelligence level ever recorded. Working with vos Savant, Jarvik created Jarvik Heart Inc., amassed more than thirty US and foreign patents in heart technology, and invented the Jarvik 2000.

"He is absolutely the most brilliant person I've ever met," said vos Savant, a longtime writer for *Parade* with her "Ask Marilyn" column. "And a hero."

In June 2000, Peter Houghton, the first lifetime-use patient, received a Jarvik 2000. This model (much more than a bridge device) was outfitted with an infection-resistant component and was enhanced by attaching the power source behind the patient's ear. It allowed Houghton to live an additional seven years, during which time he traveled extensively, hiked in high altitude, and authored two books.

Speaking at the 2016 Arents Awards, Jarvik noted that more than fifty thousand patients had received artificial hearts since 1982 and that life-extending heart technology was available in hundreds of hospitals all over the world. That's largely because of Robert Jarvik's creativity, love of science, and what one heart surgeon called "Mozartian genius."

Betsey Johnson

Fashion Designer

For one Syracuse University legend, it started with a prom dress.

Or, as fashion icon Betsey Johnson described it, "the dorkiest ballerina-type frock."

"For my senior year [of high school], I practically made my prom dress," she once told a reporter. "I don't think my parents paid more than $50 or $60 for it. Then I encrusted it, stamped on the diamonds and sewed on the dripping pearls. I wasn't a designer back then, but I had my dancing school [background]. That was like one big prom, especially during the recitals. I should have been a costume designer."

Instead, as Johnson revealed in a 2015 Council of Fashion Designers of America Lifetime Achievement Award video, she started designing clothes to fit her own body, something she described as a normal body, and realized if she stuck to designing what she herself loved, future customers might like her designs as well.

And, oh, what designs she fabricated.

For the last five decades—an eternity in designer years—Johnson's crazy, colorful, whimsical, head-scratching, spectacular sense of fun fashion has given America one of the world's most distinctive voices.

That shouldn't surprise Syracuse alumni.

Johnson graduated Phi Beta Kappa from Syracuse in 1964, and shortly thereafter she won *Mademoiselle*'s Guest Editor Contest and was selected to work at the magazine as an intern. Her predecessors in that position? Joan Didion and Sylvia Plath.

She also pushed herself into the middle of the Andy Warhol pop art revolution, the youthquake boutique vibe, and a seriously gritty New York City music scene (most notably, Max's Kansas City). It was in these late night clubs that she reconnected with rocker (and SU alumnus) Lou Reed, his seminal band the Velvet Underground, and Reed's Welsh-born guitarist John Cale, whom she married in 1968.

Betsey Johnson. ERIC THAYER / Reuters Pictures.

"We were a bunch of poor, frantic, lonely, creative kids," she told the *New York Times* in 2012. "Everyone was taking speed. Not me. I only took diet pills."

If mid-1960s Manhattan was one of the "wild sides" of the planet, then the middle of the decade was the time when millions of baby boomer women began rejecting the constrained feminine ideal that dominated the 1950s. And it was Johnson, with her frantic haircuts, fake eyelashes, and stark lipstick, standing at the forefront of the attack on cultural norms.

It started with her time as the in-house designer for New York City boutique Paraphernalia, where she unveiled neon green, pink, and yellow microskirts stuffed into tennis-ball cans or silver motorcycle jackets. After that, Johnson started her own boutique called Betsey Bunky Nini, where Warhol ingenue Edie Sedgwick, the supposed inspiration for some of Bob Dylan's most remembered songs, worked as Johnson's fit model.

From this Upper East Side location, Johnson began "draping" the revolution with her "space age, silvery sci-fi dresses, see-through plastic shifts with discreet stick-on cover-ups, a 'noise dress' with metal grommets at the hem that went clink-clank when the wearer moved, elephant bell-bottoms and 14-inch metal micro-miniskirts."

The Sirens of the city soon noticed Johnson's avant-garde look, and it wasn't long before former First Lady Jackie Kennedy, ultrathin model Twiggy, and such actresses as French star Brigitte Bardot, England's Julie Christie, and Ali McGraw were showcasing Johnson-designed fashions.

"When I wore my Betsey micro-mini crossing 39th Street at First Avenue, the truck drivers coming out of the Midtown Tunnel would go crazy," McGraw once said.

The reason? Johnson-designed clothing really could stop traffic.

"I stick to my guns, my sheaths and my sexpots," Johnson once said. "And I've always kept the price of a dress at or below the price of a round-trip weekend in Puerto Rico. That's been my formula."

Notwithstanding the fact Johnson declared bankruptcy in 2012, she has always been price conscious, yet consistent in her own vibrant look as well as the rebellious designs she has practically trademarked. From "new-wave colors, skin-tight party dresses, prom-queen-gone-rogue petticoats," or "ballet skirts over a leotard," she has pushed the conservative nature of Fashion Week and the fashionistas who influence American shoppers.

"She got on the street fashion wagon before anyone," wrote *Vogue* magazine's Susie Billingsley. "She's always been way ahead of what's hip."

Some reviewers point to her work for clothing label Alley Cat, but many believe a real turning point for Johnson occurred in 1978 when the punk rock scene exploded around grunge club CBGB. That year, Johnson and former model Chantal Bacon pooled their resources to open a store in SoHo and create the Betsey Johnson label.

"She's always been either the youngest old fashion designer in the world," said fashion consultant Fern Mallis, "or the oldest young one."

She has also been honored with just about every fashion design award anyone has thought to give out. The Pratt Institute Award, the CFDA's Timeless Talent Award, the Coty Award. She's appeared on *Dancing with the Stars* and even hosted her own reality show on the Style Network.

Shocking, bold, excited, important, trendsetting, visionary, a champion—there just aren't enough adjectives to describe the fashion bulldozer that is Betsey Johnson, who shows no signs of slowing down.

In the last decade, since selling her name brand to business partner Steve Madden in 2010, she has served as the creative director for Betsey Johnson-licensed dresses, shoes, pocketbooks, perfumes, pajamas, jewelry, and bedding.

All from one sparkly prom dress.

Ted Koppel

Journalist

Perhaps if legendary Syracuse University football coach Ben Schwartzwalder had been a little more visionary and taken the young man up on his radical offer, the course of Ted Koppel's life would have taken a dramatic turn. Maybe, six decades later, we'd be talking about how Koppel revolutionized football instead of television journalism.

British-born and raised, he had been weaned on soccer and became an excellent striker for the Orange in the late 1950s—good enough to garner a few All-American votes. Convinced SU's place-kicking needed improvement, Koppel audaciously approached Schwartzwalder to offer his services. In those days, football was far less specialized, and no coach in college or the pros had a guy on his roster who did nothing but kick. Those chores usually were handled by a position player, which is why in addition to playing running back and linebacker and returning kicks, the great Jim Brown also kicked extra points.

Koppel, who had immigrated to the United States when he was thirteen, thought he could dramatically improve SU's kicking and possibly become a secret weapon. Schwartzwalder thought he was nuts.

"I still had an English accent, and I was not the imposing figure I am today," the five-foot-nine Koppel joked in a 2005 interview with the *Washington Post*. "Ben took one look at me and said, 'We don't have an extra position.' And that was that."

Koppel claims he—and not former Buffalo Bills and New York Giants standout Pete Gogolak—came up with the idea of soccer-style placekicking. As we've since learned, booting the ball with the side of your foot rather than your toe is far more accurate, which is why every kicker at virtually every level utilizes the sidewinding style. And why virtually every team at every level has a specialist who does nothing but kick.

"I was the first to think of it," Koppel said. "I was ahead of Gogolak. It would have been a big deal."

If only Koppel had patented it. He would have made millions.

Before the start of his senior year at Syracuse in 1959, he was forced to choose between soccer—which he had played since he was old enough to walk—and a job as the program director of WAER-FM, the campus radio station. "I had to weigh my chances of a career as a professional soccer player in the United States against broadcasting," he said. "I thought about it for, oh, maybe 30 seconds." After a brief pause, Koppel added with a chuckle: "I made the wrong choice. I coulda been a contender."

Ted Koppel with Frank Langella. © Syracuse University. Photo by Stephen Sartori.

Ted Koppel considers an issue on the set of ABC's *Nightline*. Douglas Kirkland / Corbis Premium Historical / Getty Images.

Instead of becoming a soccer contender, he became a journalism heavyweight.

Koppel would spend forty-two years with ABC, including twenty-five as the anchor and managing editor of *Nightline*, the first late night network television news show. In addition to receiving critical acclaim and drastically changing the format of news shows, *Nightline* was able to attract an enormous viewership and successfully battle late night ratings giants Johnny Carson and David Letterman. On the eve of Koppel's final appearance in 2005, one historian called it "the most significant addition to TV news since 60 *Minutes* was created in the 1960s."

And the reason it worked was Koppel, who had a knack for making complex issues comprehensible, and whose tenacious interviewing skills usually unearthed the truth. *Newsweek* magazine called him "the smartest man on television." The *Los Angeles Times* described him as "the undisputed reigning lion of tough TV interview journalism."

Winner of an astounding forty-two Emmy Awards and a member of the Broadcasting Hall of Fame, Koppel helped pioneer the satellite age of television news, deftly using the evolving technology to simultaneously stage interviews with three or four people from around the globe. Whether it was grilling world leaders or discussing the meaning of life with a dying college professor, Koppel got to the heart of the story.

His own story was quite compelling, too. He was born in Lancashire, England, in 1940, just a few years after his Jewish parents fled Nazi Germany. The seed for Koppel's love of journalism was inspired by Edward R. Murrow, who received acclaim for his radio reports of the bombings of Britain. Koppel's family moved to New York City when he was thirteen years old, and he admitted to having some difficulty assimilating.

Although SU would change his life for the better, it was not his first choice. In fact, it was his third. He wound up there only after Princeton rejected him and he was turned down by a Vermont college because he had submitted his fifty dollar application fee too late.

The Newhouse School didn't exist back then, so Koppel majored in speech and dramatic arts. His journalism training came while working at WAER. "I probably spent half my life at the radio station," he said.

A gifted student, Koppel earned membership into several academic honor societies. "He was incredibly focused and had a photographic memory," a college roommate recalled. "He remembers almost every conversation he ever had with anybody."

Upon receiving his bachelor of science degree, Koppel went to Stanford, where he received a master's degree in mass communications. He began work with ABC news in 1963 at age twenty-three, making him the youngest reporter at the network. Koppel's radio coverage of John F. Kennedy's assassination earned him high praise from his bosses and listeners, and he began a rapid ascent up the network ladder, serving as the Saigon bureau chief during the Vietnam War before eventually transitioning to television news.

In 1979, after fifty-two Americans were taken hostage by Iranian militants, ABC began a late night show to cover developments. By March 1980, the show became known as *Nightline*, and Koppel was chosen to be the anchor. The issue-oriented, analytical interview program was a perfect match for the big-brained Koppel, and it would completely change not only the landscape of late night television but the timeliness and format of news shows themselves.

Following a quarter century of anchoring *Nightline*, Koppel left ABC to write several books and work with the Discovery Channel, NBC News, and National Public Radio. The reverence for his work was underscored by the more than twenty honorary degrees he has received, including a doctorate of laws from Syracuse in 1982. Twice his alma mater asked him to deliver commencement addresses. At the 2000 convocation in the Carrier Dome, he urged the graduates "to listen to their conscience and use their influence and power to alleviate suffering around the world."

He had spent a lifetime traveling the globe to report about that suffering.

Football's loss was journalism's gain.

Sheldon Leonard

Actor, Television Visionary

All the world was a stage for Sheldon Leonard when he was a student at Syracuse University during the Roaring Twenties. When he wasn't studying or practicing as a member of the varsity football and swim teams, you usually could find him acting in several campus plays.

Leonard's swarthy good looks and deep, distinctive, tough-guy voice helped him become a commanding stage presence under the tutelage of famed SU drama professor Sawyer Falk. But despite his

Sheldon Leonard from the classic film *It's a Wonderful Life* with Jimmy Stewart. © Melange Pictures LLC. All Rights Reserved.

theatrical abilities and passion, Leonard had no desire to make a career of it. He realized grinding out a life as a thespian was not practical, so upon graduating in 1929 with a degree in sociology and a Phi Beta Kappa key, he took the job that made sense and cents. It was off to Wall Street to broker stocks instead of Broadway to deliver lines.

Let's just say his timing wasn't impeccable. That October brought the stock market crash that plunged America into the Great Depression. Leonard soon found himself among the millions of newly unemployed, and after thrashing about as a longshoreman, printing salesman, and lifeguard, he decided to reunite with an old love: acting.

A star would be born, not necessarily on the stages of the Great White Way, nor on the silver screens of Hollywood, where Leonard would act in more than 140 films. But rather behind the scenes, where his writing, directing, and producing genius would create some of the most iconic television shows and characters of all time.

He wound up being nominated for nine Emmy Awards, winning three times, and earned induction into the Television Hall of Fame

Sheldon Leonard (center) during a *Dick Van Dyke Show* table read with Dick Van Dyke and Mary Tyler Moore. Allan Grant / The LIFE Images Collection / Getty Images.

in 1992. Dubbed the "King Midas of television programming" for his uncanny ability to take the pulse of American audiences during the 1950s, 1960s, and 1970s, Leonard enjoyed a stretch of several months where three of his programs—*The Dick Van Dyke Show*, *The Andy Griffith Show*, and *Gomer Pyle, U.S.M.C.*—were among the ten most watched shows in America.

"What he likes in his gut, the public likes in their guts," a fellow producer once marveled about him. "On television, that's worth more than a crystal ball."

A *New York Times* critic called him "the most successful and influential independent television producer of his time." Another writer referred to him as "the father of the situation comedy."

Leonard is credited with inventing the television spin-off. He developed a sitcom in which Andy Griffith would play a sheriff in a small southern town. Leonard saved the expense of making a pilot by introducing Griffith and the other characters on *The Danny Thomas Show*. Viewers fell in love with the characters and concept, and *The Andy Griffith Show* started airing not long after, running for eight years. In 1964, there was a spin-off of the spin-off when Jim Nabors, who played the gas station attendant on the Griffith show, was given his own series, *Gomer Pyle, U.S.M.C.*, which ran for five years.

For his *I Spy* series, which debuted in 1965, Leonard cast a young comedian named Bill Cosby to play opposite Robert Culp. It was a bold move at the time because Cosby was an African American, and no black actor had played a leading role on a network television series. Cosby initially struggled to make the transition from comedian to serious actor, and network officials pressured Leonard to replace him.

"I felt Bill would work the kinks out and be just fine, and that the unspoken reason the executives wanted to find somebody else is that they were concerned how their network affiliates in the South might react," Leonard recalled. "I told the execs not to worry and give Bill a chance. But they persisted. They became adamant and I finally said, 'If you replace him, then you'll have to replace me, too. End of discussion.'"

Actor and producer stayed, and the program became a ratings winner and was critically acclaimed. Three decades before Cosby's star plummeted after dozens of sexual abuse accusations, he helped open the door for other black actors. And that wouldn't have happened had Leonard not stood his ground.

"After that, I felt I left my mark on television," the legendary director said in a 1994 interview with the *Syracuse Post-Standard*.

Following Wall Street's collapse, Leonard played the real-life role of starving actor for several years before making his Broadway debut in 1934 in a play titled *Hotel Alimony*. "Out of an inherent sense of decency, I was tempted to ignore *Hotel Alimony* as though it had never happened," wrote critic Burns Mantle. "Reviewing is a dirty job, but someone has to do it." Despite the skewering, Mantle and other critics were kind to Leonard, and the actor's

performances in ensuing plays would earn him rave reviews and a steady stream of work.

During this time, Leonard also acted in a few nondescript movies, and by the end of the decade the siren call of Hollywood was too hard to resist. The Brooklyn native became a prolific character actor, often portraying snarling, underworld figures who talked out of the sides of their mouths and carried gangster nicknames like Pretty Willie, Harry the Horse, Louie, Lefty, and Blackie.

Leonard worked with some of film's biggest stars, sharing the screen with Humphrey Bogart, Lauren Bacall, Errol Flynn, Spencer Tracy, and Katharine Hepburn. While on the set of *To Have and Have Not*, Leonard played matchmaker, introducing Bogart to his future wife, Bacall. "It was quite an extraordinary thing to see," Leonard recalled in an interview with *Modern Times Magazine*. "Bogey, the cool sophisticate, turned into a teenager around [Bacall]."

None of Leonard's roles would be more enduring than that of the bartender who threw Jimmy Stewart into a snowbank in *It's a Wonderful Life*. Initially perceived as a disappointment, the Frank Capra film has come to be revered as a classic.

Television intrigued Leonard from the start, and he joined Danny Thomas in 1953 before eventually branching off on his own. His timing couldn't have been better because the medium was rapidly ascending into an immensely popular form of entertainment in post–World War II America. Always the innovator, Leonard was credited with introducing motion picture filming techniques to the small screen.

And he was more than willing to share his creative ideas. "I learned how to be a producer by watching what Sheldon did," said Carl Reiner, who worked with him on *The Dick Van Dyke Show*. "Sheldon mentored more people in our business than anyone else I know."

Those students included Academy Award-winning director Ron Howard. It was Leonard who convinced Howard's father that playing Griffith's son, Opie, on the television series would not ruin the boy's life.

Leonard's kindness extended to Syracuse, where he established fellowships to study television audiences, and where he returned frequently to lecture. It was a relationship he maintained until his death at age eighty-nine in 1997.

More than two decades later, his influence on television endures. The characters Sheldon Cooper and Leonard Hofstadter on CBS-TV's *The Big Bang Theory* series are named in his honor.

Floyd Little

Football Player, Entrepreneur

There were murmurs the new kid on the block was even better than two of the Syracuse University football players who had worn the Number 44 jersey before him. And that was saying something, since

Floyd Little. Athletics Department, Syracuse University, used by permission.

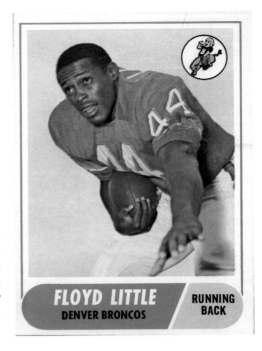

Floyd Little's 1968 NFL football trading card. Topps® trading cards courtesy of The Topps Company, Inc. Jeff Rubin, private collection.

the first notable 44 already owned six NFL rushing titles and the second 44 had won the Heisman Trophy. But when Floyd Little struggled in his first varsity football game at Boston College during the 1964 season opener, many Orange fans wondered what the hype had been about. Perhaps the coaches, reporters, and fans had been duped, gotten their hopes too high. Maybe Little wasn't cut from the same cloth as his famous predecessors, Jim Brown and Ernie Davis.

It wouldn't take long for Little to allay such concerns. In game two of his varsity football career at Syracuse—his first in front of fans at Archbold Stadium—he proved he was a worthy successor. Faster than you could say "Touchdown, Orange!" it became obvious this Little would go a long way.

Nationally ranked Kansas came to town that week, and most of the media attention focused on Gale Sayers, the Jayhawks senior running back who had earned All-American honors in 1963. The future Pro Football Hall of Famer was expected to put on a show, and the Orangemen were underdogs. On that September afternoon, however, Sayers would be upstaged by Little, who turned in one of the greatest individual performances in SU sports history.

The bow-legged, five-foot-eleven, 190-pound running back from New Haven, Connecticut, thrilled the crowd of twenty-eight thousand spectators by rushing for 159 yards and five touchdowns on just sixteen carries as the Orangemen crushed Kansas, 38-6. In addition to scoring on runs of 15, 1, 53, 3, and 19 yards, Little also caught two passes for 47 yards. That, along with the yardage he gained returning punts and kicks, enabled him to finish with a total of 254 yards. "That was the greatest performance by a back that I have ever seen," Kansas coach Jack Mitchell told reporters afterward—an extravagant compliment, considering Mitchell had been an eyewitness to Sayers's entertaining runs for two seasons.

It would not be the last compliment Little would receive from opposing coaches during the next three autumns. After watching him shred his defense, Penn State's legendary coach Joe Paterno quipped: "The best defense against him, I have decided, is to have

my old mother in Brooklyn say a novena." Army coach Paul Dietzel called Little "the greatest back in America."

His performance against Kansas was a harbinger of good things, as Little would go on to break virtually every record Brown and Davis had established. He'd also become the first SU football player since Joe Alexander (1918-20) to earn All-American honors three consecutive seasons, and some were convinced that Little would have gone four-for-four had he not played during an era when freshmen weren't eligible to play varsity sports.

He wound up finishing fifth in the Heisman Trophy voting his senior year, and he might have won the award presented annually to the nation's best college football player had the voting been conducted after he rushed for 216 yards in the 1966 Gator Bowl.

Little went on to earn four Pro Bowl invitations and one NFL rushing title while helping the Denver Broncos establish themselves as one of the league's most successful franchises. In 2010, his professional career finally received the recognition it merited when Little was inducted into the Pro Football Hall of Fame in Canton, Ohio. Following his playing career, he earned his law degree from the University of Denver and became a successful businessman in the automotive industry.

In 2011, several years after selling his profitable car dealerships, Little returned to Syracuse University as an assistant to athletics director Daryl Gross. During his five years on the job, he spent plenty of time mentoring student-athletes.

"It was my favorite job ever, and that's saying something because I was blessed to have some pretty good careers along the way," Little said. "I loved every minute of it because every day I got an opportunity to motivate and inspire young people. I got a chance to help them realize that Syracuse University was a place where their dreams could come true. I was living proof of that."

Little ultimately decided on Syracuse over the US Military Academy at West Point because he had given Davis his word that he would attend SU. He told Orange football coach Ben Schwartz-walder he was coming after receiving news on May 18, 1963, that Davis had died of leukemia at age twenty-three, just two years after becoming the first African American to win the Heisman.

"It was one of the best decisions of my life," Little said.

Few, including Little himself, had envisioned he would ever make it to college. His father died of cancer when he was six, and his mother raised him and his five siblings on meager earnings and welfare. He struggled in school, particularly with reading, and failed the fifth grade. And when he finally graduated from high school at age nineteen, his prospects for a successful life seemed gloomy at best.

"I was told I was too dumb to go to college," he said. "But you try going without eating for two days and see how well you would do on tests."

With the help of his high school coach, Don Casey, Little enrolled at Bordentown Military Academy in New Jersey. The prep school's structured setting did wonders for him, and Little wound up excelling in football and the classroom.

General Douglas MacArthur caught wind of his exploits and attempted to recruit him to play football for Army. Little was all set to enroll at the academy—until Davis died, and Little remembered how he gave the Heisman Trophy winner his word that he was going to attend SU during a recruiting visit a few weeks after he had dinner with MacArthur.

"There went my plans on becoming the first African American five-star general," Little joked. "But that's OK. Thanks to my hero, Ernie Davis, I wound up at the place I was meant to be all along. It's a place where my dreams came true. A place I'll always consider home."

Belva Lockwood

Lawyer, Presidential Candidate, Women's Rights Activist

Shortly after graduating from high school in the late 1840s, Belva Lockwood began teaching summer school in her hometown of Royalton, New York, not far from Niagara Falls. It was a rewarding experience until she discovered her male counterpart was earning two to three times what she was. As she later would write, this was "odious, an indignity not to be tamely borne."

Decades later, after receiving a master of arts degree from Syracuse University and a law degree from the National University Law School, Lockwood relentlessly lobbied a US congressman to introduce legislation creating equal pay for equal work for all government employees. Although the law that passed was watered down, salaries and opportunities for female civil servants improved dramatically.

Belva Lockwood. US Postal Service.

It would be one of many victories for the intrepid Lockwood, who made a life out of not suffering indignities tamely. Known for her tenacity and indomitable spirit, Lockwood clearly was a woman way ahead of her time; a woman who refused to accept discriminatory laws and who devoted decades to seeking equal rights for women, Native Americans, African Americans, and immigrants.

Despite a lack of support from family and friends—her father once told her that "girls get married; boys go to college"—she pursued her higher education and used the knowledge she gained to throw off what she called "a woman's shackles." Like more celebrated suffragist contemporaries Susan B. Anthony and Elizabeth Cady Stanton, Lockwood blazed many trails before dying at age eighty-six on May 19, 1917—just a month after the first woman was sworn in as a member of Congress and just three years before the ratification of the Nineteenth Amendment, which gave women the right to vote.

In 1884—thirteen years after graduating from Syracuse—she became the first female to run a full presidential campaign and receive votes in an election. (Victoria Woodhull ran a partial campaign in 1872 but dropped out months before Election Day.) Nearly a century before presidential longshots such as Margaret Chase Smith and Shirley Chisholm, and 132 years before Hillary Rodham Clinton's historic run in which she garnered more popular votes than

A Belva Lockwood stock certificate. Ken Florey Suffrage Collection / Gado / Getty Images.

winner Donald Trump, Lockwood's candidacy created quite the stir. This was, after all, post–Civil War America, a time when women were expected to run households, not for office. She promised to "seek equal political privileges for all people irrespective of sex, color or nationality" in order to make the United States "the true land of the free and home of the brave." She said that if elected she would appoint a reasonable number of female district attorneys and federal judges, and would even nominate a "competent woman to any vacancy that might occur on the United States Supreme Court bench."

Her campaign was considered radical and was lampooned by many political cartoonists. Some men, amused by the idea of a woman running for president, formed Belva Lockwood Clubs, which held faux rallies in which cross-dressing men pretended to be Lockwood and her supporters, delivering fake speeches and holding satirical parades. Through it all, Lockwood remained unflappable. She had been subjected to ridicule throughout her life because of her gender, so she had developed skin as thick as a tortoise's shell. As more than one hundred farmers, journalists, suffragists, and curiosity-seekers looked on at her campaign kickoff rally at a Maryland train station, she delivered a memorable quip: "I cannot vote, but I can be voted for."

Lockwood was not only thick-skinned, but realistic. She understood she had no chance of winning. But she did manage to receive at least 4,100 votes in an election won by Democratic candidate Grover Cleveland.

She would run unsuccessfully again in 1888, and although that would be her final crack at elected office, she remained an agent of change through her work as an attorney. She became the first woman to argue a case before the US Supreme Court and would be involved in a number of high profile trials. These included a successful lawsuit on behalf of the Cherokee tribe for a treaty violation, which resulted in an award of $5 million, at the time the largest monetary compensation in US jurisprudence history.

That she was even able to practice law was a victory in itself. Lockwood had been rejected by several law schools because of her gender. One school even told her she had been turned down because she "would be too much of a distraction to the male students." She wound up at the National University Law School, where a progressive-thinking vice chancellor offered to teach her outside the classroom.

After she successfully completed her studies, the school refused to issue her a diploma. Since President Ulysses S. Grant was the titular head of the school, Lockwood wrote him a polite letter telling him about her dilemma. When she didn't hear back from the White House, she wrote another letter several weeks later. This correspondence was less polite. Lockwood never received a reply from the president, but she did receive her diploma after the second letter.

She became the second woman admitted to the bar in the District of Columbia and embarked on a legal career in which she would knock down one barrier after another. She wound up practicing law until the age of eighty-one. In 1908, she became the first woman to receive an honorary doctor of laws degree from Syracuse University. Seventy-five years later, she was inducted posthumously into the National Women's Hall of Fame in Seneca Falls, New York. In 1986, the US Postal Service feted her with a stamp bearing her likeness. And in the 1990s, a crater on the planet Venus was named in her honor.

Oren Lyons

Activist, Ambassador

The concept of "playing hurt" has never been lost on faithkeeper and Onondaga Nation chief Oren Lyons. And that's not surprising, because as a Native American growing up on land claimed and then dominated by foreigners from other continents, there has always been pain. How could there not be?

Inside the Onondaga Nation, there were numerous social challenges. Away from home, the realities of the early 1950s included racism and cultural ignorance. It meant the decision to attend Syracuse would have been particularly daunting.

A talented artist but a high school dropout who had joined the Army (Airborne) to avoid the likelihood of failure in a "white" school, Lyons's consideration of a university degree was a massive leap of faith at a time when people of color were almost nonexistent on private school campuses.

Lyons ultimately earned his high school equivalency diploma and returned to the Onondaga Nation. The Onondagas are one of six nations of the Iroquois Confederacy, which also includes the Seneca, Cayuga, Oneida, Mohawk, and Tuscarora tribes. For almost a thousand years, the nations have honored their Creator by playing lacrosse.

Oren Lyons addressing the United Nations. UN Photo by Eskinder Debebe.

Oren Lyons poses with Yoko Ono, John Lennon, and Leon Shenandoah during a protest of Highway 81 running through Onondaga Nation land in 1971. Courtesy of Joe Heath.

Orange lacrosse coach Roy Simmons Sr. was fully aware of Lyons's capacities as a goalie and extremely talented illustrator. It took repeated calls, but the Hall of Fame coach "finally convinced the [Syracuse] admissions committee that this skilled artist deserved a chance." That opportunity came in the mid-1950s, a time when Syracuse's lacrosse program not only featured the coach's son, Roy Simmons Jr., but also arguably the greatest lacrosse and football player of that era, Jim Brown.

In one game, a 1957 contest where Brown scored six goals to beat Army, 8-6, it was Lyons who preserved a perfect 10-0 season by making clutch save after save.

"Oren was on his knees at one point and he stopped three straight shots within a matter of seconds," Simmons recalled of his quiet All-American goalkeeper, who was playing with torn knee ligaments. "He would stop shots no one else would even think of stopping. You could see that he was in pain [but] you always knew Oren would be out there when it counted, no matter what."

Lyons's life has consistently echoed that last sentiment.

Time and time again during the next sixty years, the chief of the Onondaga's Turtle Clan would blaze ambassadorial trails by serving as an advocate for Native Americans and indigenous people throughout the world. He would also become a strong voice for the planet itself.

Those dirt paths and paved roads brought Lyons to places such as the United Nations, the famed Pine Ridge Agency (site of the infamous Wounded Knee incident), Moscow, New Zealand, Rio de Janeiro, and seemingly every corner of the globe as he sought (or fought) to inform governments and the media about original inhabitants or environmental destruction.

Along the way, he also would coauthor or contribute chapters to numerous books, such as *Exiled in the Land of the Free: Democracy, Indian Nations and the U.S. Constitution, Treaty of Canandaigua 1794,* and *Spiritual Ecology.* He's also been featured in a major documentary produced by Leonardo DiCaprio (*The Eleventh Hour*) and won numerous honors, including the National Audubon Society's Audubon Medal, the Elder and Wiser Award of the Rosa Parks Institute for Human Rights, the Ellis Island Medal of Honor, and an honorary doctor of laws degree from Syracuse University.

Lyons has even had an international living center at SU named after him: Oren Lyons Hall on Euclid Avenue. At the building's rededication in 2007, Chancellor Nancy Cantor recognized Lyons and spoke of "his contributions as a scholar, athlete, teacher, author, artist, diplomat, environmentalist, human rights activist, historian, and faithkeeper." Her acknowledgment of him and the Onondaga people also led to the creation of the Haudenosaunee Promise, which provides scholarships to eligible Haudenosaunee students.

But accolades are not what has motivated Lyons.

What has always mattered was honorably representing his people. It started with the Red Power movement of the 1960s, but by 1971 it grew to include blocking Route 81 from expanding onto Onondaga tribal lands. During that protest, he was joined by former Beatle John Lennon and his wife Yoko Ono. In 1972, his organization of the Trail of Broken Treaties (a caravan "march" on Washington, DC) was widely noted. It was followed by his presence at a bloody 1973 standoff in South Dakota at Wounded Knee.

"At first, I wanted to defend the Iroquois," said Lyons, who was born a Seneca but was adopted into the Onondagas. "Then my sights broadened to embrace other Indians. Then I saw this had to include defending indigenous peoples all over the world."

So he has done that, traveling tirelessly to rally people for important causes.

During the 1990s, he journeyed to Russia three times to meet with Soviet leader Mikhail Gorbachev, and he spoke at the Global Forum of Religious and Parliamentary Leaders for Human Survival. That same decade, he spoke in Brazil at the United Nations Conference on Environment and Development, known by many as the Earth Summit. In the millennial year of 2000, he went to the United Nations to address religious leaders at the World Peace Summit. A year later he attended the first World Conference against Racism.

"We have probably fifty years to change our direction," Lyons said in 2001. "If we don't, we're facing a bitter end. There's a point of no return when you can't fix the environment."

There has also been a need to explain distinct points of view that are sometimes obscured by cultural differences.

As Lyons once told SU's *Alumni News,* "the white man's version [of the sale of Manhattan] is literal. But the Indians have no concept of buying land. It would be like selling part of the air. The Indians thought they were agreeing to share the land. Where the white man says, 'This land is mine,' the Indian says, 'This land is ours.'"

That countless citizens of the world have thought about the land, water, or air they breathe is tribute to the advocacy of Oren Lyons. The 1958 graduate and Hall of Fame lacrosse player may have stopped shots on his knees and stood strong at Wounded Knee, but he has never gone to his knees when it came to the truth.

Mike McAlary

Columnist

He came to Syracuse University as a transfer student, and before he'd written a single story for the *Daily Orange* he was selected as the school paper's sports editor.

He was that good. And like a lot of the twentieth century's greats, he died young.

Born in Honolulu but raised in the Flatbush section of Brooklyn and then in Goffstown, New Hampshire, Mike McAlary started writing in high school. He had freelanced for the *Boston Globe* and *Tennis Illustrated* before he even arrived on the SU campus during the summer of 1976. When he moved back to the Boston area after graduating, he covered sports, but his heart seemed to favor crime.

What followed was one of the most distinguished (and controversial) journalism careers ever, with the *New York Daily News* and *New York Post* both spending millions in bidding wars to feature his column.

Like city columnists before him—notably Jimmy Breslin, Murray Kempton, and Pete Hamill—McAlary seemed to spring from the pages of a Damon Runyon column or Mickey Spillane novel. Much of that achievement was by design, and after his passing in 1998, classmates remembered how he had boasted during his time at SU that he would be the next Breslin.

"He had the ability to get sources to talk to him," *New York Times* editor and *Daily Orange* alumnus Tom Coffey told *Syracuse University Magazine*. "He had great instincts for what people wanted to read."

Mike McAlary. Pat Carroll / New York Daily News Archive / Getty Images.

"Most cops look down on newspaper reporters, but they didn't look down on him," New York City deputy police commissioner John Timoney told the *New York Times*. "I think it was the toughness. He was a tough guy, physically and mentally, and wasn't afraid to go into bad neighborhoods or call somebody a dog. And he looked like a cop himself."

The fact that McAlary was willing to risk it all for a story, to go where others felt uncomfortable, to wait up and drink with the cops, or to take on corrupt police systems regardless of the circumstances was just part of his makeup.

He'd had good practice drinking and brawling during his time at Syracuse. Finishing his shift at the *Daily Orange* (with a wildly talented group of 1979 classmates like Maura McEnaney and Mike Stanton, who also won Pulitzer Prizes), McAlary often would move to the Orange, a hole-in-the-wall bar on South Crouse Avenue around the corner from Marshall Street. Stories of his wildness were legendary, but as former *Daily Orange* editor-in-chief Jim Naughton recalled, "Even back then, Mike was cultivating his 'man of the people' persona."

McAlary's first major "cops and crime" adventure may have happened in 1986, when he started detailing the corruption of New York's Seventy-Seventh Precinct (Brooklyn North) by getting a number of policemen to open up and tell him what was really happening at the station house. It led to a 1987 nonfiction book called *Buddy Boys* that became the basis for the movie *Cop Land*, a gritty 1997 thriller featuring Sylvester Stallone and Robert De Niro.

That same year, McAlary broke his biggest story, a nine-part, three-month expose of police brutality that led to his winning the 1998 Pulitzer Prize for Commentary. His searing work on the Brooklyn police station torture of Haitian immigrant Abner Louima for the *Daily News* solidified his position as a tabloid reporter who would not back down.

McAlary wrote four books—*Buddy Boys: When Good Cops Turn Bad*; *Cop Shot: The Murder of Edward Byrne*; *Good Cop, Bad Cop: Detective Joe Trimboli's Heroic Pursuit of NYPD Officer Michael Dowd*; and *Sore Loser: A Mickey Donovan Mystery*. But he is remembered less for those manuscripts than for his relentless commitment to the dirty truth. For daily newspaper readers of the 1980s and 1990s, there were few journalists anywhere who could touch him.

And while others will continue to win journalism prizes and accolades, few ever will have an author of Nora Ephron's stature write a Broadway show about a Syracuse grad that survived scandals (some of his own making), a near-fatal car crash, or the crushing weight of cancer and chemotherapy while working feverishly on the Louima story. In fact, one story that stands above many tells of McAlary walking out of a chemotherapy session to get the first interview with Abner Louima.

McAlary died of colon cancer at forty-one in the city he eagerly watched over. The day after his death, the *New York Times*, a paper he never wrote for, used the headline "Mike McAlary, 41, Columnist With Swagger to Match City's."

It was a headline his friends claimed he would have liked. And while his death was greatly mourned by the Syracuse alumni who had written alongside him at the *DO*, his imprint lives on via books, movies, and plays. The Ron Howard-directed film *The Paper* was reportedly made with McAlary in mind. And Ephron's 2013 Tony Award-winning Broadway show *Lucky Guy* was performed in 2013 by Tom Hanks starring as McAlary.

F. Story Musgrave

Astronaut

To escape the pain and chaos wrought by alcoholic parents, Franklin Story Musgrave occasionally would sneak out of his family's farmhouse at night so he could lie in fields and gaze at the stars. During these respites, the future astronaut would let his imagination run wild, dreaming about what it must be like to be up there in the cosmos.

Decades later, Musgrave would discover firsthand what it was like to be up there—participating in a record-tying six space shuttle missions while helping launch the Skylab space station and repair the Hubble Space Telescope. The Syracuse University alumnus was sixty-one years old at the time of his last mission in 1996, making him at the time the oldest-ever space traveler. But even at that age, he approached his NASA assignments with the wonderment and curiosity of that child who once peered at the heavens in amazement.

"If I had to boil my 30 years of experience with NASA down to one sentence, I'd say it's the quest for meaning," Musgrave said in a 1997 interview with *Syracuse University Magazine*. "What does it mean to be human? What is our place in the universe? That is what space is all about. It's about a whole bunch else, too, but I think at the root, that's the motivation. It's the journey that counts. It is the quest, the pursuit of meaning."

And few have traveled more meaningful or varied journeys than Musgrave, whose unquenchable curiosity prompted him to take his alma mater's "knowledge crowns those who seek her" motto to a whole new stratosphere. Despite his enormous achievements as a space traveler, you'd be selling him short by merely referring to him as an astronaut. For this renaissance rocket man is so much more.

After graduating from SU with a degree in statistics and mathematics in just two and a half years, Musgrave went on to earn five more degrees, including a doctorate in medicine from Columbia University and three other advanced diplomas, ranging from an MBA to a master's in literature.

Pretty good for a high school dropout.

Musgrave grew up on his family's dairy farm in Stockbridge, the bucolic Massachusetts hometown of famed artist Norman Rockwell, whose paintings often featured tender American family moments. Musgrave's early life was hardly Rockwellian, with two alcoholic parents and a father who was a bully—mean and abusive.

"Even going back to my absolute earliest memories, I was a survivor," Musgrave said in a 1997 interview with *Stars Magazine*. "Even at age 3, I looked at things that were going on around me, and I said, 'There's a lot of messed-up stuff here.' I was in survival mode even then."

Amazingly, he did not allow the family trauma and turmoil to dull his optimism, to turn him into a cynic. Eager to explore the world, Musgrave quit school just before graduation and joined the Marine Corps. Since he had been driving and fixing tractors and farm machinery since he was five, he opted to become an airplane mechanic. The technical manuals he studied taught him the value of a formal education and piqued his interest in going to college.

A pilot friend saw something in him and suggested he apply to Syracuse after he got out of the US Marines. To this day, Musgrave has no idea why the pilot, who was a Penn State grad, recommended SU, but he will be forever grateful because the Hill would be the place where he literally learned he could shoot for the stars.

Although Musgrave had passed the requisite tests for his high school equivalency certificate, some members of SU's admissions committee were reluctant to take a chance on a young man without a diploma. Fortunately, statistics professor Morris Budin reviewed Musgrave's application and suggested the university give him an opportunity. Budin's faith would be rewarded several times over.

To say Musgrave immersed himself in his studies would be a gross understatement. During one semester, he took twenty-four credit hours, plus a night course at University College. This, while also earning a varsity letter with the SU wrestling team and becoming a member of the Phi Delta Theta fraternity.

"When I was at SU," he said in a 1983 *Daily Orange* interview, "I didn't know what I wanted to do or where I might go, but I, ambitiously, with enthusiasm, tore up everything that was within

F. Story Musgrave converses with students during a 2015 return to campus. © Syracuse University. Photo by Stephen Sartori.

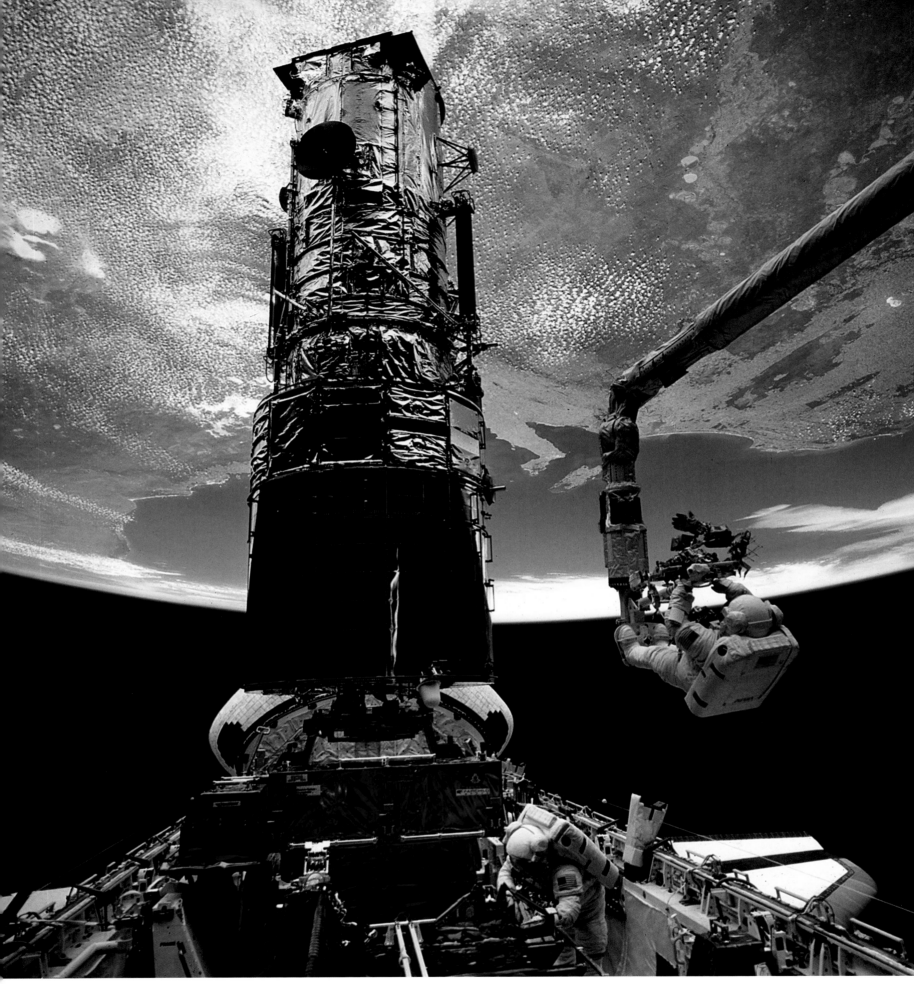

In 1993, astronaut F. Story Musgrave played a leading role in fixing the Hubble Telescope. Courtesy of NASA.

my grasp. I didn't know where it was going to lead, but I had a very open mind."

He wound up graduating cum laude and landed a job as a data processor for Eastman Kodak Company in Rochester, New York. But Musgrave's formal education was far from over. In 1959, he earned an MBA in operations analysis and computer programming from the University of California at Los Angeles. A year later, he received a bachelor of arts in chemistry from Marietta College and was accepted to Columbia's medical school, where he earned a medical doctorate in 1964. He then began teaching at the University of Kentucky and picked up a master's of science in physiology and biophysics. In 1987, he officially completed his formal education, earning a master of arts in literature from the University of Houston.

A turning point occurred in 1967 when NASA announced that it was looking for scientists to become astronauts. Musgrave couldn't apply fast enough.

"It was an absolute epiphany," he said. "It was clear everything I'd ever done, every path I'd been on, was leading to that."

It took more than a decade for him to make his first space flight. It was well worth the wait, especially the spectacular views of planet Earth, which had a visceral impact on him. "You look with your stomach," he said. "That's where you feel it."

During his distinguished NASA career—which resulted in him being inducted into the Astronaut Hall of Fame—Musgrave was involved in the design and development of the Skylab program and was the lead spacewalker in the repair of the Hubble. Astronomers will be beholden to him for decades to come because of his handiwork on that telescope. Between his space flights and all his pilot hours, he estimates he has flown twenty-five million miles—"enough frequent flyer miles," he jokes, "for a one-way trip to the sun."

After leaving the space program, Musgrave joined Walt Disney Imagineering as a consultant and later Applied Minds Inc. as a concept artist. The father of seven children, he created a palm farm and nature reserve on his estate in Florida. He also kept busy as an entertaining and highly sought-after speaker.

He returned to Syracuse University numerous times through the years, including in 1985 to receive an honorary degree, and most recently in 2015 as a favor to his good friend Professor Marvin Druger for a ceremony at Holden Observatory.

"I'll never forget that Syracuse opened the door for me back when I needed it, when I was down," said Musgrave, who showed his school spirit by unveiling an SU pennant during a 1983 space shuttle mission. "I've got a tremendous affection for this place. This is where it all began for me, where I began my intellectual pursuits and my analytical interests in life. I find strength in roots, and when I need strength I go back to where I came from, and what I was back then."

Six decades later, he remains what he was then—a student of everything. The quest for meaning continues.

Joyce Carol Oates

Author

Singer-songwriter Paul Simon once wrote the words, "In the clearing stands a boxer / And a fighter by his trade / And he carries the reminders / Of every glove that laid him down / Or cut him till he cried out / In his anger and his shame / 'I am leaving, I am leaving' / But the fighter still remains."

It is a fitting image for one of America's greatest writers: Joyce Carol Oates, a fierce 1960 graduate of Syracuse who in sixty years of writing has fearlessly chronicled the barren, compromised, hurting places of the heart and mind.

But where did this amazing writer come from? The one whose father kept old issues of *The Ring* magazine and used to take his young daughter in the early 1950s to Golden Gloves boxing matches in Buffalo. Or the one who would stand alone in the dark watching the traffic.

As Oates famously wrote in a diary (presented in Greg Johnson's book *Invisible Writer: A Biography of Joyce Carol Oates*), she would "get up and walk outside, at 2 or 3 in the morning, and watch the cars go by on Transit Road, wondering who was in them . . . An almost overwhelming sense of—curiosity, exhilaration, loneliness, wonder."

It does Oates no justice then to write of "the dark lady of American letters" because that phrase cannot contain (or fully frame) the farm girl who came to Syracuse University as an English major from Millersport, New York, with an insatiable desire to read everything and write the stories, poems, and novels that demanded she revise her work "tirelessly, monomaniacally" in pursuit of perfection.

If Oates has been magnificent on the printed page (and engaging and giving in her postcollegiate life as a professor at Princeton), some part of that outcome is a function of a haunted childhood (family fears of losing their farm) and various experiences at Syracuse that often found Oates wandering the streets of the Salt City.

Joyce Carol Oates. Syracuse University Portrait Collection, University Archives.

"I did things students usually don't do, at least in those days," she said in a 2006 *Syracuse Post-Standard* interview. "I would walk down into the city of Syracuse and take really long walks all alone, even in neighborhoods maybe a young girl shouldn't have been alone in. Nobody else would do that. I was just drawn to walking. I would walk a lot, all around Syracuse."

Oates also worked in SU's library as often as she could (for one dollar an hour) to pay fees and fines she incurred for remaining in the Phi Mu sorority. She wrote about her experience in a 2002 *New Yorker* magazine story:

> I had always loved libraries, but working in the stacks of a library with a large multifloored collection was a daunting prospect. My memory of those months is of a labyrinth so dimly lit (stacks not "in use" were dark; you had to switch them on when you entered) as to inspire hallucination—a universe, or a graveyard of books. Not very encouraging to a nineteen-year-old whose hope was to be a writer someday....
>
> I would work at the library until it closed at 11 p.m., then I would return to the sorority house where I now boarded, find a place that was quiet amid the general noise and hilarity of my sisters, and study until 1 or 2 a.m. To be poor is not only spiritually demeaning but impractical: you find yourself doing things you would not wish to do, out of an inability to do that which you might wish to do.

Which was to write. And so she has, producing more than one hundred highly regarded novels, books, essays, collections of poems, and collections of short stories. She's also won dozens of major awards, including a Guggenheim fellowship (1967), four O. Henry Awards for short stories (1967, 1973, 1983, 2001), the 1970 National Book Award for *them* (published by Vanguard Press), the F. Scott Fitzgerald Award for Achievement in American Literature (1998), a National Humanities Medal (2010), the Bram

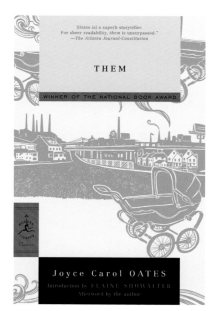

them. Courtesy of Penguin Random House LLC.

Stoker Award for Best Fiction Collection (2011, 2012), the Norman Mailer Prize for Lifetime Achievement (2012), and the Stone Award for Lifetime Literary Achievement (2012). She has also been a Pulitzer Prize finalist for literature on five occasions stretching from 1970 to 2015, and often has been in the running for the Nobel Prize in Literature.

"I can only write if I have a sense of the place," she said in a 2006 interview. "People who read my novel set at Syracuse, called *I'll Take You There*, who went to school with me at that time, are kind of astonished, because they can see I've used the landscape of Syracuse University but I've changed just about everything. I've changed the people, some of the buildings have different names ... so people feel really unnerved."

Interestingly, Oates actually started receiving writing acclaim as a teenager, first winning the Scholastic Art and Writing Award in high school, and, then, during her first year at SU, capturing the *Mademoiselle* College Fiction Contest for a short story titled *In the Old World*.

She would go on to become class valedictorian in 1960, and forty years later would receive an honorary degree from Chancellor Kenneth Shaw. Her work—both published and unpublished—is available for reading at SU's Special Collections Research Center, which has been collecting Oates's writings since 1989.

Aspiring writers would be wise to study the woman who wrote the 1987 book *On Boxing* and observed, "If the boxing ring is an altar, it is not an altar of sacrifice solely, but one of consecration and redemption."

Sean O'Keefe

Leader

Sean O'Keefe shrugged his shoulders when asked about an impressive and peripatetic career that has seen him run NASA, a major university, the US Navy, and seemingly a hundred other things.

"I couldn't keep a job," he humorously told the *Daily Orange* in 2016. "I had to keep moving on before someone caught me."

The truth is O'Keefe has kept moving on because he is a man in demand—an energetic, natural-born leader and problem solver for whom no crisis seems too big. Serving his country and others is in his DNA.

O'Keefe earned a master's in public administration at the Maxwell School in 1978 and then joined the federal service as part of the inaugural class of Presidential Management Interns. After several years on the Senate Appropriations Committee staff, he was appointed comptroller and CFO at the Pentagon in 1989 and secretary of the Navy in 1992 by President George H. W. Bush. He was called back to public service at the White House in 2001, when President George W. Bush appointed him deputy director of

Former secretary of the Navy Sean O'Keefe (left) standing on an aircraft carrier. Courtesy of Sean O'Keefe.

the Office of Management and Budget and later asked him to lead the nation's space agency as NASA administrator. He subsequently went on to be chancellor of Louisiana State University and CEO of the US division of Airbus Group. In 2016, he joined SU alumna Donna Shalala and others on a bipartisan panel of the National Academy of Public Administration to advise the presidential campaigns on the federal transition process.

O'Keefe has twice taught as a Syracuse endowed professor. From 1996 to 2001, he was the Louis A. Bantle Chair of Business and Government Policy. Then, in 2015, he became the seventeenth person in Syracuse history to be named a University Professor; he also was awarded the Howard and Louise Phanstiel Chair in Strategic Management and Leadership. The Arents Award winner also somehow has found time to serve as a distinguished senior advisor for the Center for Strategic and International Studies, Syracuse's partner research institution in Washington, DC.

O'Keefe (*standing to left, with mustache*) served several presidents, including George W. Bush. Courtesy of Sean O'Keefe.

O'Keefe's humility and intelligence have allowed him to face major challenges. These have included the Navy's 1991 Tailhook Association scandal—an event that exposed widespread sexual harassment and incidents of sexual assault by naval aviators—and the tragic space shuttle Columbia accident which took the lives of seven astronauts in 2003.

"We can either go about the business of dealing with the [Tailhook] incident and beat everybody to death to ensure that it never happens again, or we can get about the task to change the culture of the Navy," he said in 1992. His solution was to demolish "outdated Navy attitudes on sexual harassment" and begin to restore integrity.

O'Keefe has never run from strategic challenges or even from physical ones, such as the 2010 Alaskan plane crash that left five dead and gravely injured O'Keefe, his son Kevin (an SU freshman), and two others. It took eighteen hours for rescue teams to locate the plane and extract the four survivors. During that time, O'Keefe came to grips with the reality that his close friend and mentor, Alaska's US senator Ted Stevens, who years earlier had hired O'Keefe on the Senate Appropriations Committee staff, had not survived the crash.

O'Keefe also was a pioneer in giving another Syracuse graduate, Eileen Collins, a very key mission in outer space. "I have always been a big Eileen Collins fan and confidently entrusted her with command of a most critical shuttle mission—the first shuttle return to flight after the Columbia tragedy," he said. "This was her second mission command, and she performed brilliantly. She set an operational standard for the rest of the [NASA] flights of the program to complete the International Space Station."

For his role in advancing the spirit of exploration during his NASA tenure, the International Astronomical Union named asteroid 2003 SK85 for O'Keefe.

As of 2018, Professor O'Keefe was happily teaching graduate courses and was widely regarded as one of SU's most prominent (and eminently likable) faculty members.

His service continues to know no bounds.

Lou Reed

Musician

Transformer.

An apt description for a daring young musician named Lou Reed.

And a spot-on title for his fabled album featuring one of rock's most iconic songs: "Walk on the Wild Side."

Reed graduated from Syracuse University in June 1964, largely transformed, and spent the next five decades radically altering rock and roll with bands like the Primitives, the Velvet Underground, the Killers, and Metallica, and often as a solo performer.

At best, the Lou Reed story was rarely pretty or clean. More often it was messy and filled with imagery about crack cocaine,

Lou Reed (center) playing at a Syracuse University fraternity. Onondagans Reference Collection, University Archives.

racism, AIDS, and poverty that never embraced the pop sweetness of moon-in-June lyrics that successfully propelled popular music in the 1950s and early 1960s. In practice and on the world's stages, Reed embraced what *Rolling Stone* magazine once described as an "articulate aural nightmare of men and women caught in the beauty and terror of sexual, street and drug paranoia, unwilling or unable to move."

As legendary music critic Mikal Gilmore wrote in 1979, "Lou Reed doesn't just write about squalid characters, he allows them to leer and breathe in their own voices, and he colors familiar landscapes through their own eyes. In the process, Reed has created a body of music that comes as close to disclosing the parameters of human loss and recovery as we're likely to find. That qualifies

One of Lou Reed's legendary albums was *Transformer*. Photo © Mick Rock 1972, 2019.

him, in my opinion, as one of the few real heroes rock and roll has raised."

Born in Brooklyn and raised on Long Island, Reed found his way to Syracuse in the fall of 1959. At one point during his freshman year, he returned home "depressed, anxious and socially unresponsive." It led to his parents implementing electroconvulsive therapy, a process that Reed later recalled in his 1996 book *Please Kill Me*. "They put the thing down your throat so you don't swallow your tongue, and they put electrodes on your head," he wrote. "The effect is that you lose your memory and become a vegetable."

After recovering and overcoming that treatment, Reed returned to Syracuse and made SU his creative playground. "Along with his generally outrageous behavior and innate desire to shock, Reed displayed a characteristic savvy during his time at SU," wrote Anthony DeCurtis, author of the 2017 book *Lou Reed: A Life*. "His rebelliousness aside, Reed took care to avoid getting kicked out of school. He pushed the college to the limits of its tolerance."

From hosting a late night radio show called *Excursions on a Wobbly Rail* for WAER-FM, to playing guitar in a local band, to befriending fellow musician and prodigy Garland Jeffreys, to studying creative writing and poetry with Bollingen Prize-winning professor Delmore Schwartz, Reed aggressively sampled the written and musical world around him.

"At four in the afternoon," recalled Jeffreys later, "we'd all meet at the Orange Grove (a local bar). Me, Delmore and Lou. That would often be the center of the crew. And Delmore was the leader—our quiet leader." The gathering also likely included future Velvet Underground guitarist Sterling Morrison (who also attended SU) and Ithaca College drummer Maureen "Moe" Tucker, musicians who would help Reed change rock and roll.

Reed's Velvet Underground (where Tucker was a significant rarity as a female stand-up drummer) did not become a huge commercial success in part because critics would repeatedly use phrases such as the "poet of destruction," "too daring," "rebel," "experimenter," "proto-punk," "sexual deviant," or "noise rocker" in an attempt to explain Reed's genius. Not surprisingly, cultural icons such as Andy Warhol and David Bowie sought out Reed, with Bowie and his guitarist/arranger Mick Ronson helping to create Reed's massive 1972 worldwide hit "Walk on the Wild Side."

Reed would follow that 1972 success with concept albums like *Berlin*, the live *Rock 'n' Roll Animal*, *New York*, and *Sally Can't Dance*, but these avant-garde efforts did not approach the wider acceptance found with *Transformer*. Even his 1967 album *The Velvet Underground and Nico* (with its legendary Warhol cover of a simple banana) never cracked the top 150 on the *Billboard* album charts. It was almost universally banned from commercial radio and record stores because it was too daring. Today, the album/CD/download is revered as one of the most important and influential rock statements of all time. *Rolling Stone* pegged it as the thirteenth greatest ever.

It was so influential, Czech president Vaclav Havel has suggested it inspired him to become the leader of his country.

Reed, who died in 2013 at the age of seventy-one, probably offered a wry smile when told his music had so shaped lives and cultural values. But he would also undoubtedly suggest Syracuse University, where he graduated with honors as an English major, was his launching pad for what he ultimately produced and shared with the world. So much so that in 2007 he founded the Lou Reed/Delmore Schwartz creative writing scholarship and allowed "Head Held High," a Velvet Underground song, to be used in advertising for SU.

As he told music critic David Fricke during the 1990s, "I know my obituary has already been written. And it starts out, 'Doot, di-doot, di-doot.'"

That humility would miss the point that individual songs like "Walk on the Wild Side," "Sweet Jane," "Heroin," "Venus in Furs," "I'm Waiting for the Man," or "Rock and Roll" made Reed a musical immortal whose fans always knew he was a live-wire transformer.

Lorimer Rich

Architect

During a return to Syracuse University for his sixty-second class reunion in 1976, Lorimer Rich was asked to reflect on the numerous buildings and monuments he had designed during his storied architectural career. "Oh, once in a while I did a good one," the octogenarian said, smiling impishly. "The others, I don't want to talk about."

In reality, he designed a lot of good ones, including more than twenty post offices and federal buildings, as well as the Women's Building, the old White Hall, and the Lowe Art Center for his college alma mater.

But the work he's best known for is the Tomb of the Unknowns, which rests on a majestic hill at Arlington National Cemetery overlooking the Potomac River and Washington, DC. Each year, hundreds of thousands of visitors view the Rich-designed marble monument, ranking it up there with the Lincoln Memorial, Washington Monument, and the Smithsonian museums as the most popular tourist attractions in our nation's capital.

Constructing things that would stand the test of time was in Rich's genes. His grandfather had been an architect who designed clipper ships, while his father, a Civil War veteran, specialized in interiors. The third-generation Rich would attend Syracuse with aspirations of designing public buildings. His talent and drive were readily apparent soon after he started taking classes.

"As a student at Syracuse, Mr. Rich was a faithful and consistent worker," Professor Frederick Revels wrote in the January 1929 issue of SU's *Alumni News*. "From the beginning, he was thoroughly interested in the study of architecture in its broader

Designed by SU alum Lorimer Rich and sculptor Thomas Hudson Jones, the Tomb of the Unknowns is one of the most visited monuments in Washington, DC. PAUL J. RICHARDS / AFP / Getty Images.

aspects and unusually aggressive in the accomplishment of the assigned work."

Upon graduating with a bachelor's degree in 1914, Rich headed to Europe to study art and architecture. His education would be interrupted by World War I. A private first class in the US Army, Rich spent a few years as a "muddy boots" soldier fighting in the often rain-drenched trenches of France.

Following the war, he studied architecture at the American Academy in Rome, Italy, and landed a job in New York City with McKim, Mead & White, a legendary firm that was at the forefront of a Big Apple building renaissance. Rich spent eight years there, working mostly on buildings, college facilities, and monuments before breaking off on his own in 1928.

Within a year he would be awarded an architectural assignment that would profoundly change his life and legacy.

Congress announced an open, nationwide competition in which architects were encouraged to submit designs for a monument in Arlington National Cemetery to memorialize the remains of unknown soldiers from World War I. More than eighty architects

Lorimer Rich. Photo by Katherine Young. Syracuse University Portrait Collection, University Archives.

submitted applications, and a jury that included architects, members of the military, and Gold Star Mothers selected the proposal submitted by Rich and sculptor Thomas Hudson Jones as the winner.

The project would take several years to complete. First, a crew of seventy-five men had to cut a fifty-ton block of marble from Yule Creek Valley in Colorado and ship it by train to West Rutland, Vermont, where craftsmen had to chip it to its final size (roughly six feet wide, twelve feet long, and eleven feet high) before transporting it to Arlington, Virginia.

Under the supervision of Rich and Jones, the same sculptors who created the Lincoln Memorial statue carved three Greek figures in robes onto the Tomb. One figure represents victory, another valor, and the third peace. Inverted wreaths can be found on three of the panels. On the back of the shrine is the inscription: "Here rests in honored glory an American soldier known but to God." The monument was completed on April 9, 1932. Decades later, smaller monuments would be added commemorating unknown soldiers from World War II and the Korean and Vietnam Wars.

Rich's work of art received rave reviews and attracted national attention, branding him as one of America's top architects and opening up opportunities for even bigger projects. He would go on to design numerous public buildings of significance, including the headquarters and administration buildings of Fort Jay on Governors Island in New York, St. Luke's Church in Brooklyn, and several post offices in the Big Apple and beyond.

Columbia University hired him as a professor, and in 1940 SU feted him with an honorary doctorate.

When pressed to name the job he's most proud of, Rich would usually joke: "My next one. I say, 'God, give me a good one next.'" But in a 1977 interview, he finally answered the question, saying the Madison Square Station post office in Manhattan was the one he liked best.

Unlike Frank Lloyd Wright, his good friend and arguably America's most famous architect, Rich never desired to design private residences. "I seem to do my best on the larger scale," he said.

When he turned eighty, he decided to leave the hustle-and-bustle of the Big Apple and return to his hometown of Camden, New York, about an hour northeast of Syracuse. The homecoming enabled him to devote more time to a lifelong passion—trout fishing. Although he scaled back, he continued working right up until his death at age eighty-six on June 2, 1978. And one of his projects included the Tomb of the Unknown Soldiers of the American Revolution in nearby Rome, New York. At its unveiling near Fort Stanwix National Park during America's bicentennial celebration, Rich quipped: "I'm known for the Unknowns." Later, he reflected on the lasting impact of an architect's career. "You leave little footprints in bronze, stone and concrete," he observed. "You're immortal—for better or for worse."

Fittingly, President Jimmy Carter honored Rich posthumously by allowing his ashes to be buried at Arlington Cemetery. There, in Section 48, Lot 288, Grid S-23, you'll find the obscure World War I soldier's grave marker in the shadow of the well-known tomb he designed for posterity.

William Safire

Columnist, Author, Presidential Speechwriter

A man of letters, words, and sentences. A writer of columns, speeches, and books. All done while carrying the mantle of "a conservative virtuoso in a chorus of liberal voices."

Meet William Safire.

Syracuse University dropout. *New York Herald Tribune* "legman." Public relations executive. White House speechwriter. Revered *New York Times* columnist. Regular guest on NBC's *Meet the Press*. Pulitzer Prize-winner for Distinguished Commentary. Author of more than twenty books. Two-time SU commencement speaker. The individual *Time* magazine once called (for his *Times Sunday Magazine* "On Language" column) "the nation's amateur arbiter of [word and grammar] usage."

He also was presented the 2006 Presidential Medal of Freedom by George W. Bush, who noted that Safire provided "a voice of independence and principle often skeptical about our government but never cynical about our country."

Born William Safir in New York City to a successful thread manufacturer, the youngest of three sons graduated from the Bronx High School of Science in 1947 before heading off to SU. In less than two years, he was writing for the *Daily Orange*, broadcasting a radio show called "Meet the Prof," and producing a documentary on Onondaga County's trout season.

But he also felt he "could get a better education interviewing John Steinbeck than talking to an English professor about novels."

William Safire receives the Presidential Medal of Freedom from George W. Bush. Associated Press / Pablo Martinez Monsivais. © 2019 The Associated Press.

Safire arranged the infamous "kitchen debate" between Vice President Richard Nixon and Soviet premier Nikita Khrushchev at a Moscow trade fair in 1959. © Elliott Erwitt / Magnum Photos.

That didn't mean he thought little of education. Although he left Syracuse and an academic scholarship following his sophomore year (to begin work for the *Herald Tribune's* personality columnist Tex McCrary), Safire never stopped wanting to learn.

"Frankly, because I dropped out [of Syracuse], I've always felt a goad to continue my education, my self-education," the 1997 Arents Award winner once said. "I think that's also why I collect books. I collect William Cobbett, who's the only guy ever kicked out of both England and America for libel. One of my [other] favorites was Brann the Iconoclast. I don't remember his first name, but he owned a publication down in Texas back in the 1880s called *Iconoclast*. Somebody got so upset with one of his editorials, they shot him. That was back in the good ol' days, when people took their columnists seriously."

Safire's first exposure to important columnists likely came via McCrary, who hosted an early 1950s radio show and liked shaping opinion rather than reporting it. With Safire urging McCrary to start a public relations firm—a field Safire saw as "adventuresome"—the two men used a 1952 basketball game at Madison Square Garden to stage a successful rally for General Dwight D. Eisenhower.

Safire and McCrary filmed the "Draft Ike" event and then got aviator Jacqueline Cochran to personally fly the footage to Paris, where the Eisenhowers lived. The raucous rally reportedly moved the general to tears and influenced his formal entry into the upcoming presidential election. It also gave Safire an early understanding of how to shape major political outcomes.

Seven years later, in 1959, Safire was officially working in public relations for McCrary, representing Herbert Sadkin's "typical American house" at a Moscow trade fair. Impulsively, Safire placed Eisenhower's vice president, Richard Nixon, and Soviet premier Nikita Khrushchev at a kitchen table in the United States Exposition. The manufactured moment turned into what journalists historically labeled the "kitchen debate" because it featured representatives

from two global superpowers figuratively arguing "the comparative merits of capitalism and communism amid gleaming domestic appliances." The heated encounter, which Safire ensured was photographed, showed Nixon jabbing Khrushchev in the chest.

That image ultimately played a significant role in presenting Nixon as a no-nonsense anti-Communist and influenced the Californian to run for the 1960 presidency. It also encouraged Safire, who had changed the spelling of his last name to match verbal pronunciation, to open his own communications firm and work on a number of Nixon's political campaigns.

By 1968, he had joined Nixon's staff as a speechwriter, and one of his most infamous speeches was thankfully never given. It was called "In Event of Moon Disaster" and was prepared for President Nixon to read if the three astronauts of Apollo 11 were unable to return from their historic July 1969 mission.

Safire held that role in the Nixon White House until 1973 when he left for the *Times*. Years later, when asked if he felt any stigma from his association with the only US president ever to resign from office, Safire commented, "I did in 1973. When I joined the *Times*, nobody would talk to me. They thought I was a Nixon plant."

Safire was anything but that. A conservative with a libertarian bent, the *Times*'s odd-man-out columnist showed his readers "how men behave along the corridors of power." His droll "kick them when they're up" philosophy was guaranteed to create enemies whenever the pundit prodded the powerful.

"I'm writing to expose the fallacies and phoniness of some of the things I used to write," he wryly observed.

In 1977, President Jimmy Carter's budget director Bert Lance was forced to resign after Safire's Pulitzer Prize–winning commentary exposed questionable financial and banking practices. Twelve years later, Safire took the West German government to task for not disclosing that country's involvement in the construction of a Libyan poison gas factory. When Safire called it "Auschwitz in the sand," German bureaucrats were furious.

Columns like his unforgiving attacks on CIA director Bill Casey during the Iran-Contra scandal presented Safire as a columnist who always delivered "forceful expression with clarity and wordplay." He also delivered for Syracuse, speaking twice at commencement (1978 and 1990) and emceeing a celebration honoring Chancellor Melvin Eggers's twentieth anniversary at SU. Safire also gave approximately ten thousand books and rare Nixon impeachment documents to Syracuse University, where students study in the William Safire Seminar Room on Bird Library's sixth floor.

Safire died in 2009, but more than twenty years earlier his Syracuse roommate Robert Menschel led a charge to create the Safire Chair in the College of Arts and Sciences. In typical Safire fashion, the man of letters commented, "I don't really think it'll make me immortal. It'll probably just make a lot of people ask, 'Who'd you say that chair's named after?'"

Hopefully, William Safire was wrong about that observation.

George Saunders

Author

It is frigid in Syracuse, a fierce wind blowing up the Hill like arrows from an unseen archer. The late afternoon lighting is somber, moody. Shadows dart between brick and stone. In the courtyard between the Maxwell School and Tolley Building, a solitary man stands next to the Abraham Lincoln statue—the one known as *Seated Lincoln*—which is covered in a light dusting of snow.

The men, one frozen, the other carved, are in communion.

"I'm trying," Syracuse University creative writing professor George Saunders tells Lincoln. "I'm trying. I'm doing my best."

The statue is mute. It does not need to respond.

Seated Lincoln was designed by artist James Earle Fraser in 1929 and gifted to SU by the sculptor's estate in 1968, twenty years before Saunders would receive his master's degree from Syracuse. The statue appears to show the sixteenth US president at what Saunders calls "his lowest, most sad, most defeated" moment.

That anguish, though, winds up being inspirational. Since the late 1990s, Saunders has toyed with an idea for a novel. During a visit to see his cousin in Washington, DC, the best-selling author and Syracuse alumnus takes a side trip to the crypt where a grieving Lincoln once held the body of his dead son, Willie, in 1862.

Back at Syracuse, Saunders stares at the Lincoln statue. For twenty years.

He will tell a reporter that the president "looks like someone who's just been beaten at something, [has] just lost."

That sense of loss is crucial to Saunders's writing. A master of the deeply moving short story (notably, among many superb entries, *Tenth of December*), he initially fears climbing the mountain that is a novel, the long-form story that Big Abe requires. How should Saunders capture Lincoln's grief? How does one feel the pain of a country at war with itself? With the weight of a dead son in his arms? With a horrified wife facing her own demons?

Everything, as Saunders sees it, is broken.

George Saunders. © Syracuse University. Photo by Stephen Sartori.

Finally the story reveals itself.

After many confessions at the foot of a Syracuse statue, which sits just outside the professor's Tolley Building office, Saunders confronts his obsession head-on. He begins writing in 2012, setting the story in the Oak Hill Cemetery of a Washington, DC, neighborhood. Willie will not be quite so dead. Nor alone. He will exist in the bardo, a way station between life and death found in Tibetan Buddhist culture. Saunders works his way through the intricate plotting that will confound readers wanting linear story lines. In 2017, he finally publishes the story he promised to the statue.

Saunders's debut novel, *Lincoln in the Bardo*, became the equivalent of a home run on the first pitch. It immediately climbed to the top of the *New York Times* best-seller's list and received global critical acclaim, earning Great Britain's prestigious Man Booker Prize as the world's finest work of literature for that year.

The novel further enhanced Saunders's reputation as one of the literary giants of the twenty-first century. And it continued Syracuse University's sterling literary tradition, with Saunders the latest member in a powerful lineup of influential Orange authors, poets, songwriters, and professors that includes Stephen Crane, Joyce Carol Oates, Lou Reed, Tobias Wolff, Raymond Carver, Alice Sebold, Jay McInerney, Mary Karr, Cheryl Strayed, Nana Kwame Adjei-Brenyah, and Drew Taggart.

Saunders already had established himself as one of the planet's premier short story authors before writing *Bardo*. His honors included four National Magazine Awards and Guggenheim and MacArthur Fellowships. He had also become a man in demand, making frequent guest appearances on popular television talk shows (*The Colbert Report, Charlie Rose,* and *Late Night with David Letterman*). Critics and readers alike raved about Saunders's ability to capture "the pathos of everyday life."

The popularity of *Bardo* elevated him to another stratosphere. Not long after it hit number one, a seven-hour audio version of the book was released with stars such as Ben Stiller, Julianne Moore, Lena Dunham, Keegan-Michael Key, Don Cheadle, and David Sedaris reading passages. In Hollywood, actors Megan Mullally and Nick Offerman, longtime friends of Saunders, began adapting the film rights. The novel also earned him induction into the American Academy of Arts and Letters, a prestigious honor society of the country's leading writers, artists, composers, and architects. Its august membership includes famed writers Mark Twain, Kurt Vonnegut, Pearl S. Buck, Henry James, Willa Cather, and Edith Wharton.

"It is a great honor, finding oneself beside so many great artists," Saunders said before his induction in 2018. "My main goal at this point is to somehow live up to it."

While writing remains his first love, teaching is a close second. Saunders hasn't allowed the fame and acclaim to change him or his commitment to his graduate students at Syracuse. He gives back what he's received in hopes of continuing the Orange literary tradition.

"Teaching in our program [at Syracuse] is a complete joy, especially with the quality of the students we get," he says. "The best young writers in the world come to Syracuse to study."

Donna Shalala

Public Servant

One wonders if the Syracuse University graduate student from Cleveland, the one who occupied the Syracuse chancellor's building as a student protester in 1970, could ever have imagined the administrative greatness to come.

Did the woman who later said, "It was here [at Syracuse] that I was intellectually disciplined by outstanding teachers and scholars . . . and went to great parties," know that she was pointed toward a career filled with notable achievements?

Perhaps only Donna Shalala knows for sure, but it's likely everyone who ever encountered one of SU's most accomplished alumni immediately saw the drive, energy, and supreme intelligence of this dedicated woman.

And if a list of her fabled accomplishments fails to paint a complete picture, the list is nonetheless needed, if only because it helps frame the breadth of her many accomplishments:

- Master's and doctoral degrees from Syracuse University, plus an honorary doctor of laws in 1987;
- Spencer Fellow; Guggenheim Fellow; visiting professor at Yale;
- Assistant secretary of the US Department of Housing and Urban Development during President Jimmy Carter's administration;
- Youngest president ever at Hunter College (age thirty-nine);

Donna Shalala. © Syracuse University. Photo by Stephen Sartori.

- First female president of a Big Ten university (Wisconsin), and only the second to lead a major research university;
- Secretary of health and human services during President Bill Clinton's two terms, and the first Lebanese American to hold a cabinet post;
- Winner of the Presidential Medal of Freedom, the nation's highest civilian honor, presented by President George W. Bush in 2008;
- President of the University of Miami from 2001 to 2015;
- President of the Clinton Foundation from 2015 to 2017, and;
- Elected to the House of Representatives from Florida's Twenty-Seventh Congressional District in 2018.

As she told *Syracuse University Magazine* in 1987, "I've spent most of my career trying to get three things done: pursuing excellence, making sure more people had opportunity and helping poor kids. I have an ambitious agenda for the world."

That agenda started young, when Shalala signed up to play Pigtail League softball in Cleveland for George Steinbrenner, the future owner of the New York Yankees.

"All we needed to do," Shalala recalled of Steinbrenner's coaching, "was 'learn to throw overhand and slide' and we'd be champs. We did and we were. But even if we hadn't won, the lesson paid off. If we acquired the appropriate skills, we could play hardball with anyone. It was my first feminist experience."

In truth, her first feminist moments were probably shaped by her mother, a teacher who went to law school at night (while holding down two jobs), graduated, and became a practicing attorney—all while simultaneously achieving a national ranking as an amateur tennis player.

Shalala's father, who settled in Cleveland's Lebanese-Syrian neighborhood, was a "civic activist," and, in Shalala's words, "a real leader." His commitment to that lower-middle-class enclave rubbed off on his daughter. So, apparently, did leadership.

"When Donna Shalala was ten years old," recounted President Bush while awarding the Medal of Freedom, "a tornado struck her—struck her house and her neighborhood near Cleveland. Her parents searched throughout the house for young Donna but couldn't find her anywhere. She was finally spotted down the road, standing in the middle of the road directing traffic. Even at a young age, she was ready to take charge."

"I promised myself only one thing," Shalala told Syracuse graduates in 1987. "That I would never play it safe."

She backed her words with action during her four years at Syracuse in the late 1960s and early 1970s as she threw herself into movements promoting peace, civil rights, and women's rights. At a time when gender bias was rampant in society, she found encouragement at SU.

"They [SU's Maxwell School administration] figured out if they educated some women, that we were going to get the jobs of the future," said Shalala, who went to Iran as one of America's first Peace Corps volunteers before entering SU as a graduate student.

For the next fifty years, her relationship with Syracuse was highly engaged, with Shalala frequently returning (or hosting events in Washington, DC) to benefit Maxwell. During one visit to SU, at a 2007 symposium on women in science and academia, her keynote was entitled "On the Other Side of the Glass Ceiling."

She's so proudly Orange, she even created a patchwork quilt made from her Syracuse academic regalia. It hung in the home of the woman whose "concern for humanity is genuine and evident throughout the spectrum of her life's work."

In retrospect, Shalala, a winner of Syracuse's George Arents Award, has always taken note of real or perceived barriers before smashing them. "She had a reputation for never, never shying away from speaking truth to power," said current Maxwell professor Sean O'Keefe. "She's not a partisan. She's a public servant."

Which is why President Bush warmly discussed Shalala's reputation for fairness when he awarded her the Presidential Medal, noting that her fully committed "efforts helped more Americans live lives of purpose and dignity."

William Shemin

Medal of Honor Winner

Ten months after joining the US Army on October 2, 1917, nineteen-year-old William Shemin found himself hunkered down in a trench in northern France fighting the war that was supposed to end all wars and make the world safe for democracy.

German gunfire had taken a severe toll on the Forty-Seventh Infantry Regiment. Casualties were many. Roughly 150 yards from where Shemin was holed up, several fellow soldiers lay wounded in an open field. Injuries to his commanding officers had put Shemin in charge, and the young sergeant was determined not to leave without his wounded comrades. Over the course of three days, he managed to bring back three of them. His bravery was not without cost. The explosion of a German grenade embedded shrapnel in his back, perilously close to his spine. A stray bullet grazed off his helmet and caused him to go deaf in one ear.

Eventually, Shemin lost consciousness and was taken to a hospital, where he spent three months convalescing before returning to the States.

After World War I ended, Shemin enrolled in Syracuse University's School of Forestry. He played football and lacrosse for the Orange and graduated in 1924 with a degree that enabled him to open a highly successful nursery and landscape business in the Bronx.

Following the war, he received heartfelt letters from the comrades whose lives he saved and from his commanding officer, who

William Shemin's daughter, Elsie Shemin-Roth (center), received her father's posthumous Medal of Honor from President Barack Obama in a 2015 ceremony in the Oval Office. Mark Wilson / Getty Images.

recommended him for the Medal of Honor. "With the most utter disregard for his own safety, [Shemin] sprang from his position in his platoon trench, dashed out across the open in full sight of the Germans, who opened and maintained a furious burst of machine gun fire," wrote Captain Rupert Purdon.

But despite the eyewitness accounts, Shemin's recommendation wasn't even considered because he was Jewish.

In those days, military medals and honors often were denied to people based on religion, ethnicity, and skin color. Shemin never dwelled on the slight. Saving three lives was reward enough for him. He moved on.

Years later, Shemin's daughter, Elsie Shemin-Roth, met one of the men whose life her father saved. Jim Pritchard told her that anti-Semitism was the reason the medal had been denied. "It devastated me," Shemin-Roth said in a 2015 interview with the *Syracuse Post-Standard*. "I never let it go. Dad wasn't about medals. He just said, 'Let's move on.' I knew I couldn't approach it again."

Although she followed her father's "marching orders," she never could let it go. It continued to gnaw at her. In 1999, twenty-six years after her father's death at age seventy-six, Shemin-Roth decided she had to do something about righting this historical wrong. And she would do so with the same tenacity her military veteran father had ingrained in her as a child. Thus began a thirteen-year campaign in which she worked with congressmen, senators, and review boards, arduously plowing through enough bureaucratic red tape to cover the Washington Monument. Her determined efforts finally paid off in 2015 when President Barack Obama phoned to say that her dad was going to receive his long overdue medal. "We had a lovely, lovely conversation," Shemin-Roth said. "He's a mensch."

She and nearly sixty family members were on hand for the June 2, 2015, ceremony at the White House as Shemin became the first

Syracuse University graduate to receive the nation's highest military honor. Shemin-Roth used the occasion to acknowledge other Jewish veterans who never received their due. "I accept this on behalf of them, too," she said. "Though my father always told me his war experience was never about medals, I knew in my heart that he was deserving."

In addition to red, white, and blue, Shemin also bled Orange, and she passed that love of his alma mater on to four generations of his family. Shemin-Roth and her two siblings—Emmanuel (a.k.a. Manny) and Ina—graduated from Syracuse, as did Manny's wife, Rhoda. And the family tradition has been carried on by a granddaughter and four great-grandchildren.

Manny served as a member of the board of trustees from 1997 to 2009, and he and his family have been generous donors through the decades, funding a lecture series on fashion design in the College of Visual and Performing Arts, an auditorium in Shaffer Art Building, a student lounge in Winnick Hillel Center, and a resource room for academic support in Manley Field House.

Wilmeth Sidat-Singh

Student-Athlete, War Hero, Pioneer

He was one of the greatest athletes you never heard of—a pioneering African American quarterback who was compared to the Tom Brady and Peyton Manning of his day, and was also a sharpshooting, fancy dribbling Steph Curry-like guard who starred on the best basketball teams in the world.

Sadly, racial bias and a fatal flight while serving his country as a Tuskegee Airman during World War II prevented Wilmeth

Wilmeth Sidat-Singh as a Tuskegee Airman in 1943. Athletics Department, Syracuse University, used by permission.

Sidat-Singh from fulfilling his enormous potential as an athlete and a person.

Still, in his short, heroic life, Sidat-Singh was able to make a lasting impact. His exploits at Syracuse University in the late 1930s as one of college football's first black quarterbacks and as the leading scorer on an unbeaten basketball team paved the way for African American athletes such as Jim Brown, Ernie Davis, Dave Bing, Floyd Little, Don McPherson, Donovan McNabb, Pearl Washington, and Carmelo Anthony. Today, it is commonplace to see blacks playing quarterback, with NFL stars such as Russell Wilson, Patrick Mahomes, and Cam Newton leading the way. But until the 1990s, there were few blacks playing the position collegiately or professionally because of racial stereotypes. So Sidat-Singh was a true trailblazer, a man decades ahead of his time.

Wilmeth Sidat-Singh's retired Number 19 basketball jersey hangs in the Carrier Dome. Photo by Scott Pitoniak.

Along the way, he was forced to deal with the cruel segregation policies of the day. Twice during his collegiate career he was not allowed to play in games because schools south of the Mason-Dixon Line had Jim Crow rules that forbade their teams from competing against teams with African Americans on their rosters. Because of his light complexion and his surname (his stepfather was born in India), Sidat-Singh was billed as a "Hindu" athlete. However, before a 1938 game against the University of Maryland, a black sportswriter named Sam Lacy outed him in the *Baltimore Afro American*, one of the nation's prominent black newspapers of that era. Sidat-Singh was forced to sit. Syracuse, a national championship contender, wound up losing the game, 13-0. The next season, Sidat-Singh led the Orange to a 53-0 victory against Maryland in Syracuse at old Archbold Stadium.

Interestingly, Sidat-Singh came to SU from DeWitt Clinton High School in New York City with the intention of playing only basketball. But that all changed when Orange assistant coach Roy Simmons Sr. watched one of his intramural football games during his sophomore year. Simmons couldn't help but notice the quick-footed, pinpoint-passing young man playing quarterback for one of the dormitory teams. Although it was just a game of touch, it quickly became apparent to Simmons's trained eye that Sidat-Singh was as adept with an oblong ball as he was with a round one.

After watching the kid deliver one tight spiral after another, he decided to do a little pitching of his own. "I went over there and stopped the game," Simmons recalled during an interview in the mid-1970s. "I said, 'Singh, you don't belong here. You belong down on that other field (Archbold Stadium) with the varsity. With your ability you could make the football team, and you could make it with ease.'" Sidat-Singh, who had played football in high school, was intrigued by what Simmons had to say. The following season, he took the coach up on his offer. Neither he nor Simmons would be disappointed.

The greatness that caught Simmons's eye during that touch football game was there for the college football world to see during the final nine minutes of a 1938 clash with upstate rival Cornell at Archbold. With 35,000 spectators looking on during an unusually hot October day, Sidat-Singh led Syracuse to a 19-17 victory by completing six passes for 150 yards and three touchdowns in a six-minute stretch in the fourth quarter.

Grantland Rice, perhaps the most famous sportswriter of all time, was at the game and couldn't help but gush, calling it the most exciting college football contest he had ever covered. Employing the flowery prose of that era, Rice wrote: "A new forward-pass hero slipped in front of the great white spotlight of fame at Syracuse today. The phenomenon of the rifle-shot event went beyond Sid Luckman and Sammy Baugh. His name is Wilmeth Sidat-Singh." Rice's syndicated account of the game was carried in virtually every newspaper in the country. Headline writers had a field day. "Singh's Slings Sink Cornell," read one. "It Don't Mean a Thing If It Ain't Got That Singh," read another, playing off a popular song from that era. It wasn't merely that SU had upset the top football team in the East, but rather the spectacular manner in which the victory was accomplished that made it such a huge sports story.

Segregation prevented Sidat-Singh from pursuing a professional football career because the NFL banned blacks until 1946. And there was no National Basketball Association or organized professional hoops league in the late 1930s, but there were national tournaments, and Sidat-Singh helped lead barnstorming teams from Harlem and Washington, DC, to titles.

Though sports was his first love, Sidat-Singh was much more than an athlete. An honor student majoring in zoology, he aspired to follow in the footsteps of his stepfather, Samuel Sidat-Singh, who had opened a doctor's office in Harlem, and his biological father, Elias Webb, who was one of the first African American pharmacists.

But a month after the Japanese attacked Pearl Harbor, Wilmeth put his dreams of pursuing a medical career on hold. He applied and was accepted as a member of the Tuskegee Airmen, the only African American unit in the US Army Air Forces, and won his wings as a pilot. News of his decision to become a Tuskegee Airman prompted many African Americans to volunteer for the then-segregated branches of the US military.

Wilmeth quickly established himself as a top fighter pilot, but died during a training mission on May 9, 1943, over Lake Huron when the engine of his P-40 failed and he drowned after parachuting.

He was buried in Arlington National Cemetery, with prominent African Americans such as heavyweight boxing champion Joe Louis and famed singer Cab Calloway in attendance.

Six decades later, in 2005, Syracuse University honored Sidat-Singh by retiring his Number 19 basketball jersey at a ceremony during a basketball game in the Carrier Dome. Eight years later, the University of Maryland played a "forgiveness" football game against Syracuse, in which players from both schools wore Number 19 decals on their helmets and Terrapin officials officially apologized to Sidat-Singh's relatives.

While those ceremonies brought closure to his family and attracted some national media play, Sidat-Singh remains largely forgotten—even in Syracuse, where his jersey hangs from the Dome's rafters but still draws "Who's he?" responses from diehard Orange fans. And that's too bad, because he deserves to be remembered as a star student-athlete and patriot.

Aaron Sorkin

Screenwriter, Director

A Few Good Men. The West Wing. The American President. Moneyball. The Social Network. Molly's Game.

Heard of these Hollywood blockbusters?

They all have something in common. Syracuse alumnus Aaron Sorkin's fingerprints, his intricate plotting, amazing words, and assured direction are all over them.

In fact, given his numerous honors (an Academy Award for *The Social Network*, five Emmys for *The West Wing*, Golden Globes for *The Social Network* and *Steve Jobs*), the case is easily made that Sorkin is one the world's most famous screenplay writers. He's even played himself in two television series, *30 Rock* and *Entourage*.

Aaron Sorkin jokes with students before receiving an honorary degree from his alma mater in 2012. © Syracuse University. Photo by Stephen Sartori.

But if you listen to Sorkin, his fame was unexpected.

"I grew up believing, and continue to believe, that I am a screw-up," Sorkin once said in talking about his writing prowess. "That growing up with my family and friends, I had nothing to offer in any conversation. But when I started writing, suddenly there was something that I brought to the party that was at a high enough level."

That self-effacing candor wouldn't surprise Sorkin's SU's friends.

For the kid who attended Syracuse from 1979 until he graduated from the College of Visual and Performing Arts in 1983, his first year in Central New York was very rocky.

As Sorkin told Syracuse grads during a famous May 2012 commencement speech:

> I had a play analysis class—it was part of my [freshman] requirement. The professor was Gerardine Clark. The play analysis class met for 90 minutes twice a week. We read two plays a week and we took a 20-question true or false quiz at the beginning of the session that tested little more than whether or not we'd read the play. The problem was that the class was at 8:30 in the morning. It met all the way down on East Genesee. I lived all the way up at Brewster/Boland, and I don't know if you've noticed, but from time to time the city of Syracuse experiences inclement weather. All this going to class and reading and walking through snow, wind chill that's apparently powered by jet engines, was having a negative effect on my social life in general and my sleeping in particular.
>
> At one point, being quizzed on *Death of a Salesman*, a play I had not read, I gave an answer indicating I wasn't aware that at the end of the play the salesman dies. And I failed the class. I had to repeat it my sophomore year; it was depressing, frustrating and deeply embarrassing.
>
> And it was without a doubt the single most significant event that occurred in my evolution as a writer. I showed up my sophomore year and went to class, and I paid attention, and we read plays and I paid attention, and we discussed structure and tempo and intention and obstacle, possible improbabilities, improbable impossibilities, and I paid attention, and by God when I got my grades at the end of the year, I'd turned that F into a D. I'm joking: it was pass/fail.

"He was a foul-up," legendary SU department chair Arthur Storch would later say. "But by his third year, he had become his class representative and turned his college life around."

Interestingly, where the City of Syracuse was once a make-or-break test market for Broadway shows, Sorkin's first sniff of his Great White Way potential came about because of a script called *Removing All Doubt* that he sent to Storch. SU's legendary Syracuse Stage artistic director liked Sorkin's writing and invited him to stage an October reading in Syracuse.

Shortly thereafter, Broadway producers optioned the play, and while *Doubt* hadn't yet lit up bright lights on Forty-Fifth Street between Broadway and Eighth Avenue, Sorkin soon began writing *A Few Good Men* (on cocktail napkins at first) about US Marines accused of murder.

"Arthur's reputation as a director, and as a disciple of Lee Strasberg, was a big reason why a lot of us went to SU," Sorkin told the *New York Times* for Storch's obituary. "As a freshman you didn't speak to him, and it was unlikely he'd know your name. But he'd generally zero in on two seniors who he felt were worth his time, and I was one of those seniors."

During Sorkin's senior year, Storch, who had directed *The Owl and the Pussycat* on Broadway in 1964, told him: "You have the capacity to be so much better than you are."

The professor's prodding became relentless.

"He started saying it to me in September of my senior year [and] was still saying it in May," Sorkin recalled. "On the last day of classes, he said it again, and I said 'How?' And he said, 'Dare to fail.'"

Sorkin would not forget that advice or his time at Syracuse. SU alumni who have listened closely to the dialogue of *The American President* might have heard a shout-out uttered by a lobbyist counting up potential votes involving environmental legislation: "Senator Storch. Senator Clark. Senator Wagner. Senator Sabo. And the other senator from Indiana."

As Sorkin later explained, "They're all my old teachers [from Syracuse]. Arthur Storch. Jim Clark. Brent Wagner. Linda Sabo and Gerri Clark."

It has not all been roses for Sorkin. Along the way, he has battled drug addiction, which resulted in a 2001 arrest during the second season of *The West Wing* for possession of crack cocaine and marijuana.

"I had what they call a 'high bottom,'" he once commented. "I didn't lose my job or injure anyone when I was high. But the hardest thing I do every day is not take cocaine. You don't get cured of addiction—you're just in remission. With cocaine, you always feel like you're a rock star, and everything you're writing is fantastic. When I got clean, I was terrified of writing. I didn't think I could do it at all."

Given his drug habit, he also didn't think he could write other than at night.

"The first time I wrote in the daytime I was so proud," he recalled. "Now my firewall is [daughter] Roxy. I'd let her down if I relapsed."

The truth is that Sorkin could, can, and does write spectacularly. That's been underscored by his Oscar-winning adapted screenplay for *The Social Network* (2010), Academy Award nominations for *Moneyball* (2011) and *Molly's Game* (2017), and his critically acclaimed 2018 Broadway interpretation of Harper Lee's *To Kill a Mockingbird*.

Near the end of Sorkin's 2012 Syracuse commencement address, he told his audience: "Develop your own compass, and trust it. Take risks, dare to fail. Remember the first person through the wall always gets hurt."

Great advice from one of SU's finest writers.

Mary Spio

Engineer

A young girl named Mary Spio sits in Ghana watching the 1988 Eddie Murphy movie *Coming to America*. It is about a fictional African prince leaving his homeland and landing in New York City. The prince is unprepared for the differences between his country, Zamunda, and the United States. To fit in, he decides to start at the bottom and get a job at a "McDowell's" in Queens selling cheeseburgers.

A similar situation will later unfold for eight-year-old Mary Spio. The imaginative girl born in Syracuse while her father was a student at Syracuse University will come of age in Ghana during a time of military control and social unrest. Free movement is not allowed. She is forced to stay in the house. But Mary sees things on TV and thinks anything is possible in America.

What she knows of outlandish space-age concepts like *Star Trek*, *Star Wars*, or NASA shuttle missions comes from her family's small television. That "magic box" allows her to conjure up new worlds and unrestricted intergalactic travel. It allows her to escape her confinement. She imagines herself moving around inside the television. She grasps that everything televised was created by someone.

Years later, Spio begs her parents to let her enroll in an American high school. As she gets on the plane for the United States, her

Mary Spio. © Syracuse University. Photo by Stephen Sartori.

father offers his daughter some words of encouragement. "My child, my dream for you is to always see our world with that sense of wonder," he said. "And my hope is that you'll make magic wherever you point your focus."

He believes she will come back to Ghana after she graduates, but Spio determines she wants something different. She essentially runs off to New York City and, like Murphy's Crown Prince Akeem, takes a low-paying job at McDonald's.

But this is where reality stops imitating art. The passionate young woman with a wildly futuristic vision grasps how her imagination can empower an amazing future.

In one of those rare moments of fate, the girl raised in Ghana, the one not born of royalty, sees an advertisement for the US Army. She thinks about unimaginable opportunities and decides to join. But just as she's about to sign on the Army's dotted line, the recruitment officer goes to lunch. In the same building, Spio spots a different officer. He invites her to join the Air Force.

In the real-life Mary Spio story, the Army's loss was the Air Force's gain because Spio, an American citizen by birth, started a rapid rise through the air corps beginning as a satellite communications technician. Her excellence ultimately took her overseas to Desert Storm and then to a quiet room for an Air Force scholarship test. To say she did well on the Outstanding Airman exam is a massive understatement. In fact, Spio scored the highest of anyone in the European Region and was immediately entitled to study at any university in the United States.

Without hesitation, and to honor her father, she picked Syracuse University (the only school she applied to), and its highly acclaimed electrical engineering program. Four years later, Boeing selected Spio as one of only three engineers for a prestigious position helping to launch rockets and communications probes into deep space. Their goal was to distribute movies via satellites (the Boeing Digital Cinema system), and their first effort featured *Star Wars Episode II: Attack of the Clones*.

Fast forward to 2017, when Spio was honored as one of four Syracuse Arents Award winners. She had become the CEO and president of CEEK VR Inc., a developer of innovative virtual and augmented reality content solutions. She is recognized as a digital cinema pioneer, and her intuitive and joyful vision have allowed her to create technologies for such global titans as Apple, Lucasfilm, Coca-Cola, Berkshire Hathaway, Universal Music Group (with more than thirty labels), Gatorade, and Microsoft Xbox.

"My career is just one big evolution," she explained in the video preceding her Arents Award. "It's evolved with how media has evolved. I guess wherever I go, it's basically where media is going. I just stay ahead of it."

That cutting-edge commitment helps explain how CEEK's virtual reality experience for Universal's heavy metal band Megadeth led to the Universal Music Group winning a prestigious Silver Clio award that beat out Disney's Star Wars and Intel's Lady Gaga

Experience. The Universal Music virtual reality experience also won a 2017 Grammy Award for Best Metal Performance.

It also meant when 2018 movies like Steven Spielberg's blockbuster *Ready Player One* showcased futuristic new worlds in a massive virtual reality galaxy called the OASIS, Mary Spio had already been acknowledged as a true pioneer in content development and media exploration.

True to her earliest visions, Spio has generated several patents in real-time streaming, digital cinema technology, and virtual reality engineering. Spio also is a novelist, TEDx Talk speaker, screenwriter (*A Song for Carmine*), and best-selling author of *It's Not Rocket Science: Seven Game-Changing Traits for Uncommon Success*. In that book, Spio set out to inspire millennials "to move beyond their comfort zones [and] into creating impact and significance."

An innovation and entrepreneurship evangelist, Spio has worked with the US Department of State on global innovation and entrepreneurship outreach programs while winning innovation and outstanding achievement awards from such organizations as Boeing and *Essence* magazine. NBC News named her one of 100 History Makers in the Making.

"I set out to create my own imagination," said Spio, who has been compared in her inspired thinking to Apple's Steve Jobs and Facebook's Mark Zuckerberg.

And so she did.

With joy, passion, and spectacular results.

Kathrine Switzer

Marathon Runner, Women's Rights Advocate

On April 19, 1967—two years before Neil Armstrong set foot on the moon and took one small step for man and one giant leap for mankind—Kathrine Switzer toed a starting line and took one giant leap for womankind. On that dank New England day, the Syracuse University junior became the first woman to officially enter and complete the Boston Marathon. By finishing that race, Switzer started a revolution that would profoundly alter the course of her life and the lives of women around the globe.

"I had no intention of changing the world when I plopped down my two dollar entry fee," Switzer recalled. "My goal was to run a marathon, 26.2 miles. It was as simple as that."

Switzer prepped for one of the most famous moments in sports history by training with the Syracuse men's cross-country team in late 1966 and early 1967. The journalism student gladly would have trained with the women's team, but there was just one problem—there wasn't one at Syracuse, or at any other college for that matter.

While running with the Orangemen, Switzer befriended Arnie Briggs, a chatty fifty-year-old who served as the team's assistant coach. Briggs loved to regale Switzer with tales about the fifteen Boston Marathons he had run. One night, Switzer told him that she intended to run Boston herself. At first, Briggs scoffed. He barked that the distance was too long for "fragile" women to run. This angered Switzer, who pointed out that women had run the marathon before, just not officially. After jawing back and forth a bit, Briggs agreed to take her under his wing.

She and Briggs checked to see whether there were any rules prohibiting women from entering and discovered that there weren't, despite the accepted notion of that era that females weren't capable of running marathons or companies or countries. She decided to sign up for the race as K. V. Switzer because it wouldn't call attention to her gender, and she thought "it sounded cool using initials in your name like J. D. Salinger, the author of *The Catcher in the Rye*."

Flanked by Briggs, boyfriend Tom Miller, and Orange cross-country runner John Leonard, Switzer was a bundle of nerves by the time the marathon started. Two miles into the race, she briefly considered quitting, not because she was gassed but because she was assaulted. That's when race organizer Jock Semple attempted to rip off the Number 261 bib pinned to her SU sweatshirt because he didn't want women competing in "his" race. Semple had a handful of her shirt until Miller, an ex-football player and Olympic-caliber hammer thrower, sent the race director sprawling. All of this was captured on film as news photographers clicked away. Briggs told the dazed and confused Switzer to run like hell, and she followed his advice.

"Now, [Semple's] hurt, we're in trouble and we're going to get arrested," she wrote in her 2007 autobiography, *Marathon Woman: Running the Race to Revolutionize Women's Sports*. "That was how scared I felt, as well as deeply humiliated, and for just a tiny moment, I wondered if I should step off the course. I did not want to mess up this prestigious race. But the thought was only a flicker. I knew if I quit everybody would say it was a publicity stunt. If I quit, Jock Semple and all those like him would win. My fear and humiliation turned to anger."

So she kept running, even after Semple showed up again several minutes later riding in a race officials bus and screaming at Switzer in a thick, Scottish brogue: "You all ere in beeeeeeggg trouble!" Despite bloody, blistered feet, she crossed the finish line in four hours and twenty minutes. The photos of Semple accosting her were splashed in newspapers and magazines around the world. They sparked a furor and wound up being included in the *Life* magazine book *One Hundred Photographs that Changed the World*.

Race officials immediately disqualified Switzer and her running mates, even though there was nothing in the marathon's bylaws about it being a male-only event. But that disqualification didn't really matter. Switzer had become a hero to women everywhere. And her work in creating opportunities and equal status for females in sports and other fields would not stop there. After traversing those 26.2 miles, she would embark on a new marathon as a leading women's rights advocate.

Kathrine Switzer didn't allow an attack by the race director to prevent her from becoming the first woman to officially run in and complete the Boston Marathon in 1967. Paul Connell / Boston Globe / Getty Images.

Five years after her audacious debut, women were welcomed to compete in the Boston Marathon. Two years after that, Switzer became the first woman to cross the finish line at the New York City Marathon. She went on to run more than forty marathons and form an international running program for international cosmetics giant Avon Products Inc., organizing hundreds of races in nearly thirty countries for more than a million women. She also successfully led the drive to make the women's marathon an official Olympic event, just as it had always been for the men. Her advocacy continues today

through her foundation, 261 Fearless Inc., which uses running as a vehicle to empower and unite women across the globe.

"I'm so proud of what we've been able to achieve empowering women not only here, but in Japan and Africa and South America, where women have long been treated like third-class citizens," Switzer said. "Running has given so many females the belief and courage to overcome the obstacles in their lives; to get that college education or get out of an abusive relationship or seek a better job. It's all about moving forward, even when you might not feel like it."

During her SU commencement address in 2018, Switzer held up the Number 261 bib she wore during her historic Boston Marathon run. © Syracuse University. Photo by Stephen Sartori.

In 2011, she was inducted into the National Women's Hall of Fame. And in 2017, at age seventy, she celebrated the fiftieth anniversary of her historic race by running and completing the Boston Marathon. On that day, amid roaring applause, race officials announced that Switzer's Number 261 bib was being permanently retired in her honor.

"One of the things that I learned from Arnie Briggs was that running can make you a hero in your own life," she said. "And I'm not just talking about competing in marathons or 5Ks or 10Ks. Just getting out there and putting one foot in front of another for any distance, no matter how short or even if you have to walk, gives you a sense of accomplishment and can be so personally uplifting. And that can carry over into every aspect of your life."

On May 13, 2018, Switzer's journey came full circle, when she returned to the place where she earned undergraduate (1968) and graduate (1972) degrees to deliver the commencement speech.

"Sometimes the worst things in your life can become the best," she said during an address in which she brought the Carrier Dome crowd to its feet by holding up her famous marathoner's bib.

Dorothy Thompson

Journalist

Imagine a reporter once described as "a volcanic columnist in eruption." A person British Prime Minister Winston Churchill once said had "shown what one valiant woman can do with the power of the pen. Freedom and humanity are her grateful debtors."

That was Dorothy Thompson, the energetic Syracuse graduate who foresaw Europe's failure "to counteract totalitarianism and indifference toward its victims" in the early 1930s as a threat to the very foundation of the United States. For her heroic attacks on Adolf Hitler, she was the first Western journalist expelled from Nazi Germany in 1934.

The daughter of a Methodist minister, who received free tuition at SU because of her father, Thompson graduated from SU in 1914 and went on to become a grassroots organizer for the Central New York suffrage movement. She emerged as the first American woman to work as a foreign news bureau chief (for the *Philadelphia Public Ledger*), and in 1937 became the first woman to deliver SU's commencement address. She also is believed to be the first SU alum to appear on the cover of *Time* magazine (June 12, 1939).

Fluent in German and aggrieved by social injustice, she forcefully spoke her mind through newspaper columns, magazine articles for *Women's Home Journal*, and radio commentary. At the peak of her popularity in the 1930s, when she rivaled First Lady Eleanor Roosevelt for American influence, her "On the Record" column for the *New York Tribune* was carried by more than 150 newspapers and reportedly reached ten million readers.

But she could also offend, as evidenced when St. Louis radio station KWK pulled her show because "she was too belligerent" and "against everybody." Even her first husband, the 1930 Nobel Prize-winning author Sinclair Lewis (*Babbitt*, *Elmer Gantry*), felt Thompson was over the top and incessant in her analysis of international affairs. Peers called it "perpetual emotion." *Time* suggested it was "vehement sincerity." The marriage didn't last, but the strong woman certainly did.

Thompson challenged many, including what she called "the specious feminism of the women's magazines, which persist in finding cause for jubilation every time a woman becomes, for the first time, an iceman, a road surveyor or a senator. [That] see-what-the-little-darling-has-done-now-attitude ought to be outlawed."

That was Thompson, a media tempest capable of inspiring the 1942 movie *Woman of the Year*, with her character portrayed by legendary actress Katharine Hepburn.

Dorothy Thompson speaks during Syracuse's 1937 commencement. Syracuse University Portrait Collection, University Archives.

Born in the Buffalo, New York, suburb of Lancaster in 1893, Thompson realized it was easier for a woman to get a journalism job in Europe than in the United States. To achieve her goal, she moved to Vienna, Austria, to begin work as a foreign correspondent (or stringer) for syndicated American newspapers.

Shortly thereafter, she scored what *Time*'s 1961 obituary called an exclusive 1932 interview with Germany's fast-rising dictator Adolf Hitler. For the next two years, as Hitler rose from German chancellor to all-controlling führer, Thompson consistently produced "high-profile articles on the terror against Jews and political opponents in Germany," many of which were published in the *Jewish Daily Record*. She was famously expelled from Germany in 1934 but never stopped attacking Hitler or his Nazi party.

Words clearly were her weapons. Envisioning America's future, Thompson wrote plainly in 1935:

> No people ever recognize their dictator in advance. He never stands for election on the platform of dictatorship. He always represents himself as the instrument [of] the Incorporated National Will. When our dictator turns up you can depend on it that he will be one of the boys, and he will stand for everything traditionally American. And nobody will ever say "Heil" to him, nor will they call him "Führer" or "Duce." But they will greet him with one great big, universal, democratic, sheep-like bleat of "O.K., Chief! Fix it like you wanna, Chief! Oh Kaaaay!"

After the war's end in 1945, Thompson took up new targets, including Israel's creation and the "invasion of the Arab world." For this, she was considered an anti-Semite.

Thompson was undeterred and apparently unbothered by various media assaults. As one opponent, Alice Roosevelt Longworth, once noted, Thompson was "the only woman in history who has had her menopause in public and made it pay."

Thompson died in Lisbon, Portugal, at sixty-seven, of a heart attack brought on by bronchitis.

"If I had to do it all over, of course, I'd do a lot of things differently," she once observed of her career. "One knows increasingly less in this world. So much truth is clouded over by propaganda and misinformation. But I don't believe in regrets. I have written objectively and honestly."

Today, Thompson's pioneering work is rarely discussed. But the woman sometimes called the First Lady of American Journalism was not forgotten by President Barack Obama in 2015 when he spoke at the White House Correspondents' Dinner and acknowledged Thompson by saying: "It is not the fact of liberty, but the way in which liberty is exercised that ultimately determines whether liberty itself survives."

Not a bad shout-out for the woman the *Saturday Evening Post* called in 1940 "The Girl From Syracuse." The girl who took on Hitler.

Mike Tirico

Sportscaster

There's no truth to the rumor that Mike Tirico was born with a microphone in his hand. But his broadcasting career did begin really, really early in life—and with an audience of one. As a kindergartner in Queens, New York, in 1975, the sports-crazed Tirico would plop himself in front of the television set and pretend to announce games into one of his mother's large kitchen spoons.

"I guess you could say I was trying to get a head start on my competition," Tirico said, chuckling. "The broadcasting bug bit me earlier than most people in my profession."

Actually, if he had his druthers, the man *Sports Illustrated* calls "the most versatile play-by-play voice of his generation" would have made a life playing sports. But after being humbled by his inability to hit curve balls while trying out for his high school baseball team as a sophomore, Tirico decided calling games might be his true calling.

Trading bat for mic proved life-changing. Around the same time he struck out as an athlete, he read a story about how his favorite sportscaster, Marv Albert, had attended Syracuse University. Tirico decided that's where he wanted to go, too.

He showed up on campus in the summer of 1984 as a broadcasting and political science major and wasted little time making an impression, becoming the first freshman in at least a decade allowed to do play by play of Orange football and basketball games

Newhouse alumni family:
Can't come to the **50Forward gala?**
Enjoy a "slice" of the celebration from home!

▲ MIKE TIRICO '88, *PLAY-BY-PLAY COMMENTATOR, ESPN*

A caricature of Mike Tirico featured him with Varsity pizza boxes.
Newhouse Network, Syracuse University, used by permission.

for WAER-FM. By his junior year, he had been hired as a weekend sports anchor at WTVH-TV, the Syracuse-area CBS affiliate, and a year later was promoted to sports anchor and director.

ESPN hired him in July 1991, and over the next twenty-five years Tirico's talent would be on national display as he established himself as the network's preeminent play-by-play man. Working for ESPN and its broadcast partner ABC, Tirico became the voice of Monday Night Football, the British Open, Wimbledon tennis, the NBA, and college football and basketball. "Mike is one of the most versatile on-air talents in the industry and of our generation," said John Wildhack, a former ESPN executive who worked closely with Tirico and is now athletics director at Syracuse. "He can do anything—and do it well."

In July 2016, Tirico moved to NBC Sports, where his assignments have included the NFL, horse racing, and Notre Dame football. But his biggest job has been hosting the network's Olympic coverage, duties he inherited from fellow Newhouse alumnus Bob Costas, who had worked a record eleven Olympiads in that role. That Tirico would follow in Costas's footsteps was only fitting. In 1987, Tirico received the first Bob Costas Scholarship, and the two men have been good friends ever since. "I don't know of anyone more prepared to do the Olympics or any other assignment for that matter," Costas said when asked about Tirico succeeding him in the host's chair. "There's no one who works harder and prepares as thoroughly as Mike."

Tirico has been known to do twenty-four hours of research for a single three-and-a-half-hour broadcast, poring over newspaper stories, interviewing players and coaches, and watching tapes and practices. That work ethic was ingrained during his undergraduate days, when he not only worked for WAER but also wrote for the *Daily Orange* while taking a full course load in his dual major.

"Without WAER, a whole bunch of us who are doing this now would not be doing this now," Tirico said in a 1999 *DO* interview. "Me and Sean McDonough and all of us—we were so into learning the business and learning to act like professional adults and getting guidance and leadership from those who were there before us. It's become a fraternity for the people involved there. We'd hang out on Friday nights when people were going to happy hour, and we'd be putting together a football pregame show that not many people would listen to. But it was an invaluable experience for us."

Tirico's popularity stems not only from his preparation but also from his sincerity. "I'm me on the air," he said in a 1991 *Syracuse Post-Standard* interview. "The me that's on the air is the me that's going to sit here and have a slice of pizza with you, have a beer with you."

As the *New York Times* pointed out in a 2017 profile, Tirico's shtick is that he doesn't have a shtick—and that might just be why he appeals to such a broad audience. "I don't want to be the story," he said. "I'm not into the whole opinion thing. Where I'm rooted is in the games. I just love watching games."

Tirico's "realness" also resonates with his peers. In 2010, the National Sportscasters and Sportswriters Association voted him Sportscaster of the Year. Seven years later, he was back on campus to speak to students, as he often does, and receive the Marty Glickman Award for Leadership in Sports Media from the Newhouse School. One of his messages to aspiring broadcasters is that it's up to the individual. "If you overwork," he said, "you have the opportunity to get lucky and things happen."

Tirico's hard work, dating back to those kindergarten broadcasts, clearly paid off.

Dwayne "Pearl" Washington

Basketball Player

Dwayne Washington's hoop dreams began as a four-year-old on the asphalt, bent-rimmed playgrounds of a Brooklyn neighborhood one writer said "looked like bombed-out London during World War II." The basketball quickly became a yo-yo in the hands of the kid who would be nicknamed Pearl after former New York Knickerbockers' star Earl "the Pearl" Monroe. Washington's uncanny, Harlem Globetrotter-like moves electrified fans and demoralized defenders. By age ten, Pearl was playing against and dribbling past the likes of NBA stars World B. Free and Sly Williams in pickup games.

Word spread quickly about this playground phenom. People recall scrimmages on the courts at King Towers in Harlem where the crowds were so big that some fans had to climb trees or head over to the roofs of nearby tenements to catch a glimpse of the Pearl in action.

His legend would grow exponentially at New York's Boys and Girls High School. Highlights included an upset of the nation's top-ranked team and an 82-point game his senior season. After being intensely recruited by more than three hundred colleges, Pearl announced on national television he would attend Syracuse University in the fall of 1983.

"I can't underscore how big a moment that was for our program," said Orange Hall of Fame coach Jim Boeheim. "I believe at that point we officially went from being an Eastern program to a national program. Everybody knew who the Pearl was. I'd get off a plane in Los Angeles and somebody would say, 'There's Pearl's coach.' Pearl was the guy who opened the door for us and enabled us to land recruits not just from the East Coast or the Midwest, but from the entire country."

Washington would indeed have a Pied Piper effect on recruiting, with high school stars such as Derrick Coleman, Billy Owens, and John Wallace eventually following in his footsteps. Even players from as far away as California wanted to come to snowy Syracuse and play basketball there because of Pearl.

"From 3,000 miles away, he turned me—a white, suburban kid from So-Cal—into a Syracuse basketball fan," said Mike Hopkins,

Pearl Washington was a magician with a basketball in his hands. Collegiate Images / Getty Images.

Pearl Washington as he appeared on a Syracuse schedule card. Athletics Department, Syracuse University, used by permission.

who would go on to play and coach at SU. "That's the kind of magnetism he had."

And that magnetism extended to the fans. Washington's decision had an immediate impact on SU's athletic coffers as two thousand additional seats were sold, guaranteeing that Pearl would play in front of a record six thirty-thousand-plus crowds in the Carrier Dome his freshman season.

Dome denizens would not be disappointed. His first of many indelible moments came in his fifteenth game as a collegian, when he heaved in a half-court shot at the buzzer to beat Boston College, 75-73. "That shot made me a permanent part of Syracuse basketball," Washington said nearly three decades later. "I had so many great moments during my playing days there, but that one's hard to top."

Boeheim agreed.

"That was a historic moment for our program," he said. "The instant that thing went through there was an explosion in the building. As long as they play basketball at Syracuse, people will talk about that shot."

"It was," added Washington's teammate Sean Kerins, "the moment Pearl officially arrived."

The victory would prompt an enterprising vendor to begin producing and selling T-shirts reading: "And on the eighth day,

God created Pearl." It also enabled the Orangemen to crack the top twenty the following week. They would remain there the rest of Pearl's career.

Almost a year later, Washington worked his late-game magic again, hitting a fifteen-foot jumper with eight seconds to go as Syracuse nipped second-ranked Georgetown by a point. During his junior season, in 1985-86, Washington put the team on his shoulders after star teammate Rafael Addison was injured, averaging 17.3 points per game as the Orange went 23-4 in the regular season. In the semifinals of the Big East Conference tournament, Washington scored 28 points as SU nipped Georgetown, 75-73, in overtime. "What you have to remember," said Boeheim, "is that Georgetown team played suffocating defense . . . and there's Pearl scoring 28 on them and just dominating them from start to finish. They had no answer for him whatsoever. It was one of those nights he was unstoppable."

Although his team would fall to St. John's in the championship game, Pearl was voted the tournament's most valuable player.

Not long after a stunning defeat to a Navy team led by David Robinson in the Dome, Washington announced he was going to skip his senior year and enter the NBA draft and turn pro. The New Jersey Nets drafted him thirteenth overall, and most believed Pearl would become a star. But the magic he displayed on the playgrounds, in high school, and at Syracuse disappeared. He spent just three seasons in the NBA, averaging 8.5 points and 3.7 assists per game. After toiling in the minors for a few years, Washington returned to Syracuse to complete the thirty-one credit hours he needed for his degree. During that time, he became the third player in school history to have his number retired.

Though he never guided the Orange to a Big East title and enjoyed only limited success in his three NCAA appearances, Pearl made a lasting impression on the basketball program. He averaged 15.7 points and 6.7 assists per game as Syracuse went 81-27. But his impact transcended those statistics. His decision enabled the Orangemen to lure blue-chip prospects who wouldn't have considered them before. It also enabled them to lead the nation in attendance. By the time he left, they were averaging 26,255 fans per game, a jump of nearly 6,000 per game from the year before his arrival. In his three seasons, he played in front of crowds in excess of 30,000 thirteen times. "Pearl's the reason there was that guy in line waiting to buy the 31,000th seat," Boeheim said.

Sadly, Washington encountered some serious health problems after his playing days. In 2015—two decades after surgery for the removal of a brain tumor—he received the diagnosis that he had another tumor, and this time it was malignant. A year later, he died at age fifty-two. To honor his memory, Syracuse University painted his Number 31 on the Dome's basketball court.

Vanessa Williams

Entertainer

Vanessa Williams still doesn't know who wrote the words on her birth certificate or why. But the "Here she is, Miss America!" inscription would prove prophetic. As would the audacious words she penned next to her photograph in her 1981 Horace Greeley High School yearbook: "See you on Broadway."

Not long after completing her sophomore year as a musical theater major at Syracuse University, Williams became the first African American crowned Miss America. And four years later, we would indeed see her on Broadway singing, dancing, and acting her way across the stages of the Great White Way.

Intent on excelling in all facets of entertainment, a la one of her idols, Bette Midler, Williams went on to become an immensely successful recording artist, climbing to the top of the *Billboard* charts several times on her way to selling nearly twenty million albums. She also established herself as a critically acclaimed actress on screens big and small, landing leading or supporting roles in more than twenty films and fifty television shows.

An astute business woman, she became heavily involved in promoting cosmetics and her own clothing and jewelry line. And in 2012 she added "author" to her list of accomplishments, collaborating on an entertaining mother-daughter memoir titled: *You Have No Idea: A Famous Daughter, Her No-Nonsense Mother, and How They Survived Pageants, Hollywood, Love, Loss (and Each Other)*.

Vanessa Williams meets with President Ronald Reagan in the White House in 1984. Courtesy of Enter Talking / Mellian Group.

Williams's boundless talent and versatility earned her eleven Grammy Award nominations, a handful of Emmy nominations, a Tony nomination, seven NAACP Image Awards, a Mary Pickford Lifetime Achievement Award for Entertainment Excellence, an Arents Alumni Award from her alma mater, and an Oscar for her rendition of a Disney movie song.

"It's been an incredible journey since my freshman year," she told SU students, parents, and faculty at the 2008 College of Visual and Performing Arts convocation in the Carrier Dome, the day before receiving her bachelor of fine arts, twenty-five years after leaving campus.

That the daughter of two elementary school music teachers would become a multidimensional, international entertainment star did not come as a shock to those who knew her during her Syracuse days. Her wide-ranging talents and supreme self-confidence were apparent the instant she arrived from Greeley High School in Chappaqua, New York, an upper-middle-class, predominantly white enclave about thirty-five miles north of the Big Apple.

"When I first saw her on stage, in a campus production, I knew she was something very special," recalled Norma DeLuccia, a College of Visual and Performing Arts piano instructor, in a 1995 *Syracuse University Magazine* interview. "She obviously had so much talent and a beautiful voice. She was so gorgeous and her presence was awesome. She just projected herself in so many ways."

Although she disliked beauty pageants in general, Williams was coaxed into competing for Miss Greater Syracuse and Miss New York State in 1983, and she won both crowns. That qualified her

In 2008, Vanessa Williams returned to campus twenty-five years after her undergraduate days to receive her SU diploma. © Syracuse University. Photo by Stephen Sartori.

for the Miss America pageant that fall, and thanks in large part to her evocative singing, she wound up capturing the talent competition and the bejeweled tiara.

Many applauded her for breaking a color barrier. But some were angered. Williams received loads of hate mail and even death threats from racists, and she also encountered criticism from certain segments of the African American community who questioned whether her green eyes and light-skinned features made her black enough.

Despite the animus, Williams handled her role with grace. Pageant officials called her the most popular and most-booked Miss America ever. But the crowning achievement of her young life would be tarnished by scandal when, weeks before the end of her reign, she was forced to resign after unauthorized nude photos of her were published in *Penthouse* magazine.

It appeared Williams's career was over, that she never would be able to recover.

Though crushed by the dramatic turn of events, she leaned on the love of her parents, brother, and close friends, and she slowly regained the self-confidence that had enabled her to reach such dizzying heights before her fall.

"Some wounds never totally heal," Williams said in a 2006 *Parade* magazine interview. "But I've lived a lot of life since then. I always knew I would bounce back. I heard all of the bad stuff, but I just kept thinking it's a matter of time and persistence. I also thought, 'These people don't know how hard I've trained. They don't know me.' When the dust settles, there's a sense of clarity, and people can see who you are. You have to have fire. You have to have a dream and some kind of drive and vision to propel you."

Four years after the debacle, she released an album—*The Right Stuff*—that produced four top ten singles and earned her three Grammy nominations, including one for best new artist. Her second album, *The Comfort Zone*, was released in 1991 and gave her

a number one hit and her signature song—"Save the Best for Last"—which wasn't written for her but included lyrics that mirrored her own redemptive story.

Around the same time, she inherited the lead role from Chita Rivera in the Broadway play *Kiss of the Spider Woman*. A *New York Times* reviewer raved about Williams, describing her as "an irresistibly alluring temptress.... Whenever she's on stage, the temperature in the Broadhurst Theater shoots up about 20 degrees. The air-conditioning bills are going to be hell to pay, but the box office is bound to start jumping as word of her performance gets around."

Before long, Hollywood came calling. By 1996, she was starring with Arnold Schwarzenegger in *Eraser*, performing at the Super Bowl, and singing "Colors of the Wind"—her hit single from the movie *Pocahontas*—at the Academy Awards. Williams would become well known as Teri in the feature film *Soul Food* and even more popular for such humorous roles as Wilhelmina Slater in the TV series *Ugly Betty* and Renee Perry in *Desperate Housewives*.

One of her most memorable nights in television occurred during the fall of 2015 when she returned to the Miss America pageant as head judge. After performing her song "Oh How the Years Go By," Williams received a public apology on stage from pageant chair Sam Haskell for the treatment she received back in 1984.

In 2008, SU officials decided that Williams's acting and singing performances had fulfilled the remaining credits for her degree and asked her to come back to campus to receive her diploma and deliver the College of Visual and Performing Arts convocation address. "It's a very emotional homecoming for me today," she told the audience, which included her mother and two of her daughters. She described how painful it had been to break the news of her title resignation to her parents. But she also talked about how the experience "helped me become the woman I am today." She mentioned how persistence helped her put the pieces of her shattered life back together.

Near the end of her speech, she touched her blue cap.

"This," she said, "is another crown for me to wear."

7 Alumni Memories of 'Cuse

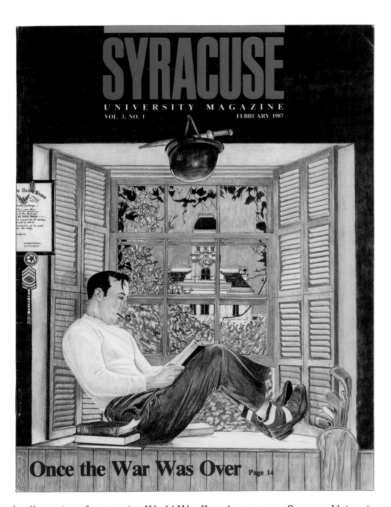

An illustration of a returning World War II student veteran. Syracuse University News and Public Affairs Reference Collection, University Archives.

The cow barn at the State Fair Grounds. That was my first address at Syracuse in the fall of 1946. I shared a cozy little room with ninety-two other [World War II] veterans, no two of whom ever seemed to go to bed or arise at the same time. It was Army-style living all over again—two-tiered bunk beds and waiting in line for the toilet facilities, plus a twenty-minute ride by shuttle bus to and from the campus.

Classroom life was similarly strained. I remember a stunned Lyle Spencer, dean of the journalism school, facing over 250 students in Maxwell Auditorium for an introductory journalism class. It had never before numbered a tenth of that size. I also recall taking an English class in a drafty Quonset hut, hastily erected in the shadow of the football stadium. In midwinter its only heat came from a pot-bellied coal stove, around which professors and students huddled in coats, scarves, and gloves.

It was not an easy time for any of us—the university with its resources stretched, the faculty faced with huge classes, the veterans striving to get on with their lives. But we all persevered. We veterans survived and so did the university. Both were tested to their limits, and I think were better for the experience.

—THEODORE LUSTIG
Class of 1948

MY PARENTS, Mark and Christina (Clair) Frega, met at Syracuse University their senior year in the spring of 1985 in a class called "Interpretation of Fiction." Following a Valentine's Day letter that my father signed "Your Friend in Fiction," they went on their first date at Hungry Charley's, and the rest is history. I grew up with a love and passion for SU instilled in me by my father.

Some of my earliest memories are driving up from New Jersey in April to see lacrosse games in the Carrier Dome. It was through my father's connection to the lacrosse team that I first learned about Pan Am 103, because it was Roy Simmons Jr. and the national championship men's lacrosse team who went over to Lockerbie the following year to bring the "Medicine Game" to that still-healing and grieving community.

Since I was a little girl, I envisioned myself attending SU, and grew up learning lacrosse from watching the Powell Brothers and attending lacrosse camps hosted by Gary Gait. In the spring of my junior year of high school, I was diagnosed with Hodgkin's lymphoma, a blood cancer, and my dreams of playing lacrosse at SU were put on hold.

The following spring, in the darkest days of my cancer treatment, I was accepted to Syracuse. My childhood dream had been attained. This admission was something tangible I held on to, and it would allow me to thrive when I arrived on campus to begin my freshman year in August 2012. I showed up just days after being released from the hospital for the final time.

My journey with cancer inspired me to become a physician. I wanted to devote my life to caring for cancer patients. I made the club lacrosse team only a few months following cancer treatment. My father passed away unexpectedly in the spring of my sophomore year, but my last memory of him was a quick trip he made to Syracuse to watch a lacrosse game together.

When it came time to apply for the Remembrance Scholarship, I dived deep into the archives in Bird Library. I learned of a student named Turhan Ergin, a theater major and member of the lacrosse team, whose life was cut short by the Lockerbie bombing, much like my father's life had been cut short.

My greatest accomplishment and memories at SU are of my time as a Remembrance Scholar my senior year. I later learned Turhan's father was a well-known surgical oncologist. I now felt a very deep connection to both my father and Turhan.

Now, in my final years as a student pursuing my degree at Upstate Medical University, I have continued to make going to lacrosse games at the Carrier Dome a priority as I pursue work in oncology.

—KATHERINE FREGA
Class of 2016

THE FIRST 'A' I ever received from Professor Bill Glavin was a long time coming and included a note I never forgot. "You could be a very good writer," it read. "But you're going to have to work very, very hard."

I knew I was a work in progress when I arrived at SU from a rural high school near Buffalo, New York. Still, I was already writing music and concert reviews for the *Daily Orange* and my hometown paper, the *Buffalo Courier-Express*. I thought I knew a fair amount. Actually, I didn't have a clue.

I struggled to get a C in my first class with Glavin. Yet I realized I had learned something, not only about writing but perhaps myself, and signed up for another. For Bill's classes, we read Joan Didion, Tom Wolfe, Gay Talese, and the other emerging voices of journalism

Syracuse football fans watch a game in Archbold Stadium in the 1930s. Athletics Department, Syracuse University, used by permission.

at the time. We went over student papers line by line, debating everything from verb usage to story construction. Such attention to detail can be excruciating, especially when it is your paper being critiqued. Still, I slowly improved, learning Glavin's rules for eloquent writing along the way. Such tips include:

- Write about people. That's how to make issues and trends come alive.
- Emphasize nouns and verbs, not adjectives and adverbs.
- Never write something that you would be reluctant to say aloud.

In my senior year, I received my first A from Bill for a story I did about the renovation of the Landmark Theatre in downtown Syracuse. I had spent several weeks going to the scene, talking with the workers and architects, sitting far back in another empty row, observing what was going on, and imagining what it all could become.

The last time I saw Professor Glavin I was dropping off my daughter for another semester. (She had followed her parents to SU.) Walking through Newhouse III, I happened upon Bill in the commons area and we soon fell into an easy conversation about our recent travels, new writers we had discovered, and baseball, a passion we both shared. A half-hour later, our talk was still crackling when Bill looked at his watch and said he had to run.

That's the last time I ever saw him. Too soon he died of cancer at the age of sixty-seven.

As with any great teacher, though, Bill's influence continues to this day. I dig out his rules to writing when I'm struggling with another piece. More importantly, I've talked about his insights to the writing classes I've taught over the years. They never had the good fortune to be taught by Bill Glavin, but many have become better writers because of him.

—TIM WENDEL
Class of 1978

WHEN I TELL PEOPLE that John F. Kennedy was our commencement speaker back in 1957, they say, "Oh, boy. You and your fellow graduates were fortunate." And I tell them, "We sure were."

JFK was a young, up-and-coming senator from Massachusetts at the time. A lot of people were talking about him running for president, and after listening to his commencement address that sunny June day in Archbold Stadium, I could see why. I remember him being very charismatic. He had this great energy about him, this great vigor—and it was contagious. He came across as a leader.

He weaved in a few political jibes, but his speech was more about encouraging us newly minted graduates to become involved in public service. I remember him delivering a line about how you can either be a hammer or an anvil. You can either endure the blows dealt by society or you can try to do something about them. He acknowledged that politics could be a dirty business, but that we shouldn't let that stop us from getting involved and trying to make things better.

He struck a very responsive chord that day. Regardless of your politics, you couldn't help but like the man. Very impressive. There were about six thousand of us at Archbold that afternoon, and I think every one of us walked out of there inspired and feeling very good about this young man who, three years later, would become the thirty-fifth president of the United States.

—VINCENT ROGERS
Class of 1957

WE KNEW NOVEMBER 28, 1998, was going to be an emotional day. Not only were we seniors about to play our last football game together in the Carrier Dome, but we also were about to play it against a Miami program that had been a national standard-bearer and a nemesis. From the time we had arrived on campus four years earlier, we had set a goal of supplanting the Hurricanes. We knew that to be the best, you have to beat the best. So, to say we were a little excited coming out of the tunnel that day would be a huge understatement.

During the introductions, I remember waving a towel so rapidly I'm surprised my arm didn't come out of its socket. And we obviously carried that energy with us into the game as we routed the Hurricanes, 66-13, to clinch our third consecutive Big East Conference title. Near the end of that game, I jumped up on a bench and held up my helmet to salute the crowd. I just wanted to say thank you to the fans, the coaches, and the professors. I couldn't help but think about how much Syracuse University had done for me. I definitely arrived there as a boy and left there as a man.

I had enjoyed so many special moments in the Dome. In addition to all the football victories, there was that time when I came off Jim Boeheim's basketball bench as a sophomore and helped beat the team I grew up rooting for—the Georgetown Hoyas. But my proudest moment in that building came in May 1999, when my

Donovan McNabb salutes the crowd following his last SU home football game in 1999. Athletics Department, Syracuse University, used by permission.

teammates and I received our degrees. The entire group of guys I started with had graduated, and that enabled us to earn the academic national championship that year in college football. My dad and mom never had the opportunities to get a degree. For me to be the first in my family to be able to do that made it all the more special.

—DONOVAN MCNABB
Class of 1999

WE HELD EACH OTHER'S HANDS as the clock wound down in overtime. The seconds were split between nervous silence, cheering, and chants of "Let's go Orange!" with 35,446 of our closest friends. Running on two hours of sleep, the adrenaline of College Game Day kept my friends and me going as we neared our eighteenth hour at the Dome for Syracuse's first-ever matchup against Duke in the ACC. We high-fived and hugged each other, screaming as the clock hit zero, with Syracuse's 91-89 victory shining bright on the scoreboard. I'll always remember it, because it's the day I learned what it means to be part of Orange Nation.

It's spending long days with your friends, laughing, talking, and cheering. It's having someone who is there for you to hold on to through wins and losses, success and failure, not just on the basketball court, but in life.

When the cheering comes to an end, the stands empty, and we leave our beloved alma mater, the spirit of Orange Nation stays with us. It's in the memories of days spent in the Dome, on the Quad, along Marshall Street, and all the other places that made SU home. It's the sense of pride when someone recognizes the block S we wear so frequently, and the bonds it helps create when we meet people who love Syracuse as much as we do. It truly is a nation, one filled with support, love, kindness, and dedication, through everything.

I will always cherish the memories I have from Syracuse. It gave me the gift of lifelong friendships; of people I get to share those memories with. That's what Orange Nation is all about, and I will always be proud and grateful to be part of it.

—JESSICA PETERS
Class of 2014

I ARRIVED AT SYRACUSE UNIVERSITY in the fall of 1961. I don't know what I expected of SU or even what I expected from a college education. I know for certain I didn't expect to get what I got. In fact, I got two educations. The first was a wonderful liberal education. The second was an education in political action.

1961 really was a bridge year. The world was changing and we were at the beginning of that change. Many questioned a Greek system that supported fraternities and sororities that segregated by race or religion. Women were beginning to ask why curfews were necessary. We wanted to know why the university acted in loco parentis.

My mind was opening to ideas I'd never thought of before. Comparative religion gave me an interesting lens for looking at the world and campus. Art history courses gave me a new way to think about interrelated cultures. Reading French novels exposed me to yet another way of seeing the world.

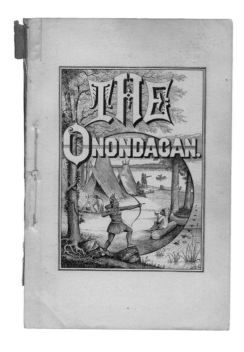

First *Onondagan* yearbook.
Onondagans Reference
Collection, University
Archives.

Meanwhile, in other parts of the country students were "sitting in" at lunch counters and being arrested or beaten. Blacks were challenging segregation in schools and everywhere else. For me and many of my friends, it was interesting to follow their efforts. We believed in equality and social justice, but I don't think I thought it might have a direct impact on us here in Central New York.

And then the rate of change sped up. In August of 1963, Dr. Martin Luther King Jr. led the March on Washington. Weeks later there were picket lines in downtown Syracuse organized by the Congress of Racial Equality, one of the civil rights groups involved in the Washington march. The city was tearing down housing in the most African American ward in the city.

As the protests continued, more and more SU students and faculty started showing up on those picket lines. On campus, some graduate students started the Syracuse University Committee on Equality. SUCE became the nucleus around which the civil rights movement grew on campus, and both faculty members and students attended meetings.

It was at one of those meetings that a group of us agreed we were willing to engage in civil disobedience. We were ready to sit in and take the consequences. As expected, we were all arrested and spent a night in jail. On returning to campus, I don't remember there were any consequences from the university, but I was called before the Dean of Women; it seems I had broken curfew.

Just weeks after my arrest, John F. Kennedy was shot. I remember my then boyfriend, now husband, walking across Walnut Avenue and telling me the president had been shot. I think every student and faculty member knows where they were on campus that day.

Like I said, it was a time of radical change as the civil rights movement morphed into the antiwar movement. There were teach-ins at Hendricks Chapel where we could listen to various views. There were antiwar demonstrations on campus. Hardly a day went by when students weren't discussing the draft.

In the spring of 1965 a number of churches were bombed in Jonesboro, Louisiana. Over spring break a group of SU students decided to go down to help rebuild one of the churches. There were three carloads of students heading south. We came to the church construction site one morning to find a board leaning against a tree with a bullet hole in it. A warning from the Klan.

Upon our return, a fine arts student made a beautiful silver cross, which we sent to the congregation. The cross never made it to church as the church was bombed again.

I graduated in the spring of 1965, and thinking back on my years at Syracuse, I'm grateful for the excellent liberal arts education I received. I'm equally grateful for studying in an environment that gave me the freedom to learn outside the classroom. As an adult, those two lines of inquiry have come together and made me a richer and more involved person.

—JAN STRAUSS RAYMOND
Class of 1965

THE YEARS I WENT TO SYRACUSE (2002-6) were some of the coldest and snowiest on record. Maybe it was all the hard studying (or partying?), but I don't remember the weather. My freshman year, the Syracuse men's basketball team won the NCAA national championship with fellow frosh Carmelo Anthony and Gerry McNamara. Some friends scraped together funds to carpool down to the Final Four in New Orleans, but I stayed on campus.

My then boyfriend, a Syracuse senior, snuck me into a Marshall Street bar to watch the championship game. When we won, everyone poured onto the street in wild celebration. Someone lifted me onto their shoulders, giving me a perfect bird's eye view as students stripped naked, climbed trees, and screamed in glory at the historic win. This was before the time of Facebook, so you can imagine my surprise the next day when my parents called from Oregon to say I was the front-page picture on CBSSports.com! It's a night I'll never forget!

The following October I was at a party on South Campus when I ran next door to use a friend's bathroom. After waiting a few minutes, I started banging on the door, hollering that I had to pee. To my sheer shock and mortification, Carmelo himself sheepishly opened the door. He was playing for Denver and back on campus for an NBA exhibition game at the Dome. I was so stunned, I could only stammer a few words before bolting past him into the bathroom.

My senior year, six girlfriends and I shared a decrepit house off Euclid Avenue with a rotting porch and a family of raccoons nesting in the attic. It was paradise. As Newhouse students, we felt lucky to attend one of the best journalism programs in the country. We worked hard, played hard, and pushed each other to be better. Coincidentally, that year five of us also had part-time jobs at various bars and cafes along Marshall Street (myself at Faegan's). On Parents Weekend, over BBQ and beer pong, our fathers collectively bragged they'd raised daughters who "paid their own way through college." From that day forward, our house was known as the Brothel, a title my girlfriends and I still use on our group chats and emails to this day.

As I write this, I am now pregnant with my first child and can say with absolute confidence that if my child doesn't "bleed Orange" he/she will at least be expected to *wear* Orange.

—STEPHANIE BURTON MOLDAN
Class of 2006

I'D BEEN TO EVERY HOME FOOTBALL GAME since arriving on the Hill in the fall of 1973, Ben Schwartzwalder's last season as coach of the Orangemen. The weather conditions on October 9, 1976, were without a doubt the worst I'd ever experienced. Official attendance was generously announced as 11,223 that day. The ticket counters must have failed math.

The ancient cement bowl that was Archbold had no seats per se. Patrons sat on the same piece of concrete that the person behind them put their feet on. When it rained—as it did in torrents that day

Fans at old Archbold. Courtesy of Scott Pitoniak.

for three straight hours—the water would cascade all the way down from the top row to the bottom row, and onto the track surrounding the field. Anyone that dared to sit down got a wet bottom almost immediately.

By halftime, the field had become a quagmire, with just a few courageous patches of grass visible. The uniforms of both teams shared the same dark brown, mud-caked coloring. Only the players' helmets distinguished our Orangemen from the boys from Tulane.

Not surprisingly, neither team could get anything going in the muck, and as the game splish-splashed to its soggy conclusion it appeared as if this mud bowl was going to end in a scoreless tie.

Then, miraculously, in the final minute, Syracuse mounted its only real drive into Tulane's territory. With just seven seconds remaining, junior kicker Dave Jacobs sloshed on to attempt a twenty-five-yard field goal. It was now or never. This was before there was overtime, so we were looking at the game ending 0-0. We held our collective breath as the snap came back and Dave kicked the ball. He somehow split the uprights. Our loyalty (insanity?) of sticking it out to the windswept, rain-soaked, bitter cold end had been rewarded with a 3-0 victory. We were so elated you'd have thought we'd won our second national championship.

A bunch of us soaked-to-the-bone students left the stadium floating on a euphoric cloud of camaraderie from witnessing a dramatic, if not epic Orange victory. Next stop, the Varsity, to grab some slices and a pitcher, relive the game, strategize that night's activities and watch the Tulane banner on the wall be turned upside down by a member of the football team in recognition of having vanquished the Green Wave.

As we left Archbold, we made our way over to Crouse to go down to M Street. At Crouse, immediately at our feet, was a glistening steep hill of inviting deep green grass wet with the rain that had fallen all day. As was our custom, my roommate, who would be my best man six years later, and I lay in the grass and rolled down the hill. Picking up speed as we neared University Place at the bottom.

This act of youth always caused uncontrollable laughter as we knew there was no way to stop until we reached level ground.

I have come back to campus at least three to four times every year since to cheer on the Orange, through good times and bad. Each time I leave the Dome I am eventually on the top of the green hill that aprons Crouse. I no longer roll down it. Not because of societal constraints, but because Father Time is not so forgiving to sixty-year-old joints. In my heart, though, I am transported back to when we were bulletproof and had our whole lives in front of us. And especially if it's raining, I smile inside remembering a muddy slog on a distant, gray October day.

—ED SHAW
Class of 1977

IT IS A LITTLE KNOWN AND TRUE FACT that my room—106-C—at Flint dormitory burned to a crisp early in my sophomore year. There was no arson involved here, but merely extreme misfortune. Some sort of electrical overload started a fire which caught on a sheet and the next thing you know at one o'clock in the morning the room is a ball of fire.

Naturally, my roommate, Roger Holstein, and I, spring into immediate action and grab the fire extinguisher at either end of the hall. Just as naturally, they are empty because everyone's been putting them to proper use—having water fights throughout the semester.

With nothing to douse the blaze, it grew in intensity, and the dorm had to be evacuated at one in the morning on a very cold November night. The sight of people half-naked and, in some cases, barefoot in the snow was most disquieting.

—BOB COSTAS
Class of 1974

WE'D BEEN PREPARING FOR IT FOR WEEKS, but like most things in life, it didn't go as planned.

A week before election night 2016, our presentation director showed the news staff and management our versions of the post-election front page. It was supposed to be a smooth night of production with Hillary Clinton projected to win handily. We still had versions for if Donald Trump won, but realized it was unlikely based on the polls.

Then the night came and the pendulum started swinging.

Would we have to run an undecided headline atop the front page? It looked as if Trump won, but our normal 12:30 a.m. deadline had come and gone and there still wasn't a president-elect. You can't be taught how to prepare for those moments. At 2 a.m. when a new president is finally named and it's your call on when to send the paper to print, nothing beats that adrenaline.

In the newsroom, we had an assistant sports editor doing a second read on a news coverage story and a sports copy editor going over the main A1 story on Trump's win. Our sports editor sprinted to the Quad after rumors of a possible student protest after covering an SU men's basketball game just a few hours before.

It was a student newspaper. In a nutshell: organized chaos.

The paper was sent a few minutes after 3:30 a.m. with the "Trump Wins" headline. You can imagine the smile on my face the next day when the student-produced DO with full coverage sat next to other papers with "Too Close To Call" headlines.

—JUSTIN MATTINGLY
Class of 2017

AFTER WHAT WE HAD BEEN THROUGH [in World War II], we were eager to settle down and build a life for ourselves. Many of us couldn't have done that without the GI Bill. Some of us who were injured were unable to work for a living, and many of us could never have afforded to go to college on our own. Syracuse and the GI Bill gave us a chance we never would have had.

It was a big adjustment for us. When we were let out from the service, we were mature young men and ladies, but we were used to following orders and having our lives scheduled for us. For the first time in our lives, we had to learn self-discipline. It was an entirely new life. But our professors were very understanding as we made this dramatic transition. One of the things I remember most was the kindness of our instructors. They were always there for us, in and out of class.

—FRANK SCHNELL
Class of 1950

AS AN UNDERGRADUATE and graduate student at SU, I have many great memories, but one I remember well is the time me and the other students who were to portray the mascot for the 1990-91 school year were at cheerleading camp at a university in Tennessee. After the "Woody B. Orange" costume was retired (with the name not well known), a brand new one was created that summer and tradition stated we needed to come up with a new name. After much consideration, we came up with the name Otto as the other choice. Opie didn't seem like a good fit, given it rhymed with Dopey. Once we got back to campus to start the fall semester, the mascot crew and cheerleaders started calling him by the new name and slowly Otto caught on with everyone associated with the university. By the time I graduated in May 1992, most fans knew our mascot as Otto! Now three decades (how is that possible????) after that meeting in that college dorm at camp, I continue to be thrilled that I was part of a legacy that will be with the university forever.

—MITCH MESSINGER
Class of 1992, MS 1993

THE INNOCENT COMMENT seemed odd at the time.

"I hope that no one we know was on that plane," our friend said shortly after my roommate and I walked into our South Campus apartment on Lambreth Lane.

The three of us, all seniors at Syracuse University, had just taken a final exam at Newhouse and were looking forward to decompressing a bit on a Wednesday afternoon before heading down to the Carrier Dome for a men's basketball game against Western Michigan that night.

It was Dec. 21, 1988, and we were about to find out that our lives had been forever changed.

There was no internet or Twitter at the time, so news didn't travel as fast as it does today. But, as the afternoon progressed, we became glued to the television set as details about the plane began to emerge and that innocent comment proved prophetic. That plane was Pan Am Flight 103 and it exploded over Lockerbie, Scotland. The bombing was an act of terrorism and killed all 259 people on board, including thirty-five Syracuse students who had spent the semester studying abroad.

Soon our apartment phone began to ring (there were no cell phones back then, either) as concerned parents, friends, and former students began to ask us all kinds of questions—including if anyone we knew was on the plane. Unfortunately, the answer was yes.

Wendy Lincoln was from North Adams, Massachusetts, my roommate's hometown. She had given us a ride to the grocery store once when we were living at Skytop and didn't have a car. As the day went on we learned that we knew others. Some from class, others through friends, and more through social activities like pickup basketball, student government, and intramurals.

"These were some of our best and brightest," Chancellor Melvin Eggers told us.

And he was right. These were our brothers and sisters in orange. They were people who shared similar dreams; people with whom we stood side by side and cheered on the Orange at the Dome; people that we walked the Quad with in the middle of a Syracuse winter—and they were gone. Our world, our innocence, our invincibility had been taken away by terrorists, and it hurt. It still does.

The days after the bombing remain a blur. Shock and grief will do that to a twenty-one-year-old, but the circumstances we endured are nothing compared to the pain the families of the victims dealt—and are still dealing—with.

As the years have passed, the pain—although a different type of pain—remains. You remain thankful for the memories our friends were able to make studying abroad, but are sad that so many of their stories were never told to the ones who loved them most. You realize that they have been gone from this world longer than they were here, and anger surfaces when you stop to think about all of the opportunities that were so unfairly taken from them. The chance to celebrate the holidays with their families. The chance to return to campus and be with their friends. The whole life that they had in front of them. Graduation. Career success. The chance to find a life partner to continue their journey with and enjoy all of the experiences that so many of us enjoy today.

All taken away by the cowardice of terrorism.

Each time I visit campus, I make it a point to stop by the Place of Remembrance, where I pause and read each of the thirty-five names. Usually there is a smile or two, and maybe a small laugh as I recall a memory. Of course there are tears as well. There is also a sense of determination each time I wipe my cheek and turn away to face the world again. Evil will not win. Evil cannot win. It wouldn't be fair to them.

—STEVE BRADLEY
Class of 1989

Remembrance Scholar.
© Syracuse University.
Photo by Stephen Sartori.

MY TIME AT SYRACUSE was the best four years of my life. My favorite memory is camping out and attending the Syracuse versus Villanova basketball game on February 27, 2010. My friends and I camped out the night before, but because it was so cold they moved us inside the Dome during the night. It was so much fun camping out and staying up all night with my best friends. In the morning, the College Game Day crew from ESPN began the day with a live broadcast from inside the Dome at 9 a.m. After the live broadcast we spent the day painting our faces and getting ready for the big game. The game tipped off at 9 p.m. and it broke the NCAA on-campus attendance record with an announced crowd of 34,616. There was so much energy in the building that night, and Syracuse won, 95-77! It truly was an amazing day on the Syracuse campus. It's a day I will always remember.

—KARI WILMOT
Class of 2011

IT STARTED IN A DORM ROOM on the Mount. The late Marc DeCosta (a.k.a. Coz, class of 1980) was a creative visionary who launched and starred in what became a Syracuse musical phenomenon in

Air Band. Courtesy of Laurence D. Nayman, private collection.

the late 1970s. Known as the Air Band, a group of students started lip-syncing their favorite hit songs in a Day Hall dorm room, circa 1976. Playing tennis rackets as guitars, a lacrosse stick as a bass, and squeezing a pillow as an accordion, they took SU by storm. Their creative flair and promotional extravagances led them from dorm lounges and Orange coffeehouses (SUCH and Two Below) all the way to the 1978 and 1979 Dance Marathon stages at Archbold and Manley Field House. It even included paid gigs at various clubs in Syracuse, like the Firebarn and Poor House North.

At the outset, the Air Band did not use real instruments (this was long before the Karaoke era), but they progressed to the point where their mastery of props (guitar, bass, drums, sax, organ) led many casual observers to believe they were a tightly choreographed cover band. There were mishaps when a dry ice stunt went awry, and brief moments of glory when "groupies" rushed the stage. Those groupies were actually fellow dorm residents who enjoyed playing the role of screaming rock fans just as much as the band enjoyed pretending to play instruments. It seemed that everyone had bought into DeCosta's dream.

In addition to the lead singer Coz, there was Steve Latour, a.k.a. Lebeau, who started with a desk lamp as a saxophone, and John Barrows, known as Mr. Bop, on trash can drums; Larry Nayman played a faux guitar, and there was a mysterious bassist known only as the Electric Jaw. The Air Band performed an eclectic mix of contemporary pop/rock hits with a jazz infusion, forming a repertoire that included the Beatles, Boston, Billy Joel, Lynyrd Skynyrd, Maynard Ferguson, the Sanford Townsend Band's "Smoke from a Distant Fire," and Bobby Darin's "Mack the Knife."

For three years the Air Band was the toast of the Hill, creating indelible memories for those matriculating at SU in the late 1970s.
—LARRY NAYMAN
Class of 1979

THE DROUGHT against our fiercest football rival had dragged on for sixteen long years. Along the way, there had been plenty of unhappy times in State College's "Happy Valley," old Archbold, and the Dome. So, I guess it wasn't surprising that when we finally beat Penn State, 48-21, on October 17, 1987, some called it the biggest win since Syracuse won the national title in the 1960 Cotton Bowl. It was a masterfully executed game plan in all facets of the game—the architect of that plan was our coach Dick MacPherson. But in this historic moment, it was Ben Schwartzwalder, coach of that national championship team and the last team to beat Penn State on October 17, 1970, who was carried off the field.

Coach Ben always had an open invitation from Coach Mac to visit and address the team. When he came to watch practice Coach Mac would cancel post-practice conditioning (wind sprints) so Coach Ben would have our undivided and enthusiastic attention. The break from sprints was like Christmas morning. When rumors swirled that Coach Ben may come to practice, we were all on watch, regularly glancing onto East Colvin Street hoping to spot his silver convertible Oldsmobile. "BEN ALERT!" would replace the din of aggressive demands of coaches, player taunts, and bodily collisions.

We were always grateful for the relief from sprints his visits allowed, but there was something more significant about those visits. Unbeknownst to us, he was a link to our history. Although we were too young (and cool) to recognize and articulate our place in that history, those moments with Ben were uniquely profound and magical—we were inspired by his presence.

Coach Ben is SU football royalty—coach of our only national championship team. He also coached the first African American Heisman Trophy winner and only winner of the coveted award in our history. We knew Coach Mac truly treasured those moments; his affection for Coach Ben was infectious. We also saw the response of assistant coaches who showed respect and reverence for the legendary coach who embodied the storied history of Syracuse football.

When he was carried off the field, it was not just about that moment of victory in a single game, it was a celebration of our SU football family and history. The great SU tight end John Mackey always talked about standing on the shoulders of those who came before him. In that moment, the players of 1987 put that history on our shoulders and Coach Ben got one more ride.
—DON MCPHERSON
Class of 1988

WE HAVE MANY FAVORITE MEMORIES at Syracuse University, but the most outstanding was a meeting at a freshman mixer in 1951. I was a junior. I decided to check out the new crop of freshman ladies.

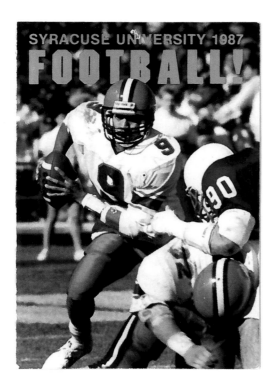

Don McPherson sparked an Orange football revival. Athletics Department, Syracuse University, used by permission.

One in particular caught my interest and I asked her to dance. After a bit, I suggested that we go to the Orange (the favorite watering spot) for a beer. She was not so sure, but I told her that my Army surplus Jeep was parked outside, so she agreed. At eighteen, after her first beer ever, I dropped her off at her living center and went back to my fraternity and sat down with our president who was a WWII Army captain veteran. I told him that I met the girl I would marry. He asked me her name and I said Jan, but I did not remember her last name as it was difficult. I called the Living Center the next day and asked for Jan. "Which Jan?" they asked, as there were three. On our first real date, she told me she had a serious boyfriend at Cornell, and it turned out that he was also a Kappa Sigma. So the challenge was to replace him, and I had the advantage of distance. At the time I was a member of the tennis team and we played Cornell and stayed in the frat house there, and I met her friend. I lost my set, but won my lady.

After graduating in 1952, Janet Streithof Blaich and I ultimately married, had three sons, lived in Boston, New York, Grand Rapids, Basel, Switzerland, Eindhoven in the Netherlands, and finally Aspen, Colorado. On June 4, 2018, we celebrated our sixty-fifth wedding anniversary.

—ROBERT I. BLAICH
Class of 1952, honorary degree 1990

I AM FROM THE UKRAINE. My favorite memory from SU was the game against Duke in 2017, and the buzzer-beater by John Gillon. I cursed the whole first half of the game in Ukrainian, because we were losing so badly. During the break I said to myself—no more curses, just pray! It is more constructive ☺. Have faith! I prayed the whole second half and John scored that crazy 3 points at the buzzer! I became insane. And I said: "Thanks, God, everything is possible with your help!"

—OLEKSIY ANOKHIN
Class of 2017

LET ME TELL YOU ABOUT MY FIRST DAY, freshman year. It was August 26, 1973. Shaw Hall. In those days we had to register for classes at Archbold Gym. In 110-degree heat, we ran from line to line hoping to get into the classes we wanted. Sophomore year we moved into DellPlain. I was so excited to be in a co-ed dorm! We froze to death watching football in Archbold Stadium and cheered on the basketball team at the Manley Zoo. Of course they were the Orangemen then, and we had an Indian as our mascot. Our bookstore was a little yellow house next to Bird Library, and there was no student union. Bird was our student union. We could talk and eat on the first two floors, and that was where we met our friends.

My School of Nursing is no longer there, but I remember my capping and pinning ceremonies, both in Hendricks Chapel. I also remember fraternity parties, Kimmel Dining Hall, the Dingleman, Marvin Druger, the Quad in the snow and the Quad in the sunshine, the Orange on Thursday nights, and a THB at Cosmos, Spectrum Records, graduation day on May 14, 1977, in Manley Field House—and so much more.

What I remember most are the incredible, amazing, indescribable, life-lasting friendships we made. I met my best friend in the halls of Shaw in 1973—she is my heart and soul—and we're still going strong. Finally, I am proud to say all three of my children graduated from Syracuse, so I have had the pleasure and excitement to be on campus in recent years. I wore my SU Alumni Parent button with pride, and felt lucky to be able to relive those happy years.

—ROBIN WEISS SHECTER
Class of 1977

NINE THOUSAND MILES. Thirty days. Twenty missed classes. Six cities. Five beds. Four hotels. One incredible month. In the spring of 2013, I had the opportunity to see each of the Syracuse men's basketball team's final nine games in person—from the Big East Tournament to the Final Four. As part of Sour Sitrus Society, I was one of a handful of students chosen to travel with the men's team to every tournament game. I could not wait to play trumpet in the mecca of basketball for the Big East Tournament. The atmosphere in the building was amazing. Even though we lost to Louisville in the Big East Final, Syracuse played great and carried a ton of momentum into the NCAA Tournament.

After a quick twenty-four hours in Syracuse after the Big East Tournament, I was off to San Jose for a week, cheering the team to victories over Montana and California, even though we were playing three thousand miles from the Dome. Wins over Indiana and Marquette in the East Regional in Washington, DC, meant watching the team celebrate and cut down the nets—truly a once-in-a-lifetime experience. Barely twelve hours after the Elite Eight win, I was back on a plane with one thing on my mind: Atlanta. Although the Final Four game against Michigan didn't end up going how Syracuse fans would have wanted, playing trumpet in the Georgia Dome is something I can safely say I will *never* get to do again. Regardless of the outcome of the last game, I would not trade those four weeks for anything. Appearing on national television and sitting courtside for incredible Big East and NCAA tournament runs by the Orange is something I will never forget.

—JEREMY PHILIPSON
Class of 2014

Old Archbold Stadium. Athletics Department, Syracuse University, used by permission.

WE HAD TO GO TO SYRACUSE UNIVERSITY to meet and fall in love with someone from our same small Pennsylvania town. We're Jack and Bonnie, and this is our story.

I (Jack Garner) was a 1963 graduate of South Williamsport High School. Bonnie Eiswerth was a 1965 graduate of cross-town rival, Montoursville High School. We had attended the same sports events, but sat on the opposite side of the field or court. After getting respective undergraduate degrees from St. Bonaventure University and Lock Haven State, we both found ourselves pursuing master's degrees at Syracuse. Mine was in journalism at the Newhouse School. Bonnie was getting an MS in education.

Unbeknownst to us, we had a mutual friend named Meg who knew we were both from Williamsport, but also knew we weren't aware of each other or of our roots. She thought it'd be a lark to arrange a meeting where we would accidentally discover that coincidence. Then, who knows?

In the fall of 1969, I was in my second year of the two-year master's program, and financing it by being a resident advisor. I had been an RA in Marion Hall for 1968-69, and was now the dorm director of DellPlain Hall. Bonnie was in her first year of grad school and was an RA in Shaw.

On Oct. 6, 1969, at 11 p.m., I heard a knock on the door of my director suite. There was Meg and another girl (Bonnie). Meg said they came to borrow "the sangria can." (The RAs shared a big aluminum farmer's milk can to use at parties. They'd throw any liquid they had into it and call it sangria. Believe it or not, after nearly a half century, we still have that can.)

I asked the ladies to come in and offered them something to drink. But, since I'd had a party the night before, it ended up being a glass of water. Bonnie saw some photos on the wall from my photography class, and my camera. She held it up, and noticed an address sticker on its bottom with "South Williamsport, Pa." And that got the conversation started. We discovered we had mutual friends in Williamsport and had been to the same events, especially involving our rival high schools. Heck, while getting her undergraduate degree, Bonnie had even student-taught at South Williamsport (though, of course, this was after I'd graduated).

We hit it off from the start.

I'm lousy remembering names, and realized in the days immediately following, that I'd gotten Bonnie's last name wrong. But I was able to clarify it with a little investigation. Now, to ask her out.

Coming on October 18 was the football game of the year, the annual Syracuse-Penn State game at old Archbold Stadium. (It's hard to imagine how huge this game was in the days before Big East, ACC or Big Ten memberships. Both universities were prestigious independents and archrivals.)

I finally called Bonnie late in the week of the big game. Though Bonnie could imagine her mother saying she should never accept such a last-minute request, she agreed. Because I was a higher-ranking dorm director, I had two tickets, and Bonnie only had one. Outside the stadium, I scalped hers for a then astronomical twenty-five dollars. When I tried to give Bonnie the money, she said: "Keep it. You sold it." I said, "Yes, but it was your ticket." We went back and forth, and I finally said, "I got a better idea—let's go to dinner on it." SU lost a defensive battle, 15-14.

After the game, we headed for Soo Lin's on Erie Boulevard, ate Chinese, and drank Tahitians. And we never looked back.

Though Bonnie was in the first year of a two-year graduate program, a national tragedy changed the schedule. When the National Guard killed four at Kent State University on May 4, 1970, the university was closed and only the RAs remained on campus. Bonnie had lots of time and access to a near-empty library, and was able to finish her thesis early. She then took two summer courses and had her MS degree by early August.

On August 15, 1970, we were married, in our hometown of Williamsport, Pennsylvania. We moved to Rochester, New York, where I worked for the Gannett newspapers, first in news, but eventually as the national film critic for Gannett. Bonnie was a science teacher in the Brighton and Pittsford school districts, eventually got a second master's degree in school administration from SUNY Brockport, and finished her career as the assistant superintendent for technology at BOCES. Meg's little lark of coincidence led to a half century of marriage, three children, six grandchildren, and continued cheers for Syracuse University football.

—JACK AND BONNIE GARNER
Class of 1970

SU RAISED A TON OF MONEY back in the day with an annual forty-eight-hour dance marathon to benefit the Muscular Dystrophy Association. I participated twice. Each couple was responsible to raise their own money and the funds were all pooled to raise a huge amount each year. Everyone raised money with pledge cards, as many of the walks and fundraisers in the 1970s required. But most of the couples competed to be the largest fundraising groups for some kind of incentive or prize. The fraternities and sororities always won that competition, but I think they actually had a prize for the "Greek" winner and then for other couples that were not in a frat or sorority.

One of the years my partner and I decided to compete, and to do so, organized a one-mile road race with a $50 entry fee. We offered a $500 prize to the winner which would be donated to the MDA in their name. Many of the other Dance Marathon couples put a runner in hoping they would get the top prize. Just about all the frats did.

This was not your average road race. In addition to the run, there were five checkpoints along the way where participants would stop and chug a beer. The race started on the Quad, and the checkpoints were at Hungry Charley's, Sutter's Mill, the Orange, the Jabberwocky, and the Rathskellar in the basement of Slocum Hall.

All of the bars donated the beer, provided a table where the beers were stacked and waiting for the runners to arrive, so we got that at no cost. The race started on the Quad, ran down through the Marshall Street area and finished at the top of the steps at Hendricks Chapel. This was meant to be reminiscent of the movie *Rocky*. It was a huge success. We grossed about $1,200, and after giving the winner his $500, we made around $700 for the MDA.

The winner wound up being a member of the Phi Psi fraternity that ran on the track team, and when he finished, he leaned over the rails at the top of the stairs and deposited the beer he drank into the bushes!

—MIKE VADALA
Class of 1978

I WAS BLESSED to be involved in some really memorable football games during my four years at Syracuse. There was the Kansas game, where I rushed for 252 yards, and the Independence Bowl in 1979, which we won after having to play our entire regular-season schedule on the road while the Carrier Dome was being constructed. And, of course, who can ever forget the night we opened the Dome the following season.

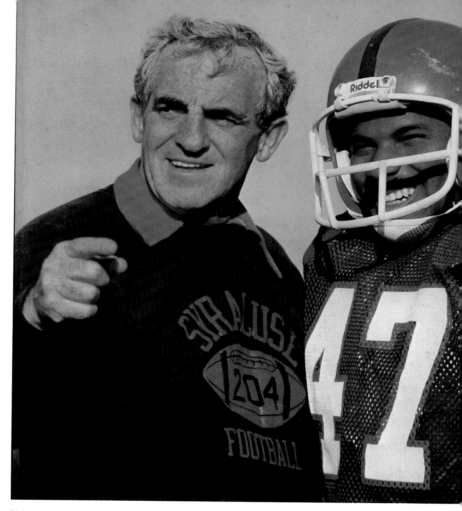

SU's all-time leading rusher Joe Morris with Coach Dick MacPherson. Athletics Department, Syracuse University, used by permission.

But the most meaningful game for me was my last college game on November 21, 1981. We beat West Virginia at home that day. My mom wasn't supposed to be there because she was going to my younger brother Jamie's high school game back in Massachusetts, and I understood completely, because he was the baby of the family.

However, after our game ended, Coach Dick MacPherson grabbed me by the arm and said, "Joe, I want you to see someone." I followed him and there was my mom, grinning ear to ear. Apparently, she had watched the first half of Jamie's game, then hopped in her car and drove all the way to Syracuse to see the end of my game. I'm just surprised she didn't get pulled over for speeding on the Mass Pike and Thruway. I had tears in my eyes as I picked her up and hugged her. Mom has since passed, but I'll always have that special memory.

It just spoke to what a loving mother she was.

—JOE MORRIS
Class of 1981

ONE DAY IN ENGLISH CLASS the student in the next seat handed me a carefully folded note. It read: "Dear Beautiful Hair—How about meeting me for conversation after this class? Signed, R.B. (P.S., I'm sitting two seats behind you.)"

I glanced around to see what I thought was the tallest, most fascinating-looking man I had ever seen! He asked me for a date and that weekend we went to the new and daringly dark Pilots Club downtown. I felt very sophisticated to be suddenly dating a former paratrooper who appeared worldly, witty, well-traveled, and brilliant!

One night we were munching popcorn at the movies when a newsreel came on and showed several paratroopers jumping out of war planes and landing in a wooded area. Suddenly, R.B. got up and left his seat. I followed, thinking he must be sick. I found him leaning heavily against the wall near the theater entrance visibly very shaken.

"Didn't you ever notice I had an ugly nose?" he asked. I hadn't.

R.B. then told me that when a plane he was in during the war had been fired at, he and his buddies had jumped out. He landed in a tree, and a small branch ripped open his nose. Many months of hospitalization, pain, trauma, and plastic surgery followed, and he said it seemed then that his dreams of becoming a doctor would never materialize.

The full impact of what these veterans had gone through for us did not fully penetrate my still-immature mind until I had met, and learned to know and respect, many of these veterans over my four years at school.

—CLAIRE LAYTON GENK
Class of 1949

MY MOM CAME UP TO VISIT ME my junior year in 1998 the same weekend that a 5-3 Syracuse football team hosted number sixteen Virginia Tech with the Big East title hanging in the balance. The Orangemen came into that year with a lot of hype, but had just lost to West Virginia and fallen out of the rankings for the first time all season. I remember it felt like our backs were up against the wall. To have any chance of fulfilling its destiny, SU would have to win this game.

My friends and I had season tickets in the student section. Rather than sit separately in the nosebleeds, we bought a scalped ticket on Marshall Street for my mom and then snuck her in with the rest of the students. I was excited for her but I was also extremely nervous because I knew how much Syracuse football tended to make us yell and curse.

I probably don't need to tell you what happened. The Hokies raced to a 21-6 halftime lead, but Syracuse stormed back in the second half. The two teams traded leads, and Virginia Tech went up 26-22 with less than five minutes left. Donovan McNabb began leading the Orangemen on a drive from their own seventeen-yard line. As Syracuse approached the goal line, I turned to my mom and said: "All right, if they score here, we are storming the field." "Okay," she responded, before thinking about it for a few seconds and then asking, "What does that mean?"

Commencement joy in 2015. © Syracuse University. Photo by Stephen Sartori.

I quickly explained the logistics, just in time for McNabb to hit tight end Stephen Brominski in the corner of the end zone as time expired. Syracuse won and everyone made a beeline directly for the field, including my mom.

The best part was that as we stood there celebrating, McNabb came running toward us with his hand raised high. He ran near my mom and high-fived her. At the time, I would have killed for that high-five. But if anyone else had to get it, I'm glad it was my mom.

—SEAN KEELEY
Class of 2000

I WAS PART OF THE FIRST CLASS of "open Ottos"—the first group of mascots that did not come exclusively from Lambda Chi Alpha fraternity. In fact, we were the group that named Otto. Auditions were held in the spring of 1990, my junior year. I was thrilled to hear that I was selected to the team of mascots. While I had only one year "in the suit," it was a fantastic year.

There is something magical about being Syracuse's mascot. Although I wasn't much of an athlete, I was able to expand my horizons by learning some stunts with the cheerleaders. I quickly learned the sheer stamina it takes to run around in costume.

Being Otto presented some great opportunities for travel, and some interesting experiences. I recall being carried off the field at Boston College by the entire BC marching band. We also spent a week in Hawaii for the Aloha Bowl. It gets hot in the tropics in an Otto costume! But it was an unforgettable week.

Spending just one year in the costume (my senior year) meant that I largely did not know what I was doing, but I still had a lot of fun being Otto. It was by far my most special experience at Syracuse University.

—BRIAN LAPIS
Class of 1991

I STILL REMEMBER VIVIDLY ATTENDING, by happenstance, the Arents Award ceremony at the end of my senior year in the spring of 1959. At the time I was just passing by one of the buildings on campus, and decided to stop in to see what was happening inside. The ceremony on stage was celebrating the achievements of three of Syracuse University's most distinguished alumni. The honorees were Vernon L. deTar (class of 1927), Eric Faigle (1928, G'30) and Clare Brown Williams (1931). Dean Faigle was the beloved dean of liberal arts.

I was mesmerized, hearing the achievements of these three alumni, and thrilled to watch Chancellor Tolley bestow the highest honor an SU alum can receive to these outstanding individuals. As a graduating senior that year, I reflected on all I had personally accomplished in four years, and was now looking ahead, with these three Arents awardees as my new role models.

Little did I dream that seventeen years later, I would receive a phone call from Chancellor Eggers telling me I had just been selected to receive the Arents for Excellence in Government. I was literally awestruck and speechless, and didn't realize at the time that he was speaking about the same award that I had seen presented to those three distinguished alumni seventeen years earlier. In 1976, I received my award at a beautiful dinner at a lovely building at the edge of campus. The other awardees that year were Floyd Little (1967, Athletics) and Lee J. Topp (1951, Business).

Each year, I try to come back to watch others receive this most significant recognition from our alma mater. I will always cherish the rich memories of my four years on campus, as well as my years since then contributing to the ongoing alumni activities of the boards and association with the colleges.

Thank you, Syracuse University.

—NANCY HARVEY STEORTS
Class of 1959

WHEN YOU ARE SIXTEEN, five foot six, and buy your pants in the "husky" section of the men's clothing shop, your dreams of becoming a successful athlete are pretty much over. But since I was a huge sports fan (especially basketball), I knew that I had to find another way to stay close to the action—and sports writing seemed to be the answer.

So, I joined the high school newspaper sports staff, and when I got to Syracuse, I began writing sports stories for the *Daily Orange*. But by senior year (1970-71), even though I was friendly with most of the basketball players, I didn't feel that I was actually *contributing* anything to the hoops program at SU.

Then, ten minutes into the first home game of that season in Manley Field House, I had an epiphany. It was very evident that there had been no excitement, no vitality, and no rhyme or reason to the music that had been played over the field house speaker system when our players emerged from the locker room and ran onto the court before the start of the game. I immediately realized that I was the right person to change that. So, without checking with anyone at all connected with the university, I mentally named myself the Official SU Basketball DJ during the next time out.

It turned out to be a really simple task to ascend to that lofty position. At halftime, I searched for and quickly found the building's "audio room" which was staffed by one undergrad who I did not know. After he informed me that he was responsible for every aspect of the sounds in the building, I asked him if he minded if I composed a different music cassette to be played at each home game that season when the players ran onto the court and did their pregame warm-ups? The guy said "No," and that was that.

I knew that producing what I now refer to as "SU's first mixtape" would not be difficult since my roommate Steve Palmer (1972) had equipped our room with a top-of-the-line cassette recorder, turntable, tuner/amplifier, and speakers.

As I began to plan out the composition of my first tape, I recalled that at the start of a home game two or three years earlier the Zoo denizens in Manley went wild when the "sound guy" played the *Lone Ranger* theme (the *1812 Overture*) as the players came out of the locker room. But I needed to add one more "bell and whistle" to that routine—so before every home game, I had a friend of mine create a large SU on a huge piece of white paper that the players would run through to the *Lone Ranger* TV show theme music.

Then came time to record the rest of the first "Intro Tape." It was then that I first decided to talk with as many players as possible to find out what their favorite types of music were. Their unanimous choices were "soul" and "rhythm & blues." And some of them specifically asked me to include some of their favorites like Jackie Wilson's "Higher and Higher," JJ Jackson's "But It's All Right," Eddie Floyd's "Knock on Wood," and the Beatles' "Get Back" on every individual tape.

"'Get Back'?" I repeated. "How is that a soul song?" "It's not—it's an inside joke," conceded one of the players. "At our early season practice game at Kansas, Tommy [Green, SU's starting senior point guard] was totally embarrassed on the court by their All-American JoJo White. We've been calling Tommy 'JoJo' ever since." That's when I remembered that the opening stanza of "Get Back" was:

JoJo was a man who thought he was a loner
But he knew it couldn't last
JoJo left his home in Tucson, Arizona
For some California grass

So, for those of you who have been scratching your heads for the past fifty years wondering about "Ira's" choice to mix in "Get Back" with the other danceable and lively songs on his tape, now you know.

Each week I would fill out a cassette with powerful songs by artists like Sly and the Family Stone, Aretha Franklin, Stevie Wonder, James Brown, the Parliaments, and Wilson Pickett. We made the postseason for the only time in my four years at SU that season—and I like to think that I played a small part in the team's success.

—IRA SILVERMAN
Class of 1971

THE EXPERIENCE that impacted me the most was my semester abroad in London. Having never been to Europe before, it was truly eye-opening. After a short period of provided housing, we had to find our own flats, so I learned about different neighborhoods, tube stops, and budgeting. The classes were wonderful and offered courses that took advantage of what makes London unique—from Shakespeare classes with a teacher from the Royal National Theatre to learning about art at the National Gallery to attending performances in both London's West and East End districts.

However, the real value of this opportunity was that I experienced another culture and my perspective on the world shifted— whenever I hear of an event occurring in Europe now, it has real meaning to me—in a way it never did before. I also took a tour of Europe after that semester, and that certainly changed my life as that is how I met my first husband!

—SUSAN HUGHES
Class of 1980

AS A JOURNALISM STUDENT I wrote for the DO covering campus housing, not usually a source of big news. But the proposed closing of a dilapidated, but beloved, off-campus house called the Ostrom

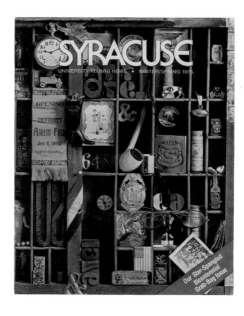

Mementos from bygone days. *SU Alumni News.* Syracuse University, used by permission.

Co-Op, led to a campus protest with thousands of students marching in demonstration. It was the biggest journalistic effort I'd ever be part of and the resulting story was on the front page of the DO's seventy-fifth anniversary edition, with my byline. The most memorable thing that day was when a certain vice chancellor dismissed the massive turnout of student protesters saying, "It's a nice spring-sunny day. You can get people to come out for almost anything."

And I think he had a point. It had been another long Syracuse winter and this was a perfect day. Very few of those "protestors" really knew much or cared about the Ostrom Co-Op, but as undergraduates of the late 1970s who grew up watching the protest marches and demonstrations of the 1960s, it was our chance to get out there and show "the man" we would not be moved! For a short while, there was a singular spirit of togetherness and of students standing up for something important, even if that something was somewhat elusive.

—JOHN BARROWS
Class of 1980

WE VETERANS were serious students who studied hard. But if the ideal student is one who prepares for lifelong learning for the life of the mind, who develops habits of thinking and problem-solving that will last a lifetime, then we vets were probably not ideal. We were in a rush and interested only in career payoff, because we felt we had lost three, four, five years of our lives to the war. We wanted to get on with our careers and interrupted lives.

I suppose a more ideal student experience would be to fully participate in the rites of passage and traditions of the university and to have sufficient leisure time to enjoy a certain maturation of learning. But we were in a hurry. We were going to school full time and working part time to supplement our small monthly government checks. Many of us had families. We just didn't have time to join fraternities or to have a full undergraduate social life.

We were also rather serious about studying. None of us would flunk out if we could help it. We weren't going to go back home and say we had failed. And we were grateful to the government for giving us this chance. And most of us, having gone on to build productive lives, are proud of having repaid that debt.

—FRANK FUNK
Class of 1949

IN SEPTEMBER OF 1947 I was accepted as a Teaching Assistant at Syracuse and graduated from there with a master's degree in mathematics in June 1949.

There was absolutely no comparison between my college years at D'Youville and my graduate years at Syracuse. D'Youville had a total enrollment of about three hundred students—all female. SU was bursting at the seams with returning GI veterans. When I started there, the enrollment was close to fifteen thousand, with a

Published in 1947 by Gabe Josephson, *Vic the Vet* was a cartoon book about a World War II veteran studying at Syracuse University under the GI Bill. Josephson, a decorated veteran of the Battle of the Bulge, graduated from SU in 1950 and enjoyed a successful career as a cartoonist, illustrator, and freelance artist. Gabe Josephson Collection, University Archives.

ratio of about seven men for each woman. I taught college algebra and trigonometry to classes in the engineering school.

These classes were made up almost entirely of male students. Almost all of them were veterans and were a good deal older than me. I was also a math tutor for the athletics department. These were younger fellows who those days needed at least some credits in math to stay in college and play sports. They may have been whizzes on the basketball court or on the football field, but they didn't know beans about algebra. It was quite a challenge for me to shepherd them through their final exams in math so they could continue to excel in sports.

—ALICE STAEBELL SMITH
Class of 1949

I ATTENDED SYRACUSE UNIVERSITY from fall 1975 until May 1978; I graduated from the S.I. Newhouse School of Public Communications with a bachelor's of science degree in public relations in three years by attending summer school at Utica College, which at the time was part of SU. I pledged Kappa Kappa Gamma during the fall of my freshman year, and formed lasting friendships with my "sisters" that I still enjoy today. Greek life was an important part of my university experience in many, many ways.

I lived in Watson Hall my freshman year, the first year the dorm became co-ed after only housing male students for many years. I remember my mother's disapproval of the girls' restroom on my floor because the urinals were still there. She was thrilled when I moved into my sorority house the following year. I was fortunate to have a car on campus, so that meant that my friends and I could socialize off campus at popular venues such as TC's near South Campus, the Dandelion in Fayetteville, and Uncle Sam's off of Erie Boulevard. Popular on-campus bars included the Orange, Hungry Charley's, and the Jabberwocky.

Frequently, after a night of revelry, or a late night studying in Bird Library, comfort could be found at the Dingleman food truck parked on the corner of Comstock and University Place for great fried egg sandwiches, or a short drive to Abe's Donuts, where the fresh, hot honey buns came out of the oven in the wee hours each morning.

Oh, the memories of a wonderful college experience! After a rewarding career in financial communications in New York City, I moved back to Central New York and have been teaching public relations courses at the Newhouse School for a decade and a half—a most rewarding way to come full circle in my Syracuse University experience.

—DONNA (NOBLE) STEIN
Class of 1978

IN MY JUNIOR YEAR I was living in Lawrinson Hall, the tallest building on campus. One day, I got onto the elevator and wound up sharing my ride down with Tommy Myers, the safety on the football team. My jaw dropped, and we actually had a great conversation. Needless to say I followed his career from that point on. Unfortunately, he wound up getting drafted by the New Orleans Saints, who were just awful back then. It was tough being an "Ain'ts" fan, but I just focused on Tommy, who had a great career, going to several Pro Bowls and eventually coaching with the Saints. If it was not for this chance meeting and conversation I can only guess who I would have followed. I suppose there was a grad student who never left school who might have been a candidate. His name? Jim Boeheim!

—BILL ASTIFAN
Class of 1972

MY FIRST APPEARANCE at good old Syracuse University occurred more than six decades ago on November 17, 1956. A high school friend of mine, Bob Hallock, had a sister, Carol, attending SU, and he invited me to hop on a bus and travel over the brand new Thomas E. Dewey Thruway from Albany to Syracuse to visit her and attend the football game against Colgate at Archbold Stadium.

We saw little of Carol, who was much too busy with her own football weekend activities to be able to shuffle around with a couple of high school guys. Luckily, Bob had an aunt who lived just off of Euclid Avenue (on Ackerman) and we were able to stay there and walk back and forth to the university.

The game was the highlight. We had awful seats (concrete of course) in the lower end zone of the west side of Archbold Stadium. But they turned out to be great seats as Number 44—Jim Brown—spent most of the game running into our end zone or kicking extra points over our goal posts. In fact, he personally scored six touchdowns and converted seven extra points good for 43 points that set the NCAA record that lasted for thirty-four years until 1990.

Football program from 1956 Syracuse-Colgate football game. Athletics Department, Syracuse University, used by permission.

player-representation agency. Not only did I jump at the opportunity, but I offered to become the point person for my group.

Our task was to build a social media marketing plan for the agency to continue to grow its presence among its peers and potential clients. Because of my professor's close connection with the agency, I went from leading the project to getting hired as the agency's sole intern in Colorado Springs, and then getting admitted to law school in San Diego.

Years later, I began representing the agency's principal owner as his attorney. My story is a true reflection of how strong the Syracuse alumni network is and how Orange alumni look out for each other when it comes to pursuing dreams and goals. Because of my great experiences at SU, I try to give back the same way and help fellow alumni whenever possible.

—JONATHAN M. STAHLER
Class of 2011

After the game, we hit Marshall Street and managed to get into the Savoy Restaurant. The Varsity was too full. But the Savoy was all right. It had great toasted sticky buns. It also was one of Brown's favorite go-to food spots. He wasn't there that day, of course, or he would have been mobbed. At any rate, the Varsity is still there. The Savoy is long gone.

Most everyone had left by the time we headed back to Bob's aunt's home. It was very quiet. The fading sunlight filtering through the late-fall branches of the campus trees created a soft, hazy orange glow that seemed to be begging me to make Syracuse my choice for college.

I did so in the fall of 1958.

With an orange beanie on my head, per the rule for an incoming freshman in those days, a slide rule (our nonelectrified calculator) in one hand and a portable typewriter (also sans electricity) in my other hand, I began my efforts to obtain my degree. I graduated in the summer of 1962 and obtained a graduate degree two years later.

Neither diploma was accomplished without a massive struggle that included eight o'clock (in the morning!) classes, Saturday morning labs, numerous windblown, frozen-nose trips over the Quad, scrounging up money for a jawbreaker (two hamburgers on a sub roll) from the Dingleman food truck, working for the *Daily Orange*, and many other "experiences" that stamped Syracuse University as an overwhelming and forever part of my life.

—JAMES M. ALBRIGHT
Class of 1962 (BS) and 1964 (MS)

I ATTENDED SYRACUSE UNIVERSITY knowing I wanted to pursue a career in sport management and entertainment law. This dream started becoming a reality when one of my favorite sport management professors (an SU alum) presented our sport communications class with an opportunity to work on a project with a top NFL

8 "Let's Go Orange!"

A Rich Sports Heritage

Joyous Orange players form a human pile seconds after defeating Kansas to win the 2003 NCAA men's basketball championship. Bob Rosato / Sports Illustrated / Getty Images.

2003 NCAA Basketball Championship

The final furious seconds of the 2003 NCAA basketball championship game were playing out in the Louisiana Superdome, and for a fleeting, deflating moment, Jim Boeheim flashed back to the Nightmare on Bourbon Street he had experienced sixteen years earlier in this very same building. It appeared as if history were about to repeat itself and Syracuse was about to be edged at the end again, the way it had in 1987 when Indiana's Keith Smart hit a dagger-in-the-heart jumper to deny the Orangemen their first NCAA hoops crown.

Kansas, which had trailed by as many as 18 points, had shaved the lead to three. Momentum had shifted to the Jayhawks side. "I'm not thinking good thoughts when Kansas is bringing the ball down the court on that final possession," Boeheim recounted in the book *Slices of Orange*. "We had just missed a few free throws—just like '87—and I looked to the corner, and I saw (Michael) Lee open, just like Keith Smart was."

This time, though, thanks to a marvelous heads-up play by SU's Hakim Warrick, Lee's shot wound up in the stands instead of the basket. Warrick, a six-foot-nine forward with elastic arms, came over to the corner and swatted away Lee's potential game-tying 3-point attempt with 1.5 seconds remaining. "It actually worked out for us because we had our centers out and we had put Hakim in at center," Boeheim said. "We didn't do it for defensive reasons, but rather because I wanted to have our best ball-handlers and shooters on the floor. If we had our centers in, it is doubtful one of them would have come out to contest Lee. But Hakim was thinking like a forward, so he went out there. It was an incredible play on his part. I still don't know how he got to that ball."

After the block, the Jayhawks inbounded the ball and were way off with their final desperation shot. The Orangemen had an 81-78 victory and the school's first NCAA hoops title. The ghost of Keith Smart had been exorcised. There was a new signature play in SU hoops history, a more joyous one—Warrick's block. "Same building,

177

same part of the court, similar situation," Boeheim marveled. "If that shot had gone in . . ." He paused for a second, then finished his sentence, saying, "they probably wouldn't have let me back in town."

Instead, he became the toast of the town.

While Warrick's block was *the* play of the game, two precocious freshmen were *the* players of the game. Forward Carmelo Anthony, whose back was so stiff that he had difficulties tying his sneakers before the game, finished with 20 points, 10 rebounds, and 7 assists, while guard Gerry McNamara hit a championship game record six 3-pointers in the first half—some from as far away as the French Quarter—to build SU's sizable cushion. Senior captain Kueth Duany contributed 11 points, while reserves Josh Pace and Billy Edelin combined for 20 points, 6 steals, 10 rebounds, and 4 assists.

"The excitement this team has brought, the attitude of never giving up, and continuing to play hard is a life lesson for every kid who lives in the Syracuse area, and for the adults, too," said Boeheim, whose team erased second-half deficits fifteen times while compiling a 30-5 record. "This team showed that you can be behind, you can be struggling, you can do some silly things sometimes, but you can still overcome all that. If you keep playing and keep working together all the time, anything's possible."

The college basketball prognosticators had low expectations for Syracuse basketball heading into the season. Few questioned the team would be more talented than its predecessor, which had lost eight of its final twelve to wind up in the National Invitation Tournament, a.k.a. the "runner-up tournament." But even with the arrival of the highly touted Anthony and McNamara, none of the pundits believed a team that started two freshmen and two sophomores could make the quantum leap from missing the NCAAs one year to winning it all the next.

However, sometimes talent trumps experience, sometimes youth is not wasted on the young, and that clearly was the case

Precocious freshmen Gerry McNamara and Carmelo Anthony were the catalysts behind SU's first NCAA hoops title. Athletics Department, Syracuse University, used by permission.

with these young Orangemen. "I guess we wound up defying the conventional wisdom that says you can't win without experience," said Duany, the only senior scholarship player on the team. Known to his teammates as Gramps, Duany saw something special in this group the first day of practice in Manley Field House. "I think Melo and G-Mac and Billy Edelin were in so many pressure games in high school and in AAU leagues that the pressure didn't bother them," he said. "They arrived here with a big-game mentality. I had to keep reminding myself these guys are only freshmen and sophomores. There are times when they play like seniors, and sometimes they play like grad students. It's interesting to note that they ended their first practice of the season by huddling up and chanting in unison: "Final Four."

Talk about a good omen.

Though they lost their season opener to Memphis at Madison Square Garden on November 14, 2002, notice was served as Anthony scored 27 points, at the time a school record for freshmen, and McNamara added 14. The Orangemen then reeled off eleven consecutive victories, including a 76-69 win over eleventh-ranked Missouri. They continued to open eyes by storming back from double-digit deficits to defeat second-ranked Pittsburgh and ninth-ranked Notre Dame in the Carrier Dome in February. But it wasn't until the Orangemen came away with victories at three of the toughest venues in college basketball—Michigan State, Notre Dame, and Georgetown—that outsiders began taking them seriously.

After losing to Connecticut in the Big East tournament semifinals, the Orangemen received an NCAA bid and were sent to Boston, where they defeated Manhattan in the opener before coming back from an 18-point deficit to defeat second-round opponent Oklahoma State. From there they went to Albany for the East Regionals. The Pepsi Civic Center became like a mini Carrier Dome as SU escaped with a surprisingly close victory against Auburn before trouncing Oklahoma to reach the Final Four. In the semifinals in New Orleans, they continued to impress with an 11-point victory versus Texas. That set the stage for the title game between Boeheim and Roy Williams, two coaches who had never won a national championship.

Thanks to Warrick's block, the Orange prevailed. Surrounded by family and players past and present on the Superdome court following the victory, Boeheim shed a tear as he peered at the scoreboard to make sure this wasn't all a dream. Later, he and his wife, Juli, led a procession of hundreds of adoring Syracuse fans Pied Piper-style through New Orleans's French Quarter. Before calling it a night, a fan presented Juli with an orange velour cowboy hat that her husband wound up wearing at several functions honoring the team in Syracuse. The nation witnessed Boeheim's self-deprecating side when he traded barbs with David Letterman on national television and felt his pride when he and Anthony rang the opening bell at the New York Stock Exchange. (The Dow wound up climbing 147 points that day.)

Five days after knocking off the Jayhawks, more than 25,000 fans congregated in the Carrier Dome to say thanks amid an atmosphere that resembled a high-energy rock concert. During the ceremonies, Boeheim emerged from a cloud of smoke holding aloft the championship trophy. The crowd roared its approval. School spirit had never been higher.

"This is honestly the coolest thing I've ever lived through," student Tiffany Roy said the day after the title game. "Last night and today were worth every snowy day, every cloud in the sky, every dollar we paid to go here."

1959 National Football Champs

After the Syracuse University football team suffered its third consecutive bowl loss following the 1958 season, patience in the Salt City was starting to wear thin with Coach Ben Schwartzwalder. Yes, the man had resurrected the Orange program from the dead, but there was a growing sentiment, particularly among some sportswriters in Syracuse and beyond, that Schwartzwalder was one of those good but not great coaches who couldn't win the big one. The decorated World War II paratrooper who had survived jumps on D Day appeared unfazed by the criticism. "I don't resent it," Schwartzwalder told an assistant. "The writers write what they see."

What the writers and everyone else would see in 1959 would be one of the greatest college football teams of all time. Ol' Ben finally would win the big one, and all the little ones leading up to it. That season, the Orangemen dominated college football like it had never been dominated before, winning all eleven of their games and becoming the first team in history to lead the nation in total offense (451.5 yards per game) and defense (96.2 yards per game). Led by their Sizeable Seven line and their Four Furies backfield, they atoned for previous bowl futilities and struck a blow for Eastern football with a convincing 23-14 victory against the second-ranked Texas

Longhorns in the Cotton Bowl. (Fifty years later, the game would be inaccurately portrayed as a down-to-the-last-play nail-biter in the movie *The Express*.)

Their aggressive defense pitched five shutouts that season, holding four different opponents to negative rushing yardage, including a minus-88-rushing-yard performance versus Boston University. Led by future Heisman Trophy winner Ernie Davis and a backfield that threw a nation-leading twenty-one touchdown passes, the SU offense did its part, topping college football with a 39 points-per-game scoring average. Syracuse's talent was so abundant that during a nationally televised 38-6 annihilation of UCLA in the Los Angeles Coliseum, football Hall of Famer Red Grange told viewers: "If Syracuse's first team is the number one team in the country, then their second team must be number two."

Despite losing their starting quarterback to a season-ending injury during camp that August, the Orangemen opened the 1959 season with a 14-point victory. They then pummeled their next five opponents—Maryland, Navy, Holy Cross, West Virginia, and Pittsburgh—by an average score of 38-2, setting up a battle of unbeatens against Eastern archrival Penn State on the road in Happy Valley. The seventh-ranked Nittany Lions made things interesting by blocking a punt and returning a kickoff for a touchdown. They threatened to tie the game at 20 with about six minutes remaining, but Gene Grabosky stuffed running back Roger Kauffman on a 2-point conversion attempt. After Davis accidentally stepped out of bounds at the Syracuse seven-yard line on the ensuing kickoff, it appeared that momentum had shifted Penn State's way.

"But we didn't panic," recalled team captain Gerhard Schwedes. "We knew we had a great line, and we knew we could run out those final six minutes."

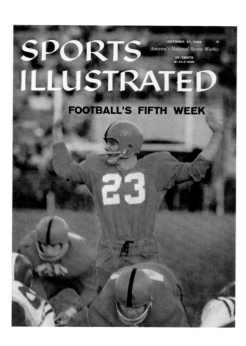

On October 27, 1958, quarterback Chuck Zimmerman became the first Syracuse University athlete featured on the cover of *Sports Illustrated*. Richard Meek / Sports Illustrated / Getty Images.

Syracuse's 1959 national championship football team. Athletics Department, Syracuse University, used by permission.

One of the strong suits of SU's national title team was its Sizeable Seven line, led by All-American guard Roger Davis. Athletics Department, Syracuse University, used by permission.

Ben Schwartzwalder with 1959 team captain Gerhard Schwedes and All-American guard Roger Davis. Athletics Department, Syracuse University, used by permission.

1959—Game by Game

Syracuse 35, Kansas 21

Syracuse 29, Maryland 0

Syracuse 32, Navy 6

Syracuse 42, Holy Cross 6

Syracuse 44, West Virginia 0

Syracuse 35, Pittsburgh 0

Syracuse 20, Penn State 18

Syracuse 71, Colgate 0

Syracuse 46, Boston University 0

Syracuse 36, UCLA 8

Syracuse 23, Texas 14

And that's what they did, imposing their will and methodically moving all the way to the Nittany Lions one-yard line as time expired, preserving a 20-18 victory.

"Ernie and I received a lot of credit that season, but our line was the heart and soul of the team," Schwedes said, referring to two-way linemen Fred Mautino, Gerry Skonieczki, Roger Davis, Bruce Tarbox, Maury Youmans, Bob Yates, and Al Bemiller, collectively known as the Sizeable Seven. "And as good as those guys were, our second line was nearly as good." SU steamrolled its next two opponents—Colgate and Boston University—by a combined score of 117-0, then traveled across the country to trounce seventeenth-ranked UCLA by four touchdowns.

In those days, the national champion was declared before the bowl games, but the SU coaches and players realized that distinction would ring hollow if they lost their Cotton Bowl showdown with second-ranked Texas. During the first day of pre-bowl workouts, Davis severely pulled a hamstring while fooling around kicking field goals. "It really was touch-and-go whether he'd be able to play," said Pat Stark, one of SU's assistant coaches. "On game day, it was still really tight, but Ernie wasn't going to miss this game. He would have played with crutches if he had to." Syracuse won the toss, and on its third play from scrimmage, Davis turned a half-back option pass from Schwedes into an eighty-seven-yard touchdown. "The funny thing about the play is that Ernie ran the wrong pattern," Schwedes said. "But he wound up in the right place—their end zone." Davis scored again later in the half, on a one-yard run. He also scored a 2-point conversion and had a long interception return to set up another touchdown.

Sadly, the game was marred by fights after several Longhorn players shouted racial epithets at Davis and SU's two other African American players—John Brown and fullback Art Baker. "It was an

Program from 1960 Cotton Bowl in which the Orange defeated Texas, 23-14, to win the national football championship. Cotton Bowl Athletic Association.

unfortunate and ugly thing, but guys like Maury Youmans immediately came to their defense," Stark said. "We were like a family and I think that made us even closer."

The victory put an exclamation point on SU's perfect season and removed that "can't win the big one" albatross from Ben Schwartzwalder's neck. Nearly thirty years later, *The Sporting News* ranked the 1959 Orangemen as the tenth greatest team in college football history. It was a team for the ages; a team that has stood the test of time.

The Legend of 44

Had famed running back Jim Brown had his way, 33 would have become the most famous number in Syracuse University history. That's the number he wore while playing football at Manhasset High School in Long Island, where he won thirteen varsity letters, and the number he wanted to don for the Orangemen. But senior Vince Vergara already had 33 by the time Brown joined the SU varsity in 1954, so the sophomore running back requested another double-digit number, and longtime equipment manager Al Zak tossed 44 his way. Fifty-one years and three College Football Hall of Fame induction ceremonies later, a large replica of the number made famous by Brown and fellow All-Americans Ernie Davis and Floyd Little was hoisted to the Carrier Dome rafters, signifying that it would never be worn again. Here are 44 tidbits about these revered double digits.

1. On November 12, 2005, 44 became the first football number retired at SU.
2. In the mid-1980s, the university's zip code was switched from 13210 to 13244.
3. In 1988, the university's phone exchange was switched from 423 to 443.
4. Brown was the first player to make Number 44 famous. He earned All-American honors during his senior season in 1956, scoring a then NCAA-record 43 points in a single game while leading SU to a Cotton Bowl berth. He would have scored 44, but he missed one of his extra point attempts.
5. Davis followed in Big Jim's footsteps, helping the Orange win a national championship in 1959. Two years later, Davis became the first African American to win the Heisman Trophy.
6. Little was the next great Number 44. He broke most of his predecessors' records while becoming only the second football Orangeman to earn All-American honors three times.
7. Brown, Davis, and Little are all members of the College Football Hall of Fame. Brown and Little also are enshrined in the Pro Football Hall of Fame.

Forty-four is back!

The number 44 has legendary status at Syracuse University. *SU Alumni News.* Syracuse University Alumni Reference Collection, University Archives.

8. Twenty-five football players have worn the number at SU.
9. Halfback Gifford Zimmerman was the first, in 1921.
10. Fullback Rob Konrad was the last, in 1998.
11. Larry Csonka was offered the number before his senior year (1967), but he declined, sticking with Number 39.
12. Joe Morris, the school's all-time leading rusher, also was offered the jersey before his senior season (1981), but he stuck with Number 47.
13. Damien Rhodes, a highly recruited running back from suburban Syracuse, was offered it his freshman season (2001), but he chose Number 1 instead.
14. Davis ultimately chose SU over Army because of the opportunity to follow Brown and wear his old number.
15. Little decided to accept Syracuse's scholarship offer the day Davis died of leukemia.
16. Tom Stephens wore the number for the two seasons between Brown and Davis.

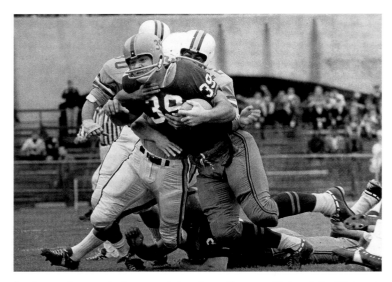

It often took several players to bring down Syracuse University's All-American fullback Larry Csonka. Athletics Department, Syracuse University, used by permission.

SU's football backfield in 1966 (*left to right*): Quarterback Rick Cassata, running backs Floyd Little and Tom Coughlin, and fullback Larry Csonka. Athletics Department, Syracuse University, used by permission.

17. William Schoonover wore the number for the two seasons between Davis and Little.

18. Retiring football's 44 was the brainchild of former athletics director Daryl Gross.

19. Davis was the first overall pick of both the NFL and AFL in 1962. (The Buffalo Bills actually offered more money than did the Browns, who acquired him in a trade with the Washington Redskins.)

20. Brown was the fifth pick overall in the 1957 NFL draft.

21. Little was the sixth overall pick in the 1967 NFL draft.

22. Little and Michael Owens are the only 44s to rush for more than one thousand yards in a season.

23. The number remained in mothballs from 1969 until 1977, when Mandel Robinson, a highly touted recruit from North Syracuse, was given the jersey. The pressure proved too much, and he transferred to Wyoming, where he wound up having a one-thousand-yard rushing season.

24. While looking for a successor to Davis, SU assistants offered the number to three different high school running backs at the same time. Jim Nance, Billy Hunter, and Nat Duckett arrived on campus in the summer of 1961 expecting to receive Number 44 once Davis graduated. Head coach Ben Schwartzwalder's solution was to put the famous jersey back into storage.

25. Nance led the Orange in rushing his senior season and went on to become the New England Patriots' all-time leading rusher. Hunter, a three-year letterman, became the longtime head of the NBA's player union. Duckett also earned three varsity letters.

26. Other football numbers retired by SU: Csonka's 39, John Mackey's 88, Don McPherson's 9, Donovan McNabb's 5, Joe Morris's 47, and Tim Green's 72.

27. Derrick Coleman's Number 44 has been retired in basketball. John Wallace also wore 44 in hoops, and his number is expected to be retired, too. Danny Schayes, who played eighteen seasons in the NBA, also was a 44.

28. For several years there was a popular campus bar named 44's that was located on Marshall Street, better known as M Street.

29. Brown was cool with the idea of retiring the number. Little wished the number was still available to prospective recruits.

30. Michael Owens was wearing Number 44 when he scored the most famous 2-point conversion in SU history to help the Orange beat West Virginia and preserve their unbeaten season in 1987.

31. Number 22—half of 44—is the most famous number in SU lacrosse history, having been worn by All-Americans Gary Gait, Charlie Lockwood, and brothers Casey, Ryan, and Michael Powell.

32. John Mackey, the superb tight end who wore Number 88 during the early 1960s, liked to joke that he was twice the player Number 44 was.

33. Brown's Number 32 was retired by the Cleveland Browns.

34. Although he never played for the Browns because he was stricken with leukemia, Davis had his Number 45 retired by the team.

35. Little's Number 44 was retired by the Denver Broncos.

36. Davis still holds the SU record for highest average yards per carry for a game (15.7), season (7.8), and career (6.63).

37. Little had three punt returns of more than ninety yards in his SU career.
38. Brown had seven 100-yard rushing games in 1956 and averaged 123 yards per game that season.
39. Rob Konrad was the only fullback to wear the number.
40. Clarence Taylor (1925), Henry Merz (1933), and Rich Panczyszyn (1967-69) were the only quarterbacks to wear 44.
41. Three two-way linemen—Francis Mazejko (1939), Richard Ransom (1940), and Jack O'Brien (1945)—wore 44.
42. Brown also lettered in lacrosse, basketball, and track and field at SU.
43. Davis played one year of varsity basketball.
44. Little ran track.

Bernie Custis

After leading the Orangemen in total offense three consecutive seasons, Bernie Custis was hoping to continue his quarterbacking career with the Cleveland Browns, who had selected him in the eleventh round of the 1951 National Football League draft. But there weren't any opportunities in those days for African Americans to become signal callers in the NFL, so Custis opted to play in the Canadian Football League, where he became the first black quarterback in professional football history. He spent four seasons with the Toronto Argonauts and two seasons with the Ottawa Roughriders. Syracuse University Portrait Collection, University Archives.

Six in the City

Jonny Flynn was so exhausted he no longer could feel his legs beneath him. Which is why during either the fourth or fifth overtime of that 2009 Big East Conference tournament quarterfinal game against Connecticut, the Syracuse University point guard looked up at the Madison Square Garden ceiling and sought divine intervention.

"Lord, just get this game over with," Flynn prayed and pleaded. "Doesn't matter who wins. Let's just get it over."

His prayers wouldn't be answered until the sixth overtime as the Orangemen took a lead they would not relinquish, beating the Huskies, 127-117, in the second-longest game in college basketball history.

Flynn's reputation for being a marathon man was enhanced that March night—and morning—as he played sixty-seven of a possible seventy minutes, scoring 34 points, including 26 in overtime. "The (sellout crowd of 19,375) got their money's worth, and then some," he said. "I don't think anybody left. I think a bunch of them were as gassed as we were."

That game—which tipped off on March 12 and didn't conclude until 1:22 the following morning—took three hours and forty-six minutes to complete. Of the combined 244 points, 102 were scored after the regulation buzzer sounded. Eight players fouled out. Six players recorded double-doubles, including Flynn, who had 11 assists to go with his game-high point total, and Paul Harris, who had 29 points and 22 rebounds.

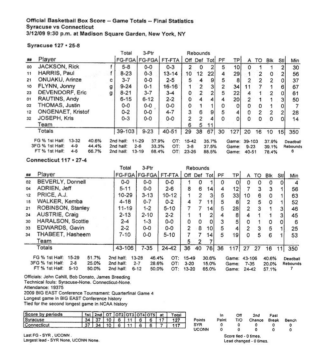

No basketball game in Syracuse history lasted longer than the six-overtime, Big East Conference men's basketball contest with Connecticut at Madison Square Garden in 2009. SU beat UConn, 127-117. Athletics Department, Syracuse University, used by permission.

People forget that game appeared to be over in regulation when Eric Devendorf swished a jumper at the buzzer after taking an improbable length-of-the-court pass from Harris. Immediately after sinking the twenty-eight-footer, Devendorf leaped onto the scorer's table and pounded his chest in celebration. But after reviewing the shot on courtside monitors, the officials ruled the ball had not left Devendorf's hand before the buzzer sounded. The basket was waved off, sending the game into overtime.

By the fourth extra session, six-foot-seven swingman Kris Joseph had to jump center because SU's post players—Arinze Onuaku, Rick Jackson, and Kristof Ongenaet—had fouled out. When Devendorf fouled out in the fifth overtime, SU coach Jim Boeheim had no choice but to insert walk-on Justin Thomas, who had not played a meaningful minute all season. At the end of the fifth overtime, Flynn huddled with his teammates and told them: "If we can win one tip, we'll win the game."

With UConn's seven-foot-three center Hasheem Thabeet fouled out, the Orange finally won a tip, and Andy Rautins drained a jumper that gave SU its first lead since regulation. Syracuse went on to outscore the Huskies 17-7 in the final overtime to make the weary Flynn a prophet.

"During the fourth overtime, I looked at the guys at the scorers' table and said, 'What in the world are we a part of right now?'" Boeheim said. "I mean, we're down in five different overtimes and come back every time. How incredible is that?"

When it was mentioned that the longest game in college basketball history—a 1981 matchup between Bradley and Cincinnati—went seven overtimes, Boeheim astutely pointed out: "Yeah, but that was before the shot clock. Those guys were holding the ball. I would make the case this is something none of us have ever seen or are likely to ever see again."

One of the Big Apple tabloids summed up the game later that morning with the headline "Six in the City," a clever takeoff on the popular *Sex and the City* television series and movies. By the following week, orange T-shirts with that phrase were being sold on campus.

Just in case Flynn & Co. didn't get their fill of basketball from that game, SU played another overtime period while beating West Virginia in the semifinals. That set up a championship matchup with Louisville. The Orangemen led at halftime, then understandably ran out of gas as the Cardinals copped the title with a 76-66 victory. Flynn, who played an astounding 181 of a possible 195 minutes of basketball in four days, was named the tournament's most outstanding player, and Devendorf, who set a record with 84 points, earned a spot on the all-tournament team.

Ben Schwartzwalder

When a longtime mentor recommended he apply for the Syracuse University head football coaching job following the 1948 season,

Ben Schwartzwalder initially acted as if someone had suggested he take the helm of the Titanic after the ship hit that iceberg. Schwartzwalder was well aware that the school's once-proud football program had fallen on hard times, winning but nine games over the previous four seasons. He groused to his friend that "Syracuse is a graveyard for football coaches."

Schwartzwalder figured he was better off staying at Muhlenberg (Pennsylvania) College, which he had guided to a 25-5 record and a national small college championship in three seasons. He figured another, more advantageous big-school opportunity eventually would come along.

But a few weeks after blowing off Syracuse, he had a change of heart after a change in philosophy at Muhlenberg. The school's president called him and told the coach he was doing too good a job and that other schools in the Mid-Atlantic Conference were complaining. Schwartzwalder thought his ears were deceiving him when the president told him it would be better if he didn't win so many games.

Suddenly, the SU job didn't seem so bad after all. So he applied and was hired, but he wasn't greeted with open arms by prominent alumni and benefactors. They clearly were underwhelmed.

In an interview years later, the droll Schwartzwalder joked: "The alumni wanted a big-name coach and they wound up with a long-name coach."

They also wound up with a Hall-of-Fame coach who would resuscitate a moribund program that was coming off a 1-8 season. The peak came in 1959, when the Orangemen scaled college football's Everest and won the national title with an 11-0 record that was capped by a 23-14 victory against Texas in the Cotton Bowl.

During Ol' Ben's twenty-five-year reign, SU went 153-91-3 and made seven bowl appearances. His teams recorded twenty-two consecutive nonlosing seasons and churned out a long line of All-American running backs, including Jim Brown, Ernie Davis, Floyd Little, and Larry Csonka—each of whom is enshrined in the College Football Hall of Fame.

A paratrooper in World War II, Schwartzwalder earned a Bronze Star, a Silver Star, and a Purple Heart for his heroics during the D-Day invasion of Normandy, and he rose to the rank of major. Over time, the laconic coach with the trademark crew cut and stern countenance built the program in his tough image. "When you think of a hard-nosed, old-school football coach, you think of Ben Schwartzwalder," said Dick MacPherson, who eventually followed in his cleatsteps and performed a similar football revival job in the 1980s. "He was right out of central casting."

Schwartzwalder's absent-mindedness was legendary (he once wore his pajama bottoms to practice). As his wife once explained: "He simply refuses to clutter up his mind with anything but football."

Success came slowly for Schwartzwalder at SU. It took him awhile to convince school administrators that if they truly wanted to field a successful team they would need to increase the number of

What's in a (Nick)Name?

Colorful nicknames have long contributed to our enjoyment of sports. Here's a look back at some Syracuse University favorites.

Pearl	Dwayne Washington
Coach Mac	Dick MacPherson
The Louie and Bouie Show	Louis Orr and Roosevelt Bouie
The Zoo	Student section in Manley Field House
G-Mac	Gerry McNamara
Coach Q	Quentin Hillsman
Sizeable Seven	Linemen on SU's 1959 national championship football team (Fred Mautino, Maury Youmans, Bob Yates, Bruce Tarbox, Al Bemiller, Roger Davis, and Gerry Skonieczki)
Roy's Runts	Name for Coach Roy Danforth's vertically challenged basketball teams of the early to mid-1970s
Melo	Carmelo Anthony
Otto, Saltine Warrior, and the Dome Ranger	Mascots
Sweet D	Dennis DuVal
The Elmira Express	Ernie Davis
The General	Sherman Douglas
Air Gait	Revolutionary lacrosse shot invented by Gary Gait
Otto's Army	Student section in the Carrier Dome
Poetry in Moten	Lawrence Moten
Red	Tony Bruin
Slugger	Roy Simmons Jr.
Fast Eddie	Eddie Moss
Sour Sitrus Society	SU Pep Band
The Loud House	Carrier Dome
Kangaroo Kid	Vaughn Harper
Four Wheel Drive	Defensive line of the mid-1980s (Tim Green, Blaise Winter, Bill Pendock, Jamie Kimmel)
Bug	Jimmy Williams

Louis Orr and Roosevelt Bouie—pictured here on Syracuse's 1979-80 basketball schedule—were nicknamed the "Louie & Bouie Show." And what a show they were, leading the Orange to one hundred wins and four NCAA tournament appearances in their four seasons together. Athletics Department, Syracuse University, used by permission.

Kid	Greg Kohls
Pride of the Orange	SU marching band
Coach P	Paul Pasqualoni
Ol' Ben	Ben Schwartzwalder
Four Furies	SU's backfield on the 1959 national championship team (Ernie Davis, Dave Sarette, Gerhard Schwedes, and Art Baker)
DC	Derrick Coleman
Buffalo Bill	Bill Hurley
The Braintree Butcher	Tom Stundis
The Blond Bomber	George Hicker
Fab	Fabricio Melo
Shack	Dale Shackleford
Z or Z-Man	Lazarus Sims

(Right) SU's 4-2 victory against North Carolina in the 2015 championship game marked the first NCAA women's title in Orange history. Athletics Department, Syracuse University, used by permission.

(Below) Goalie Jess Jecko holds up the national field hockey championship trophy after Syracuse defeated North Carolina in the 2015 title game. Athletics Department, Syracuse University, used by permission.

HOME OF CHAMPIONS

Syracuse University has fielded thirty national championship teams through the years, including fifteen in lacrosse, six in crew, three in basketball, and three in cross-country. The Orange also has captured titles in football, women's field hockey, and boxing.

Twenty-four individuals have won national championships, including eight in boxing, seven in wrestling, six in gymnastics, two in track and field, and one in cross-country. Five athletes have won multiple titles: wrestler Gene Mills (1979 and 1981), wrestler Jim Nance (1963 and 1965), gymnast Leo Minotti (1950 and 1951), boxer John Granger (1954 and 1955), and distance runner Justyn Knight (2017 and 2018).

According to the university's website, boxer Al Wertheimer was the first individual to win a national championship (1932), while the 1904 men's rowers were the first SU team to take national honors. Knight won the school's most recent national championship when he finished first in the indoor five thousand meters on March 9, 2018.

Coach Ange Bradley's field hockey team capped a 21-1 season in 2015 with a 4-2 victory against North Carolina in the NCAA finals, marking the first national title by a Syracuse women's team or individual.

Not all the titles are recognized by the NCAA, since sports such as boxing and crew are not sponsored by college sports' major governing body. The boxing, wrestling, and gymnastics programs have since been dropped by the school. Here's a look at SU's team and individual national champions:

Team

Men's crew (1904, 1908, 1913, 1916, 1920, and 1978)

Men's lacrosse (1920, 1922, 1924, 1925, 1983, 1988, 1989, 1990, 1993, 1995, 2000, 2002, 2004, 2008, and 2009)

Men's basketball (1917-18, 1925-26, and 2003)

Men's cross-country (1949, 1951, and 2015)

Women's Field Hockey (2015)

Football (1959)

Boxing (1936)

Individual

BOXING

1932	Al Wertheimer (126 lb.)
1936	Ord Fink (155 lb.)
1936	Ray Jeffries (165 lb.)
1942	Salvatore Mirabito (heavyweight)
1947	Jerry Auclair (125 lb.)
1949	Marty Crandell (heavyweight)
1954	John Granger (139 lb.)
1955	John Granger (139 lb.)

WRESTLING

1959	Art Baker (191 lb.)
1963	Jim Nance (heavyweight)
1965	Jim Nance (heavyweight)
1967	Tom Schlendorf (191 lb.)
1979	Gene Mills (118 lb.)
1980	Gene Mills (118 lb.)
1992	Mark Kerr (190 lb.)

GYMNASTICS

1950	Leo Minotti (rope climb)
1950	Gene Rabbitt (side horse)
1951	Leo Minotti (rope climb)
1953	James "Corky" Sebbo (tumbling)
1964	Sydney Oglesby (long horse)
1992	Jason Hebert (vault)

TRACK AND FIELD

| 2012 | Jarret Eaton (60-meter hurdles) |
| 2018 | Justyn Knight (5,000-meter) |

CROSS-COUNTRY

| 2017 | Justyn Knight |

(Above Right) John Desko has coached the Orangemen to five NCAA lacrosse titles. Athletics Department, Syracuse University, used by permission.

(Below Right) In 2015, the Orange won its second cross-country national championship. Athletics Department, Syracuse University, used by permission.

scholarships so they would be on par with competitors such as Penn State and Pittsburgh. After going 14-14 in his first three seasons, the Orange enjoyed a breakthrough campaign with a 7-2 record and the school's first bowl appearance. Though SU was crushed 61-6 by Alabama in the Orange Bowl on January 1, 1953, the program was finally pointed in the right direction.

By the late 1960s and early 1970s, Syracuse's football fortunes sagged once more. Several black players accused Schwartzwalder of being a racist and staged a boycott that attracted national media attention. That incident, along with the continued deterioration of outdated Archbold Stadium and a reduction in support from the administration, resulted in a severe talent drain and a 2-9 record by Schwartzwalder's final team in 1973. Despite the sad ending, he departed as the winningest football coach in school history. In 2015—twenty-two years after his death at age eighty-three—a statue of Schwartzwalder was unveiled in Plaza 44 near the Ensley Athletic Center on South Campus.

Syracuse clearly wound up being a launching pad rather than a graveyard for his coaching career.

Dick MacPherson

Dick MacPherson became such a beloved figure in the Syracuse community that the Onondaga County Republican Party approached him about running for mayor after he retired from coaching in 1993. Though flattered, the personable, garrulous man who resurrected Syracuse University football politely declined. Coach Mac had no desire to become Mayor Mac, despite the fact he probably would have won in a landslide.

The transformation in the public's perception of MacPherson had been dramatic. Just a decade earlier, with the Orange program

Gregarious, personable coach Dick MacPherson led a football renaissance in the late 1980s and early 1990s and became one of the most beloved figures in Orange history. Athletics Department, Syracuse University, used by permission.

mired in mediocrity, Syracusans wanted to run him out of town instead of for political office.

After SU opened the 1986 season with four consecutive losses, angry fans formed the "Sack Mac Pack" in hopes of getting MacPherson fired. The feeling was that the native of Old Town, Maine, had been given more than enough time to turn things around, and to that point had produced just a 25-34-1 record in five and a half seasons. Fortunately, SU athletics director Jake Crouthamel didn't listen to them. "Jake was an old football coach, so he could see that we were on the verge of getting this thing turned around," MacPherson recalled in his familiar R-dropping New England accent in a 1997 interview. "I'll always be grateful for him sticking his neck out for me."

Crouthamel's patience would be rewarded, and the "Sack Mac Pack" would be disbanded. Led by their promising junior quarterback Don McPherson, the Orangemen rebounded to win five of their final seven games to finish 5-6 and lay the foundation for one of the most remarkable seasons in SU history. In 1987, the 'Cuse went 11-0-1 and finished fourth in the final polls, their highest ranking since winning the national championship twenty-eight years earlier. The string of victories included a thrashing of Penn State, snapping a sixteen-year losing streak to the Nittany Lions, and a last-second, 1-point victory against West Virginia when running back Michael Owens scored on a 2-point conversion.

MacPherson received national coach of the year honors for reviving the program following a long dry spell. "That was such a special group of young men and such a special season," MacPherson said. "Just about everything fell our way. It put an exclamation point on the fact we were back."

They were back all right—with a vengeance. The 1987 campaign began a string of fifteen consecutive winning seasons that saw the Orangemen make twelve bowl appearances, winning eight of them and tying one.

"They were down when I got there and then the university made a huge commitment to turn things around," said MacPherson, the third winningest coach in school history, with a 66-46-4 record. "There were a lot of things in place. The Dome was brand new and that really helped recruiting. And Syracuse had such a great tradition that we could sell to young people. I knew it was going to take some time to make the situation better. And thank God I had a guy in my corner who was willing to be patient."

Following a 7-4-2 season in 1990 that was capped with a 28-0 victory against Arizona in the Aloha Bowl, MacPherson left to coach the New England Patriots for two seasons. His time as an NFL coach did not go well, as the Pats won just eight of thirty-two games, and Mac was fired.

Not long after coming back to the Salt City, he was approached about that political run. With a gift of gab and a gift for making friends, Coach Mac seemed a natural. "To be mayor of Syracuse, New York, would have been a fascinating job, but I realized me and politics would not have been a good match," said MacPherson, who

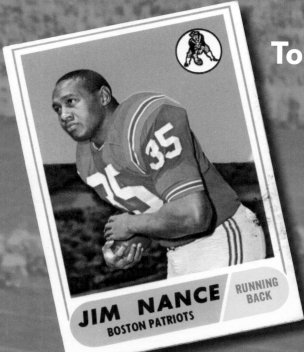

Topps in Their Field

Here are some Orange football stars who have been immortalized with their own Topps trading cards: Jim Nance's 1968 NFL card with cards for Ernie Davis, Jim Ringo, Joe Morris, and Art Monk. Topps® trading cards courtesy of The Topps Company, Inc. Jeff Rubin, private collection.

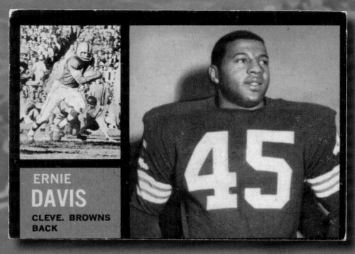

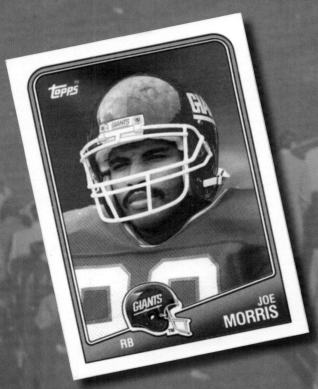

spent nearly two decades providing commentary on SU football broadcasts. "Even though you know you've made the right decision, you've got to convince a council or other people that it's right. All of a sudden you are not the head coach. You become a mediator, and I don't feel I ever was a good mediator. I wouldn't want to run anything where people run me and tell me how to run my business."

Although he never became an elected official, Coach Mac did become an elder statesman and goodwill ambassador for the university and its football program. His achievements at UMass and SU were recognized in 2009 when he was inducted into the College Football Hall of Fame.

More than one thousand mourners paid their respects after MacPherson died in 2017 at age eighty-six. In his eulogy at the funeral in a packed Hendricks Chapel, esteemed broadcaster Sean McDonough recounted how he was nearly forced to leave Syracuse for financial reasons. Shortly after informing MacPherson, McDonough was mysteriously offered an academic scholarship, salvaging the college career of one of sports' most prominent voices. McDonough says that moment changed his life. MacPherson never took credit for it.

Carmelo Anthony

Not long after senior guard Kueth Duany met highly touted basketball recruit Carmelo Anthony in the summer of 2002, the two headed to Manley Field House for an impromptu pickup game with several other Syracuse players. Known for his ability to shut down the opposition's top scorer, Duany paired up against Anthony. It was no contest. The rookie wound up schooling the veteran. The hype was justified. "Let's just say I came away impressed with how developed his game was," Duany recalled, chuckling at the memory. "I couldn't wait to see our opponents try to stop him."

They quickly discovered what Duany had already realized—that stopping the player known as Melo was akin to stopping a tornado. The six-foot-eight forward with the sublime scoring skills and the incandescent, Magic Johnson–like smile would go on to average a double-double for the 2002-3 season (22 points and 10 rebounds per game), and he would earn consensus All-American and national freshman of the year honors while leading the Orange men to their first NCAA basketball title.

Although Anthony would spend just one season at Syracuse before joining the NBA, his brief time on campus would be long enough to make an impact that would last for generations.

Coach Jim Boeheim knew Anthony was going to be a special player the first time he laid eyes on him in 2001. Syracuse assistant coach Troy Weaver had caught Melo's extraordinary act before other college coaches did and convinced his boss to do something he rarely did—make a long, in-season recruiting visit. Anthony was a junior at the time, and Boeheim grudgingly agreed to accompany Weaver to see him play in Baltimore. "Coach told me, 'Troy, this

better be worth my time and trouble,'" Weaver recalled. "I assured him it would be as worthwhile a recruiting trip as he ever made. After watching Melo for just five minutes, Coach turned to me and said, 'This kid is the best player in the country.'"

There were times when Boeheim couldn't help but marvel at Melo's men-against-boys performances for the Orange. "You could be from another planet and not know a thing about basketball and see that he was far and away better than the other nine guys on the court," he raved. "Some stretches, he was unguardable."

That certainly was the case during SU's 81-78 victory against Kansas in the NCAA championship game in the Louisiana Superdome in New Orleans as Anthony scored 20 points, grabbed 10 rebounds, and handed out 7 assists. What made the performance even more impressive was that Anthony played with a back so tight that by the second half he could barely bend over to tie his shoes. Despite the limitations, he gutted it out for thirty-seven minutes. "You spend a lifetime dreaming of playing on a stage like this," he explained afterward. "There was no way I was coming out of that game until the final buzzer sounded."

At a teary-eyed press conference just seventeen days after winning the national championship, Anthony announced that he was leaving school to play in the NBA. "I never for one moment tried to talk him out of it," Boeheim said at the time. "In my mind, it was the right decision. He's ready to go."

Anthony mentioned how he wanted to repay his mom for her years of love and sacrifice, and an NBA contract would help him do just that. He said he was somewhat torn about his decision. "I was still uncertain until about fifteen minutes before the press conference started," he said. "I loved Syracuse University, I loved my teammates and Coach Boeheim. But like coach told me, you've accomplished in one year everything a college player could hope to accomplish. But no matter how long I play this game, nothing will ever top the feeling of winning the national championship. That was as good as it can ever get."

Two months later, the Denver Nuggets drafted him third overall, and he would go on to become a perennial all-star with them and the New York Knicks. He wound up leading the league in scoring during the 2012-13 season and won Olympic gold medals with the US basketball team in 2008, 2012, and 2016. The Olympic experiences were even more special because he was reunited with Boeheim, who was an assistant coach for the US team.

Anthony returned to campus on September 24, 2009, to participate in the ribbon-cutting ceremonies at the $19 million Carmelo K. Anthony Basketball Center. He got the ball rolling on the project by donating $3 million, the largest single donation ever made by a former SU athlete. "For Carmelo to step up like he has, it just means the world to me personally," Boeheim said. "I told him when we won the national championship that he didn't have to do anything else for me ever again. The reason we have this [state-of-the-art] building is because Carmelo did this."

In the not-so-distant future, Anthony is expected to be reunited with his college and Olympic coach when he's inducted into the Naismith Memorial Basketball Hall of Fame in Springfield, Massachusetts.

David Tyree

Steve Sabol, an Emmy Award-winning producer for NFL Films, called it the greatest play in Super Bowl history, adding that it "defied logic, history, gravity, and just about anything else you care to mention." A writer agreed, describing the mind-boggling play as "an insult to physics and Albert Einstein."

Indeed, David Tyree's leaping catch in which he pressed the football against his helmet and somehow maintained possession after crashing to the ground in Super Bowl XLII was one of those impossible, I-don't-believe-what-I-just-saw sports moments. And it was all the more memorable because it occurred on football's biggest stage, enabling the New York Giants to sustain a crucial late-game scoring drive in a 17-14 victory against a New England Patriots team that had sought to become the first in NFL history to finish a season 19-0.

The odds that quarterback Eli Manning's thirty-two-yard desperation pass would be caught during the final minute of that February 3, 2008, game were extremely low. The odds that Tyree, the former Syracuse special teams star, would be on the receiving end of a miracle were even more remote.

The Giants had selected Tyree in the sixth round of the 2003 draft to tackle kickoff and punt returners. But the man who had caught only four passes for thirty-five yards heading into that Super Bowl would be pressed into action as a third receiver. The former Orangeman proved up to the moment, catching a touchdown pass that gave New York a 3-point lead. But that reception paled in comparison to the spectacular grab Tyree later made to set up the Giants winning score.

The play earned him a permanent spot in football lore. It's come to be known as the Helmet Catch and Catch 42, a reference to Super Bowl 42 and Joseph Heller's classic *Catch 22* novel. It justified the Giants drafting him after a successful career at SU that saw Tyree block 6 punts and accumulate 229 receiving yards in a game against Virginia Tech. It also enabled another Syracuse alumnus, Giants coach Tom Coughlin, to win his first of two Super Bowls against the Patriots.

Justyn Knight

The most decorated distance runner in Syracuse University cross-country and track-and-field history always dreamed big.

"I believe in setting almost impossible goals for myself," Justyn Knight said in a 2017 interview with *Syracuse University Magazine*. "I think by putting the bar so high you almost can't see it, it forces you to work even harder, push yourself to the limit. And if you wind up doing the nearly impossible instead of the impossible, you'll still be pretty happy with what you achieve."

Knight should be ecstatic with what he achieved—an Orange running career that will be nearly impossible to match. In addition to winning two individual NCAA titles (cross-country in 2017 and the five thousand indoor meters in 2018), he was the pace-setter for the Orange men's national cross-country crown during his freshman season in 2015. Toss in a dozen All-American honors, sixteen Atlantic Coast Conference titles, and four runner-up performances in NCAA meets, and you can see why SU cross-country and track-and-field coach Chris Fox compared Knight to Orange basketball legend Carmelo Anthony.

"Justyn is a once-in-a-lifetime talent, just like Carmelo," Fox said before Knight's senior year. "He's the type of runner that can take you to the Promised Land immediately, which he did. And

David Tyree's Helmet Catch is regarded by many as the greatest play in Super Bowl history. Robert Sabo / *New York Daily News* Archive / Getty Images.

Justyn Knight shows his school pride while winning the 2017 NCAA cross-country national championship. Photo by Michael Scott. Athletics Department, Syracuse University, used by permission.

the great thing for us is that unlike Carmelo, who rightly left for the NBA after winning the national championship his freshman year, we get to have Justyn all four years."

One of Knight's post-SU goals is competing in the Olympics—he missed qualifying for the 2016 Summer Games in Rio de Janeiro by one second—and winning a gold medal in the 5K. "To achieve that would be the ultimate," said Knight, a native of Vaughan, Canada, a Toronto suburb. "Do that, and people will say you are the best in the world."

Fox believes an Olympic medal is within reach. "People forget that Justyn came to running relatively late," Fox said of the young man who was named the Atlantic Coast Conference's Cross-Country Runner of the Year three times. "He didn't really start doing this until his sophomore year of high school, so he's still learning about training and preparation and race strategy. . . . He's just entering his running prime. He has a good ten, twelve years of world-class running in front of him."

Before turning pro, Knight earned his bachelor's degree in social work from the David B. Falk College of Sport and Human Dynamics. His goal is to become a guidance counselor. "Ever since I was young, I've enjoyed helping people work through challenges so they can realize their potential," he said. "I definitely believe it has helped me become a better teammate. I've had people encourage me along the way, and I try to do the same."

"Sportscaster U."

Few schools in the country are more closely associated with a profession than Syracuse University has become with sports broadcasting. The two go together like a microphone in a hand. Turn on your television on any given night and begin surfing the channels carrying sporting events, and there's a good chance you'll hear the voice of someone who studied at SU's S.I. Newhouse School of Public Communications. That's how ubiquitous Newhouse sportscasters have become. They're everywhere. No wonder *Sports Illustrated* once called it the "incubator" of American sportscasters, lauding SU's "dazzling record" of turning out not only the most but the best in the business.

Interestingly, the man regarded as the father of "Sportscaster U." didn't graduate from Newhouse because the school didn't exist back in the late 1930s when Marty Glickman was a student. An Olympic sprinter and Syracuse football All-American, Glickman's popularity on campus resulted in him being asked to host a sports highlight show on local radio station WSYR for fifteen dollars a week.

By accident, he found his calling, and after graduating he went on to make a name for himself as a New York City broadcaster. He did a little bit of everything—including radio play by play of the New York Knicks and football Giants, pre- and postgame shows on New York Yankees and Brooklyn Dodgers broadcasts, and anchor work on several Big Apple television stations. "He had a way of making

Marv Albert. © Syracuse University. Photo by Stephen Sartori.

you feel like you were inside Madison Square Garden," recalled Hank Greenwald, a Newhouse alumnus who became the longtime voice of the San Francisco Giants. "When you listened to Marty, you could smell the cigar smoke wafting up to the ceiling. In a medium like radio where you can't see what's happening he gave you the word picture you needed."

His descriptions became so vivid that he once was asked to broadcast a circus to the blind. He gladly accepted the assignment and became the eyes for those who could not see the elephants, clowns, or men on the flying trapeze. One critic called Glickman "the Michelangelo of play-by-play broadcasting."

Marv Albert, another famous SU broadcasting alumnus, began keeping stats and doing research for Glickman while attending Abraham Lincoln High School in Brooklyn. "He was very giving to me and other aspiring young broadcasters," Albert said. "When I discovered that Marty had attended Syracuse, that sealed the deal for me."

It also would seal the deal for Syracuse's most decorated and best-known sportscaster, Bob Costas. He grew up listening to Glickman, then Albert, and decided SU was the place for him, too. Winner of twenty-eight Emmy Awards and a record eight national sportscaster of the year honors, Costas would keep the pipeline of announcing talent flowing to Newhouse. Like Glickman, Albert, Greenwald, Dick Stockton, Andy Musser, and Len Berman before him, Costas would inspire and mentor another generation of "mic" men and women, including Mike Tirico, Sean McDonough, Ian Eagle, and Beth Mowins.

"You've had not only great sportscasters, but great broadcasters that have come out of Newhouse, and the radio [program] and journalism school that preceded it," Albert said. "Not only Marty, but media giants like Dick Clark and Ted Koppel cut their teeth there. I think when you choose your profession and start looking

Sportscasters Beth Mowins, Bob Costas, Mike Tirico, and Sean McDonough share a laugh with sports agent Sandy Montag (*third from right*) and SU athletics director John Wildhack (*far right*). © Syracuse University. Photo by Stephen Sartori.

at schools, you naturally look at places that have produced people who have succeeded at the highest levels. A reputation is developed, and although I'm admittedly biased here, I don't think any school comes close to Syracuse when it comes to producing top-notch broadcasters."

Albert believes the bond formed among Newhouse alumni and current students has contributed to the school's success. "I think that goes back to Marty," he said. "He was extremely generous with his time for young broadcasters. And I think those of us who benefited from his mentorship have attempted to make that part of the school's tradition."

Newhouse's world-class faculty and state-of-the-art facilities also have contributed greatly, as has the opportunity to cover major college sports for WAER-FM and local television and radio stations. "We have been particularly fortunate that the athletics department has permitted WAER the right to broadcast SU's football, basketball, and lacrosse games in competition with the commercial stations that carry them," former Newhouse dean David Rubin said in a 2002 interview with *Syracuse University Magazine*. "They didn't have to do that; most schools don't. But, as a result, our students get chances to broadcast college athletics at the highest level. No Ivy League school can give you the opportunity to broadcast a Final Four NCAA basketball game or a major college football bowl game. We can, and we do."

Beth Mowins

Beth Mowins loved sports, so when she was growing up in North Syracuse in the 1970s and 1980s, it was common to see her with a basketball or a softball in her hands. And it also was common to see her gripping a Mr. Microphone. See, in addition to dreaming about playing professional basketball or softball, Mowins also fantasized about becoming a sports announcer.

In preparation for that career, she would provide play by play of sporting events on her Mr. Microphone, and would also be inspired watching former Miss America Phyllis George analyzing football alongside Brent Musburger and Jimmy "the Greek" Snyder on CBS's *NFL Today* show. George's presence in a then predominantly male world gave Mowins hope that she could one day do that, too.

After graduating from Lafayette College, where she was captain of the women's basketball team, Mowins returned to her hometown and received a master's degree in broadcast journalism from SU's Newhouse School in 1990. After graduating, she embarked on a bunch of small radio jobs before joining ESPN in 1994. Over time, she did play by play on a wide array of events, including men's and women's college basketball, softball, soccer, and volleyball.

In 2017, Mowins made broadcasting history when she called the *Monday Night Football* game between the Los Angeles Chargers and Denver Broncos for ESPN. It marked the first time a female announcer had done play by play on a nationally televised NFL game, and only the second time a woman called a regular-season NFL game. (Gayle Sierens was the first, when she called a regional game for NBC in 1987.) Later that season, Mowins became the first female play-by-play announcer for the NFL on CBS in its fifty-eight-year history when she called the Cleveland Browns-Indianapolis Colts matchup.

"Beth will show up and do a game and do as good a job as any of the men," said NBC Sports announcer and SU alumnus Mike Tirico. "She is a ceiling-breaker, a pioneer, and there will be more women (calling the NFL) going forward."

Though she tried to deflect credit for her groundbreaking debut, she understood the significance.

"If there are little girls or boys out there who want to do this, chase it," she said. "Show people what you are capable of."

Mowins has been doing that since her play-by-play days holding that Mr. Microphone.

Quentin Hillsman

It's fitting that a basketball coach known for being a fashion plate would hail from a place called Suitland, Maryland. Quentin Hillsman's sartorial splendor can be traced to his youth and the example his father set. Horace Hillsman subscribed to the theory that to be your best, you should look your best. Which is why in his various jobs as an entrepreneur, engineer, and computer technician, the elder Hillsman always made sure he was impeccably attired in suit and tie.

His son took notice, and the man known on the Syracuse University campus as Coach Q could easily be referred to as Coach GQ, after the men's fashion magazine *Gentleman's Quarterly*. "My dad believed that if you liked the way you looked, you most likely will do a better job, have more self-confidence," said Hillsman, who has

SU women's basketball coach Quentin Hillsman, best known as Coach Q. Athletics Department, Syracuse University, used by permission.

guided the Orange women's basketball program to heights never visited before. "I'm fortunate enough to coach a sport a lot of people love, and I do so in the public eye. I'm always repping the University, so I want to try to look sharp and neat."

At SU, Hillsman has become known for wins as well as for his wardrobe. He took a program that suffered nine losing seasons in ten years and turned it into a national championship contender, guiding the Orange women to seven NCAA tournament appearances in his first dozen seasons at the helm. The highlight, so far, occurred in 2016 when they made it all the way to the title game, which they lost to a dynastic Connecticut team that was in the midst of winning four consecutive national crowns. "That season gave us a view of what's achievable," he said. "A national championship no longer is out of the realm of possibility."

After one-year stops as an assistant coach at four different universities, including Alabama and Siena, Hillsman came to the Orange in 2005 as an assistant. He had no intention of making Syracuse his permanent residence. He thought his shot at a head coaching job would come elsewhere, several years down the road. But just a year after arriving on the Hill, he was named interim head coach, and that temporary tag was removed within a year. Former athletics director Daryl Gross's faith in promoting him was rewarded big-time as Hillsman established himself as the winningest coach in program history with ten twenty-win seasons in his first twelve years.

And, yes, along with the wins he accumulated a few more suits to go along with his spiffy ties and color-coordinated eyeglasses. While working with a Syracuse-based clothier, he had the words "Just Win" embroidered in orange thread underneath some of the collars.

He's lost track of how many suits he owns, but each year he thins out his wardrobe, donating several suits to a program that helps men who need them for job interviews.

In his case, the clothes definitely have made the man.

Orange Lacrosse a Family Affair

Football had been his first love, and Roy Simmons Sr. was quite good at it, quarterbacking Syracuse to a 22-4 won-lost record in his three varsity seasons, one of which resulted in the Orange receiving a Rose Bowl invitation that the school declined because of budgetary concerns.

But the man known as Simmie would wind up making an even greater impact in a sport that had been foreign to him until his undergraduate days—lacrosse. Simmons discovered the Native American game purely by accident. He was walking across campus one day when he noticed some students tossing a ball around with funny, netted sticks that he surmised were meant to be used for crabbing. He stopped to inquire, and before you knew it he was whipping the ball around and was hooked.

Simmons tried out for the varsity and was a natural from the start. A rugged defenseman, he helped Coach Laurie Cox's Orange stickmen win national titles in 1924 and 1925. Simmons wound up taking the coaching reins from his mentor following the 1931 season. From that point until his retirement in 1970, he guided the Orangemen to a 251-130-1 record, the highlight being the 10-0 squad in 1957 that featured All-Americans Jim Brown, Jim Ridlon, Oren Lyons, and Roy Simmons Jr.

Orange alumni Roy Simmons Jr. and Roy Simmons Sr. excelled as coaches and players at their alma mater. Athletics Department, Syracuse University, used by permission.

His son would wind up being one of Simmie's greatest contributions to the success of the program. The younger Simmons, nicknamed Slugger, succeeded him as coach and led Syracuse to six national championships.

Roy Simmons III also would go into the "family business," playing for the Orange before becoming a longtime assistant. And, in the spring of 2018, a fourth generation would be represented, as team captain Ryan Simmons capped his collegiate playing career by scoring the winning goal in a triple-overtime victory against Army in the Carrier Dome. The feat was witnessed by his father from the sidelines and his grandfather in the stands. Ryan wore Number 16 that day, the same number his father, grandfather, and great-grandfather had worn before him.

All told, a Simmons had contributed to 786 of the program's first 902 victories.

"When your family has been coaching at a school for more than 85 years, people will say it's a tradition," Roy Simmons Jr. said in a 2016 interview. "And I'll say, 'Yes, it's a tradition, until you lose. Then, it's nepotism.'"

No nepotism here. Just a string of championships.

John Desko replaced Simmons Jr. in 1999, and the winning ways continued, as the Orangemen tacked on five more national championships. And, yes, one of Desko's sons—Timothy—would play for SU, too.

Syracuse lacrosse's family ties don't stop there. Two sets of brothers—the Gaits and the Powells—also would contribute greatly to the coaching success enjoyed by the three Roy Simmonses and Desko. Identical twins Gary and Paul Gait showed up in the late

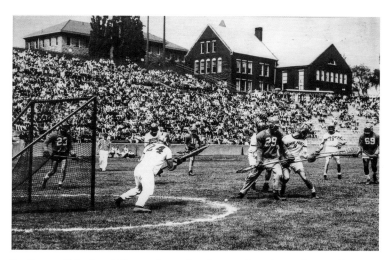

Jim Brown (Number 69) scored a goal and assisted on three others as Syracuse defeated Army, 8-6, in a lacrosse game at Archbold Stadium on May 18, 1957. Earlier in the day, Brown helped the Orange beat Colgate in track by winning the high jump and discus, and taking second in javelin. The lacrosse victory was Syracuse's only win versus Army between 1934 and 1980. Visible in front of the crease is Orange teammate Roy Simmons Jr. (Number 29), who went on to win six NCAA national championships, and, like Brown, secure election into the National Lacrosse Hall of Fame. Courtesy of John Desko. Athletics Department, Syracuse University, used by permission.

1980s and helped the Orange dominate college lacrosse like it had never been dominated before or since. SU won fifty-one of the fifty-six games they played, including the last twenty-seven, while capturing three national championships. The twins combined for seven first-team All-American selections, two national player-of-the-year awards, two NCAA Final Four MVP awards, and 309 goals and 146 assists—an average of nearly 8 points per game.

"It's like having Magic Johnson," Roy Simmons Jr. said, when asked to put the otherworldly play of the brothers into perspective. "Only, there's two of him." It was a spot-on analogy because the twins from British Columbia, Canada, did for lacrosse what Magic had done for the National Basketball Association—help revolutionize and popularize their game. And like Magic, the former Los Angeles Lakers star, they also helped their team win.

The explosion of interest in lacrosse is directly attributable to the flamboyant, innovative style of play created by the Gaits. Their impact on the game landed both of them in the National Lacrosse Hall of Fame. And after his professional playing career, Gary continued to bleed Orange, returning to his alma mater to coach the women's lacrosse team to multiple Final Four appearances.

The Gaitses figured to be an impossible act to follow, but the Powell brothers—Casey, Ryan, and Mike—succeeded in carving out a legendary act of their own at SU. The three of them combined for 445 goals, 881 points, nine first-team All-American selections, four NCAA championships, five NCAA player-of-the-year awards, and six attackman-of-the-year awards. "The reason I recruited Casey and Ryan is so I could get Mike," Roy Simmons Jr. liked to joke, even though he was retired by the time the youngest of the clan arrived from his hometown of Carthage, New York, about eighty-five miles north of campus.

Mike Powell handled the pressure of following in the cleatsteps of his brothers and the Gaitses, scoring a school record 307 points, the last coming on a game-winning goal versus the Naval Academy in the 2004 NCAA title game. "Ever since I was a kid, I'd dreamed of getting the goal that won the championship," he said after becoming the first player in history to win two Tewaaraton Awards (college lacrosse's answer to the Heisman Trophy). "And after all this time it finally came true. Scoring the last goal of the season. Scoring the last goal of my career. Scoring the game-winning goal. There's nothing better than that."

And by doing so, he kept a family tradition—and a Syracuse University tradition—going strong.

Air Gait

He was known for his behind-the-back passes and shots that weren't only entertaining, but also effective. Of all the derring-do practiced by Gary Gait, none received more publicity than his "Air Gait" shot in a May 30, 1988, NCAA semifinal lacrosse game against Penn in the Carrier Dome. That's when the inventive

Gary Gait's never-seen-before "Air Gait" shot from behind the net was so unstoppable that college lacrosse officials eventually banned it. Athletics Department, Syracuse University, used by permission.

player leaped through the air from behind the net and stuffed the ball under the crossbar.

"He did something no one had seen before," said SU coach Roy Simmons Jr. "Watching that shot was like being there the first time someone slam-dunked a basketball."

It was such an unbelievable move that it was outlawed because the rules makers argued that it was tough enough for a goalie to stop shots in front of him, let alone behind him.

Ange Bradley

Most Syracuse University alumni are probably familiar with Orange national championships in football (1959) and men's basketball (2003). But it's likely a smaller number could identify the only SU women's team to win an NCAA title. Or name the diminutive former goalkeeper, the Delaware Blue Hen record holder for shutouts, who led Syracuse to a field hockey national championship on a frigid November 22 in 2015.

It was head coach Ange Bradley's fierce determination and steely fitness demands that helped guide Syracuse to a historic 4-2 win over North Carolina at the University of Michigan's snow-encircled Ocker Field. The win capped off a spectacular 21-1 season record, and among those on hand to witness the win (against a Tar Heel team playing in its sixteenth NCAA title match) was Syracuse chancellor Kent Syverud.

Led to a postgame press conference, her hair soaked from the ritual ice bath afforded champions, Bradley looked at the assembled media and said, "I'm numb. I've been chasing this dream for twenty-five years. I have no feeling because it's so unreal."

But it *was* real, and like other famous Syracuse coaches, Bradley's list of accomplishments warranted her hard-earned joy. She'd won more than 80 percent of her games at Syracuse while recruiting and coaching thirty-one All-Americans (including 2015 Honda Award recipient Alyssa Manley). Bradley was also the architect of ten consecutive NCAA tournament invitations and a two-time winner of the NFHCA National Coach of the Year.

She had also mastered coaching psychology, and she frequently drew on an undergraduate college course involving rats, certain stimuli, and desired results. As Bradley once told the *Daily Orange*, performance behaviors are dictated by a combination of frustration, desperation, and inspiration.

"Probably the most important thing in coaching is understanding people and what moves them and their spirit," Bradley said. "Everyone thinks coaching is all about inspiration, but an opponent gives desperation and frustration."

What Bradley gives Syracuse players is the chance to win every game they play in. And her players have admired her for it.

Said center back Elise Lagerweij, a member of the 2015 championship team, "The thing about Coach Ange is that she sees more in us than we see in ourselves. That's why she pushed us further than we thought we could go. She saw our potential. She saw the person and player we could become and then did absolutely everything to get that out of us. I think that's the key to what makes her such a great coach. The boundaries I saw for my own abilities? They didn't exist to her. She transformed me from being a center forward to the best center back in the country. Most coaches wouldn't dare to ask something like that from one of their players."

Ange Bradley did because nothing usually gets by her.

Syracuse head coach Ange Bradley is hoisted onto her players' shoulders after winning the 2015 NCAA field hockey championship. It was SU's first women's national championship. Athletics Department, Syracuse University, used by permission.

SYRACUSE UNIVERSITY'S OLYMPIANS

1900	Myer Prinstein (track and field)
1904	Myer Prinstein (track and field)
1908	Marquis Frank "Bill" Horr (track and field)
1912	Charlie Reidpath (track and field)
1920	Al Woodring (track and field)
1924	Chet Bowman (track and field)
1928	Ray Barbuti (track and field)
1936	Ed O'Brien (track and field)
1936	Marty Glickman (track and field), Ed O'Brien (track and field)
1956	Siegbert Wirth (soccer)
1964	James Edmonds (rowing), Anthony Johnson (rowing)
1968	Anthony Johnson (rowing)
1972	Anthony Johnson (rowing)
1976	Mike Plumb (rowing)
1980	Gene Mills (wrestling), Thomas Darling (rowing), William Purdy (rowing)
1984	Jose Betancourt (wrestling), Thomas Darling (rowing), Drew Harrison (rowing), Chris Catalfo (wrestling)
1988	Jason Morris (judo), Thomas Darling (rowing), Drew Harrison (rowing)
1992	Jason Morris (judo), Anthony Washington (discus), Jose Betancourt (wrestling), Tracy Rude Smith (rowing), Drew Harrison (rowing), Allen Green (rowing)
1996	Jason Morris (judo), Anthony Washington (discus), Miroslav Vucetic (swimming), Jose Betancourt (wrestling), Jose Gonzalez (swimming), Drew Harrison (rowing), Don Smith (rowing), Jason Gleasman (wrestling), Chris Saba (wrestling)
2000	Jason Morris (judo), Anthony Washington (discus), Adrian Woodley (track and field), Sam Okantey (track and field), Djordje Filipovic (swimming), Don Smith (rowing)
2004	Boldizsar Kiss (swimming), Helen Tanger (rowing), Froukje Wegman (rowing), Chris Liwski (rowing)
2006	Stefanie Marty (ice hockey)
2008	Carmelo Anthony (basketball), Anna Goodale (rowing), Helen Tanger (rowing), Jim Boeheim (basketball), Chris Liwski (rowing), Phil Wheddon (women's soccer), Jason Morris (judo)

Myer Prinstein (*far right*) poses with members of a Syracuse relay team during the 1901 season. Onondagans Reference Collection, University Archives.

2010	Stefanie Marty (ice hockey)
2012	Shannon Taylor (field hockey), Carmelo Anthony (basketball), Jim Boeheim (basketball), Uhunoma Osazuwa (track and field), Natalie Mastracci (rowing), Mike Gennaro (rowing)
2014	Stefanie Marty (ice hockey)
2016	Carmelo Anthony (basketball), Jim Boeheim (basketball), Uhunoma Osazuwa (track and field), Flings Owusu-Agyapong (track and field), Katie (Hursey) Zaferes (track and field), Michael Gbinije (basketball), Alyssa Manley (field hockey)
2018	Akane Hosoyamada (ice hockey)

Jim Konstanty

Known as Big Jim, bespectacled Casimir James Konstanty became one of the most versatile athletes in Syracuse history, lettering in baseball, basketball, boxing, and soccer before graduating with a degree in physical education in 1939.

Eleven years later, after a circuitous journey through professional baseball, Konstanty shocked himself and the sports world by winning the National League Most Valuable Player Award and being named professional Athlete of the Year by the Associated Press. His MVP was a milestone moment in baseball history because it marked the first time a relief pitcher had received the award. Only three relievers have accomplished the feat since—Rollie Fingers (1981), Willie Hernandez (1984), and Dennis Eckersley (1992).

Konstanty was thirty-three years old when he enjoyed his career year in 1950. He appeared in a then major league record seventy-four games, recording sixteen wins and twenty-two saves as the Philadelphia Phillies "Whiz Kids" won their first pennant in thirty-five years. The Phillies would be swept by the New York Yankees in that World Series.

Five years later, Konstanty would help the Yankees capture an American League pennant with a 7-2 record and eleven saves. His work against and for the Bronx Bombers prompted Hall of Fame manager Casey Stengel to comment: "Konstanty is one of the greatest I've ever seen in the clutch." The six-foot-two right-hander spent eleven seasons in the big leagues, posting a 66-48 record and seventy-four saves in 433 games.

Syracuse would send twenty-three players to the major leagues before disbanding its varsity baseball program after eighty-three years in 1971. Only one of those players would be named the best of the best: Jim Konstanty.

Discontinued Varsity Sports

Baseball	1889-90 to 1970-71
Boxing	1924 to 1956
Men's Golf	1925 to 1973
Men's Gymnastics	1947-48 to 1996-97
Rifle	1921 to 1973
Men's Swimming and Diving	1915-16 to 2010-11
Women's Swimming and Diving	1976-77 to 2010-11
Skiing	1933 to 1977
Men's Tennis	1950-51 to 1971-72
Water Polo	1924 to 1931
Wrestling	1922 to 1999-2000

Gene Mills

People referred to him as "mean Gene the pinning machine," and the nickname fit because in four varsity wrestling seasons at SU Gene Mills posted a 144-5-1 record, which included a then NCAA-record 107 pins. The New Jersey native captured two national championships in the 118-pound class and became the first athlete in school history to earn All-American honors four consecutive years.

And he was every bit as dominating on the world stage, posting a career record of 1,356-46-1 with 866 victories by pins. He won three world titles.

Yet for all the success Mills enjoyed, he remains haunted by the one opponent he couldn't defeat: President Jimmy Carter. It was a

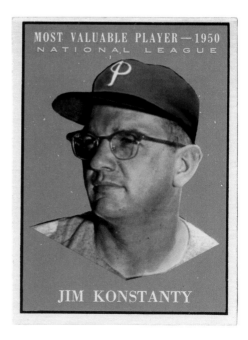

In 1950, Orange alum Jim Konstanty won the National League Most Valuable Player award after pitching the Philadelphia Phillies into the World Series. Topps® trading card courtesy of The Topps Company, Inc.

Syracuse's Gene Mills pinned seven straight opponents to win the 1981 NCAA wrestling championship at 118 pounds. For his efforts, he was named Most Outstanding Wrestler for the tournament. Athletics Department, Syracuse University, used by permission.

foregone conclusion that Mills was going to win a gold medal at the 1980 Olympics in Moscow, but those golden dreams never materialized because Carter decided the United States would boycott the Summer Games to protest the Soviet Union's invasion of Afghanistan. Mills and other members of the US Olympic team were devastated that politics had poisoned the world of sports.

"What did it wind up accomplishing?" Mills asked in an interview thirty years later. "It was meant to punish the Russians, but the only people it wound up punishing were the athletes who had worked a lifetime to get to this point only to have the rug pulled out from underneath them. I know it's not healthy and I know there are a million things more important, but I think about it almost every day. It's business I'll never be able to finish; it's a goal I'll never realize."

Following the boycott, he returned to SU for his senior season and took his anger out on his opponents, going 35-0 and literally pinning his way through the NCAA tournament to win his second title. Shoulder and knee injuries prevented him from competing in the 1984 and 1988 Olympics.

After his dreams were dashed, he went to work on helping other wrestlers to realize theirs, first as an assistant coach under Ed Carlin at SU, then as one of the nation's most successful scholastic coaches at Phoenix High School in Central New York.

The Syracuse Eight

Many who followed the 2016 saga of NFL quarterback Colin Kaepernick and the controversy involving athletes kneeling for the "Star-Spangled Banner" know that during the late 1960s and early 1970s, numerous athletes staged protests about conditions they felt warranted discussion and change.

In 1966, boxer Muhammad Ali refused to fight in the Vietnam War and found himself arrested, convicted for draft evasion, and

The Syracuse Eight. Courtesy of the Syracuse 8, LLC.

stripped of his right to fight. Two years later, Olympic sprinters Tommie Smith and John Carlos raised black-gloved fists on the Mexico City medals podium to protest oppression of African Americans in the United States. Almost immediately, they were suspended from the US team and sent home.

Something similar took place at Syracuse University when nine African American football players boycotted spring practices in 1970 to challenge the racism they faced on campus and from their coaches. For their troubles, the nine saw their athletic careers terminated despite an intervention on their behalf by SU's legendary Number 44, Jim Brown.

Incorrectly identified by the media as the "Syracuse Eight," the nine players—Greg Allen, Richard Bulls, John Godbolt, Dana Harrell, John Lobon, Clarence "Bucky" McGill, Alif Muhammad (then known as Al Newton), Duane Walker, and Ronald Womack—quickly ignited a wave of anger, including threats as well as teammate and SU fan boycotts. They did find support on campus from Charles Willie, one of SU's first African American professors; Allen Sullivan, then a graduate student in the School of Education; education professor John Johnson; and Rev. George Moody, director of the Martin Luther King Jr. On-Campus Elementary School where the players met to strategize. The nine men ultimately sat out the 1970 season and never played again.

Jim Brown summarized the players' objectives in his foreword to David Marc's 2015 *Leveling the Playing Field: The Story of the Syracuse Eight.* "Did they succeed? Look at the things they were asking for in 1970: an end to race discrimination in assigning player positions, an end to race discrimination in academic support for student athletes, medical care that prioritized the health of the athletes above patching them up for the next game, and a diverse coaching staff capable of relating to the needs of all the team members."

Syracuse later acknowledged "unintentional" racism was prevalent within the university and the athletics department, and instituted changes within the football program and wider university. It led to the assistant coaching appointments of Carlmon Jones in the fall of 1970 and varsity wide receivers coach William Spencer (for head coach Frank Maloney's staff) four years later.

More than three decades later, in 2006, the Syracuse Eight were awarded the Chancellor's Medal for Courage, an official apology, and long-denied letterman jackets.

As Greg Allen told the *Players' Tribune* in 2015:

We were trying to help the white players as much as ourselves. Yes, one demand we had was for a black coach, but everything else was for the team in general—better medical care, and so on. We were taken aback by the fact that: How come the white ball players had now turned against us and didn't want us back on the team and were threatening to boycott if we came back on the team? In the end, the chancellor's report stated that there was institutional racism at Syracuse—but we, the victims, were being more victimized by our teammates who we were trying to help. It wasn't a matter of trying to split the team or just being rebellious, it was a matter of trying to make the university that we loved greater and better.

Syracuse was formed in 1870 by the Methodist Church so that people of color, Native Americans and women would have an opportunity to go to a university. The first class at Syracuse was something like 43 percent women and people of color. So what happened since 1870, when there were only one percent people of color when we attended?

What happened was that one hundred years after Syracuse was founded, nine men made SU a better university and initiated a meaningful commitment to equality, diversity, and inclusion.

Lon Keller and the New York Yankees Logo

After graduating from Syracuse University with a degree in fine arts in 1929, Lon Keller embarked on a career as an illustrator that would see him design more than five thousand program covers for sporting events. He was so prolific and so respected among his peers that he became known as the Norman Rockwell and Babe Ruth of sports illustrators.

Of his numerous designs, none was more recognizable than the Uncle Sam hat-on-the-bat emblem of the New York Yankees. It continues to be used by the team today and is arguably the most famous and familiar logo in sports history.

This legendary New York Yankees logo was designed by Syracuse alumnus Lon Keller in 1946. Major League Baseball trademarks and copyrights are used with permission of Major League Baseball Properties, Inc.

Keller was commissioned by Yankees co-owner Larry Mac-Phail in 1946 to design a logo to strengthen the team's advertising opportunities following World War II. He had been hired because of his reputation for designing hundreds of major college football program covers as well as his work with World Series programs. His first drawing used the word *Yankees* in script with a top hat placed above the *k*. It was first seen on the cover of the team's spring training roster in 1946.

MacPhail was pleased with the outcome but wanted Keller to develop it a bit more. The artist added a baseball to surround the *Yankees* script, changed the *k* to depict a baseball bat, and positioned the top hat directly above the bat. The new logo premiered on the team's spring training roster in 1947 and was an instant hit. From that point on, it's been used in virtually every Yankees correspondence and publication, and has remained unchanged.

Interestingly, Keller also would design the logo for the Yankees' crosstown rival, the New York Mets, in 1962. Because their formal name was the Metropolitans, Keller opted to feature the Big Apple's skyline with skyscrapers such as the Empire State Building as the backdrop on a baseball logo in the Mets' orange and blue team colors.

Art was Keller's ticket out of a Spartan childhood in New Jersey, where his father ran a five-and-dime store and money was always tight. Keller earned a scholarship to study fine arts at SU and wound up graduating in 1929, the year of the infamous Wall Street crash. His extraordinary talent enabled him to find plenty of work during the Great Depression. For nearly forty years, his work graced the covers of some of the most famous sports events in the United States and brought him many accolades, including induction into the New York Sports Museum and Hall of Fame in 1991.

Keller continued drawing and painting up until his death at age eighty-seven in 1995. At the time, SU was working on coming up with a new logo and mascot. Keller's children said their father would have "loved to have been a part of that project."

Billy Connors

Billy Connors achieved national sports fame at age twelve, six years before showing up on the Syracuse campus and four decades before contributing to the New York Yankees dynasty. As a precocious pitcher, Connors helped lead Schenectady to the 1954 Little League Baseball World Series title in Williamsport, Pennsylvania. That achievement earned him and his teammates an appearance on NBC's *Today Show* and pregame introductions at the Polo Grounds in New York City before that fall's Major League Baseball World Series opener.

Connors's prowess on the mound and basketball court led him to SU, where he would letter in both sports. A quick-thinking point guard, he averaged 6 points per game for the Orange hoopsters, but he was much better on the diamond, guiding the 1961 Orangemen to a 16-3 record and their only appearance in the College World

Series. The Chicago Cubs liked what they saw and signed him to a contract following his sophomore year.

Despite a pedestrian big-league playing career (0-2 won-lost record and a 7.53 earned run average in twenty-six games with the Cubs and New York Mets), Connors went on to enjoy enormous success as a three-time Yankees pitching coach and confidant of team owner George Steinbrenner. Known as the pitching whisperer, Connors was part of five World Series titles, while serving as the team's vice president of player personnel from 1996 to 2012. During that time, he was credited with helping Yankees Hall-of-Fame relief pitcher Mariano Rivera develop the cutter pitch that enabled him to record more saves than any player in major league history. Connors also played a role in the success of several other pitchers, including Andy Pettitte, Orlando Hernandez, Doc Gooden, and CC Sabathia with the Yankees, and Greg Maddux and Rick Sutcliffe with the Cubs.

The Yankees honored him with a moment of silence before a game following his death at age seventy-six in 2018.

Ya Gotta Regatta!

In Malcolm Alama's book *Mark of the Oarsmen*, we learn that Syracuse University's first chancellor, Alexander Winchell, was opposed to muscular sports of all kinds and refused to allow students to form a crew when the idea was first broached by two freshmen in 1873, just three years after the school was founded.

When Winchell learned that undergrads Charles Holden and George Hine were going to hold a regatta on Onondaga Lake and offer prize money donated by downtown Syracuse merchants, he had a snit. He wrote letters of displeasure to friends and community figures, but his attempts to torpedo the idea were too late because Holden and Hine already had captured the imagination of the community and interest from crews from Rochester, Buffalo, and New York City. Thousands of spectators showed up to watch the races. The daring duo thought the enormous success of the regatta would change Winchell's mind, but it didn't.

Rowing wouldn't be taken seriously until a more forward-thinking chancellor, James Roscoe Day, embraced the idea in 1900. Day convinced benefactor Lyman Cornelius Smith, a local typewriter tycoon, to provide financial assistance, and SU football coach Edwin Regur Sweetland offered to take on the additional duties of coaching the team in order to earn a little extra money. The first organized crews would become known as the Syracuse University Navy, but they didn't get off to an auspicious start, and Sweetland resigned in 1902.

James A. Ten Eyck, a professional sculler and coach of the US Naval Academy's first crews, took over, and a golden era of SU rowing ensued. During Ten Eyck's thirty-five years as coach, the Orangemen won the Intercollegiate Rowing Association's (IRA) regatta—regarded as the national championships—five times. A year

before Ten Eyck's death at age eighty-six in 1938, the university built and dedicated a boathouse in his honor.

Another seminal moment in the program's rich history would come in 1959, when Loren Schoel coached SU to victory as the US representative in the Pan American Games. That same year, Schoel recruited a superb rower named Bill Sanford who would become varsity captain in 1963 and go on to coach for thirty-four years, producing an IRA varsity eight champion in 1978 and a varsity four champ in 1981. The 1978 championship was SU's first national rowing title in fifty-eight years, the boat powered by a crew of Gerald Henwood, Andy Mogish, Bill Purdy, Bill Reid, John Shamlian, Art "Skip" Sibley, Ozzie Street, and David Townsley. Several of the rowers would go on to compete in international competitions. Purdy wound up qualifying for the 1980 Olympics in Moscow but was not allowed to compete because of the Olympic boycott.

Through the years, the men's and women's teams have churned out a number of Olympic rowers, most recently Natalie Mastracci, who won a silver medal at the 2012 Summer Games in London, and Mike Gennaro, who was an alternate on the US men's team.

From 1952 through 1992 and again in 1994, SU served as hosts of the IRA on Onondaga Lake, staging a huge regatta that undoubtedly would have made Holden and Hine burst with pride and Chancellor Winchell explode with anger. Crowds in excess of fifteen thousand people would gather on the shores and in the park for the three-day event. Over time, the partying and boozing of the spectators overshadowed the races themselves. One scribe described the scene as "rowing's Woodstock." By the early 1980s, race officials stopped allowing alcohol to be brought into the park. Flooding forced the races to be moved in 1993. After returning to Onondaga the following year, the regatta was moved to Cooper River in Pennsauken, New Jersey.

Alexis Peterson, Brianna Butler, and Brittney Sykes

In life—and on the basketball court—good things often come in threes. And that certainly was the case for the Syracuse women's hoops team from 2015 to 2017, when the backcourt trio of Alexis Peterson, Brianna Butler, and Brittney Sykes took the Orange to heights never visited before.

The national media recognized them as the best guard combination in women's college basketball, and Peterson, Butler, and Sykes lived up to the hype. Teaming with twin forwards Briana and Bria Day, they led fourth-seeded Syracuse into the 2016 NCAA national championship game in Indianapolis against Connecticut's mighty Huskies. While Syracuse ultimately lost its first-ever final, its talented backcourt helped change national perceptions of Coach Quentin Hillsman's Orange.

Peterson, who finished her senior season averaging 23.4 points per game, was the first Syracuse player ever picked as conference

Brittney Sykes helped lead the Orange women's basketball team to the 2016 NCAA title game. Athletics Department, Syracuse University, used by permission.

Seattle's Storm, and Butler was taken as the twenty-third pick in the 2016 WNBA draft by the Los Angeles Sparks.

Not bad for one backcourt.

Al Davis

Al Davis earned a bachelor's degree in English literature from Syracuse University in the spring of 1950. However, there was something he coveted even more from his alma mater but didn't receive, and it would gnaw at him and motivate him for the rest of his compelling, nonconformist, often mysterious life. A frustrated jock who wound up becoming the influential, maverick owner of the three-time Super Bowl-winning Oakland Raiders, Davis had hoped to earn a varsity letter from the Orange in football, but, alas, it was not meant to be. The man who coined the phrase "Just win, baby" played junior varsity football, baseball, and basketball at SU, but he wasn't talented enough to make the big squads. "I didn't do as well at Syracuse as I dreamed or hoped to," he told his old classmates at a New York City reunion in 1992. "I just didn't do it."

What he did do at Syracuse was acquire a wealth of football knowledge that would serve him well, first as a coach at the college and pro levels and then as a talent evaluator when he became the Raiders principal owner in 1972. At SU, Davis lived with the jocks in the temporary Quonset hut barracks known as the Shacks that sprung up on campus to accommodate the influx of GI Bill students after World War II. When it became apparent he wasn't going to make it as an athlete, Davis became a student of football, often attending classroom strategy sessions taught by SU assistant coach Bud Barker.

Legend had it that some of Davis's best lessons occurred outside the classroom. After being cut from the varsity, he reportedly still attended practices, observing intently from the stands or on Hendricks Hill just above Archbold Stadium. He took copious notes about Coach Ben Schwartzwalder's then revolutionary unbalanced line, wingback offense.

Davis developed a passion for literature at SU but had no intention of putting his English degree to use as either a writer or teacher. "It was pointless," he said. "I remember thinking, 'What am I studying English for when all I want to do is coach?'" After graduating, the Brooklyn native landed his first job as the offensive line coach at Adelphi College. He would later work as an assistant coach for the Baltimore Colts and as the offensive line coach at the Citadel and the University of Southern California. In 1960, he returned to professional football as the receivers coach for the Los Angeles Chargers of the newly formed American Football League.

After three seasons with the Chargers, Davis became the youngest head coach and general manager in professional football when the Oakland Raiders hired him at age thirty-three. He earned the league's coach-of-the-year honors in 1963, and three years

player of the year. She finished as the school's all-time assist leader and ended up second in points scored and third in steals (including one contest where she set a school single-game record with 10).

But statistics fail to tell the story of a fierce, five-foot-seven, second-team All-American who once scored 45 points in a game while epitomizing Coach Q's attacking style. Peterson triggered Hillsman's offense by driving to the basket, shooting the 3, pressuring the ball on defense, and stealing passes. She did it all.

Next to her were her "sisters in solidarity," Sykes and Butler. Coming off two devastating knee injuries, the athletically explosive Sykes persevered so she could combine with Peterson and Butler to lead Syracuse to a 30-8 season with tournament victories over perennial powers South Carolina and Tennessee in the Sioux Falls Regional. She also set the team record for most career starts (137) and was a first-team All-Atlantic Coast Conference selection her senior year.

Butler was the rare individual who always had the green light to shoot the triple, regardless of court location. Butler was hesitant by nature to shoot first if she thought she could find an open teammate, but Coach Q was adamant the guard launch them early, late, often, and without worry.

The result? Butler left Syracuse holding the record for threes made and for playing the most minutes in SU history. She also set the NCAA single-season record for threes (129), and climbed to twelfth all-time in NCAA history for successful 3-point shots (373).

How did things turn out for the mighty trio after their days on the SU campus? Each was drafted by WNBA teams, with the highly popular Sykes taken seventh by the Atlanta Dream, where she was the leading rookie scorer and second in the 2017 Rookie of the Year voting. Peterson went fifteenth (third pick of the second round) to later, as commissioner of the AFL, he helped broker the merger with the established NFL. He then returned to the Raiders as owner, a position he held until his death at age eighty-two in 2011.

During his nearly five-decade reign, Davis's Raiders established themselves as the winningest franchise in all of sports. Davis relished his renegade role, as did many of the unsavory characters who played for him. His teams came to be known for their fearless and, some would say, dirty tactics. And Davis would prove to be a thorn in the side of his fellow owners and former commissioner Pete Rozelle, going so far as to sue the league on several occasions.

But Davis also proved to be a civil rights activist who used his influence to break down barriers. He was the first man to draft a black quarterback in the first round (Tennessee State's Eldridge Dickey in 1968), the first man to hire a Hispanic coach (Tom Flores in 1979), the first man in the modern era to hire an African American coach (Art Shell in 1989), and the first man to hire a woman as CEO (Amy Trask in 1997). His groundbreaking hires resulted, in part, from the sensitivity he developed at SU, where he roomed with Bernie Custis, one of the first African American quarterbacks in major college football.

For a long time after graduating, Davis had nothing to do with his alma mater. The hard feelings, he said, were the result of his former coaches not being helpful during his job searches. But thanks to the intervention of former classmate and former SU football standout Luke LaPorta, the fences were mended. Davis wound up donating several hundred thousand dollars to renovate the football locker room. In 1985, Davis returned to campus and received something that had eluded him during his undergraduate days. The man not good enough to make the Orange varsity was named an honorary LetterWinner of Distinction.

Dave Meggyesy

Most longtime baseball fans are familiar with Jim Bouton's landmark 1970 book *Ball Four*, which revealed the inner workings of professional baseball. A year later, a former Syracuse football player who played seven seasons in the NFL took things a lot further by releasing a radical work promoted as "the roughest sports book ever written" and one designed to expose "the dehumanizing quality of the game—the fraud, payoffs, racism, drug abuse, and violence."

Dave Meggyesy was familiar with challenging authority. The son of an Ohio union organizer, Meggyesy came to Syracuse in 1959 and played for the Orange from 1960 to 1962. Selected in the seventeenth round of the 1963 NFL Draft by the St. Louis Cardinals, the ferocious outside linebacker retired after the 1969 season just as numerous national and political issues were rising to the surface.

The first contentious point for Meggyesy probably happened when NFL Commissioner Pete Rozelle mandated how players

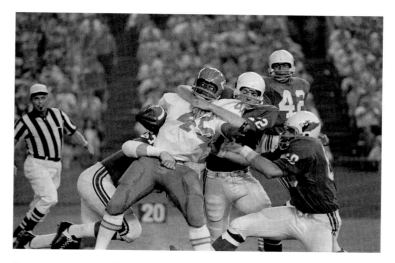

Former Orange football standout Dave Meggyesy (lower right) played seven seasons in the NFL before publishing a provocative book designed to expose the "the dehumanizing quality of the game." Bettmann / Getty Images.

should stand during the playing of the national anthem. Foreshadowing a similar controversy fifty years later, Meggyesy refused to "line up along the sideline, holding your helmet in your left arm, against your armpit, and your right hand on your heart, while turning toward the flag."

Instead, Meggyesy bowed his head and let his Cards helmet hang by his side. Worst of all, he began shuffling his feet.

"For me, it was two things," Meggyesy told the *New Yorker* in 2018. "No. 1, being told how to salute the flag—don't tell me what to do!—and, No. 2, was my antiwar sentiment. I just thought, this is bullshit—the indignity of realizing the NFL is supporting the war by being super patriotic. I'm protesting that they're trying to support the Vietnam War with Nixon and Agnew and the boys."

Told by the Cardinals to end his protest, Meggyesy went the opposite way. He began hosting activist meetings, organizing buses for Washington, DC, protesters, and sending signed letters to local congressmen. The result? He was benched before the season ended, and out of the league by year's end. He was twenty-seven.

But Meggyesy wasn't done with the NFL. Retreating to northern California, he entered Jack Scott's Oakland-based Institute for the Study of Sport and Society and proceeded to write *Out of Their League* (published in 1971). Suddenly, he was appearing on national TV shows detailing actual and ongoing abuses of football players.

In one interview, on the *Dick Cavett Show*, Meggyesy announced college football players were "one of the most exploited minorities in the country." That sentiment, plus an African American football player protest at SU, helped guarantee Meggyesy's return to Syracuse.

"In the fall of 1970," Syracuse Eight member Dana Harrell later recalled, "the late David Ifshin, the SU student government president, invited Meggyesy back to campus to speak. Dave had just written *Out of Their League*. He had played for SU and the St. Louis Cardinals until 1969. But SU's Administration would not give the students a permit to use Hendricks Chapel (HC), claiming concerns about damage if the students got excited."

"Ifshin and the white students 'took' HC the night of the speech," said Harrell, recalling how Meggyesy's talk was even broadcast on the radio. "We [the Syracuse Eight] met with Meggyesy and he supported us and because of the student support for the SU 8 and because we were founding, active members in [a group that] worked closely with student government, Ifshin asked one of us to speak and introduce Meggyesy. The night of the speech, Hendricks was [standing room only] with an over-flow crowd outside, and I delivered a speech entitled 'Tell the Truth.'"

The truth was something Meggyesy cared about passionately, and before he retired in 2007, one of SU's greatest football players would teach courses at Stanford, coach high school football, and, starting in 1979, work for the NFL Players Association as their Western regional director.

According to author David Harris (*The League: The Rise and Decline of the NFL*), "Meggyesy was the first to come along and say Rozelle's attempt to portray the league as a wholesome, all-American engagement of sportsmen was incomplete. That, on one level, it was a business and a meat factory."

Or, as Meggyesy told *Sports Illustrated* in 1987,

Football emerged out of Social Darwinism and the industrial period in American history. It is based on violence, on the conquest and defense of territory. The ball is just a little marker of where you are. I think the game fits in with the whole idea of corporate America. The values of being aggressive are being tested in the business world. Are we competitive? Can we beat the other guy? The game now is an ode to materialism. It certainly doesn't stand for any spiritual or ethical values. The stuff that surrounds the Super Bowl is just one big corporate self-congratulation. It's so ostentatious it makes you want to puke.

Because of Meggyesy's honesty, *Sports Illustrated* concluded that universities started "offering courses in the sociology of sport and [using his] book as a text. Journalists would begin writing more about the human dimensions of football, trying to understand the sport, not only for the pleasure and escape it can be, but also for its importance as a reflection of the greater world."

It's one clear way a Syracuse alumnus influenced the language and contemporary integrity of sport.

Dome Announcers

"Nervous? You bet. *Terrified* too. Suppose I say the wrong thing or I open my mouth and nothing comes out but my lunch!"

That was how public address announcer Carl Eilenberg felt September 20, 1980, the night the Carrier Dome opened.

His voice was the first one transmitted through the Dome's new speaker system welcoming fifty thousand fans to SU's first Dome event. Outside the Dome, limos bearing Syracuse football players in tuxes were arriving at a building that, during the next four decades, became one of the most talked about NCAA athletic venues ever.

For Eilenberg, becoming the "Voice of the Dome" was more a lucky accident than a plan. He was already one of several local radio and TV announcers doing PA work at Manley Field House and Archbold Stadium. But because he played noontime pickup basketball with coaches and administrators at Manley, he was known by Tom Benzel, the former SU athlete tasked by the university to oversee the building and opening of the Dome. As he did for occasional pickup games, Tom picked Carl as the Dome announcer in 1980.

Eilenberg would hold that position for twenty-six years, announcing more than one thousand football, basketball, and lacrosse games until he turned the title and microphone over to Michael Veley in 2006. "During those twenty-six plus years, I was eyewitness to thrilling performances by student-athletes from all over the world," recalled Eilenberg. "I literally had a front row seat to history, record-setting performances and legends getting forged. And the only real advice (or warning) I ever got was from our taciturn and right-to-the-point athletics director Jake Crouthamel when he looked me square in the eye on opening night, paused for effect, and then said, 'Don't screw it up.'"

By 2018, Veley, the chair and director of the Falk College's sport management department, had announced more than six hundred Carrier Dome events, including Orange (Midnight) Madness, the NCAA Men's Basketball East Regionals, NCAA Men's Lacrosse tournaments, NBA exhibition games, SU commencement, the Dalai Lama's One World Concert event, and ESPN Game Day ceremonies. "I've been a part of four NCAA record attendance crowds for basketball," said Veley, "and announced games between the two winningest coaches in college basketball history. I also got to call SU's upset of number two ranked Clemson in football and great jersey retirements. Plus, the most successful women's basketball team in program history which was the national runner-up in 2016."

Dino Babers and Eric Dungey

At his first press conference as Syracuse University football coach in 2016, Dino Babers asked the roughly seventy-five media members, administrators, players, and boosters in attendance to close their eyes while he painted a word picture.

"Visualize this," he began. "You're in the Carrier Dome. Your house is filled. The feeling is electric. The noise is deafening. You have a defense that's relentless. You have a special teams [unit] that has been well-coached. You have an offense that will not huddle.

Coach Dino Babers and quarterback Eric Dungey celebrate on the Carrier Dome field after the Orange upset defending national champion Clemson in 2017. Athletics Department, Syracuse University, used by permission.

And you have a game that's faster than you've ever seen on turf. Open your eyes. That's going to be a reality. That's going to be Syracuse football."

Many in attendance broke into applause. Some appeared ready to run through a wall for the guy. But some also remained skeptical, and that skepticism would grow when Babers's teams started fast but stumbled to 4-8 records in each of their first two seasons with him at the helm. During those disappointing finishes, the always upbeat Babers kept preaching "faith without evidence." And that faith would be rewarded with resounding evidence in 2018 as he led Syracuse to its best record and first top twenty-five ranking in nearly two decades. As promised, the Orange would become an offensive juggernaut, scoring 40 or more points eight times and 50 or more points on five occasions.

The presence of quarterback Eric Dungey was one of the reasons Babers accepted the challenge of rebuilding a program that had won just 48 of its previous 131 games. The hypercompetitive

Dungey had shown promise as a freshman, the season before Babers's arrival. And he would wind up flourishing under the new Orange coach, establishing or tying sixteen school records while becoming the first SU quarterback to pass for more than ten thousand yards, while also rushing for more than two thousand yards in his career. A crowning moment for coach and quarterback would occur in the Carrier Dome on October 13, 2017, as Syracuse scored a monumental upset, knocking off defending national champion Clemson, 27-24. The victory proved the Orange could compete with college football's elite and prompted thousands of delirious fans to flood the field in celebration.

Afterward, the charismatic Babers delivered a memorable postgame locker room speech that went viral. In it, he repeatedly asked his players, "Whose House?" and each time they responded emphatically, "Our House!" It had the feel of a revival, and that was fitting, because Babers, with a huge assist from his tough-as-Dome-concrete quarterback, had helped revive SU football in a manner similar to the jobs done by predecessors Ben Schwartzwalder in the 1950s and Dick MacPherson in the 1980s.

Syracuse 17, Top-Ranked Nebraska 9

The wizards of odds in Las Vegas had established the Syracuse University football team as 24-point underdogs heading into their September 29, 1984, game in the Carrier Dome against the top-ranked Nebraska Cornhuskers.

Many believed the point spread should have been much larger.

After all, the Cornhuskers were riding a 24-game regular-season win streak and had clobbered the Orange, 63-7, the season before in Lincoln, Nebraska. And SU was coming off a 19-0 loss to lowly Rutgers the week before Nebraska came to town—an eight-turnover performance so pathetic that the Dome fans booed the Orange players and coaches off the field.

The oddsmakers weren't the only ones anticipating a romp. That week, *Sports Illustrated* splashed a photo of a Cornhuskers player scoring a touchdown on its cover. They called Nebraska the "Big Red Machine."

What occurred that September afternoon was arguably the most remarkable upset in the nearly 130-year history of Syracuse football, as the Orangemen knocked off the Cornhuskers, 17-9, in front of 47,280 spectators. Up in the press box, Ben Schwartzwalder, who had coached SU to the 1959 national championship,

leaped to his feet when the final gun sounded. "I still can't believe it," he said, chomping on an unlit cigar. "This, and the Cotton Bowl win over Texas on New Year's Day 1960 . . . That's the only other win I can remember that compares to this one."

Led by All-American defensive end Tim Green, Syracuse limited a team that had been averaging 531 yards per game to just 214. The Orange forced seven punts, caused two fumbles, intercepted a pass, and stopped Nebraska cold on a crucial fourth-and-one.

Running back Jamie Covington rushed for ninety-nine yards, but the unsung hero for SU was quarterback Todd Norley, who had been jeered off the field after a three-fumble, two-interception performance the week before. Roughly five minutes into the third quarter, Norley and wide receiver Mike Siano connected on one of the most dramatic plays in SU history—a forty-yard touchdown pass in which Siano out-leaped two defenders near the goal line. The score gave SU the lead for good.

In the joyous locker room afterward, Green hugged Norley and bellowed above the din, "This is why I came to Syracuse. I wanted to be able to experience moments like this one."

The win was a watershed moment for the program, laying the foundation for the 1987 season in which SU would go 11-0-1 and finish number four in the final Associated Press poll.

SU receiver Mike Siano (shown on this schedule card) caught the decisive touchdown pass as the Orange defeated top-ranked Nebraska in a 1984 game in the Carrier Dome. Athletics Department, Syracuse University, used by permission.

9 Serving the Country and the World

A Syracuse veteran states his convictions via his T-shirt. © Syracuse University. Photo by Stephen Sartori.

If knowledge crowns those who seek her, then courage surely has anointed those who served their country and the less fortunate. That has certainly been the case for the last 150 years as countless Syracuse University students, alumni, professors, and administrators played significant roles in America's armed forces, NASA, and social aid groups such as the Peace Corps, USAID, and Model United Nations.

Engagement with America's military may seem like a strange endeavor for a university founded as part of a religious movement (Methodism) in 1870, but Syracuse has enjoyed one of the strongest and longest-standing relationships with the US military of any university. One example is SU's vaunted ROTC program, which is the longest running active program of its kind in the country.

Another (and perhaps more telling) example was the Servicemen's Readjustment Act, otherwise known as the GI Bill, that was instituted in 1944 and gave educational "hope" to millions of World War II veterans and prisoners of war returning home. What is often not recalled is that many universities did not want veterans on their campuses.

That was not the case at SU, which invited a transformation from a small undergraduate liberal arts college to a major research university. Chancellor William Pearson Tolley, in support of an emergency plea from New York governor Thomas E. Dewey, embraced the concept of service members on campus, and between the 1945-46 and 1948-49 academic years, SU's enrollment nearly quadrupled, going from about 5,700 to just under 20,000.

Tolley's operational genius was to suggest Syracuse was a "Victory University," and his open-door welcome to eight thousand veterans (more than half of whom were married) would change SU forever. As David May, former editor of *Syracuse University Magazine*, wrote in February 1987: "Because Syracuse welcomed [vets] more enthusiastically than most universities, the veterans changed Syracuse more than most—perhaps more than any."

That GI Bulge expansion of enrolled students required a massive infrastructure. Virtually overnight, SU was forced to build housing (including a cow barn at the New York State Fairgrounds, a trailer camp in the apple orchard at Drumlins, and rough barracks known as Quonset huts at Skytop), classrooms, laboratories, dining halls, studios, and offices. In a sense, it was SU that was invaded, but the happy outcome was national relevance and a commitment to those who had served.

Concepts such as personal and vocational counseling or speech and hearing therapy (for wounded vets) would set the research table for a different chancellor seventy years later when Kent Syverud was inaugurated in 2014. In Syverud's first formal remarks to the university community, he said he would revisit and embrace Tolley's approach to veterans and military families, telling a packed Hendricks Chapel that he wanted Syracuse "to become the best place in the world for veterans." By 2017, *Military Times* was recognizing Syracuse as the number one military-friendly private university in the United States, and the campus population would feature more than one thousand student veterans.

SU's connection to the military went beyond welcoming veterans. Orange football coaches in the 2000s, such as Doug Marrone, Scott Shafer, and Dino Babers, took their teams to the Fort Drum Army base near the Canadian border for intensive summer practices and leadership seminars. For many years, Syracuse football teams wore the stylized X of the Tenth Mountain Division on their uniforms.

Behind the direction of Vice Chancellor Michael Haynie, SU would emerge as a national leader in recognizing the needs of America's veterans. For many, including those who served in the War on Terror that began with the bombing of New York City's World Trade Center and the US Pentagon on September 11, 2001, Syracuse became a place of transformation.

This was most evident in the design and development of the Entrepreneurship Bootcamp for Veterans, the Office of Veteran and Military Affairs, and the Institute for Veterans and Military Families—a brand new $60 million National Veterans Resource Complex on SU's campus that will open in 2020. That facility will serve as the gateway to veteran commitment, lasting far beyond any one administration.

Syracuse's understanding of service shapes the DNA of nearly every graduating class. Whether it is the Peace Corps or NASA, Syracuse has long been connected to the service thread.

In fact, the creation of the Peace Corps owes much to Harlan Cleveland, the third dean of the Maxwell School. As President John F. Kennedy's undersecretary of state, Cleveland saw to it that Syracuse was selected as one of the first Peace Corps training centers.

SU alumni F. Story Musgrave and Eileen Collins are astronauts who have been shining stars while serving NASA's space program. Musgrave was the only astronaut to fly on six space shuttles, while Collins became the first female pilot and commander of a space shuttle. Collins served under Maxwell MPA graduate Sean O'Keefe,

who was NASA's chief administrator from 2001 to 2005. A former Secretary of the US Navy under President George H. W. Bush, O'Keefe led the space program during challenging times, including the aftermath of the space shuttle Columbia accident in 2003.

SU's involvement in space exploration was evident again when His Royal Highness Prince Sultan bin Salman bin Abdulaziz Al Saud of Saudi Arabia, who received a master of social science degree from the Maxwell School, was selected as a NASA specialist in 1985 and became the first Arab and Muslim astronaut to fly on a shuttle. And twenty-six years later, Orange alumnus Waleed Abdalati was appointed NASA's chief scientist.

Peace Corps

The literal and figurative roots of America's Peace Corps have a distinct Orange flavor, thanks to Harlan Cleveland, a thirty-eight-year-old Princeton-educated Rhodes Scholar who was named the Maxwell School's third dean in 1956.

A year later, Cleveland met SU's commencement speaker, Senator John F. Kennedy. Cleveland was so taken by Kennedy's vision, he volunteered to head JFK's upstate New York presidential campaign and eventually chaired the Institute of International Education committee assigned to implement one of Kennedy's campaign-trail pledges. Namely, to make the concept of the Peace Corps come to life.

By 1961, Cleveland was President Kennedy's undersecretary of state, and on September 21, 1961, Congress authorized the Peace Corps Act. Its mission: to promote "world peace and friendship" and to make "available to interested countries and areas men and women of the United States qualified for service abroad and willing to serve, under conditions of hardship if necessary, to help . . . such countries and areas in meeting their needs for trained manpower."

Cleveland wound up selecting Syracuse University as a Peace Corps training center, with ten acres of university land designated to building a replica of an African village. The center became a place where engineers, teachers, surveyors, and nurses could work on mud-brick farms simulating the living conditions they would find in Africa.

Operating from 1962 to 1966, the Syracuse site held special purpose for the Corps because of the Maxwell School's unique East African Studies Program, which had previously coordinated a development project at the Kenya Institute of Administration. While working on "the farm," volunteers faced rigorous ten-hour days for six days a week over an eight-to-ten week period. During that time, trainees were placed in fitness regimens, Swahili language instruction, and classes on American foreign policy and race relations, in addition to attending lectures on administrative management.

One trainee who came to Syracuse was Paul Theroux, a 1963 graduate of the University of Massachusetts. Theroux, who went on to achieve international fame as a travel author, started his Peace

Corps training at Camp Radley in Puerto Rico but finished on the SU farm before departing for Malawi (then known as Nyasaland).

As Theroux later wrote in the *New York Times*, "My record was so bad I was first rejected by the Peace Corps as a poor risk and possible troublemaker, and accepted as a volunteer only after a great deal of explaining and arguing. The alternative was Vietnam."

Before Theroux could complete his two-year stint, he was chastised by the Peace Corps brass in Washington and "terminated." He claimed he'd been framed for an assassination plot against Hastings Kamuzu Banda, Malawi's president for life.

Syracuse closed its Peace Corps program in 1967, but not before it had trained more than two thousand volunteers, making it third among all university training centers.

Homer Wheaton

Homer Wheaton attended Syracuse University's College of Law from 1902 to 1904, but he left school before graduating and eventually became the sports editor of the *Evening Gazette* in Worcester, Massachusetts. His true calling, though, was to be a soldier. It was something he had dreamed about while a high school student at St. John's Military Academy in Manlius, New York, and was the reason he quit his newspaper job and enlisted as a National Guardsman in 1916, despite being thirty-three years old, well above the draft age.

The man known as Wheat wound up fighting for the 101st US Infantry in Mexico that year and in France a year later, after the United States had entered World War I.

While "over there" he wrote several letters that his old newspaper published. In one of them, he showed his trademark sense of humor. "Just eight lines to let you know that I am still very much alive, although perhaps not the best risk in the world from an insurance

Homer Wheaton was the first man from Onondaga County to perish in combat in World War I. He was posthumously awarded France's Croix de Guerre and the first Distinguished Service Cross in American history. Institute for Veterans and Military Families, Syracuse University, used by permission.

standpoint. Have been promoted to Corporal but strange to say the President hasn't called on me for advice as to the conduct of the war."

That letter, published in the *Gazette* on February 27, 1918, would be his last. Unbeknownst to the paper at the time, it ran the same day Wheaton sacrificed his life to save the lives of his comrades by using his body as a shield from the blast of a grenade in their bunker.

Sergeant Edward Creed, of Wheaton's 101st regiment, later filed this report: "A grenade squad of five men were picked to make a raid through No Man's Land. They were in a dugout, loaded down with grenades, awaiting the order to advance. One grenade fell to the floor. The firing pin had been drawn. In five seconds, the grenade would explode. The five men stood in terror, knowing that when it exploded they would be killed. Corporal Wheaton did not try to pick up the grenade. He did not hesitate. He threw his body over the grenade. It exploded under him, killing him. The other four men were saved."

A few weeks before that fateful day, Wheaton's commanding officer told him a story about an Australian soldier who had saved his fellow soldiers' lives by throwing himself on a grenade. Wheaton told his captain that "was a heroic gesture, the ideal way for a soldier to die."

Wheaton became the first man from Onondaga County to perish in combat in World War I. He was buried at the Oise-Aisne Cemetery in Seringes-et-Nesles, France, not far from the battlefield where he drew his last breath.

In recognition of his valor and heroism, he was posthumously awarded France's Croix de Guerre and the very first Distinguished Service Cross in American history, the second highest honor bestowed by the US military. Some, though, believe Wheaton is deserving of the highest honor—the Congressional Medal of Honor. In 2018, members of the Onondaga Historical Association petitioned local politicians to take up his cause.

In Worcester there is a public square bearing his name. There once was a Homer J. Wheaton American Legion Post on the SU campus. There remains a street and playground named after him in the Salt City.

Forrest Vosler

It's not often a deceased war hero—a winner of the Congressional Medal of Honor, and one already buried in Arlington National Cemetery—graduates from college. But that's exactly what happened in 2015 when Army Air Corps technical sergeant Forrest "Woody" Vosler, who died in 1992, was awarded an associate of arts degree in liberal arts by Syracuse chancellor Kent Syverud.

A radio operator on a B-17 in the 303rd Bomb Group (358th Squadron), Vosler's Flying Fortress had once smashed into the frigid North Sea following a World War II bombing mission over the German seaport of Bremen. That Vosler was still alive after such a horrific mission suggests a staggering will to survive.

Forrest Vosler receives the Medal of Honor from President Franklin D. Roosevelt on August 31, 1944. Courtesy National Archives, photo no. W15663.

Vosler was only twenty at the time of his fourth sortie, and his bomber was severely damaged and forced from formation during a bombing raid on December 20, 1943. Repeated attacks from an estimated thirty enemy fighters and antiaircraft guns on the ground left Vosler with bleeding wounds to his legs, thighs, chest, arms, and both eyes. Despite his visual impairment, Vosler continued firing a machine gun at vague shapes before finding his radio by feel, fixing damaged elements, and communicating the crashing bomber's distressed location.

As if that weren't enough, when the plane—nicknamed Jersey Bounce Jr. (after a Benny Goodman hit record)—went into the water, Vosler crawled out onto its wing and, sensing a badly injured crewmember slipping below the waves, went into the sea to keep the tail gunner from drowning.

On August 31, 1944, less than nine months after Vosler's crew was rescued by a fishing boat in the English Channel, President Franklin D. Roosevelt hosted Vosler and his parents in the Oval Office to bestow America's highest military honor on the young man from Livonia, New York.

Required by his doctors to remain seated during the presentation to Vosler, Roosevelt apologized to the young airman before beckoning him to approach his desk and lean over the president's chair. In a moment Vosler never forgot, Roosevelt whispered, "Son, you know I've given out many of these medals. But I want you to know, Sergeant, that this is the finest medal I've ever had the privilege to give out."

True to his humble Central New York roots, Vosler would later say, "If he [Roosevelt] told that to everyone, I don't want to know about it." He also was fond of saying that the Medal of Honor, which was first awarded during the Civil War in 1863, was "not something you win. It's something that happens to you."

Vosler, who married his SU sweetheart Virginia and matriculated at Syracuse in 1945, initially had been unable to complete his degree because of the wounds to his eyes. But Syverud rectified that situation when the Institute for Veterans and Military Families reviewed Vosler's transcript and recommended the former contact officer for the Syracuse Veterans Administration receive his degree posthumously. It was accepted by Vosler's son, Steve.

ROTC: Reserve Officer Training Corps

There was a time shortly after World War II when a freshman or sophomore taking a class at Syracuse University might find nearly twenty percent of the students in uniform. That was because SU had long featured one of the oldest and most respected on-campus Army ROTC programs of any American university.

There was also a time during the late 1970s when women couldn't go from college directly into military flight school, but when that rule was changed, SU Air Force ROTC cadet Eileen Collins was completely prepared to take advantage of it. Because of her grades and outstanding performance in Syracuse's Air Force ROTC, Collins was one of the first women ever selected for flight school and the first female NASA space shuttle commander.

"I wanted to go into the Air Force from the time I was about fifteen," Collins said. "I joined [Syracuse's] ROTC because I wanted to be part of the military and I wanted to be an officer."

That sentiment has been shared by thousands of SU students since the university first activated a small Student Army Training Corps with four companies (and a thirty-five-member band) on October 1, 1918. Less than a year later, Sidney F. Mashbir, who had served in Army intelligence during World War I, began coordinating the US War Department's establishment of a formal (and permanent) military department known as ROTC.

Serving as SU's first ROTC commander, Lieutenant Colonel Mashbir taught military science and tactics while presiding over 120 men who were simultaneously receiving infantry training. The program would continue to expand through the years, and during World War II, Syracuse would train more Army and Air Force officers than any other educational institution in the United States, not counting the military academies.

SU's Army ROTC (the Stalwart Battalion) and Air Force ROTC (Detachment 535) remain active on campus and frequently lead local high school programs at events such as the Junior ROTC Fitness Challenge in the Carrier Dome.

Not surprisingly, SU's ROTC has launched numerous individuals toward significant military careers, including Max Baratz, who at one time was the oldest serving general officer on active duty in age, time, and pay grade as a major general. Another example is Major

Syracuse University first activated a small Student Army Training Corps with four companies on October 1, 1918. It was the forerunner to SU's long-standing ROTC program. Syracuse University Photograph Collection, University Archives.

A member of SU's Reserve Officer Training Corps (ROTC) trains on the Syracuse campus. © Syracuse University. Photo by Stephen Sartori.

General Franklin Blaisdell, former commander of the Twenty-First Space Wing at Peterson Air Force Base in Colorado Springs. At the time, the Twenty-First was the largest wing (with forty squadrons based in ten foreign countries) in the Air Force.

Margaret Hastings

While many military histories have been written about famous generals or decisive battles, it's rare when a woman plays a pivotal role in a wartime setting. Even more unusual are stories where the heroine, an enlisted servicewoman, survives a horrific plane crash before heroically helping lead wounded men to safety.

In this case, the woman would be briefly hailed by the national media as a hero. And then, true to the age, largely forgotten.

That's what happened to Corporal Margaret Hastings, a post-World War II Syracuse University student from Owego, New York, who joined the Women's Army Corps in 1944 at age thirty and

Margaret Hastings's epic tale of survival following a WWII airplane crash influenced the writing of Mitchell Zuckoff's best-selling book *Lost in Shangri-La*. Bettmann / Getty Images.

found herself assigned to an Army Air Force base in mountainous Papua New Guinea. Then, on May 13, 1945, as the war in the Pacific was winding down, she accepted an unauthorized Sunday sightseeing flight into Papua New Guinea's uncharted interior to see a mysterious village that myth-building pilots had nicknamed Shangri-La.

For twenty-one of the AAF C-47 transport plane's twenty-four passengers and crew, it was their last flight ever. For Hastings, it started a nearly two-month-long jungle ordeal that led to one of the largest rescue efforts of the era.

That Hastings survived the dense, clinging rainforests and deadly steep ravines can only be viewed as a testament to her fierce determination that she, Lieutenant John McCollom, and Sergeant Kenneth Decker would survive.

More than sixty-five years later, Hastings emerged from the jungle once again when investigative journalist Mitchell Zuckoff brought the Army's three survivors to life in his 2011 book *Lost in*

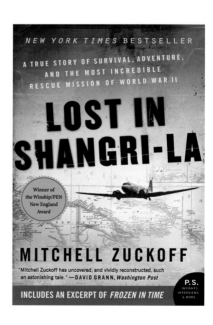

Book cover from *Lost in Shangri-La* by Mitchell Zuckoff. Copyright © 2011 by Mitchell Zuckoff. Reprinted by permission of HarperCollins Publishers.

Shangri-La (HarperCollins). In Zuckoff's gripping narrative, Hastings is presented as a strong woman capable of surviving an abrupt crash, gangrenous infections, burns, an injury nearly requiring amputation, and an unforgiving landscape capable of threatening the three at every turn.

Eventually, Hastings's group stumbled into a Stone Age village Zuckoff described as a place "time never knew existed." The kind of place where the local tribe, capable of headhunting and cannibalism, had "tamed fire but hadn't discovered the wheel."

Margaret Hastings handled the near prehistoric conditions with ease, even making friends with the chief's wife before the Army Air Force evacuated the survivors via gliders.

The "queen of Shangri-La" eventually returned to Central New York, where she attended SU for two years, majoring in engineering while living in the women's dorm known as Nottingham Cottage. She worked at Griffiss Air Force Base in Rome, New York, before dying in 1978 at age sixty-four.

And while her story lay dormant for more than six decades, thanks to Zuckoff, Hastings's heroism was rightly restored.

Rorke Denver

If there's one Syracuse University alumnus to accurately provide the general public with an up-close look at military service, it may be retired Navy SEAL commander Rorke Denver. That's because for five years Denver, a former two-time NCAA lacrosse national champion and 1996 graduate, was arguably America's most visible serviceman.

Denver's acting career started with a key but uncredited appearance as Lieutenant Rorke in the 2012 Hollywood movie *Act of Valor*. It was uncredited because as an active SEAL, Denver's full name couldn't be listed for security reasons.

Two years later, the honorable-mention All-American lacrosse player followed his silver screen appearance with two episodes in the outdoor hunting show *MeatEater* before getting asked to star in the 2016 Fox reality TV show *American Grit*. During the same time, he also appeared on talk shows hosted by Conan O'Brien, Mike Huckabee, Charlie Rose, and Michael Shure.

Adding to his cinematic and TV efforts, Denver also began writing in his spare time, and his first book, *Damn Few: Making the Modern SEAL Warrior*, hit shelves and websites in 2013. It was followed in 2016 with *Worth Dying For: A Navy SEAL's Call to a Nation*, coauthored with Ellis Henican.

"I initially got called by my commanding officer to meet some Hollywood guys," said Denver of his invitation to size up *Act of Valor* directors Mike McCoy and Scott Waugh. "I was one of the guys they talked to and, like all good SEALs, we're pretty secretive. We said, 'No.'"

McCoy and Waugh persisted in wanting real soldiers for their script and after rigorous auditions (and approvals from the US

Navy, Department of Defense, and the Pentagon), Denver was selected with seven others to depict special operations SEAL commandos facing terrorists and drug runners.

With more than 190 deployments during thirteen years of combat service in Iraq and Afghanistan under his belt (plus leading BRAVO Platoon of SEAL Team Three in Iraq's violent Al Anbar Province), Denver's realistic performance helped drive *Valor* to a strong opening weekend and more than $80 million in box office receipts.

Waleed Abdalati

Waleed Abdalati whiled away many a youthful day painstakingly reenacting the Apollo 11 moon landing. After swigging some Tang (the official drink of astronauts) in his best friend Matt's kitchen, the boys would head to the backyard shed, which doubled as their spacecraft. "We'd get in, shut the door, do a countdown, and bang ourselves violently against the walls of the shed for a while," Abdalati recalled in a 2014 *Syracuse University Magazine* interview. "And then we'd stop, step out, and be on the moon, right there in Matt's backyard."

Decades later, during a two-year stint as NASA's chief scientist, Abdalati's boyhood dreams of space exploration would become adult reality as he oversaw the successful landing of the Curiosity rover on the planet Mars.

"Watching that unfold—viewing the console room as the first images came down to the mission control team—was truly amazing," said Abdalati, who earned a bachelor's degree in mechanical and aerospace engineering from SU's College of Engineering and Computer Science in 1986. "It's a story of blood, sweat and tears, triumph, failures along the way, and success—a really powerful story that illustrates the emotional and human element to all we do at NASA."

Abdalati joined NASA after receiving his doctoral degree from the University of Colorado-Boulder (UCB) in 1996. He spent a dozen years there before returning to UCB's Cooperative Institute for Research in Environmental Sciences as a geography professor and director of the Earth Science and Observation Center.

He took a temporary leave to return to NASA as chief scientist in 2011, a position he referred to as "quite possibly the greatest job in the world." The job afforded him a front row seat to many fascinating technical and scientific achievements.

"What we really do at NASA is pursue answers to questions that are at the heart of the human spirit—the things people have wondered about since people began wondering," he said. "From the time humans could stand upright and look upward, they wondered about the stars."

At the end of his two-year stint, Abdalati returned to UCB to run the institute, which boasts nearly five hundred researchers, faculty, and administrative staff and close to two hundred students. In 2012, he came back to SU to deliver the College of Engineering and Computer Science's convocation address. He encouraged the graduates to shoot for the stars. It's a concept he's spent a lifetime pursuing.

Fire at Skytop

It would read like a chapter from a Tom Clancy spy novel if it wasn't so tragically real.

In the early morning hours of January 6, 1959, a raging fire, reportedly fed by gale force winds, completely engulfed a US Air Force military barracks on Syracuse University's South Campus. The mysterious blaze would kill seven men and leave nineteen hospitalized.

Where Cold War fiction and truth intersect, unusual facts about the "security services" incident are scattered. First, each of the seven fatalities was a Russian and Slavic language intelligence specialist apparently working on sensitive translations. Second, rumors have long suggested that doors to the building, known as M-7, had been blocked from the outside. For some of the survivors, it meant their only exit into a subzero Syracuse night was by smashing small windows and bulling through snow-clogged screens.

"The fire rolled down the long corridor like a river of flame," the *Syracuse Post-Standard* reported the next day, with five of the seven dying in their beds. One man died "as he apparently staggered outside, a human torch. The seventh died in his room next to the rear exit."

"[It] went up like a matchbox," said Peter Dowling, one of the survivors.

The structure, built without a permit to hold forty-three airmen, was not scheduled to open officially until later the next month. It was reportedly never certified for occupancy by the City of Syracuse since it existed as a military installation. Such buildings were not entirely uncommon at SU during the 1950s, since Syracuse maintained more than five hundred military barracks as classrooms, dormitories, or for married student housing. All were later removed or demolished.

Strangely, the fire's exact cause was never determined (although a faulty boiler or failed chimney were suggested), and settlements for filed lawsuits were never recorded.

The names of the seven men who died were Billy Marlowe, twenty-nine; Michael Gasparri, nineteen; Edward Duggan, twenty-three; Joseph Stoll, eighteen; Frederick Browning, twenty-one; Remus Tidwell, eighteen; and Thomas Merfield, twenty-eight. Their lives were commemorated with an October 2013 unveiling of a memorial placed just off Lambreth Lane on South Campus.

Many who gathered for the dedication ceremony and were interviewed believed SU and the US military agreed not to erect a memorial or allow public grieving during the first decade after the fire because it would tip off Russian intelligence to the existence of a special language program at Syracuse.

Americo Woyciesjes

In his obituary following his death at age eighty-one in 1997, Americo Woyciesjes's daughter said her father had lived the life of three or four men. "That was part of what made him so fascinating," said Marilyn Woyciesjes. "He had so many different experiences."

That he did.

As a boxer at Syracuse University, Woyciesjes (pronounced Woy-SEE-jis) won three light-heavyweight (175 pound) championships and cocaptained the Orangemen's Eastern Regional championship team. Coach Roy Simmons Sr. called him "the most aggressive man I ever coached."

As a student, Woyciesjes earned a bachelor's degree in forestry and a master's in mycology—the study of fungi—and was inducted into several academic honorary societies. All the more impressive when you consider that this son of Ukrainian immigrants worked the night shift at Crucible Steel, and that he would run the five miles to and from campus because he didn't have any other form of transportation and believed the daily jogs would keep him in shape for boxing.

Woyciesjes was scheduled to box in the 1940 Olympics, but those Games were canceled by the bellicose developments brewing in Europe. After the attack on Pearl Harbor in 1941, he enlisted and became one of the US Marines' original "frogmen"—amphibious scouts who under the cover of darkness obtained vital preinvasion intelligence information that would be used in the bloody but victorious Battle of Guadalcanal. The missions were so dangerous that Woyciesjes carried a cyanide pill to swallow if captured by Japanese soldiers. His bravery earned him several military commendations, including the Navy and Marine Corps Medal for heroism.

An ardent naturalist, Woyciesjes used his nocturnal journeys into jungles to gather butterflies as well as intelligence. His collection would include nearly two hundred different butterflies by the time he returned to the States.

After World War II, Woyciesjes worked for Bristol Labs and Allied Chemical while earning his postgraduate degree, which he received from SU in 1955. He also set up a laboratory in his home, where he identified a fungus that led to the development of gentamicin, a "last resort" antibiotic that wound up saving thousands of lives.

He retired in the early 1970s and purchased seven hundred acres of remote, rugged land in rural Central New York, where he whiled away many hours hiking and exploring nature.

"My father was very dynamic—a perpetual motion machine who was always trying to fill his days with as much as he possibly could," recalled his daughter. "He lived his life with gusto, and he lived every day as if he would not live until tomorrow."

Gary Scott

When Gary Scott graduated with honors from SU's ROTC program in 1967, he had his pick of assignments. The newly commissioned second lieutenant chose the most difficult and dangerous one, becoming a platoon leader in the 101st Airborne during the height of the Vietnam War. Jim Bruen, who already had served in the Navy and was one of Scott's dorm mates at Sims II, tried to talk him out of taking an infantry position. But Scott was adamant. As an African American, Scott believed there was a dearth of blacks in leadership positions in the United States. He felt he could help create more opportunities if he proved his mettle in war.

So, on December 14 of that year, Scott was deployed to Southeast Asia. It would be his first and last tour of duty, as he was killed in an ambush in Hue, Vietnam.

Though his life ended, his legacy lived on. Scott had made such an impression on his dorm mates, that, led by Bruen, they created a scholarship in his memory. Each year, a senior at Scott's high school in LeRoy, New York, is awarded a $5,000 scholarship and learns about the fallen soldier's heroism.

Scott's is one of 58,000-plus names chiseled into the shiny, black granite wall of the Vietnam Veterans Memorial in Washington, DC. He also is remembered with a plaque in Hendricks Chapel and a paver in the Orange Grove on the Quad that was dedicated to him by his old Sims II friends.

In 2012, Scott's former SU classmates returned for their forty-fifth reunion.

"There was much updating on each other's lives, but, of course, Gary Scott was front and center," Bruen recalled. "He is the glue that keeps us together."

Lester McClelland

Lester McClelland's plans of returning to rural western Pennsylvania and becoming a farmer changed abruptly after he attended an ROTC summer camp at Elgin Air Force Base in Florida before his senior year at Syracuse. At that moment, the geology major began dreaming about piloting planes instead of tractors.

He enrolled in a pilot's program and decided he would join the US Air Force after receiving his degree in 1954. And that's what the former star Orange football lineman did, following a year playing professionally in the Canadian Football League.

McClelland would spend twenty-six years in the Air Force, rising to the rank of colonel before retiring from the military in 1980. Along the way, he would become aircraft commander of Air Force One, transporting presidents Gerald Ford and Jimmy Carter on 196 flights around the country and the world. "I'm thrilled to have what I consider the top flying job in the Air Force," the man known as Colonel Mac said during a 1976 interview with SU's *Alumni News*. "I'm not nervous. After a while you go beyond worrying who is riding with you, and you simply operate in the safest way possible."

McClelland began as an Air Force One copilot following Richard Nixon's inauguration in January 1969. He served on flights for Nixon's historic China visit and secretary of state Henry Kissinger's peace negotiations with North Vietnamese leaders in Paris.

Colonel Lester McClelland, an SU alum, piloted Air Force One for US presidents Gerald Ford and Jimmy Carter. Syracuse University Portrait Collection, University Archives.

Nancy Cantor presented Saudi astronaut Prince Sultan bin Salman bin Abdulaziz Al Saud with the Chancellor's Medal in 2012. © Syracuse University. Photo by Stephen Sartori.

McClelland also copiloted the flights that brought President Lyndon Johnson's body back to Washington for viewing in the Capitol Rotunda and then returned it to Texas for burial. And he was part of the somber August 1974 flight that returned Nixon and his family to San Clemente, California, following the president's resignation.

McClelland retired from the Air Force at the end of Carter's term, and then spent fifteen years as the director of flight operations for Canadair and eight years as the chief pilot for Cape Clear LLC. Although flying took up the lion's share of his time, he did manage to fulfill his dream of operating a small farm in Espyville, Pennsylvania, until his death at age seventy-four in 2007. He was buried with full military honors in Arlington National Cemetery in Virginia.

His Royal Highness Prince Sultan bin Salman bin Abdulaziz Al Saud

His Royal Highness Prince Sultan bin Salman bin Abdulaziz Al Saud of Saudi Arabia was the first Arab, first Muslim, first royal, and youngest person ever to reach outer space, which he did at age twenty-eight.

For many in Arab countries, Prince Sultan bin Salman's selection as a NASA specialist in 1985 was extremely significant. To earn the opportunity to join the seven-member *Discovery* team, it was essential NASA's candidate was a pilot, came from one of twenty-two Middle Eastern countries, and spoke English. Sultan bin Salman, who graduated with a master of social science degree from the Maxwell School, checked all boxes.

And, once selected, the prince remained true to his culture and Muslim faith. While flying nearly three million miles in just over seven days (111 orbits) as part of NASA Mission STS-51-G, he helped launch three communications satellites (with the Arabsat-1B specifically benefiting the Arab world), facilitated Saudi-designed experiments (including an ionized gas experiment for Prince Turki bin Saud of Stanford), telephoned King Fahd, and prayed the Koran. He also brought Middle Eastern food to outer space, eating fresh dates from Medina.

"The Arab world is at a turning point," said His Royal Highness, who retired as a colonel from the Royal Saudi Air Force in 1996. "The new generation is looking forward to joining the rest of the world by obtaining the most important things in that turnaround: opportunity and education. They are the keys that open the door for our future. My space flight [was] just a crack in that door."

Using his influence, the prince helped facilitate discussions between Princess Nourah Bint Abdulrahman University (PNU), the first all-female university in Riyadh, and Syracuse University. The PNU campus opened in 2011 and is the largest women's university in the world with more than sixty thousand students. For his many achievements, Sultan bin Salman was awarded SU's Chancellor's Medal in 2012.

Don Waful

Don Waful turned 103 in 2019, making him Syracuse University's oldest known survivor from World War II. His longevity alone would make the lifelong Syracuse resident notable, but what he packed into those years is even more impressive.

After earning undergraduate and graduate degrees from SU in 1937 and 1939, respectively, he joined the Army and commanded an armored division tank unit before his 1942 capture by German soldiers in Tunisia, North Africa. He managed to survive three years of captivity in Italy and Poland before attempting a daring escape once Russian forces took control of his German POW camp.

His military service later would inspire the 2002 musical *I'll Be Seeing You*, which told the story of how he met his first wife, Cassie (Olga Casciolini), during a wartime dance in Belfast, Ireland. That chance encounter included a Christmas Eve engagement (on their third date) followed by three years of complete separation due to his wartime imprisonment.

One interesting story from Waful's time as a POW in the German camp Oflag 64 included a friendship with fellow tank commander and barracks mate Fred Johnson, the future father of Major League Baseball player and manager Davey Johnson.

Always outgoing, Waful was such a devoted SU football fan that he missed just three home games between 1945 and 2019 and attended every game played at the Carrier Dome. That commitment meant Waful witnessed two of Syracuse's most memorable home football victories: A stunning come-from-behind 19-17 victory against second-ranked Cornell in 1938 in Archbold Stadium, and a last-second victory over West Virginia in the Carrier Dome in 1987 to preserve a perfect 11-0 season.

But Orange football wasn't his only love.

Waful served thirty-five years as the president of the Syracuse Chiefs minor league baseball team, playing major roles in keeping the Chiefs in Syracuse and building NBT Bank Stadium. As if that service wasn't enough, he played trombone in a big band called the Rhythm Airs into his nineties.

10 Syracuse in Pop Culture

THUNDER ROAD
Bruce Springsteen: guitar, vocals, harmonica
Garry Tallent: bass guitar
Max M. Weinberg: drums
Roy Bittan: Fender Rhodes, glockenspiel
Clarence Clemons: saxophones
Background vocals: Roy Bittan,
Mike Appel, Steve Van Zandt

TENTH AVENUE FREEZE-OUT
Bruce Springsteen: guitar, vocals
Garry Tallent: bass guitar
Max M. Weinberg: drums
Roy Bittan: piano
Clarence Clemons: tenor saxophone
† Randy Brecker: trumpet, flugel horn
† Michael Brecker: tenor saxophone
↔ Dave Sanborn: baritone saxophone
Wayne Andre: trombone
Horns arranged by Steve Van Zandt,
Bruce Springsteen

NIGHT
Bruce Springsteen: guitar, vocals
Garry Tallent: bass guitar
Max M. Weinberg: drums
Roy Bittan: piano, harpsichord, glockenspiel
Clarence Clemons: saxophone

BACKSTREETS
Bruce Springsteen: guitar, vocals
Garry Tallent: bass guitar
Max M. Weinberg: drums
Roy Bittan: piano, organ

BORN TO RUN*
Bruce Springsteen: guitar, vocals
Garry Tallent: bass guitar
Ernest "Boom" Carter: drums
* David Sancious: keyboards
Danny Federici: organ
Clarence Clemons: saxophone

SHE'S THE ONE
Bruce Springsteen: guitar, vocals
Garry Tallent: bass guitar
Max M. Weinberg: drums
Roy Bittan: piano, harpsichord, organ
Clarence Clemons: saxophone

MEETING ACROSS THE RIVER
Bruce Springsteen: vocals
Roy Bittan: piano
Richard Davis: bass
† Randy Brecker: trumpet

JUNGLELAND
Bruce Springsteen: guitar, vocals
Garry Tallent: bass guitar
Max M. Weinberg: drums
Roy Bittan: piano
Clarence Clemons: tenor saxophone
Suki Lahav: violin
Strings Arranged and conducted by Charles Calello

† Appears courtesy of Arista Records
* Appears courtesy of Epic Records
↔ Appears courtesy of Warner Reprise
Engineered by Jimmy Iovine

PRODUCED BY BRUCE SPRINGSTEEN, JON LANDAU AND MIKE APPEL
* PRODUCED BY BRUCE SPRINGSTEEN AND MIKE APPEL

© 2005 Bruce Springsteen / "Columbia" and ✹ Reg. U.S. Pat. & Tm. Off. Marca Registrada. / 82796 94175 2

BRUCE SPRINGSTEEN

BORN TO RUN

Eric Meola's *Born to Run* photo shoot produced one of the most iconic rock album covers of all time, featuring legendary musical artists Clarence Clemons and Bruce Springsteen. Courtesy of Eric Meola and Sony Music Entertainment.

Eric Meola

Imagine taking a photograph that emerges as one of the most revered and iconic images in pop culture history—a photograph that inspires a generation. That's what happened to Eric Meola when he shot the cover for Bruce Springsteen's legendary third album, *Born to Run*.

Meola, a 1968 graduate of Syracuse with a degree in English, has done far more than photograph a rising rock star. He's also

In 1972, Eric Meola was assigned to photograph Haiti for *Time* magazine. It resulted in one of his most famous images, the "Coca Kid," which was included in *Life* magazine's special 1997 issue, "One Hundred Magnificent Images." Courtesy of Eric Meola.

produced multiple covers for *Time* magazine and won the 1986 Advertising Photographer of the Year award and a 1989 Clio for Timberland.

But Meola will always get "props" for the single frame that roared out of a June 20, 1975, photo session at his Fifth Avenue studio in New York. It was there Meola shuttered more than six hundred images of Springsteen with E Street saxophonist Clarence Clemons against a stark white backdrop. In the famous shot, Springsteen, his fret hand balancing a Fender Telecaster, casually leans on Clemons while the "Big Man" appears to play one of his famous solos.

Meola was working without an assistant that day, and his cover photo came from a roll of black-and-white film featuring the two musicians in their now-famous configuration. Of those, only two showed Springsteen (who was standing on a four-inch box) looking directly at Clemons under his black fedora hat. And in only one frame is Springsteen grinning.

The Springsteen-Clemons brotherly pose became so famous that it was occasionally imitated. Cheap Trick's album *Next Position Please* appears to honor the Springsteen cover, as do Bert and Cookie Monster on Sesame Street's 1983 *Born to Add* release. The Boss and the Big Man occasionally re-created Meola's famed shot during live concerts when the stage lights were dimmed. As concert-goers recognized the famous stance and began responding, the laughing duo would immediately break apart.

As Springsteen's fame grew to massive proportions, the cover shot took on a mythical life of its own. The photo of Bruce in torn T-shirt with an Elvis Presley N.Y.C. Fan Club button and Clemons in leather pants became so popular that Meola wound up creating an expansive coffee table book called *Born to Run: The Unseen Photos*.

Syracuse Cartoonists

To make someone smile is a gift. To do it every day is a talent. To do it every day for years on end, well, that's a syndicated cartoonist.

Syracuse University has enjoyed a long tradition of generating one-panel or comic strip artists who could capture America's constant need for a good laugh.

This legendary legacy probably started most famously with *Marmaduke* creator Brad Anderson, who had been freelancing as a cartoonist in the early 1950s for the *Saturday Evening Post* and *Colliers*. The Orange advertising and illustration major, who had graduated in 1951, kept noticing that as television started taking off as a media form, popular magazines began to fold.

Anderson knew he needed to be nimble, and drawing on his time as the art director for the student magazine *The Syracusan*, he approached a cartoon syndicate in Chicago about a giant Great Dane who could cause daily mischief much like Hank Ketcham's *Dennis the Menace* (which had debuted in 1951).

Before long, *Marmaduke* was widely syndicated and seen in more than six hundred papers nationally and internationally in twenty countries.

Like Anderson, another Syracuse advertising design major who loved dogs found an SU publication that valued his talents. From 1982 to 1985, the *Daily Orange* carried a cartoon strip called *Hector* that followed the casual critiques of Robb Armstrong's two everyday "heroes" and their curious pooch.

Hector would eventually evolve into *Jump Start*, and when United Features Syndicate picked it up in 1989, Armstrong's lead characters, Joe and Marcy Cobb, provided a strong African American family living in Philadelphia (where Armstrong was originally from) that deliberately steered away from traditional stereotypes.

"But how do you know for sure you've got power unless you abuse it?"

New Yorker cartoonist Bob Mankoff's sly humor and editorial acumen led to an entire episode about Mankoff and his drawings on CBS-TV's *60 Minutes*. Courtesy of Bob Mankoff.

"No, Thursday's out. How about never—is never good for you?"

Mankoff's "How about never?" cartoon, considered one of his greatest, led to the title of his book about a life in cartooning. Courtesy of Bob Mankoff.

Another black cartoonist to gain national prominence with a different distributor (Universal Press Syndicate) was Barbara Brandon-Croft, who became America's first nationally syndicated African American female cartoonist. Her strip, *Where I'm Coming From*, first produced for the *Detroit Free Press*, provided humorous lifestyle commentary as seen from the perspective of a black female.

Anderson, Armstrong, and Brandon-Croft became three of the most famous daily cartoonists, but SU also produced a wealth of political and editorial pundits, such as Frank Cammuso (who often skewered SU for the *Syracuse Herald-Journal*) and Jim Morin (*Miami Herald*). Morin, who drew daily editorial cartoons for the *Daily Orange* before graduating in 1975, won the Pulitzer Prize twice for editorial cartooning (1996, 2017).

One additional name to note is a former wild-haired cartoonist who ultimately became the person responsible for selecting some of the world's most revered (and sophisticated) cartoons. Bob Mankoff, a 1966 graduate in psychology, became the cartoon editor for the *New Yorker* in 1997 (after years of supplying weekly bon mots), and his careful selections resulted in him being profiled on the CBS television show *60 Minutes*. The title of Mankoff's memoir, *How About Never—Is Never Good for You? My Life in Cartoons* (published in 2014), is drawn from one of his best-known creations.

"Laughter helps us function better," said Mankoff, who became *Esquire*'s cartoon and humor editor in 2017, "especially when we are trying to solve serious problems."

How true.

Martin Bandier

It's fitting that a man with the word "band" in his last name would pursue a music career.

"When I was a kid," Martin Bandier once said, "my grandmother would take me to the movie theater to watch all the great musicals, and when most people had left the theater, I would stay right until the end credits had finished so I could catch the names of all the artists who had performed the songs as well as the names of the songwriters who had written them."

Staying to see the end of movies is nice, but when Bandier arrived at Syracuse University as a seventeen-year-old, the future 1962 graduate would've had a hard time predicting he'd become CEO of Sony/ATV Music Publishing, the world's leading music publisher, and guide his artists to fifty-two consecutive weeks (during 2017-18) of Sony/ATV writers sitting atop *Billboard*'s Hot 100 singles chart.

He also would have had a tough time imagining the music catalogs he would build for the Entertainment Music Company, CBS Songs (which he sold for $125 million), SBK Entertainment, SBK Records, and EMI Music Publishing. Or that he would enable Sony/ATV to eventually control the music industry's largest music publishing assets. That collection would include more than 3.5 million songs and acts such as the Beatles, Elvis Presley, Stevie Wonder, Ed Sheeran, Drake (the most streamed artist of all time), Bob Dylan, Lady Gaga, Kenny Chesney, and Taylor Swift.

For a kid from Queens, New York, that would've required one incredible imagination. Especially in the early twenty-first century, when the music industry seemed ready to implode from the reality of downloads replacing CD sales.

As Bandier told the *Los Angeles Times*'s Randy Lewis in May 2018, "I actually endowed a school at Syracuse University, my alma mater, which is the Bandier Program for music business and entertainment industries. I did it—what, 15 years ago?—and I started to feel guilty about the students. I was saying to myself, 'God, all these kids who love music and want to be in the business—their passion was so great—am I putting them in a position of doom and gloom?' Now, we [annually] get 400 applicants for 30 spots."

That demand helps explain how Bandier's generosity to his alma mater lifted Syracuse's Bandier Program in Recording and Entertainment Industries, housed in the Newhouse School, into one of *Billboard*'s "12 Elite Music Business Schools Shaping the Industry's Future."

His extraordinary impact on the music industry has been recognized at his alma mater and beyond. Bandier received SU's Arents Award in 1994, was inducted into the Songwriters Hall of Fame (Patron of the Arts) in 2003, and, during the Grammy Salute to Industry Icons, became the first music publisher to receive the Recording Academy's President's Merit Award in 2015.

Felix Cavaliere

Good Lovin'.

Two simple words that summarize the amazing career and longevity of Syracuse alumnus Felix Cavaliere, who before finishing his premed studies in 1964 had been hired as a member of Joey Dee and the Starliters, famous for the 1961-62 hit "Peppermint Twist."

At Syracuse, Cavaliere's band was called the Escorts. But his greatest fame came as a founding member of the Young Rascals, a 1960s band that released numerous singles, including "Groovin'," "People Got to be Free," "It's a Beautiful Morning," and the legendary "Good Lovin'," which was prominently featured in the 1983 movie *The Big Chill*.

"In the early Sixties, 'city bands' were all but segregated from campus, so university bands, such as the Escorts, held sway at [Syracuse] campus functions, fraternity and sorority parties, local bars and clubs," Ron Wray wrote in a review of Syracuse music history. "While the Twist was still filtering through local city bars, the university's big band on campus, Felix and the Escorts, featured rhythm and blues as their main course."

A possible reason for that success might've been Cavaliere's membership in Sigma Phi Epsilon fraternity, and his friendships with football players Ernie Davis, Dave Meggyesy, John Mackey, and Jim Nance. Those "big men on campus" were some of Cavaliere's most devoted followers and great fans of soul music.

"In those days, SU was more of a football school than a basketball school, so I made friends with a lot of football players," Cavaliere once noted. "Being at SU and playing in a white band that was embraced by black athletes was huge for me. I guess it was my destiny, if you think about it, because I would help form the first all-white band on an all-black label [Atlantic Records]. I probably wouldn't have done that, if I had gone to school somewhere else."

So influential were the Young Rascals (who later dropped the word "Young" and performed as the Rascals) that their 1968 Greatest Hits album *Time Peace* ("one of the most enduring albums in

Felix Cavaliere and the Young Rascals (later just the Rascals), appeared on the *Ed Sullivan Show* during the mid-1960s. The musical group was voted into the Rock and Roll Hall of Fame in 1997. CBS Photo Archive / Getty Images.

the Atlantic Records catalog") was *Billboard*'s No. 1 Pop Album in September 1968. It also made clear white acts could play soul music, leading to the industry phrase "blue-eyed soul."

Cavaliere once said the Rascals' signature sound—white pop melodies steeped in muscular rock and soul—was unique for its time. "We would do a Beatles song here and there, but, instead of sounding like the Beatles, it would sound like an R&B song," he said. "I don't think our sound was intentionally planned. It just turned out that way. It was a natural progression."

"I Ain't Gonna Eat Out My Heart Anymore" was the Young Rascals' first single—a 1965 "R&B scorcher that nearly cracked the top 50." They followed it up by remaking an Olympics song called "Good Lovin'." Rocketing up the charts to number one, the song featured Cavaliere's famous "one-two-three" countdown and a sound that knew no color.

"When we first went out on the road, Atlantic didn't put our pictures on the [record] jacket because we were getting this incredible crossover, which was good for radio," said fellow Rascal Dino Danelli. "Then we'd show up in-person, and people couldn't believe we were white. A lot of that had to do with Felix's voice."

Inducted into the Rock and Roll Hall of Fame in 1997 by longtime friend Steven Van Zandt (famous for his work with Bruce Springsteen and his acting on HBO's *The Sopranos*), the Rascals ultimately gave Cavaliere the springboard to a lifetime of influential music that included stints with Ringo Starr's All-Starr Band, Little Steven, and the Disciples of Soul and as a prominent solo artist.

Draper Daniels

A famous advertising executive once opined that "an idea can turn to dust or magic, depending on the talent that rubs against it." Draper Daniels showed Madison Avenue early on that he had the Midas touch. Much of what he rubbed against turned to gold.

A 1934 journalism graduate of Syracuse University, where he served as editor of the *Daily Orange* and its counterpart humor magazine, the *Orange Peel*, Daniels became the brains behind some of the most iconic ad campaigns in history. He devised the idea for the Marlboro Man, the rough-hewn, independent cowboy who helped sell millions of cigarettes in the 1950s. He also helped create StarKist's Charlie the Tuna, Elsie the Borden Cow, the Jolly Green Giant, and Kellogg's Tony the Tiger. Later, after souring on the deleterious effects of smoking, Daniels left the world of billboards and television commercials to work in President John F. Kennedy's administration as the national export expansion coordinator.

In the 2010s, three decades after his death, Daniels's influence continued to be felt when he became the template for Don Draper, the main character in the Emmy Award-winning *Mad Men* television series that centered on the martini-lunch lifestyle of a prominent New York City ad agency. Matthew Weiner, the show's producer (and previously the producer and writer for *The Sopranos*), acknowledged he based his protagonist partly on Daniels, whom he called "one of the great copy guys." In reality, the character likely is a composite of several real-life ad execs, though the alliterative name used clearly was inspired by Daniels.

A native of Morris, New York, a village near Cooperstown, Daniels—like his father and his son, Bruce—attended SU. "He was an upstate New York farm boy," said Bruce, a 1964 graduate who enjoyed a distinguished career with the US Department of Housing and Urban Development. Draper Daniels married his college sweetheart—Louise Parker Lux Cort. In 1965, she marched with Dr. Martin Luther King Jr. in Montgomery, Alabama, and was jailed for her efforts in the civil rights movement. Bruce Daniels wound up marrying his high school sweetheart, Suzanne, who worked for the SU philosophy department while he was a student.

In a 2012 interview with the *Syracuse Post-Standard*, Bruce said he experienced an "eerie feeling" when he tuned into *Mad Men* for the first time. But he also realized that Hollywood took considerable license with the main character, who bore little resemblance in temperament and lifestyle to his father.

"It's fiction," he said. "I am very proud of my father. He was quite a guy."

Thom Filicia

Trapped.

In an elevator.

For more than an hour.

That's where highly successful interior decorator Thom Filicia found himself one day in 2003. So he did what came naturally to him. He entertained his captive audience. What he didn't know was that one of the "prisoners" was a casting director for the cable television network Bravo.

Thom Filicia (*far right*) was part of a five-man cast featured on the Bravo reality TV show *Queer Eye for the Straight Guy*. © 2004 Bravo Media, LLC.

A week later, Filicia got a call to audition for a reality television concept designed to feature five gay men with expertise in fashion, grooming, interior design, culture, and style. They would then "make over" (or make better) a heterosexual (or traditionally straight) male and bring him into the twenty-first century.

Bravo loved Thom and selected him to fill the "Design Doctor" role. Alongside Carson Kressley, Ted Allen, Kyan Douglas, and Jai Rodriguez, the show *Queer Eye for the Straight Guy* was launched in July 2003. Almost overnight, it became a national sensation, winning the 2004 Primetime Emmy for Outstanding Reality Program, and the "Fab Five" began a highly discussed residency on Bravo (filming one hundred episodes) until 2007.

After the show had been off the air for a decade, Bravo brought back an updated version of *Queer Eye* in 2018 with five new stars. Shortly thereafter, the network announced its intention to greenlight a series titled *Get a Room with Carson and Thom*, where Filicia and Kressley stylishly entered the home and retail design sector of reality television.

In the new series, Thom guided Carson, *Queer Eye*'s fashion expert, on the intricacies and nuances of renovation. Leveraging their *Queer Eye* charm, Filicia and Kressley started creating "breathtaking and affordable home (and retail) re-designs."

Filicia, who graduated from Syracuse's College of Visual and Performing Arts in 1993 and was a member of Phi Gamma Delta, is a best-selling author (*American Beauty: Renovating and Decorating a Beloved Retreat*) and was identified as a "Top 100 Designer" by *House Beautiful* and an "A-List" designer by *Elle Décor*.

Jeff Glor

Had he mastered his chemistry course during his freshman year at Syracuse University in 1992, we might never have heard of Jeff Glor. The man who succeeded the likes of Walter Cronkite, Dan Rather, and Katie Couric as *CBS Evening News* anchor probably would have followed in the footsteps of his grandfather and uncle and become a dentist. He would have spent his career peering into people's mouths instead of teleprompters.

"Chemistry was my Achilles' heel," Glor recalled. "That's when I realized (dentistry) was not for me."

He eventually settled on dual majors of broadcast and digital journalism and economics, and it didn't take long for his Newhouse professors to forecast a bright future for him in broadcasting. "He always wanted to be better," recalled Barbara Fought, who taught Glor in his first broadcast writing course at Newhouse when he was a sophomore. "I remember going home and telling my husband, 'This young man is going to go far.'"

Glor's insatiable desire to improve, coupled with his laudatory work ethic, resulted in him receiving the coveted Henry J. Wolff Prize, presented annually to the Newhouse student who is "most proficient in journalism."

A lover of newspapers since his paperboy delivery days in suburban Buffalo, New York, Glor began his career as a news writer at Syracuse's WSTM-TV during his senior year at SU. It wasn't long before he was reporting and anchoring, and attracting the attention of larger markets. In 2003, he left for Boston station WHDH-TV, and four years later joined CBS News as correspondent and coanchor on the *Saturday Early Show*, and eventually earned an Emmy for broadcasting excellence. His rapid ascent continued as he began anchoring weekend editions of the *CBS Evening News* and spearheaded several investigative stories, including the massive recall of unsafe cars by General Motors.

On December 4, 2017, Glor reached the pinnacle of his profession at age forty-two, taking over as the permanent weekday anchor of the *CBS Evening News*. In his first several months, he traveled extensively, covering several major breaking news stories, including the Parkland and Santa Fe school shootings, wildfires in southern California, and the controversial opening of the new US embassy in Jerusalem.

In May 2018, he delivered the convocation address to Newhouse graduates. He praised his former professors and said his educational experiences prepared him for the anchor job, which he held until being reassigned the following May. He also mentioned that Syracuse would always be special to him because it's where he received his diploma and met his wife, Nicole, a former SU cheerleader who wound up launching her own national fitness brand.

Peter Guber

Before Peter Guber became one of the most powerful people in Hollywood or even a successful team owner in professional sports, he was an English history major at Syracuse University concerned largely with "getting through."

"Sports and getting through," he once told SU's *Alumni News*.

But then he got scared. It was the mid-1960s, his grades were ordinary, and the Vietnam draft was breathing down his neck. "That's when I realized you could make fear work for yourself," he said. "I was a lousy student until I got that [draft] notice. I got that notice, I became a great student."

Good enough to get into NYU's Graduate School of Business, where he secured an MBA while simultaneously earning a law degree from NYU Law. And good enough to find himself recruited by Columbia Pictures for his first big job as a management trainee in 1968. He started in Columbia's casting department but would quickly migrate to creative affairs and film development.

"I remember sitting around the table at Columbia Pictures, and I was 25 or 26 years old, and I was 40 years younger than the average age of the people sitting around the table," he said. "I knew that if I could hang in just a little bit, time was on my side."

Time, luck, hard work, fear, vision, and courage were on his side. During the next five decades, Guber would lead Mandalay

Golden State Warriors co-owner Peter Guber celebrates with star guard Steph Curry after one of the Warriors' NBA Championships. Andrew D. Bernstein / NBAE / Getty Images.

Entertainment, PolyGram Filmed Entertainment, and Sony Pictures (all as chair and CEO), preside over Columbia Pictures as president, co-own and co-chair Casablanca Record and Filmworks, serve as chair of Dick Clark Productions, and co-own Guber-Peters Productions (with fellow producer Jon Peters). He also would co-own and help operate the three-time National Basketball Association champion Golden State Warriors, Major League Baseball's Los Angeles Dodgers, Major League Soccer's Los Angeles Football Club, and the emerging eSports giant Team Liquid.

His association with top movies (either as an executive, a producer, or distributor) would take up several pages, but many readers would appreciate his authorship of numerous books or his role in producing movies such as *Batman, Rain Man, Flashdance, The Color Purple, Clue, Midnight Express, Gorillas in the Mist, Innerspace, The Witches of Eastwick*, and *The Deep*.

Guber received Syracuse's Arents Award in 1989. He has also been a longtime faculty member at UCLA's School of Theater, Film, and Television as well as UCLA's Anderson School of Management.

Shirley Jackson

Four months before her death in August 1965, reclusive author Shirley Jackson returned to Syracuse University for the first time in twenty-five years. She had already published landmark works such as "The Lottery" (first published by the *New Yorker*), *Life among the Savages* (a humorous short-story collection about raising four children), and an infamous ghost story called *The Haunting of Hill House*, which best-selling author Stephen King later suggested was "one of the most important horror novels of the twentieth century."

THE LOTTERY

SHIRLEY JACKSON

Shirley Jackson's *The Lottery* has been called one of the most famous short stories in the history of American literature. Illustration © 2008 by Etienne Delessert; published by Creative Education in 2008. Image used by permission of The Creative Company.

Speaking to a group of students in Gifford Auditorium, Jackson said her education at SU "started me writing. But most of my class compositions came back criticizing me for confusing 'that' and 'which.'"

Having arrived at Syracuse after flunking out of the University of Rochester, Jackson met her future husband, Stanley Hyman, and they collectively founded the short-lived SU literary magazine *Spectre*. It led to Jackson publishing her first story, "Janice," about a teenager's suicide attempt.

Jackson and Hyman graduated in 1940 and eventually moved to Bennington, Vermont, where the California native began collecting books, hosting fellow authors like Ralph Ellison, and writing for the *New Yorker*. Her semiautobiographical first novel, *The Road Through the Wall*, was published in 1948, the same year as "The Lottery."

Written in a single morning while she cared for two children, "The Lottery" is a ritualistic depiction of a community's willingness to stone to death one of its own members—a housewife.

Jackson's final novel, *We Have Always Lived in the Castle*, was selected by *Time* magazine in 1962 as one of the ten best novels of the year. It later was adapted into a Broadway play (running only for nine performances), a musical drama, and, in 2018, a movie from executive producer Michael Douglas starring actors Crispin Glover and Taissa Farmiga.

While little known during her lifetime (because she consistently shunned media attention and self-promotion), Jackson quietly emerged as a major literary figure of the twentieth century, worthy of multiple biographies and the establishment of the Shirley Jackson Award for "outstanding achievement in the literature of psychological suspense, horror, and the dark fantastic."

Megyn Kelly

After taking a high school journalism course that included a two-day newspaper internship with the *Albany (NY) Times-Union*,

Megyn Kelly knew what she wanted to do for a career. She was going to become a journalist, and she figured Syracuse University would provide the best training to make that dream come true.

She figured right, but the script wouldn't unfold quite as planned. The woman who would become one of television's most recognizable and controversial news show hosts applied to the Newhouse School. The good news? Syracuse accepted her. The bad news? Newhouse did not.

Though deeply disappointed, Kelly decided to enroll anyway and figure it out as she went along. Thanks to a course she took with famed Maxwell School professor Robert McClure, she fell in love with political science and decided to make that her major, earning her bachelor's degree in 1992.

"My time at the University was spectacular," she said in an interview with *Women of Upstate New York*.

> I did all the things you're supposed to do in college, many of which helped me as a television anchor to this day. I fell in love. I joined a sorority. I worked two jobs to pay my room and board. I navigated the joys of living in a "triple" at Day Hall, and my first apartment at Skytop. I taught aerobics to the Syracuse lacrosse team (the one that won three national championships—yes, that was all my doing—wasn't it?). I made, and lost friends, ate late-night pizza from Acropolis, went to the computer lab to type and print out my papers—yes I am dating myself. I became part of the student senate. I had a creative writing professor who believed in me, and told me to consider grad school. I developed my IQ, but also my EQ, through the many social and campus activities SU has to offer. And both are important in my current job . . . and in life.

After graduating from Syracuse, Kelly went on to earn a JD from Albany Law School and became a highly successful corporate attorney in Chicago.

Despite her success, she longed to give journalism a try. After moving to Washington, DC, in 2003, she began making cold calls to local television stations, and her persistence paid off when she was hired by ABC affiliate WJLA-TV as a general assignment reporter. She was a natural in front of the camera, and her political science and legal background proved invaluable in her coverage of the confirmation hearings for US Supreme Court Justice Samuel Alito and Chief Justice John G. Roberts, the retirement of Justice Sandra Day O'Connor, the death of Chief Justice William Rehnquist, and the 2004 presidential election.

Following her stellar coverage of George W. Bush's election to a second term in the White House, Kelly was hired by Fox News. She would spend thirteen years there, earning plaudits even from critics of Fox's conservative agenda. Her ability to cut to the core of complex issues and conduct dogged interviews helped *The Kelly File* become one of the highest rated prime-time news talk shows. *Time* magazine named her one of the one hundred most influential people in the world, and she held her ground after being repeatedly insulted by Donald Trump during the 2016 presidential debates.

Two months after Trump's election, Kelly left Fox to work for NBC News and host a live-audience morning show. Her success there would be short-lived. Lagging ratings, coupled with her racially charged remarks regarding the appropriateness of blackface as part of Halloween costumes, resulted in a mutually agreed departure from NBC in the fall of 2018.

Warren Kimble

If his brother hadn't been driven into New York City every Saturday in the late 1930s for dancing lessons, it is possible Warren Kimble might never have emerged as "America's Best Known Living Folk Artist."

"He danced on Broadway with Ethel Merman, in the chorus," Kimble once said.

And because his parents were invested in their dancing prodigy, they left Warren alone.

"I was just given art supplies and encouraged to do artwork," he said. "And that was good for me. That was a gift."

Artistic freedom gave Kimble entrepreneurial ideas, and from a very early age he began thinking about how to sell his art, which included "crazy little angels" and painted Christmas windows.

Later, during a midlife period where Kimble dabbled in painting and sold antiques to make ends meet, he chanced into a life-changing situation. A couple building a publishing business saw Kimble's rural-themed art in Woodstock, Vermont, in 1990, and they asked permission to make lithographic prints. Kimble wasn't convinced that houses on hills, cows, and rural American landscapes would generate any demand, but the 1957 Syracuse fine arts graduate was very wrong. His nonglitzy, simple reproductions "just took off."

The artwork may not have been that of Jasper Johns or Norman Rockwell, but with more than six million prints sold, Kimble and his wife Lorraine quickly grasped that his work was important.

"My art is for the people and of the people," he said. "I'm in houses and I'm in bathrooms. I mean, please. That's the fun of it. That's what makes it real."

Kimble was able to branch away from "quaint," and his late career work included political themes such as "Widows of War," a collection of muted mixed media tied to the Iraq war. Through these pieces, he sought to speak for the wives and mothers who dealt with military separations.

A winner of an Arents Award in 2002 and the Melvin A. Eggers Senior Alumni Award in 2017, Warren Kimble painted distinct Americana themes that have consistently helped global art collectors remember and showcase simpler times.

Warren Kimble's folk art of Vermont cows, barns, and snowmen caused many to call him America's best-known living folk artist. Courtesy of Warren Kimble.

Steve Kroft

From the steamy battlefields of Vietnam to America's front lines as a *60 Minutes* correspondent, Steve Kroft has rarely backed down from a meaningful story or an all-out investigation. In fact, since September 1989, when Kroft joined the *60 Minutes* team and began working his way toward a Lifetime Achievement Emmy Award and three decades of meaningful reporting, the 1967 Newhouse School graduate has been recognized as one of America's most important journalists.

His list of topical stories (many rewarded with Emmy, Murrow, duPont-Columbia, or Peabody awards) have included wars, terrorism, assassinations, presidential elections, serial killers, sectarian violence, AIDS controversies, spies, dangerous airlines, and criminal behavior at the highest levels of corporate America. He is, in fact, the only *60 Minutes* correspondent ever to win two Peabody Awards in the same year.

Like many Newhouse alumni, Kroft served a stint in Syracuse (with local station WSYR-TV, now WSTM-TV) before moving on to stations or network assignments in Jacksonville, Miami, Dallas, New York, and London. For his excellence in journalism, Kroft was awarded SU's Arents Award in 1992.

Some of Kroft's biggest stories include Barack Obama's last interview as president, a 2015 Cold War Soviet spy feature about Jack Barsky (who lived in the United States undetected for more than a decade), and a probing 2012 investigation of a computer virus that sabotaged Iran's nuclear program. One of Kroft's most memorable interviews involved Charles Cullen, a former nurse that some authorities believed might have killed hundreds. Cullen's appearance on 60

Broadcaster Steve Kroft is best known for his investigative work on CBS-TV's *60 Minutes*. John Lamparski / WireImage / Getty Images.

Actor and SU alum Frank Langella has appeared in numerous movies, and was nominated for a 2008 Academy Award for playing President Richard Nixon. But one of his most famous roles was his 1979 portrayal of Count Dracula. MPTV images.com.

Minutes represented the first time a serial killer was interviewed on the show in its nearly five decades of Sunday night broadcasts.

Perhaps more powerfully relevant to Americans was Kroft's 2013 report illuminating America's inability to provide adequate mental illness treatment and address the number of mass shootings. That effort led to Kroft's twelfth Emmy.

Frank Langella

Profoundly uncomfortable with himself as a teenager, actor Frank Langella came to Syracuse University in 1955 for one reason. To become a Broadway star.

He figured the fastest way for him to achieve that goal was to come north from Bayonne, New Jersey, and study under SU drama department legend Sawyer Falk.

Falk quickly realized his gifted student's potential, and during Langella's senior year he became the professor's protégé. Falk's faith in him would be rewarded, as Langella went on to earn four Tony Awards and three Obies, and garner a Best Actor Oscar nomination for his 2008 role as President Richard Nixon in the movie *Frost/Nixon*. His portrayal of Nixon prompted a *New York Times* critic to write: "By the end of the movie Mr. Langella seems even more like Nixon than Nixon did."

Movie director Ron Howard was initially hesitant to cast Langella (even after having seen the Orange alumnus play Nixon on the London stage) because names like Warren Beatty and Jack Nicholson were receiving strong consideration for the role.

"The studio thought this was a bravura opportunity for one of our established studio actors, but at the end of the day, Frank was just a lock," Howard told the *Times*. "To not use him seemed almost karmically imprudent."

Compelling acting made Langella famous in film as a handsome Count Dracula in 1979's *Dracula* and as CBS chief William S. Paley in 2005's *Good Night, and Good Luck*, and on TV as KGB

handler Gabriel in the FX series *The Americans* (2015-17). His best performances, though, may have been on Broadway, the place he always intended to inhabit.

"When you're from an Italian family," he told *Syracuse Herald-Journal* entertainment critic Joan Vadeboncoeur in 1984, "you're exposed to the church and other very theatrical things. You're always seeing the priest in his robes and your mother waving a rolling pin and screaming at your father."

That same father would hire a "professional placement man," who recommended Syracuse as the ideal match. Young, ambitious Langella enjoyed himself immensely during his college years, while sampling a variety of Orange traditions.

"I loved being in a fraternity," Langella said of his time in SU's Alpha Chi Rho. "I don't think I ever left the campus except to fill up the car."

His most memorable college experiences, though, would come at Syracuse Stage under the guidance of Falk.

"I had a teacher in college who said to me, 'Frank, act in spite of your neurosis, not because of it,' and I was smart enough to know what he meant," Langella said.

Harry Rosenfeld

Most recognize the names Carl Bernstein and Bob Woodward, the intrepid *Washington Post* reporters who gained fame for their penetrating stories about the Watergate scandal that led to the resignation of President Richard Nixon. But far fewer are familiar with Harry Rosenfeld. Described fondly and fearfully as "the bulldog in a bow-tie," Rosenfeld was the metro editor who help direct Bernstein and Woodward's coverage, which won a Pulitzer Prize and changed the way Americans viewed investigative reporting.

A 1952 graduate of Syracuse's College of Arts and Sciences, Rosenfeld immediately realized there was more to the story than a simple burglary when news broke on June 17, 1972, that several men— including a former White House employee—had been arrested for breaking into the Democratic National Committee headquarters at the Watergate complex. Two weeks after the break-in, former attorney general John Mitchell resigned as head of the Committee to Re-elect the President. "I knew then that this was going pretty high up," Rosenfeld said in a *Syracuse University Magazine* interview.

He also knew that the *Post*'s coverage would be picked apart and had to be irrefutable, which is why he meticulously scrutinized the facts and questioned the veracity of sources. Over time, "Woodstein's" reportage would make the connection all the way up to the president, and on August 9, 1974, Nixon resigned. "It vindicated our hard work at a time when no other media was doing it," Rosenfeld said.

Bernstein and Woodward later would write a best-selling book, *All the President's Men*, which was turned into a movie starring Robert Redford and Dustin Hoffman. *Washington Post* executive editor Ben Bradlee was played by Jason Robards, and Rosenfeld's role, though not as publicized as the others, was played by Jack Warden.

After six decades of newspapering, Rosenfeld published *From Kristallnacht to Watergate*, a memoir that also reflected on his life as a nine-year-old immigrant in New York after having escaped Nazi Germany with his family. His life story included fond memories of taking journalism courses and covering sports for the *Daily Orange*. "It was an invaluable experience, traveling with teams, writing on deadline, doing feature stories," he said.

Fred Silverman

Time magazine referred to him as "The Man with the Golden Gut," and the moniker was spot-on because few people in television history have been better at identifying winning programs than Fred Silverman. The 1958 Syracuse graduate definitely had a knack for knowing what Americans wanted to watch.

At the time of *Time*'s designation in 1977, Silverman was president of ABC Entertainment and responsible for green-lighting or reinvigorating shows such as *Happy Days*, *Laverne & Shirley*, *Fantasy Island*, *Charlie's Angels*, *The Love Boat*, and miniseries ratings monsters like *Rich Man*, *Poor Man* and *Roots*.

A year later, he jumped ship and became president and CEO of NBC, making him the only individual ever to supervise programming at each of the three original TV networks.

Television network executive Fred Silverman was known as "the man with the golden gut" for his ability to pick hit TV shows. © Syracuse University. Photo by Stephen Sartori.

Years earlier, at CBS, while still only in his thirties, Silverman played a role in purging rural-themed hits like *Green Acres*, *The Beverly Hillbillies*, and *Mayberry R.F.D.*, and replacing them with classics such as *All in the Family*, *M*A*S*H*, and *The Mary Tyler Moore Show*.

His time at NBC (1978-81) led critics to lambast shows that didn't work (*Supertrain* or *Hello, Larry*), but *Hill Street Blues*, *The David Letterman Show*, and the miniseries hit *Shōgun* more than made up for those whiffs and added to his reputation as one of the most powerful executives in television history.

He later would move into independent television production, where he helped create and air successful programs such as *Matlock* and *Jake and the Fatman*, as well as the *Perry Mason* movie series.

"This is what I do," Silverman told the *New York Times* in 1989. "What was I going to become, an architect?"

For baby boomers who came of age watching television between 1970 and 1995, it was just as well the son of a TV repairman programmed the shows they watched. For his efforts, Silverman was inducted into the Academy of Television Arts and Sciences Hall of Fame, given the Lucy Award (honoring individuals who enhance the perception of women in TV), and, in 2018, honored with SU's Melvin A. Eggers Senior Alumni Award.

Jerry Stiller

From 1993 to 2007, Jerry Stiller came into millions of American living rooms and ranted.

First, he was George Costanza's uber-cranky father, Frank, on *Seinfeld*. Then he morphed into Doug Heffernan's outlandish (and grouchy) father-in-law, Arthur Spooner, on *The King of Queens*.

For Seinfeld aficionados, there were numerous episodes where Stiller's enraged behavior created television history. Festivus for the

Husband-and-wife comedy duo Jerry Stiller and Anne Meara returned to Syracuse one fall and posed behind an Orange football player and cheerleader display. Syracuse University Portrait Collection, University Archives.

Jerry Stiller enjoyed large, reoccurring roles on prime time television shows, such as *Seinfeld* and the *King of Queens*. M. Phillips / Wire-Image / Getty Images.

rest of us. The Manssiere (a bra for men). Stopping short (while driving). Speaking Korean (to learn if Julia Louis-Dreyfus's Elaine is getting verbally abused during manicures). Playing pool with Kramer (Michael Richards) in a small room. Grounding son George (Jason Alexander) for leaving a condom wrapper on the bed. Or hollering about the Florida retirement complex Del Boca Vista.

But long before Stiller was raising his palms upward and saying, "The hell does that mean?" he and his wife Anne Meara were making Americans laugh with their infamous comedy routines by portraying Hershey Horowitz and Mary Elizabeth Doyle. She played the tall Irish Catholic redhead to his short, curly-haired "Jewish Romeo," and together they appeared on Ed Sullivan's weekly variety show thirty-six times (often before or after gyrating plate spinners or bands like the Rolling Stones).

Born in New York City, Stiller joined the Army at eighteen and was stationed overseas in Italy. Returning to the States, he leveraged the GI Bill to enroll at Syracuse. It was a way to gain acting experience and exposure to the theater. To make ends meet, the aspiring comic performed regularly at local Syracuse clubs, even going so far as inviting Sawyer Falk, the vaunted head of SU's drama department, to see him perform at the Casablanca on Genesee Street.

"I was wonderful [that night]" Stiller told *Syracuse University Magazine* in 1997. "I come out and say [to Falk], 'What did you think?' And Professor Falk says, 'You've got to get out of here.' I say, 'Whaddya mean?' And he says, 'You've got bad habits. Bad habits.'"

Despite that assessment, the following Monday Falk chose Stiller to direct, produce, and cast an upcoming student project called *Long Live Love*. Managing the student revue took all of Stiller's time that semester (causing him to flunk every class). But it led to a postgraduate role with noted actor Burgess Meredith. Within three years of his graduation from Syracuse in 1950, Stiller met Meara (at an agent's office) and proposed. They would marry twice—the second time as a TV couple on *The King of Queens* 2007 season finale. Their legendary real-life marriage ran from 1954 until Meara's death in 2015.

Stiller and Meara were not only popular as a comedy duo but also productive as parents. Son Ben became a cinematic legend (*Meet the Parents* trilogy, *Tropic Thunder*, *Zoolander*), while actress/comedian Amy Belle Sawyer Stiller (named, in part, after SU's Falk) has appeared in numerous movies and TV shows, including a recurring role on *The King of Queens*.

Arielle Tepper

It's one thing to hit it big right out of the box. First novel. First movie role. First hit single.

It's another thing to stay in the game and consistently generate box-office winners. For 1994 Syracuse graduate Arielle Tepper, her first smash as a theater producer came freakishly early. Tepper was only twenty-six and less than five years out of SU's esteemed drama department when she launched her Broadway career by producing *Freak*, a one-man show featuring actor John Leguizamo.

But Tepper, who started off by lighting and designing sets at Syracuse, didn't stop there. During the next two decades, her Broadway productions would win more than forty Tony Awards.

Theatrical producer Arielle Tepper's Broadway shows have included *Annie*, *Hamlet*, *Spamalot*, and *The Elephant Man*. She also served as the board chair for the Public Theater in New York. Simon Luethi.

Her keen stage instincts were first evident when *Freak* won the 1998 Drama Desk Award for Outstanding Solo Performance and established the New York City native as a veteran capable of consistently thrilling Broadway and London audiences. Since then, some of Tepper's best-known shows (as lead or coproducer) have included Monty Python's *Spamalot*, *A Raisin in the Sun*, *The Elephant Man* (with Bradley Cooper), *Frost/Nixon*, *Lucky Guy* (starring Tom Hanks playing Syracuse alumnus Mike McAlary), *I'll Eat You Last: A Chat with Sue Mengers* (featuring Bette Midler), and *Hamlet* (with Jude Law).

The 2016 Arents Award-winner and SU Life Trustee also has dabbled in film (coproducing the 1999 movie *30 Days* and executive producing 2016's *Genius*), running a travel concierge business (What Should We Do), and serving as the board chair of the Public Theater, the off-Broadway stage that premiered playwright-composer-actor Lin-Manuel Miranda's sensational *Hamilton* (eleven Tony Awards).

In addition, Tepper also committed herself to philanthropy. Her $1.2 million gift to SU's College of Visual and Performing Arts (the largest ever to VPA) created the Tepper Center for Careers in Theater and made it possible for selected Orange students to work in the Forty-Second Street Theatre Row complex for an entire semester.

It gave many aspiring Syracuse undergraduates a chance to dream about hitting it big, about becoming the next Arielle Tepper.

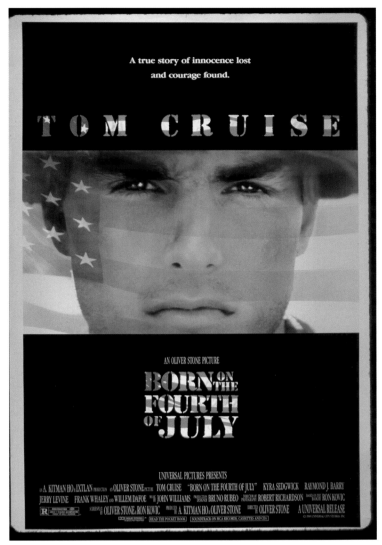

Jim Brown huddles with other actors during a break in filming from the 1967 movie *The Dirty Dozen*. Bettmann / Getty Images.

Adam Sandler wore a Syracuse shirt for numerous scenes in his 1999 hit movie *Big Daddy*. BIG DADDY © 1999 Columbia Pictures Industries, Inc. All Rights Reserved. Courtesy of Columbia Pictures.

The Tom Cruise movie *Born on the Fourth of July* was released in December 1989 and featured a scene where wheelchair-bound Vietnam veteran Ron Kovic attends a 1970 student strike at SU. What is shown in the movie (a peace rally turned violent) is not what happened in real life. © 1989 University City Studios, Inc. Courtesy of Universal Studios Licensing LLC.

(Above) The Grammy-award-winning musical act the Chainsmokers features for-mer Syracuse student Drew Taggart, the band's lead vocalist, writer, and producer. The Chainsmokers' second studio album, *Sick Boy*, was released in December 2018. Kevin Winter / Getty Images.

(Left) Eliza Orlins, a 2005 graduate of SU, appeared on *Survivor Vanuatu* and *Survivor Micronesia*. Monty Brinton / CBS Photo Archive / Getty Images.

(Below) *Survivor* contestant Brad Culpepper, father of SU football player Rex Culpepper, wore an SU baseball hat for an entire season of the CBS-TV reality show to honor his son. Jeffrey Neira / CBS Photo Archive / Getty Images.

(Above) Studio 54 cofounder Steve Rubell. Michael Abramson / The LIFE Images Collection / Getty Images.

(Below) Real Estate agent and reality TV star Josh Altman (left) has appeared on Bravo TV's *Million Dollar Listing: Los Angeles*, as well as the E! Network's *Keeping Up with the Kardashians* and *Giuliana and Bill*. The SU alum's book *It's Your Move: My Million Dollar Method for Taking Risks with Confidence and Succeeding at Work and Life* was published by HarperCollins in 2015. Randy Shropshire / Getty Images.

11   **Movers and Shakers**

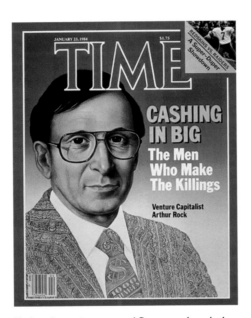

Tech industry investor and Syracuse alum Arthur Rock appeared on the cover of *Time* in January 1984. From *TIME*, January 23, 1984 © 1984 Time Inc. Used under license. *TIME* and Time Inc. are not affiliated with, and do not endorse products or services of, Licensee.

Arthur Rock

It's not often a Syracuse alum winds up on the cover of *Time*, but that honor occurred for Silicon Valley venture capitalist Arthur Rock on January 23, 1984, when the magazine featured the 1948 SU grad with a headline reading: "Cashing in Big: The Men Who Make the Killings."

This was not long after Rock, a pioneer in funding the development of Silicon Valley technology start-ups, had taken a young Steve Jobs under his wing and helped secure significant money for Jobs and Steve Wozniak's 1976 personal computer brainchild, the Apple II. As Jobs later told his biographer, Walter Isaacson, "Arthur had been like a father to me."

That relationship empowered Jobs, but it did not deter Rock from helping Apple's board choose John Sculley to lead the tech firm as CEO in 1985 and to remove Jobs from managing key areas of the company he'd cofounded.

Rock was that influential.

There was good reason, though, to trust his acumen. From his time funding the creation of Fairchild Semiconductor, Rock and his initial partner Tom Davis, were well ahead of the technology investing curve. Rock essentially invented the phrase "venture capitalist" and is one of the individuals most associated with establishing "the Valley" as a global technology hub.

Between the late 1950s and late 1980s, Rock generated financing for technology titans such as Apple, Intel, Scientific Data Systems, and Teledyne. In fact, Rock's greatest achievement may have been his role in cofounding Intel with Robert Noyce and Gordon Moore, who developed Moore's Law, a projection about the computing capacity of microchips.

At one point, according to a Silicon Valley historian, Rock's technology gems had created "hundreds of thousands of jobs and as much as 40 percent of the U.S. export market." Those investments also made Rock a billionaire at a time when that milestone was considered an astonishing achievement.

While Rock rarely sought the limelight, he was portrayed by actor J. K. Simmons in the 2013 movie *Jobs* and was featured in the documentary *Something Ventured*, which looked at the "story of risk, reward and the original venture capitalists."

Rock also is a notable philanthropist, with his most impressive giving tied to the founding, funding, and initial direction of the BASIC Fund, an initiative that made it possible for San Francisco-area children to secure private education tuition.

John D. Archbold

Can a case be made that John Dustin Archbold was the most important donor Syracuse University has ever known? Very possibly.

There have been numerous gifts to Syracuse during its first 150 years, and many of them greatly dwarf the total amount given by a single Ohio oilman. But no other donor ever rescued the university from financial failure or singlehandedly transformed its athletic prowess by underwriting an entire stadium that made Syracuse a consistent giant on the college sports landscape.

Additionally, no single Syracuse donor ever served as chair of the Syracuse University Board of Trustees for as long as Archbold (1893-1916). But if one looks around the modern Syracuse campus, there is scant evidence of Archbold's largesse.

Those with keen eyesight will find his name etched in ancient stone over the front of the Hall of Languages. Others, listening carefully, will hear contemporary students discussing workouts or intramurals at "the Arch" and know the phrase is the modern nickname for the recently renovated Archbold Gymnasium. Both of those subtle acknowledgments barely hint at the presence of a benefactor who never attended Syracuse but "bled Orange" like few others.

Born in Leesburg, Ohio, Archbold started giving money to Syracuse in 1871 (just one year after its inception) with the construction of the Hall of Languages, and continued his philanthropy with contributions for the building of Peck, Sims, and Steele Halls, plus the 1908 construction of Archbold Gymnasium. His final gift in 1915 allowed the university to purchase the Nottingham House (701 Walnut Avenue), today recognized as the chancellor's residence.

For Syracuse alumni who graduated before 1980, it was Archbold's 1905 pledge of $600,000 that allowed SU to build a world-class football facility that originally held twenty thousand spectators. It was a donation some historians believe was the first naming rights gift ever for a fully encircled stadium, and simultaneously the largest gift ever to an American university.

The result? The stadium once called "the greatest athletic arena in America" let SU race alongside Ivy League champions like Harvard, Yale, Cornell, and University of Pennsylvania during the early twentieth century, and ultimately win a football national championship in 1959.

Archbold's football stadium, designed to resemble Greek theaters (in particular the Syracuse Theater in Sicily) and Roman structures like the Colosseum, would stand for seventy-one years before the last game was played there on November 11, 1978—an Orange victory over Navy.

Photos from the era suggest John Archbold was short in stature, but he was no small donor or businessman. In fact, he was so associated with the influential oil industry that his *New York Times* obituary on December 6, 1916, suggested Archbold, one of America's earliest oil refiners, was "almost as closely identified with Standard Oil as John D. Rockefeller himself."

For Syracuse University, John D. Archbold was the original mover and shaker.

Richard Seth Hayden

She stands 151 feet tall and weighs 100 tons. Her face is ten feet wide and her waist stretches thirty-five feet around. Her index finger is eight feet long. She wears a spiked crown and clasps a book in her left hand and a torch high above her head in her right hand. She is the Statue of Liberty, and since 1886 she has been greeting visitors, including "huddled masses yearning to breathe free," from an island pedestal in New York Harbor.

When French sculptor Frederic Auguste Bartholdi finished riveting together the three hundred copper pieces that make up Lady Liberty, he proclaimed she would last forever. But fewer than one hundred years after her birth, sun and wind damage, water seepage, and pollution had taken their toll, and the statue was in dire need of repair. In the early 1980s, former Chrysler Corporation chair and Italian American immigrant son Lee Iacocca spearheaded a $230 million fundraising campaign to pay for the restoration. Once the money was secured, he chose Richard Seth Hayden, a 1960 graduate of SU's School of Architecture, to fix one of the world's largest and most beloved works of art. The project would be tricky, requiring a massive makeover while ensuring the statue looked the same as it had to those seventeen million immigrants who witnessed her majesty on their way to nearby Ellis Island to become US citizens.

Though it was a formidable challenge, Hayden was confident he and his architectural firm could pull it off because they already had tackled similar pressure-packed projects, including the restoration of the US Capitol, Senate chambers, and Supreme Court chambers in Washington, DC, and St. Patrick's Cathedral and the old Bowery Bank building in the Big Apple. In large part, it was because of those successes that Iacocca felt comfortable Hayden would get the job done.

"When I first walked into the statue it seemed so incredibly complex, it was frightening—and I've been in this business 20 years," Hayden said in a 1984 *Syracuse University Magazine* interview. "But after a year of involvement, it's become simple. After all, it's an open structure—there's no hiding the problems."

In the early 1980s, architect and Syracuse alum Richard Seth Hayden was selected to oversee the historic renovations of the Statue of Liberty. *Syracuse University Magazine.* Syracuse University News and Public Affairs Reference Collection, University Archives.

Scaffolding was set up around the statue, and many of the copper plates and twenty thousand rivets were replaced. Each new plate and rivet was treated to match Lady Liberty's distinctive bluish copper skin color. The torch and flame also had to be replaced, and numerous repairs were made to the statue's interior iron skeleton. A double-decker elevator was added to reduce waiting times for trips to the statue's crown, and space inside the pedestal was expanded to accommodate more visitors.

The massive project forced closing the monument to the public for nearly two years. But Hayden's team was able to complete the job in time for the statue's centennial celebration in 1986.

"Some structures are mute; some talk; some sing," said Hayden, a longtime member of SU's board of trustees. "We took one bursting with song and made it sing out even more. We have restored the statue's health without tampering with her dignity. And we are grateful, proud and privileged to have contributed to her immortality. Her

torch is raised; her scaffold is down . . . as the doors open on her second century, the Statue of Liberty is as strong in body as in spirit."

Steven W. Barnes

Do Horatio Alger-style stories about young boys rising from modest origins to live the American Dream still happen?

Ask Steve Barnes, the Syracuse grad who cooked cheeseburgers at Friendly's in Fayetteville. The Chittenango, New York, native who came to SU in the late 1970s because he believed the university would give him a chance.

"I was a small town kid from a humble background," said Barnes. "And not very worldly when I started college. Syracuse opened doors for me and gave me options in life."

Studying under noted Syracuse accounting professor Horace Landry, Barnes secured internships at Peat Marwick (a forerunner of industry giant KPMG) and then General Electric. According to Barnes, these experiences provided invaluable connections and stepping stones to a sensational business career.

"The internship at Peat Marwick helped me make a pivotal career choice between public accounting and industry," said Barnes. "And then, when I looked for a job after graduation, I had the advantage of recommendations from two major firms."

Not long after, PricewaterhouseCoopers came calling and put him to work on mergers and acquisitions.

Suffice to say if SU helped give Barnes options, he's certainly given much more back.

The managing director and head of private equity for North Americas at Bain Capital, plus a part owner of the Boston Celtics, Barnes and his wife, Debbie, have made numerous financial gifts to Syracuse over the years, including endowing the Barnes Family Entrepreneurship Bootcamp for Veterans with Disabilities, plus

Syracuse's chair of the board of trustees, Steve Barnes (*right*), and his son Eric during the announcement ceremonies for the new Barnes Center in the renovated Archbold Gymnasium. The Barnes Center opened in the fall of 2019. © Syracuse University. Photo by Stephen Sartori.

the Barnes Professor of Entrepreneurship. In addition to money, he has donated valuable time and expertise by serving on the board of trustees, including a four-year stint as chair.

He is a founding investor in the Orange Value Fund, a $5.5 million student-run portfolio, and his family has also provided substantial financial support to the Lockerbie Remembrance Scholarship Fund and the McLane Legacy Fund, which supports programs for students with disabilities.

The family's latest gift is the creation of the Barnes Center at the Arch, which, in 2019, transformed the Archbold/Flanagan Gymnasium complex into a world-class health, wellness, and recreation center. That center houses all campus health and wellness services—including the Counseling Center, the Office of Health Promotion, Health Services, Recreation Services, and the Office of Student Assistance—in one central location. The new complex also features a multifloor fitness center, a rock climbing wall, a multiactivity sports court, and fully accessible locker rooms and restrooms.

In making the gift, the boy from Chittenango said SU students needed a place for "extracurricular activities that ignite their passion, plus health and wellness opportunities to balance the rigor and demands of higher education."

Horatio Alger would have liked how this story unfolded.

Martha Bellinger

Here's the scenario: You are visiting Syracuse University for a campus tour, and while your parents marvel at the historic architecture of the Administration Building (now the Tolley Humanities Building), angry Orange students begin protesting the Vietnam War and Dow Chemical's campus recruitment of students. They cut the power, storm the building, chain the front door, and barricade the exits.

Might be a good time to pick another university.

Not for Watertown's Martha Bellinger, who witnessed the March 12, 1968, assault on SU's connection to an overseas war and knew immediately she wanted to attend SU. Not surprisingly, for the next four years, Bellinger placed herself at the forefront of numerous Syracuse protests and boycotts.

"I never believed in destroying property or causing physical harm to anyone," Bellinger said in 2018. "But I was pretty good at confrontational politics."

So much so that she became the first woman to run for president of SU's Student Association, provided prayers on the Hendricks Chapel steps during a large memorial service for the Kent State massacre victims, led an economic boycott of war profiteers, and guided female protesters to the chancellor's residence to address "inoperable bathroom facilities." She was crazy busy, yet she graduated as one of 1972's senior class marshals.

And Bellinger was just getting warmed up.

Between 1972 and 2004, the girl who wanted to join the Peace Corps straight out of high school secured a master's degree

in theological studies from Boston University, became the United Methodist Church's first female pastor in a conservative region of the Adirondacks, discovered her true sexuality as a lesbian ("I felt like a hypocrite, being clergy of a church that probably would not have accepted me"), added a law degree from Whittier College, and served as an openly gay Los Angeles County deputy district attorney and juvenile court commissioner.

Then, in 2005, California governor Arnold Schwarzenegger, a Republican, appointed Bellinger, a Democrat, to the Los Angeles Superior Court. From this bench, she was able to actively promote and protect LGBTQ rights while writing more than three hundred decisions on matters of family law and dependency.

Is her story over? Apparently not. Since 2010, Bellinger has written three books, including a best-selling memoir titled *From Robe to Robe: A Lesbian's Spiritual Journey*. Despite swearing she'd never rejoin the United Methodist Church, she is leading a reconciliation ministry for her denomination and the Claremont United Methodist Church.

Bettye Caldwell

Bettye Caldwell stood with six others on a New York City auditorium stage as they prepared to receive 1976 Women of the Year Awards from *Ladies' Home Journal* magazine. The esteemed lineup included First Lady Betty Ford, poet Maya Angelou, and singer Kate Smith. And although the other women's fame may have overshadowed Caldwell's, their impact did not.

As the woman credited with pioneering the early childhood education program known as Head Start, Caldwell had helped thousands of impoverished children realize their potential. She was changing the world for the better, one child at a time.

Her groundbreaking work had begun when she was a professor and chair of Syracuse University's Department of Child and Family Studies in the 1960s. It was during that time that she, in collaboration with Upstate Medical University pediatrics chair Julius Richmond, started an early education center on East Adams Street. The program, which focused on children from six months to five years old, drew national attention, with more than one thousand visitors to the center in the first year alone, including Eunice Shriver. Caldwell's research convinced her that prekindergarten education needed to be about more than just access to literacy and even basic needs like food. She believed the program could help make up for "a lack of love" some children experience.

Her themes of advocacy would soon become commonplace among education experts.

After President Lyndon Johnson declared war on poverty in his 1964 State of the Union address, Richmond was recruited to begin the Head Start program. He drew heavily upon Caldwell's research, which suggested that children born to poor families developed normally until they were about one, but then declined intellectually compared with their peers. The project concluded that the decline could be prevented or arrested through what she called "Educare"— early childhood programs that began in infancy and were integrated into the school experience.

Asked what children need, Caldwell told Syracuse.com in 2013:

> They need to be loved. They need to be spoken to, all the time. They need opportunities to explore. They need to be safe and to feel safe. They need stable figures in their lives. They need new experiences. They need to repeat experiences they enjoy. They need someone to interpret their new experiences in the world verbally. They need someone to help them find words for what they see in the world. They need an opportunity to feel love and to feel part of a family. Their wants are fairly simple, and these are needs we'd like to think would be met for every child.

What children also needed was more people like Bettye Caldwell, who was advocating on their behalf right up until her death at age ninety-one in 2016.

Renée Schine Crown

In her more than seventy years of affiliation with Syracuse University, Life Trustee Renée Schine Crown has worn many hats: student, graduate, alumna, trustee, executive committee board member, and 2000 Arents Award winner. But perhaps her most significant role has been as generous donor.

Her path to philanthropic excellence began on December 28, 1950, when Renée Schine and Lester Crown married at New York City's Waldorf-Astoria, which was transformed, as the *New York Times* reported the next day, "into a series of rose gardens" with "masses of white azaleas, cedar trees and hibiscus and apple trees in full bloom."

It wasn't long before the Crowns began a blossoming legacy of beneficence, giving to various organizations.

A 1950 graduate in fine arts, Crown has consistently ensured SU was a significant part of her family's philanthropy by helping generations of Orange undergraduates with university fundraising efforts and by creating in 1985 the nearly 200,000-square-foot Schine Student Center, named in honor of her parents, Hildegarde and J. Myer Schine.

She followed that gift up in 2002 by establishing the Renée Crown University Honors Program. SU's Honors Program was initially started in 1963 by English professor Mary Marshall for students in the College of Liberal Arts. During the 1970s, however, the program was expanded to include all undergraduate colleges, and by the 1990s the Honors Program had built a home in Bowne Hall for small student seminars and informal gatherings.

That changed more fully in 2002 when Crown, a winner of the Chancellor's Medal for Outstanding Achievement, provided

Syracuse alumnus Renée Schine Crown surveys land near Bird Library that was used for the 1985 construction of the Schine Student Center. Syracuse University Portrait Collection, University Archives.

a landmark gift that transformed the program into a showcase for the university's brightest young scholars. Led by founding director Samuel Gorovitz, former dean of the College of Arts and Sciences, the Honors Program annually began giving approximately one thousand SU students challenging research opportunities (including a rigorous senior thesis project), civic engagement, global experience, and interdisciplinary study.

Additionally, the Center for Fellowship and Scholarship Advising was developed in 2012 in partnership with the Honors Program. It was designed to help Syracuse students and alumni with the process of applying for nationally competitive awards, including Fulbright grants and Rhodes, Marshall, and Mitchell scholarships.

Of note, Syracuse students have a long tradition of success with national scholarships. Elliott Portnoy became Syracuse's first Rhodes Scholar in 1986, completing his doctoral studies at Oxford University, and now serves on SU's board of trustees. Syracuse has also produced multiple Marshall, Mitchell, Luce, Soros, and Gates Cambridge scholars, thirteen Truman Scholars, twenty-four Goldwater Scholars, and more than 150 student Fulbright award winners.

In a word, Renée Schine Crown's long-standing commitment to her alma mater has been incredibly honorable.

Angel Collado-Schwarz

Author, global scholar, island historian, university president, board member, dedicated philanthropist, multilingual communicator, radio show host. There are undoubtedly other titles Angel Collado-Schwarz has earned during his more than forty years of jet-hopping around the world, but to linger on any of them would miss understanding this Puerto Rican dynamo.

A graduate of Puerto Rico University, Collado-Schwarz earned his MBA from Syracuse in 1974 before tackling his PhD at Complutense University in Madrid, Spain. Along the way, he has served as the chair of Nazca Saatchi & Saatchi (a Latin America communications network with operations in more than twenty countries in Latin America, the Caribbean, and the US Hispanic Market), and advised the Berlin Staatsoper as well as the Film Society of Lincoln Center in New York.

For Syracuse University, he joined the Maxwell School's advisory board and is a life member of SU's board of trustees. He was named the fourth president of Carlos Albizu University in July 2014, and a lecturer at Columbia and Yale Universities.

What has made Collado-Schwarz so relevant to Syracuse students during his visits to campus is his ability to make connections in Latin America and introduce a clear understanding of how this massive marketplace functions.

Puerto Rico may be a small island, but Angel Collado-Schwarz has lived life large.

Samuel I., Si, and Donald Newhouse

During the early twentieth century, the most recognized donor at Syracuse University was probably John D. Archbold for his gifts of a stadium and gymnasium plus construction donations to numerous campus buildings. That mantle easily passed to the Newhouse family beginning in the early 1960s, when media giant Samuel Irving Newhouse Sr. made his first university-altering donation.

At the time of Newhouse's first gift, Syracuse featured a fine School of Journalism (focused primarily on print media) that originally started inside the elderly confines of Yates Castle. But in 1934, the Federal Communications Commission passed a key media act, prompting Syracuse to launch a journalism college and become the first university in the nation to offer a credit-bearing course in radio broadcasting. Thirteen years later, building on that growing student

Philanthropist and media executive Donald Newhouse speaks at SU's 2016 commencement. © Syracuse University. Photo by Stephen Sartori.

interest, SU launched WAER-FM, one of the first student-run college radio stations in the nation.

Syracuse's visionary communications initiative caught the eye of media magnate S.I. Newhouse, who had built one of the world's largest communications empires. The man who was born Solomon Isadore Neuhaus grasped that media outlets needed highly skilled journalists. At the dedication ceremony for Newhouse I in 1964, with President Lyndon B. Johnson watching, Newhouse said: "It is right and fitting that such a communications center be located within a dynamic university with world-embracing interests."

During the next five decades, the S.I. Newhouse School of Public Communications' three-building complex would sprout along University Place, with the first iconic structure designed by world-famous architect I. M. Pei. It stands, as S.I. Newhouse Jr. once suggested, as "one of the glories" of SU.

Raised in Bayonne, New Jersey, Newhouse Sr. was managing the *Bayonne Times* at age sixteen, became part owner of the *Staten Island Advance* in his mid-twenties, and became sole owner by the time he was thirty. During the next fifty years, Newhouse's Advance Publications became a worldwide leader in media platforms. It would include newspapers, magazines (notably *Vogue*, *Vanity Fair*, *WIRED* and the *New Yorker*), cable TV, and internet properties.

At his passing in 1979, Newhouse Sr. left control of the Newhouse holdings to sons, S.I. Jr. (known as Si) and Donald. Both had attended Syracuse and worked collaboratively to expand the family's vast communications empire. They also maintained a staunch commitment, via the Samuel I. Newhouse Foundation, to keep Syracuse as one of the world's most dynamic and top-ranked journalism programs.

The Samuel I. Newhouse Foundation has given millions to Syracuse on multiple occasions, making the Newhouse family one of the most generous donors in university history. Their gift in 2003 ensured the opening of Newhouse III four years later, with a keynote address from US Supreme Court Chief Justice John G. Roberts.

Today, the striking Newhouse complex, with words from the First Amendment filling windows wrapping around Newhouse III, is evidence of one family's long-standing love of Syracuse and their transformational vision for educational excellence in public communications.

John T. Connor

Some Americans might have been surprised when US president-elect Donald Trump selected ExxonMobil CEO Rex Tillerson as his secretary of state in December 2016. But a similar appointment of an industry titan took place in 1965 when Syracuse alumnus John T. Connor, previously CEO of Merck & Company, was appointed President Lyndon Johnson's secretary of commerce.

It was Johnson's first cabinet appointment following the assassination of John F. Kennedy and was based on Connor's business acumen.

Service came easily to Connor. He'd acted as senior class president at Syracuse and captained the Orange golf team in the mid-1930s before joining the Marines during World War II, working as an air combat intelligence officer. He later served as special assistant to Navy Secretary James Forrestal, playing a role in advancing penicillin production as well as assisting in the creation of legislation that established the Department of Defense.

Connor reported to Johnson until 1967, but his growing opposition to the Vietnam War and its effect on the American economy caused Connor to clash frequently with the president. Recognizing the proverbial writing on the wall, he stepped down to run Allied Chemical Corporation.

Connor's wife later indicated her husband left Johnson's administration because he "was a little bit of an idealist about government. He felt Lyndon Johnson was treating the Cabinet more like aides."

A longtime friend agreed. "He found working for L.B.J. very difficult," lawyer John Pickering told the *New York Times*. "I recall [Connor] saying once that L.B.J. thought he could snap his fingers and the business and industrial machine would just turn around."

Serving as president and chair of Allied from 1967 until 1979, Connor, a Harvard Law School graduate, frequently spoke out against President Nixon's management of the war in Southeast Asia. In the 1970s, Connor even headed the Committee of Business Executives against the Vietnam War.

Diane Lyden Murphy

In the early 1970s, Syracuse University graduate student Diane Lyden Murphy, a young mother of twins, became deeply immersed in policy and social justice issues simply because she couldn't ignore the facts. With two children in tow and limited services provided by the university, Murphy stepped forward as a feminist activist when salary equity and available day care were not only meaningful but hotly debated issues.

Under the direction of vice president of student affairs Charles Willie (one of SU's first African American professors and administrators), Murphy became the coordinator of married student programs. Blending Willie's reputation as a champion for students and her unwavering commitment to social activism, the two quickly rallied support and funding for adequate and affordable childcare.

The result? Murphy, along with volunteers, cared for children in a small space in Hendricks Chapel while a proposal for a permanent childcare center moved through the university's bureaucratic ranks.

"What emerged was a model center in the College for Human Development that offered quality campus child care and still does today," said Murphy. "Amazing faculty, such as Bettye Caldwell,

As of 2019, Falk College dean Diane Lyden Murphy (*left*) was the longest-serving active dean at Syracuse. Daylight Blue Media / Michael Barletta.

Alice Honig, Ron Lally, Ruth Wynn and Bernice M. Wright were responsible for educating students while conducting groundbreaking research."

Murphy's graduate work coincided with the evolution of women's studies as an academic discipline, and SU soon became one of the first universities to offer regular courses in that subject area. Aided by a grassroots movement, it wasn't long before an official program was fully considered.

By the time Murphy completed her PhD in social science in 1983 (her fourth Syracuse degree), a concentration in women's studies existed. Then, in 1989, while working as an associate professor of social work, the mother of five daughters was named director of women's studies. Two years later, the major was approved.

These were just the first of many women's issues Murphy would address as a researcher or administrator. Curriculum transformation and firm establishment of the Women's Studies Program in the College of Arts and Sciences marked Murphy's seventeen-year tenure as director. Under her guidance, Women's Studies would become one of SU's major interdisciplinary programs, offering opportunity for feminist study and research campus-wide and at Syracuse centers abroad.

Murphy and her colleagues also developed the first-of-its-kind, nationally modeled Rape, Advocacy, Prevention, Education Center. As a women's issues consultant to Chancellor Kenneth Shaw, she also coauthored sexual harassment policy, developed studies on gender pay equity, and pushed for adoption and domestic partner benefits and the development of platinum benefit packages for faculty, staff, and graduate students.

For more than four decades, Murphy's sought-after expertise has informed women- and family-focused efforts in classrooms and conference rooms globally.

Not surprisingly, she was appointed dean of her college in 2005 and, as of 2019, was the longest serving active academic dean at SU.

Mort Janklow

In 1972, lawyer-turned-literary-agent Mort Janklow had agreed to represent client, friend, and fellow Syracuse alumnus William Safire for a nonfiction book Safire was writing on President Richard Nixon. Given Safire's former role as a Nixon White House insider, the book promised to be explosive, with demand for the publishing rights extremely competitive.

What Janklow decided next was that New York City's biggest publishers would come to him. Only then would they get to look at select pages of the manuscript. Nothing would leave his office.

The move was unheard of, but it led to lucrative outcomes for Safire. It also led to a sea change in the publishing industry because Janklow began controlling the narrative. The literary landscape would never be the same.

"We took the publisher out of the captain's seat and put the author in it," he said. "The publisher is replaceable; the author is not."

That sentiment reflected Janklow's keen desire to change the dynamic between authors and publishers in the 1970s. From that point forward, he would land his clients the best deals possible, including a $2.25 million contract for astrologer Linda Goodman's nonfiction book *Love Signs*.

Some of Janklow's most visible clients would include presidents Jimmy Carter and Ronald Reagan, Pope John Paul II, Jackie Collins, Michael Crichton, Joan Didion, Thomas Harris, David McCullough, Jane Bryant Quinn, Anne Rice, Sidney Sheldon, Danielle Steel, Hunter Thompson, Tom Wolfe, and the Duchess of York.

At times, books from Janklow's stable of intellectual and influential authors were everywhere, and the magnitude of his influence might've been most obvious in November 1989 when the Queens native became the first agent to "run the table" on the *New York Times* best-seller lists. That month, "MegaMort's" clients topped the charts for fiction (Steel's *Daddy*), nonfiction (Nancy Reagan's *My Turn*), and paperbacks (Sheldon's *The Sands of Time*). It happened less than a year after Janklow, who had represented seven Pulitzer Prize winners, famously merged with fellow mega-agent Lynn Nesbit in December 1988.

Janklow, who started at SU at the age of sixteen, graduated in 1950 and has often given back to his alma mater by serving on the College of Arts and Sciences Board of Visitors and by founding the Janklow Arts Leadership Program.

Robert E. Johnson

A classmate of Martin Luther King Jr. at Morehouse College in Atlanta (both graduated in 1948), Robert E. Johnson was often

A classmate of Dr. Martin Luther King Jr. at Morehouse College in Atlanta, Robert E. Johnson received his graduate degree from Syracuse before becoming executive editor for *Jet* magazine. Syracuse University Portrait Collection, University Archives.

credited with building *Jet* magazine into the "most popular black news magazine in the world." But that single sentence barely begins to cover the influence Johnson held as a journalist and early supporter of the US civil rights movement.

Born in Montgomery, Alabama, but raised in Birmingham, Johnson began selling black weeklies as a youngster before founding his high school newspaper and emerging as the editor of Morehouse's collegiate periodical.

By 1953, following time in Syracuse where he earned his master's degree in journalism, Johnson was hired as the associate editor for *Jet*. Already valued as an important stringer for the magazine, the WWII veteran was quickly promoted to assistant managing editor (1954), managing editor (1956), and executive editor (1963).

Johnson would hold the executive editor position for more than three decades, and along the way he ensured *Jet* frequently featured the heroic efforts of Dr. King. In fact, Johnson was one of the first journalists to cover King's famed marches, and his coverage helped make *Jet*, a pocket-sized magazine, hugely important in the African American community.

"He was the web that connected music, culture, religion, history and social developments," said civil rights leader Jesse Jackson following Johnson's death in 1995. "He was one of the great communicators of our times."

Added *Jet* chair and CEO John H. Johnson: "During his 42 years as *Jet* managing editor and executive editor, he helped change the color of American journalism. Bob Johnson was a great journalist who inspired and taught tens of thousands of aspiring journalists, black and white."

Robert Johnson was no relation to the Johnson family that founded *Jet*, but during his management of the magazine, weekly circulation grew to nearly one million with a readership often thought to exceed seven million.

Conrad Lynn

He stood a smidgen below five feet six inches tall, but that didn't stop Conrad Lynn from casting a giant shadow as a civil rights attorney, often taking on unpopular but seminal cases in the pursuit of justice for all during his memorable sixty-year law career.

Although the Supreme Court twice declined to hear his case to desegregate the US Army, his arguments swayed public sentiment enough to convince President Harry Truman to integrate the military after World War II.

Lynn also attracted national attention for the "Kissing Case," in which two African American boys from North Carolina—a nine-year-old and a seven-year-old—were charged with rape because they kissed a young white girl while playing house. The boys were held for months without bail, but they were eventually released and exonerated after Lynn gathered thousands of signatures on a petition, convincing President Dwight Eisenhower to intervene. Lynn's defense of the "Harlem Six" in a New York City police brutality case in the mid-1960s and his controversial defense of conscientious objectors during the Vietnam War were other trials widely covered by metropolitan newspapers and the television networks.

A skilled debater in high school, Lynn landed a partial scholarship to Syracuse in 1927 and earned his degree from the College of Arts and Sciences three years later. He then enrolled in SU's College of Law, and in 1932 became one of the first African Americans to graduate from the school.

Lynn participated in some of the earliest Freedom Rides in the 1940s, when interracial groups of civil rights advocates rode buses in the South to protest Jim Crow policies. Throughout his career, he worked shoulder-to-shoulder with a variety of activists, including Martin Luther King Jr., Malcolm X, Supreme Court Justice Thurgood Marshall, and former First Lady Eleanor Roosevelt.

"What Conrad did during his lifetime was as powerful as King's accomplishments," said Stella Marrs, executive director of the Martin Luther King Multipurpose Center in Spring Valley, New York, at the time of Lynn's death at age eighty-seven in 1995. "He was a warrior for people. He gave all of us vision, hope and confidence that we can fight to make this world a better place."

Five years before his death, Lynn received the prestigious Roy Wilkins Award from the NAACP in recognition of a lifetime devoted to civil rights causes.

"No lawyer since Clarence Darrow has had such a colorful career and successfully defended so many controversial cases as Lynn," said famed attorney William Kunstler, who collaborated on some of those cases with him. "For the sake of history—whatever that is—Conrad will be remembered as a very strident voice against all injustice."

Dan D'Aniello

Already acknowledged as one of the finest high school gymnasts in the state of Pennsylvania, all muscular star Dan D'Aniello needed to do during the summer of 1964 was pass the US Naval Academy's physical examination to secure a full ride to Annapolis. That appointment would launch what D'Aniello hoped would be a dynamic military career.

But there was one small problem. The young man who had mastered the rings and parallel bars did not pass the exam. He now had a bigger problem. His single mother couldn't afford to send him to college. If he was to go anywhere, he would need a scholarship.

Enter Syracuse University and head gymnastics coach Paul Romeo with a last-minute offer to join a squad that went 7-0 and won an Eastern championship in 1963. That "rescue-ring" would shape the rest of D'Aniello's life.

Arriving at SU with virtually nothing, the future cofounder and chair of the Carlyle Group was unsure he could cut it academically and as a varsity athlete. But thanks to support from Orange faculty members, D'Aniello found his confidence. When he graduated magna cum laude from Syracuse in 1968, he was ready for the future.

The Vietnam War had other ideas, though, and D'Aniello found himself drafted. He joined the US Navy, spending the next three years as a supply officer on board the USS *Wasp*, an antisubmarine aircraft carrier famous for recovering NASA's Gemini space capsules.

After exiting the service, D'Aniello picked up an MBA at Harvard Business School before launching into one of the most spectacular financial careers of the late twentieth century. It has included administrative stops with PepsiCo, TWA, and Marriott in areas such as mergers, acquisitions, and project funding.

Business executive and major Syracuse donor Dan D'Aniello (*second from left*) received his 2017 Arents Award with Diane Nelson (*left*), Mary Spio, and Tom Coughlin. © Syracuse University. Photo by Stephen Sartori.

In 1987, he cofounded the Carlyle Group, a private equity firm based in Washington, DC, and by 2018 the firm was managing more than $200 billion in assets. But the Syracuse alumnus, who grew up believing his mother and grandmother sacrificed so that he might succeed, has always shown a most generous heart.

Already an Orange Life Trustee, D'Aniello and his wife, Gayle, made a $20 million donation to the Syracuse Institute for Veterans and Military Families (IVMF) to support the construction of the National Veterans Resource Center. Immediately, the D'Aniellos' gift, which was announced in February 2018, was one of the largest ever given to Syracuse.

"The work being done at SU, specifically at the IVMF, is simply unrivaled," said D'Aniello of the center, which opens in 2020 prepared to focus on the needs of more than twenty million veterans and their families. "The fact is that unlike any other university, Syracuse understands and appreciates the significant contributions veterans and military families play in our society. This new center will allow SU to help our nation not only respond to but anticipate the unique needs of this population by helping veterans more seamlessly transition to civilian life."

For the young man who couldn't get into Annapolis, life seems to have come full circle.

Rey Pascual

At Syracuse University, Reinaldo "Rey" Pascual received a gift that keeps on giving.

"Syracuse opened the world to me and proved everything is possible for committed people who work hard and dedicate themselves to excellence," he said. "It gave me the opportunity to learn, discover and intellectually go where I'd never gone before, thereby challenging me to succeed."

Energized by his Orange experience, Pascual has consistently given back to his alma mater, particularly in Atlanta, which he's helped become one of SU's most active alumni cities. He also became an SU trustee and served as vice chair of the board from 2015 to 2019. In 2013, he served on the search committee that selected Kent Syverud as SU's chancellor.

Born and raised in Puerto Rico, Pascual came to Syracuse and earned a degree in political science in 1985. From there he went to Creighton University's law school before settling in Atlanta and engineering a rapid rise through the ranks at Kilpatrick Stockton LLP and Paul Hastings, one of the world's most prominent law firms.

Practicing corporate law with a focus on areas such as mergers and acquisitions, corporate finance and securities, private equity, and investment management, Pascual was focused primarily on the United States but frequently worked in Latin America, where he could leverage his bilingual skills and knowledge of international business cultures.

For his efforts, he was recognized as a Leading Lawyer for Corporate/Mergers and Acquisition Law by Chambers USA and recognized as a Georgia Super Lawyer for Corporate Finance by *Atlanta* magazine. In 2002, SU honored him with the Chancellor's Citation for Distinguished Service in Law.

Pascual also cofounded and directed the United Americas Bank, the first Hispanic-owned bank in Georgia. In addition, he represented or assisted numerous Atlanta organizations, including the Metro Atlanta Chamber of Commerce, Atlanta Convention and Visitors Bureau, and Georgia Hispanic Chamber of Commerce.

In 2017, after a decade at Paul Hastings, Pascual left to establish his own firm, providing outside general counsel to many of his long-standing clients. He also helped SU establish greater visibility and presence in Atlanta via the Atlanta Regional Council.

"I've always been extremely proud to be Syracuse Orange, and could not have been more excited when Syracuse decided Atlanta was a 'geography of opportunity,'" Pascual said. "The learning and networking opportunities are simply great. Orange must do business with Orange, and, in so doing, we must give back to the institution."

Terence Todman

As the *Washington Post* reported in his 2014 obituary, career diplomat Terence Todman joined the US State Department in the early 1950s, when—according to an interview conducted by historian Michael Krenn—he said "the only thing they had blacks doing . . . was serving as messengers and secretaries."

By the time he finished serving his country, Todman had acted as an ambassador to six different nations (Spain, Denmark, Argentina, Costa Rica, Chad, and Guinea), worked as President Jimmy Carter's assistant secretary of state for inter-American affairs and, in 1990, earned the prestigious rank of Career Ambassador.

His 1974 assignment to Costa Rica represented the first time an African American was appointed ambassador to a Spanish-speaking country. Four years later, the 1952 Maxwell School MPA graduate became the first African American to hold a major European ambassadorship.

"I resented, and I still resent, the 'ghetto' assignment of blacks to Africa or Caribbean nations," he said in an oral history that Krenn began conducting in 1995. He was willing to make those strong comments because he had witnessed bias throughout his career.

One example occurred after he passed the State Department exams required for admission to the US Foreign Service. He initially was denied a position because the personnel officer felt his accent (Todman was born on St. Thomas in the US Virgin Islands) was an inhibitor to success. The officer indicated "the Foreign Service needed employees who were '100 percent identifiable as Americans.'"

"I was considered a troublemaker," Todman said of his time in the State Department. "And that was all right."

Todman's final ambassador's job before retiring in 1993 was in Argentina, where he willingly (and somewhat controversially) addressed "corrupt practices such as bribes that he believed obstructed U.S.-Argentine business."

Martin J. Whitman

There are only a handful of donor names Syracuse University students frequently discuss without even thinking about them. Archbold. Newhouse. Crouse. Bird. Hendricks. Schine. Manley. Falk.

One other name they'd instantly include is Whitman, their shorthand for the Martin J. Whitman School of Management, the endowed name given to SU's business school when Marty Whitman magnanimously gave back to his alma mater in 2003.

For Whitman, providing educational opportunities for those in need always mattered.

That social consciousness likely started in New York City, where he was born in 1924, the son of Jewish refugees from Poland who traded in felt and fabrics. Joining the Navy for World War II, Whitman served as a medic and personally saw African American sailors mistreated. Years later, after becoming one of America's most astute investors, he and his wife, Lois, created numerous scholarships for African American, Arab, and Latino students to attend college or law school.

Whitman understood discrimination and had felt it personally when Ivy League schools rejected his college applications because of his Jewish faith. Using the GI Bill, Whitman was accepted into Syracuse and graduated magna cum laude with a bachelor's degree in 1949. He followed that success by studying at Princeton and earning a master's in economics from New York's New School for Social Research.

In the decades that followed, Whitman learned the world's financial ropes, ultimately creating the Third Avenue Value Fund in 1990. He was widely known as "a patient investor and a man of profound generosity and integrity," which the *New York Times* noted was unusual, since such traits in high finance are often slighted. Known to some as the king of due diligence, Whitman was famous for "spending enormous amounts of time collecting and analyzing information before pulling the trigger on any transaction."

Whitman's famous work ethic was evident right up to the day he died on April 16, 2018, when he reportedly argued with his doctor to let him go to work.

Elected to SU's board of trustees in 2003, Whitman played tennis into his nineties and frequently taught classes or seminars as an adjunct faculty member at Syracuse, Columbia, and Yale's School of Management. He was given Syracuse's Arents Award in 2004 for excellence in business.

"Marty Whitman represented the very best of a generation that believed in hard work, education, and striving for excellence always," said Chancellor Kent Syverud. "He used his education and extraordinary intellect to achieve the highest levels of success, and yet never forgot his humble roots. He was a role model for thousands of students here at Syracuse and elsewhere, and his legacy will live on through them."

Business executive and SU alum Martin Whitman is shown speaking to students in the School of Management that bears his name. © Syracuse University. Photo by Stephen Sartori.

12 Orange Slices

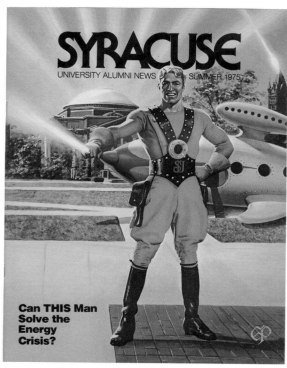

SU Alumni News was the forerunner to the present-day *Syracuse University Magazine. SU Alumni News.* Syracuse University Alumni Reference Collection, University Archives.

Before embarking on a thirty-one-year career as a professor in the College of Visual and Performing Arts in 1967, Jerome Malinowski was part of a team that designed the iconic Ford Mustang. The sports car was introduced to the public at the World's Fair in New York in 1964, and it wound up saving the Ford Motor Company and revolutionizing the automobile industry. The first in a class of vehicles known as pony cars, the Mustang inspired other brands, such as the Chevrolet Camaro and Pontiac Firebird. Malinowski also helped improve the aerodynamics of the bobsleds used by the US team at the 1988 Winter Olympics in Calgary.

Television and movie character actor Sheldon Leonard was so well known as a tough guy that when Miller Lite cast its sixth-ever commercial for the famous "Tastes Great—Less Filling" ad campaign in the mid-1970s, they selected the Syracuse alumnus to play a gangster. The punch line for the spot was, "All right, Louie, drop that beer." Unfortunately for Leonard, the ad was pulled just after it started running because Miller received complaints about the glorification of gangsters. Leonard was the second SU alumnus to appear in a Miller Lite commercial. Retired Baltimore Colts legend John Mackey had previously appeared with New York Jets running back Matt Snell in an arm wrestling spot.

A member of the Onondaga Nation, Judith Lewis Anquoe Meggesto graduated from Syracuse University's College of Law in 1978 and became the first female Native American to be admitted to the New York State Bar. Meggesto practiced as an attorney specializing in Native American Law and became both a tribal court judge and appellate county judge for various tribal nations. She died in 2001.

Although he earned first-team All-American honors as a two-way tackle at Syracuse University in 1958, Ron Luciano made his mark as arguably the most colorful umpire in baseball history. The mathematics major had a soft spot for the theater—he was an avid reader of Shakespeare. So it wasn't surprising that he would become known for his dramatic calls and humorous, pithy quotes. A regular on the Johnny Carson show, Luciano collaborated on five books, including two best-sellers—*The Umpire Strikes Back* and *The Fall of the Roman Umpire*.

Her real name was Elizabeth D. Ewart, but in Syracuse lore she's better known as the Haven Hall Rebel for the 1912 food strike she organized against the dining hall over the quality of its meals. Ninety girls signed the petition. Chancellor James Roscoe Day didn't take kindly to the protest and wound up expelling Ewart. He told her she could come back to school if she disassociated herself from the petition, but Ewart was inspired by the women's suffrage movement and stuck to her beliefs. The story was carried in newspapers across the country. In 1956, after Ewart had become Mrs. Elizabeth Reed, she attracted national attention again by winning CBS television's quiz show *The $64,000 Question*. Despite her expulsion, Reed later attended SU class reunions and said she considered the school her alma mater.

Not long after Syracuse University's Athletic Governing Board adopted the block S logo in 1893, notable football and baseball player George H. Bond bought a sweater and had the orange-colored letter sewn onto it. Bond wore the sweater during a baseball game that spring, and a tradition was born. Today, the block S is worn by all SU athletes and has become one of the most recognizable logos in college sports.

Syracuse University Magazine officially launched in 1984, but the publication can trace its roots to SU's *Alumni News*, which debuted sixty-five years earlier. In the mid-1960s, *Alumni News* started expanding its coverage to reflect societal changes brought about by the civil rights and anti-war movements. Stories began addressing not only alumni achievements but also current student issues, as well as the shifting role of higher education. *Alumni News* continued to be published after the launch of SU's magazine but eventually was incorporated into SU's main magazine.

The discovery of an unknown species of orange shrimp in the Atlantic Ocean in 1993 by Syracuse University professor Steven Chamberlain resulted in the shrimp receiving the scientific title *Rimicaris aurantiaca. Aurantiaca* means "orange" in Latin. Chamberlain and two of his graduate students—Robert Jinks and Erik Herzog—made their finding while diving in the Azores, a cluster of nine islands nine hundred miles west of Portugal. Chamberlain shipped off his information to an expert in Los Angeles who confirmed it was an unnamed species, and the new name became official in honor of SU's primary color.

Catholic priest Charles Borgognoni—known to Orange fans simply as Father Charles—served as the chaplain of the Syracuse University football and basketball teams from 1962 to 1991. "He was much more than a chaplain; he was a friend," said Floyd Little, the Orangemen's three-time All-American running back during the mid-1960s. "It didn't matter if you were Catholic or Baptist or Jew or an atheist, Father Charles just had this way about him that enabled him to connect with everybody. And he had this way of making you believe that no matter what happened out there, win or lose, everything was going to be OK."

Two Syracuse alumnae participated in the 2016 Miss America Pageant, one as a contestant, the other as a judge. Vanessa Williams, who won the crown in 1984, was back as head judge, while Allie Curtis, who graduated from SU in 2014, competed as Miss Rhode Island. Curtis did not make the top fifteen, so she didn't get to compete in the live television rounds. But she and the other nonqualifying contestants cheered their friends on from the side of the stage.

A statue of the Saltine Warrior was commissioned in 1951, with art student Luise Kaish winning a campus-wide design competition. Kaish, who studied under SU professor and world-famous sculptor Ivan Mestrovic, had a member of the Onondaga Nation pose for the bronze statue. Depicting a bow pointing skyward, it now resides on the southeast corner of the Quad in front of Carnegie Library.

Syracuse's Saltine Warrior statue. © Syracuse University. Photo by Stephen Sartori.

In 1978, astrophysicist Martin Pomerantz (SU class of 1937; honorary degree 2007) traveled to the South Pole and became the first person to observe the sun for 120 continuous hours from a single point. His images rocked the scientific community. He later endowed a professorship that advanced the work of physics professor Peter Saulson, whose groundbreaking research in multimessenger cosmology is helping to unlock the mysteries of the universe.

National Collegiate Athletic Association president Mark Emmert received a master's degree (1976) and a PhD (1983) from the Maxwell School of Citizenship and Public Affairs. Before becoming head of the governing body of college sports, Emmert served as president of the University of Washington and chancellor at Louisiana State University. The NCAA oversees more than 1,100 schools, 19,000 teams, and 460,000 student-athletes.

Syracuse University alumnus and Pulitzer Prize-winning *New York Times* columnist William Safire credited SU College of Law graduate Karen DeCrow with coining the phrase "politically correct."

From the 1950s to the demolition of Archbold Stadium in November 1978, SU was home to a small nuclear reactor that was used by the physics department. The five-thousand-square-foot reactor was housed in a two-story building next to the stadium, and it had been dormant for several years before Old Archie was razed to make way for the construction of the Carrier Dome. When it was removed, 5,500 pounds of uranium was tucked into lead crates and transported away by truck under the direction of the US Department of Energy. The reactor's generator—called a Van de Graaff—was disassembled and moved to the physics building. A producer of protons, it would continue to be used for instructional purposes.

In 1983—twenty-four years after graduating from Syracuse University—James D. Morrissey was on top of the world. Literally. That's the year he led a climb up the "forgotten" East Face of Mount Everest. Although Chinese climbers had taken the same route before, Morrissey and his team were the first Americans to scale the 29,028-foot peak from the Tibetan side. "I have found no challenge to equal it," Morrissey wrote in *National Geographic*. He first began climbing in the Adirondacks while an undergraduate at the SUNY College of Environmental Science and Forestry, which was part of Syracuse University from 1911 to 1948. After completing his training at Upstate Medical University, he became a heart surgeon in Stockton, California, and went on to scale the high peaks of Africa, South America, Alaska, and the Himalayas.

Grover Cleveland, the only US president to serve nonconsecutive terms, was a member of the Syracuse University Board of Trustees from 1883 to 1885. A former resident of Fayetteville, a Syracuse suburb, Cleveland gave up his board seat shortly after winning his first presidential election in 1884. He lost to Benjamin Harrison four years later, but rebounded to win a second term in 1892. In 1946, the present-day University College building was renamed in honor of Cleveland, the twenty-second and twenty-fourth US president.

The inscription on Jefferson Burdick's tombstone reads: "One of the greatest card collectors of all times." Many hobbyists who have devoted lifetimes to accumulating baseball cards would dispute that claim. "Greatest card collector of all time" would have been a more accurate epitaph. Burdick, who graduated from Syracuse with a two-year degree in business in 1922, not only collected more than 300,000 baseball cards but also developed the classification system for card collecting and published catalogs that became collectors' items. Before his death in 1963, the man known as the father of card collecting donated his entire collection—valued in the tens of millions—to the Metropolitan Museum of Art in New York City. Many of his mini works of art—including the rare T206 Honus Wagner tobacco card—are displayed in the same building that houses Egyptian mummies, medieval armor, and Renoirs.

After graduating from Syracuse in 1967 with a degree in illustration, Roger Schlaifer worked a bunch of odd jobs. They included medical illustrator, surrealist painter, photographer, art director, and member of the National Guard. But it wasn't until he enrolled in SU's Independent Study Degree Program and majored in advertising design nine years later that he discovered his calling. Schlaifer's luck turned when he saw how taken his daughters were with Little People dolls, created by Xavier Roberts. The dolls were accompanied by a "cabbage patch" legend, and Schlaifer expanded upon this, creating a new concept that included dubbing the dolls Cabbage Patch Kids. Roberts loved the idea and awarded Schlaifer exclusive world rights to market the concept. The cuddly critters became a billion-dollar industry, earning Schlaifer the nickname "King of the Cabbage Patch."

The Sour Sitrus Society pep band's name originated from the wrong notes the group often played when it was formed in 1970. After a rocky start, the band began hitting all the right notes and earned national acclaim for its music and its ability to fire up the home crowd. *Basketball Times* wound up calling it the best pep band in the nation.

After graduating from Syracuse University's School of Music in 1952, Donald Martino became one of America's foremost contemporary composers, with his chamber music piece Notturno earning him the Pulitzer Prize in 1974. Martino, who went on to teach at Harvard, also received four grants from the National Endowment for the Arts and was a three-time Guggenheim Fellow. After retiring from Harvard in 1993, the clarinetist spent several years composing and performing his music.

When *Forbes* magazine revealed its sixth annual "30 Under 30" listing of the six hundred most influential people under the age of thirty in 2017, there were seven SU alumni on the list, including Jessica Santana and Evin Robinson, who were selected for their co-creation of New York on Tech, a not-for-profit organization providing opportunities and proficiency in technology and innovation to underrepresented students in New York City's public high schools. Santana, one of Univision's inaugural technology anchors, did her Syracuse honors capstone project determining why Latino students who were interested in business did not pursue accounting degrees. Robinson, who started as a tech consultant for Accenture, was recognized as a Wells Fargo Millennial Activist and LinkedIn Millennial Influencer. Both Santana and Robinson earned undergraduate and graduate degrees from SU.

Renowned jazz pianist Gap Mangione, a 1965 graduate of SU and brother of legendary jazz trumpeter Chuck Mangione, produced more than twenty highly acclaimed albums. Twenty years after leaving school, he returned to his alma mater to teach a course on jazz history and serve as a consultant.

In 1990, the National Women's Hall of Fame in Seneca Falls, New York, memorialized Helen Barben with a Wall of Fame tribute. A 1923 graduate of Syracuse University with a BS in music, Barben taught for several years and became heavily involved in several historical societies. She was a founding member of the National Women's Hall of Fame and was credited with helping to keep the museum solvent.

During the 1989-90 basketball season, Syracuse University averaged 29,919 spectators per game, an NCAA record that still stands.

For nearly forty years, writer Judy Freudberg resided on *Sesame Street*, writing thousands of scripts for the landmark PBS children's television series, and even creating the sweet, bright-eyed monster known as Elmo. Freudberg joined the immensely popular and educational TV show for its third season after graduating from Syracuse University in 1971 with a degree in speech and dramatic arts. Along the way, she would create segments for celebrities such as Whoopi Goldberg, B.B. King, Ellen DeGeneres, and Maya Angelou, and would win seventeen Emmys. She also collaborated on two animated movies (*The Land Before Time* and *An American Tail*) for executive producer Steven Spielberg. She died at age sixty-two in 2012.

In a 2017 interview with *Syracuse University Magazine*, Chris Renaud, the Oscar-nominated illustrator and filmmaker behind such global box office hits as *Despicable Me* and *The Secret Life of Pets*, advised aspiring young artists to "be prepared to reinvent yourself and your skill set." They clearly are words he has lived by. Before establishing himself as one of the world's most prolific and respected film animators, the 1989 graduate of SU's College of Visual and Performing Arts traveled a self-described "convoluted" career path. His journey included everything from drawing and writing comic books for DC Comics to designing sets and children's television characters for the Disney Channel and PBS. Renaud was co-creator of the iconic, lovable Minions characters from the *Despicable Me* movie series. His films were twice nominated for Academy Awards. His film *No Time for Nuts*, which featured the popular *Ice Age* character Scrat, won an Annie Award for Best Animated Short Subject.

Bob Wheeler never met Jim Thorpe, but he may know him better than anyone ever has. While a graduate student at Syracuse University in the late 1960s, Wheeler hitchhiked across the country interviewing scores of people, including former president Dwight Eisenhower and actor Burt Lancaster, for his master's thesis on Thorpe, the Native American whom many regard as the greatest athlete of the twentieth century. His research enabled him to earn his graduate degree in history and write a defining biography, titled *Jim Thorpe: Pathway to Glory*. With a huge assist from his wife and fellow SU alum, Florence Ridlon, Wheeler was able to convince the International Olympic Committee to right a decades-old wrong and restore the gold medals Thorpe had been stripped of shortly after the 1912 Games in Sweden because of accusations of professionalism. On January 18, 1983, Wheeler and Ridlon attended the ceremony in which replica medals were presented to Thorpe's relatives.

In the early 1990s, Syracuse University alumnus David Ginsberg spent three years bicycling around the world to raise money for OxFam America, an international nonprofit organization that fights poverty and hunger in more than ninety nations. It took him 962 days and the repair or replacement of forty flat tires to negotiate the 24,616 miles—the approximate distance around the earth. His life-changing journey was not without risk. He was mugged in Moscow, pickpocketed in Bucharest and Tanzania, arrested in China, and ambushed by fire ants in Louisiana—and he ran out of water in the Gobi Desert. He raised $10,000 for thirteen schools OxFam built in impoverished countries.

On November 5, 1904, on the Oval gridiron near the present-day Carrier Dome and Quad, Syracuse University's football team obliterated Manhattan College, 144-0. It remains, by far, the most points ever scored by an Orange football team and was preceded that season by 69-0 victories versus Clarkson and Allegheny. That team, coached by Charles Hutchins, averaged 45 points per game.

Ernie Davis holds the Syracuse University record for most statues, with three. Two are on campus. The one near Hendricks Chapel on the main campus depicts him in his football uniform, holding his helmet in his left hand and a football in his right. He is shown in an action pose in his statue on the South Campus athletic complex, next to statues of fellow Number 44 legends Jim Brown and Floyd Little. There's also a statue of Davis in a letterman's jacket, holding books and a football, outside Ernie Davis Academy in his hometown of Elmira, New York.

Legendary Motown entertainment executive Suzanne de Passe may not have stayed at Syracuse for all four traditional years, but she was certainly good with the number five. As in

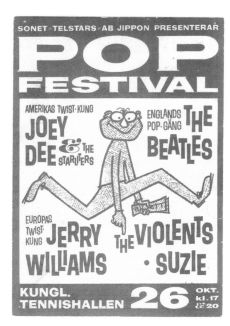

When Felix Cavaliere joined Joey Dee and the Starliters for their 1963 European tour, the Beatles were an occasional opening act. Courtesy of Rockaway Records (www .rockaway.com).

SU softball player Sydney O'Hara generated national attention in March 2017 when she hit four home runs in one game. Athletics Department, Syracuse University, used by permission.

Jackson Five, the Gary, Indiana, quintet that, with the stunning ascendancy of youngest singer Michael, dramatically altered popular music forever. The Harlem-born de Passe was working for Motown founder Berry Gordy when she discovered and helped sign the band to a deal in early 1969. Within fifteen years, she was president of Motown Productions, had been nominated for an Academy Award (cowriting the screenplay for *Lady Sings the Blues*), and won an Emmy for the TV special *Motown 25: Yesterday, Today, Forever*.

During a game on March 10, 2017, Sydney O'Hara experienced a record-tying power surge, becoming the first player in Syracuse history and just the fifth in college softball annals to blast four home runs in a single game. ESPNW recognized the feat as the top performance by a female athlete in America that week.

It's a safe bet the overwhelming majority of people who traverse Marshall Street—better known as M Street—have no clue about the thoroughfare's namesake. And that's too bad because former SU trustee Louis Marshall is a man who should be remembered. A driving force behind founding the forestry school, Marshall was a staunch defender of minority causes, arguing more cases before the US Supreme Court than any nongovernment lawyer of his era. The prominent Jewish leader took on the Ku Klux Klan during the height of its power in the late nineteenth and early twentieth century. Marshall was lauded by President Herbert Hoover and other world leaders upon his death at age seventy-two in 1929.

Syracuse has a rich tradition producing not only NFL players but also coaches. Joe Alexander, a three-time football All-American for the Orange, started the tradition in 1926 when he coached the New York Giants. Al Davis coached the Oakland Raiders in the mid-1960s, but he would gain greater acclaim as the team's owner, leading the franchise to three Super Bowl titles. Jim Ringo, an All-American center in 1952, coached the Buffalo Bills in 1976-77. Tom Coughlin coached the Jacksonville Jaguars to the AFC championship game in the team's second season of existence, and he would go on to win two Super Bowls as the Giants' head man. Doug Marrone began his NFL career coaching the Bills, and currently he is the coach of the Jaguars.

His life represented a modern version of the Great Peacemaker. He was a wise healer of tribes and a protector of his people. That was Irving Powless Jr., longtime Onondaga Nation chief. Powless died in November 2017, but for fifty years prior to his death, the leader of the Onondaga's Beaver Clan and Haudenosaunee Council of Chiefs member worked tirelessly as an advocate for Native American sovereignty. He was also an author (a 2016 book titled *Who Are These People Anyway?*), ambassador, educator, and Native American historian. In 2009, SU gave him an honorary doctor of laws degree for his decades-long work in promoting the Haudenosaunee's Great Law of Peace and for protecting the land and ways of his threatened nation. Powless was a superb lacrosse player who took pride in being able to say he was the only man to knock down Jim Brown. He also was proud to have served in the US Navy alongside his brother, Everett Powless, on the USS *Randolph*.

Four Syracuse chancellors are buried in sprawling, parklike Oakwood Cemetery, which borders the southwest side of campus. Three of the four—James Roscoe Day (chancellor 1894-1922), Charles Wesley Flint (1922-36), and William Pratt Graham (1937-42)—served in succession and were honored with residence halls or a dining hall in proximity to their final resting place. Melvin A. Eggers (1971-91) was interred at Oakwood in 1994 and has a wing of the Maxwell School named in his memory.

In honor of Number 44, the university's zip code was changed from 13210 to 13244 during the week of November 11-18, 1985. Nearly three years later, on June 30, the university's telephone exchange number was switched to 443.

If there was one book in the mid-1980s that exotically glamorized "the excesses of young fashionable urbanites," it was Jay McInerney's stunning first novel, *Bright Lights, Big City*, which he wrote after studying under SU's Raymond Carver. Using an unusual second-person narrative, McInerney, then only twenty-nine, lifted literary hedonism to new levels by taking readers on a seedy, cocaine-fueled ride into New York City's trendy nightclubs and sexually feral living spaces.

When world-famous novelist John le Carré suggests your book is "the best book I have ever read on men and war in our time," there's a pretty good chance your name is going to be remembered. That's what happened to Syracuse grad Michael Herr after his Vietnam War novel *Dispatches* was released in 1977. *Dispatches* was based on Herr's frontline journalism as a correspondent for *Esquire* magazine. But Herr wasn't quite done with Vietnam. In 1979, he contributed to Francis Ford Coppola's *Apocalypse Now*. Less than a decade later, he cowrote the Academy Award-nominated screenplay for Stanley Kubrick's film *Full Metal Jacket*.

On July 28, 1927—just two months after achieving worldwide fame for becoming the first pilot to make a trans-Atlantic flight—aviator Charles Lindbergh flew into Syracuse. And he did so in the cockpit of the *Spirit of St. Louis*, the same single-engine plane he used to fly from Long Island to Paris, France. Following a parade in downtown Syracuse, he was taken to Archbold Stadium, where thousands gave him a hero's welcome.

It was initially known as the Gallo Opera House and later became CBS-TV Studio 52. Then, in 1977, two Syracuse fraternity brothers, Ian Schrager and Steve Rubell, converted the cavernous space at 254 West Fifty-Fourth Street (between Broadway and Eighth Avenue) into a nightclub. They called it Studio 54, and it immediately joined the ranks of legendary celebrity watering holes like the Crazy Horse Saloon in Paris or London's Hard Rock Café. Schrager and Rubell, both from Brooklyn, ultimately served prison time for Studio 54's celebrated evasion of taxes, but until its first closing in 1980, Studio 54 was the place to be seen and the elite discotheque most people couldn't get into.

Athletics are a huge part of Syracuse University's identity, but sports got off to a false start because of a reluctant chancellor. In an 1872 editorial in the *University Herald* headlined "Shall We Boat?" the writer argued that SU should have a crew team because Onondaga Lake made it a natural and "would be considered a gem of a sheet were it near one of our large boating colleges." But Chancellor Alexander Winchell was fearful athletics "would interfere with the fundamental purpose of the university." It would be years before sports would gain a foothold on campus.

Among the first to use and popularize the term "information superhighway," best-selling author and Maxwell School graduate Ken Auletta was hailed as one of the twentieth century's top one hundred business journalists. Books like *The Streets Were Paved with Gold* (1979), *Greed and Glory on Wall Street: The Fall of The House of Lehman* (1986), *Three Blind Mice: How the TV Networks Lost Their Way* (1991), *The Highwaymen: Warriors of the Information Superhighway* (1997), *World War 3.0: Microsoft and Its Enemies* (2001), and *Googled: The End of the World As We Know It* (2009) revealed Auletta could consistently make complex business stories approachable. But it was his prolific media presence in the *Village Voice*, *New York* magazine, the *New Yorker*, and the *New York Daily News* that showcased his greatest influence. At one point, *Columbia Journalism Review* anointed Auletta "America's premier media critic" and suggested "no other reporter has covered the new communications revolution as thoroughly as has Auletta."

In addition to hosting the largest on-campus crowd in college basketball history (35,642 attendees at the February 23, 2019, game against Duke), the Carrier Dome also holds the record for largest crowd ever to watch an indoor professional hockey game in the United States. In what was billed as the "Frozen Dome Classic" on November 22, 2014, 30,715 spectators attended an American Hockey League contest between the Syracuse Crunch and Utica Comets.

The Carrier Dome has been home to SU basketball since 1980. Previously, the Orange played in Manley Field House (1962-80), the Onondaga War Memorial (1951-52, 1955-62), the New York State Fairgrounds (1947-52), and Archbold Gymnasium (1908-47, 1952-55).

It didn't take long for Newhouse newspaper graduate and former *Daily Orange* sportswriter Eli Saslow to make his mark in journalism. In 2014, just a decade after graduating, he won the prestigious George Polk Award for National Reporting and a Pulitzer Prize for explanatory reporting for his series about Americans living on food stamps. A writer for the *Washington Post* and *ESPN the Magazine*, Saslow also was a Pulitzer finalist for feature writing in 2013, 2016, and 2017. In 2018, he jolted Americans with the release of his book *Rising Out of Hatred: The Awakening of a Former White Nationalist*. It was a work his own newspaper called a "disturbing look at the spread of that extremism—and how it is planted and cultivated in the fertile soil of American bigotry. Yet Saslow's vivid storytelling also conveys that during this period of deepening racial division, there is the possibility of redemption."

Coach Laurie Cox and an early Orange lacrosse team. Syracuse University Photograph Collection, University Archives.

Canadian-born and Harvard-educated Laurie Davidson Cox had made a name for himself as a leading American landscape architect by the time he arrived on the Syracuse campus as an associate professor at the School of Forestry in 1915. He spent thirty-two years at SU as a professor and department chair and had a lasting impact designing parks and trails in New York City, Los Angeles, and Vermont. He also left an indelible mark by launching the Orange lacrosse program. In his fourteen seasons as coach, SU posted a .722 winning percentage and won four national championships, earning the former Harvard player acknowledgment as the father of American college lacrosse.

Veteran sportswriter Jayson Stark never thought he'd top being on a Topps baseball card. But a year later, in 2018, the Syracuse University alumnus achieved another form of immortality when he was named winner of the J. G. Taylor Spink Award by the Baseball Writers' Association of America. That meant Stark's name will forever be listed on a display in the Baseball Hall of Fame in Cooperstown, New York. The honor came just a year after friend and former Newhouse classmate Bob Costas was voted into the hall's broadcasting wing. The Spink Award was a fitting tribute for Stark, who has spent four decades covering baseball for various outlets, including the *Philadelphia Inquirer*, ESPN.com, MLB.com, and the *Athletic*.

Some people only need one name. Madonna. Bono. Pele. Ronaldo. Sting. Pink. In the advertising world, it's Mower, the moniker announcing the $200 million marketing and public relations agency run by 1966 Syracuse graduate Eric Mower. An Arents Award winner in 2015, Mower joined Silverman Advertising in 1968, and during the next fifty years he oversaw naming progressions that produced Silverman and Mower (1975), Eric Mower + Associates (1980), and Mower in 2018. It's fitting simplicity for one of the nation's largest independent full-service brands directed by a legendary chair/CEO widely respected for his visionary marketing communications acumen.

When SU graduate John Wildhack was named Syracuse University's athletics director in July 2016, he told the assembled media "to say this is a dream job would be a significant understatement." That sentiment might've seemed unusual, since Wildhack was leaving a lucrative position at sports TV network ESPN where he served as the executive vice president for programming and production. But for John Wildhack, he was coming home. Wildhack's legacy at ESPN began shortly after its humble inception in September 1979. Having graduated from SU's Newhouse School in May 1980, Wildhack would fly up ESPN's corporate ladder from production assistant to producer (he helmed ESPN's first live regular-season college football game in 1984 and first live NFL game in 1987) and then ultimately into the cable giant's executive suite. Two of his largest contract deals included a nine-year agreement with the NBA and a twenty-year renewal with the NCAA's Southeastern Conference.

Not many can say they knew immediately when they'd seen the next big thing. But it happened for musician Felix Cavaliere in Stockholm, Sweden, where the New Jersey native was playing organ for Joey Dee and the Starliters during a concert tour in 1963. The Starliters had previously scored a major hit with the song "Peppermint Twist," and the band opening for them in Stockholm was an English group called the Beatles. When the Swedish crowd went wild for the act from Liverpool, Cavaliere knew he'd seen something very special.

John Wildhack (center) spent his entire career at ESPN before returning to his alma mater as the athletics director. Wildhack is shown with ESPN's Dick Vitale and Mike Patrick. Courtesy of John Wildhack.

Irma Kalish, a Phi Beta Kappa from Syracuse, was a rarity in Hollywood. She was a comedy writer and producer during the 1960s and 1970s, working—usually with her husband, Rocky—on the biggest TV shows, including *All in the Family*, *Bob Newhart*, *My Three Sons*, *Family Affair*, and *Good Times*. A major proponent of women in television, Kalish famously employed a personal adage that "God made man before women, but then you always do a first draft before you make a final masterpiece." Many of the Kalishes' more than three hundred scripts are considered landmark episodes, and the majority are held in SU's Special Collections Research Center. Irma Kalish was awarded an Arents Award in 1997.

Described as a "gruff, intense Brooklyn native and truck driver's son," Mel Elfin brought "a scrappy and aggressive jolt" to *Newsweek*'s Washington bureau during the height of the Vietnam War, civil rights movement, and Watergate scandal, enabling the magazine to successfully challenge *Time*'s standing as the country's preeminent newsweekly. Elfin honed his craft at SU, editing the *Daily Orange* and graduating Phi Beta Kappa in 1951 with a degree in journalism. After a twenty-year stint as *Newsweek*'s Washington bureau chief, Elfin left in 1985, and a year later became an editor at *U.S. News & World Report*. During his eleven years there, he oversaw the magazine's popular college rankings guide.

Sometimes the connection to Syracuse does not involve an alum or famous visitor but rather an Orange parent. That was the case with Newhouse School advisory board member Michael Lehman, whose two daughters, Carly and Lindsay, brought their father into contact with the Syracuse Bandier Program in Recording and Entertainment Industries. That connection caused Lehman to help legendary Allman Brothers founder and organist/guitarist Gregg Allman create the need-based Allman/Lehman Endowed Scholarship for music industry students in Newhouse's Bandier program. Lehman first began working with Allman in 2004 and over the next thirteen years was instrumental in booking tour dates, helping to produce four solo CDs, and the writing of Allman's best-selling book *My Cross to Bear*. Allman, who passed away from liver cancer in 2017, was a Grammy Lifetime Achievement Award winner.

If you've traveled into or out of Asia to visit must-see destinations in the past five years, chances are strong that 2008 Orange alumnus Ethan Lin had you on his radar. Or, more accurately, his computer screen. That's because the cofounder of the Hong Kong-based travel agency Klook helped create Asia's largest in-destination services booking platform and quickly raised more than $300 million in funding. Klook's estimated valuation of $1 billion in 2018 was considered notably impressive for a travel technology start-up conceived in 2014 when the partners were planning a trip to Nepal.

He started his journalism career as a sportswriter, but when World War II erupted in 1939, Drew Middleton began covering the conflict for the Associated Press. By September 1942, the *New York Times* had signed the 1935 Syracuse graduate, and a month later he landed with Allied troops on North Africa's Algerian coast. After visiting a Tunisian battlefield, Middleton's story in the *Times* included this powerful post-combat observation: "You can follow the path of those soldiers through the wheat as you could follow the path of Pickett's charge through the summer wheat at Gettysburg. History was made here only yesterday, but today only the wind blows over the rich grass and ruffles the wheat. And there is silence in the graveyards so far from home." For nearly fifty years, Middleton reported on wars and international conflicts, including his last battlefield appointment in the Falklands during 1982. Middleton, who interviewed luminaries like Winston Churchill and Dwight D. Eisenhower, was awarded the US Medal of Freedom and Syracuse's Arents Award (for Excellence in Journalism) in 1948.

It took nearly seventy years, but because of Lieutenant Colonel William Baker's efforts, a flawed 1906 presidential decision by Teddy Roosevelt was eventually overturned. The turn of the century case involved 167 African American enlisted men wrongly given dishonorable discharges for a murder in Brownsville, Texas. Baker, a Syracuse MBA alumnus, learned of the case and by successfully righting "a wrongful disgrace" was honored at the White House in 1973 with the Army's Legion of Merit and Pace Award (for meritorious service).

For Rob Light, one of Hollywood's longtime music visionaries, the smoke-filled Bottom Line nightclub was where it all started. It was August 15, 1975, and after Bruce Springsteen finished playing his set, Light knew his calling had announced itself: the music business. Light went from running University Union concerts in the late 1970s to more than thirty years of managing, directing, and influencing the world's music scene. Guiding major acts like Barbra Streisand, Fleetwood Mac, AC/DC, Britney Spears, Bruce Springsteen, the Eagles, and One Direction, Light would rise through the music industry's ranks to run Creative Artists Agency's worldwide music business while serving the Rock and Roll Hall of Fame as one of its board members.

He taught at Syracuse for only one year, but in 1926, Australian H. Duncan Hall, a visiting professor of international relations in the Maxwell School, proposed a student model assembly that mirrored the recently created League of Nations. Maxwell dean William Mosher supported the concept, and during April 29-30, 1927, eleven upstate New York colleges sent seventy-four delegates, representing eighteen nations, to meet at SU's Slocum Hall. From that simple idea (born in a Maxwell faculty meeting focused on global citizenship), Syracuse can claim to have created the Model United Nations, an educational simulation famous for hosting more than five thousand international students annually.

In 1906, there were reportedly only seventy-five female scientists employed by academic institutions in all of America. One of them was zoologist Cornelia Clapp, among the first women to receive a PhB, which she earned at Syracuse in 1888. A graduate of what is now Mount Holyoke College in 1871, Clapp studied at MIT, Williams College, and Woods Hole Marine Biological Laboratory in the 1880s before taking exams at Syracuse for her PhB and PhD. On completing her doctoral work at SU, Clapp's dissertation on toadfish was published in the *Journal of Morphology*. Mount Holyoke named its biology building the Cornelia Clapp Laboratory in 1924.

A lifetime supporter of Syracuse, Pittsburgh Pirates CEO and chair Doug Danforth graduated from SU in 1947 with a degree in engineering, and he spent the majority of his professional career in electronics. During the 1980s, when Danforth was CEO and chair of Westinghouse, he successfully kept out-of-state investors from buying Major League Baseball's Pirates and moving Westinghouse's hometown team out of Pennsylvania. His legacy lives on at Syracuse through his endowment that created the Douglas D. Danforth Dean of the College of Engineering and Computer Science.

A self-described radio buff, Allen Smith served as the announcer at Archbold Stadium for forty-six years. His first public address gig came during a 77-0 SU victory against Hobart College in 1929, which also happened to be the first night football game at the stadium. Smith continued announcing games through the 1977 season, missing only the 1940-42 campaigns while serving in World War II. He also worked as an electrical engineering instructor at SU.

Larry Kramer once worked part time at Cosmos on Marshall Street making pizzas. But his full-time love was journalism, and during a five-decade career he held positions as a stringer at the Associated Press, editor at the *Washington Post*, founder and CEO of the company MarketWatch, publisher of *USA Today* (long America's largest-circulation newspaper), and CEO of financial news service TheStreet. Kramer left the *San Francisco Examiner* as executive editor in 1991, and by 1997 showed he was—according to the *New York Times*—one of the early print journalists to fully "understand that the power of the web lay in its ability to deliver immediate information." During the initial internet boom, Kramer created MarketWatch and in 2005 helped sell it to Dow Jones for more than $500 million.

As far as baby boomers are concerned, one of the greatest inventions ever might've been something 1977 Syracuse graduate John Sykes helped co-create for Viacom Media. The novel concept was MTV, the first-ever 24-7 cable music video channel, which launched August 1, 1981. With the words "Ladies and Gentlemen, rock and roll" (announced over footage of the space shuttle Columbia's launch countdown), MTV went live. The first music video? The Buggles' quirky new wave song *Video Killed the Radio Star*. For Sykes, who went from SU's Newhouse School to CBS Records, MTV's footprint was often like their astronaut on the moon imagery. Historic.

On the grounds of the SUNY College of Environmental Science and Forestry stands a tall oak tree known as the Robin Hood Oak. Around 1926, Syracuse professor Nelson C. Brown returned from England's Sherwood Forest with an acorn from the famous Major Oak and planted it near Bray Hill. Nearly a century later, it provides the SUNY-ESF campus with a link to Great Britain.

Author. Poet. Disability activist. Lover of guide dogs. Translator of ancient and modern Finnish literature. Syracuse professor. Steve Kuusisto easily could star in one of those "most interesting man in the world" beer commercials. His books *Planet of the Blind*, *Eavesdropping: A Memoir of Blindness and Listening*, and *Have Dog, Will Travel* are critically acclaimed texts dealing with the harsh realities of an individual who saw only "colors and torn geometries." Kuusisto's global commitment to equality for those with vision disabilities led the *New York Times* to call *Planet of the Blind* one of the notable books of 1998.

Founded in 1943 by Chancellor William Pearson Tolley, Syracuse University Press has become one of the leading publishers in Middle East studies, Irish studies, television and popular culture, peace and conflict resolution, and books about the history of New York State. The press, which celebrated its seventy-fifth anniversary in 2018, regularly publishes books of academic importance and general interest, often to critical acclaim. It has received multiple PROSE awards and grants from the National Endowment for the Humanities for special publishing projects, and was the publisher of the 2017 Robert

Syracuse professor and noted author Steve Kuusisto wrote frequently about his visual impairment and his guide dogs. © Marion Ettlinger.

Penn Warren Award-winning author Liza Wieland's novel *Land of Enchantment*.

One of the most influential people associated with the Olympics never competed in them. David D'Alessandro, a 1972 graduate of Utica College (then an extension of SU), was CEO of global sponsor John Hancock in 1999 when investigative journalism revealed International Olympic Committee members had accepted bribes from the Salt Lake City Organizing Committee. As the corruption scandal grew, D'Alessandro courageously threatened that John Hancock would quit the Olympics as a sponsor if changes weren't made. D'Alessandro's conviction forced numerous ethical reforms reshaping the Olympics for years to come.

If legendary filmmaker (and Syracuse grad) Albert Maysles, working with his brother David, had made only the infamous Rolling Stones documentary *Gimme Shelter* and nothing else, his name would stand out in the annals of great counterculturist cinema. But the Maysles brothers also filmed the Beatles' inaugural arrival in the United States in 1964 before creating more than twenty-five other major works. *Gimme Shelter*'s early 1970s fame was largely enhanced because the film featured an actual murder during the Stones' Altamount Free Concert in December 1969. The Maysles brothers were also one of the first film production companies to hire future *Star Wars* and *Indiana Jones* legend George Lucas.

For moviegoers, Diane Nelson's superhero resume is filled with plenty of Pow! Zap! and Bam! In a spectacular twenty-five-plus-year career in Hollywood, the 1989 Syracuse graduate supervised numerous aspects for movies such as *Wonder*

Woman, *Superman*, *Batman*, *Super Girl*, *The Flash*, *Justice League*, and *The Hobbit*. Along the way, the 2017 Arents Award winner also worked closely with author J. K. Rowling to ensure the cinematic development of Rowling's seven *Harry Potter* books remained consistent with the author's vision for her characters. In the process, the Potter movies and their associated merchandise grossed more than $14 billion worldwide.

The first Hispanic individual to serve in the Georgia State Senate was Sam Zamarripa, a Mexican American politician who received his MPA in public policy from SU's Maxwell School and went on to represent Georgia's Thirty-Sixth District (eastern Fulton County) for two terms. He also became secretary of the State Economic Development Committee and worked extensively on US immigration policy. In 2017, his first novel, *The Spectacle of Let: The Oliet and Obit*, was published by Floricanto Press, an influential publisher of books dedicated to enhancing Latino/Latina culture.

Few families have enjoyed a stronger connection to Syracuse University than the Kelley family. In 1913, Paul W. Kelley graduated from the College of Law, starting a tradition that has seen more than twenty family members follow in his footsteps. They include children, grandchildren, great grandchildren, cousins, and nieces.

Vera Farmiga won a Kennedy Center American College Theater Award for her performance in *The Seagull* during her senior year at Syracuse in 1995. It would be a harbinger of good things, as Farmiga went on to earn an Academy Award

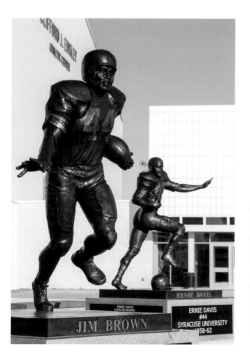

SU football players Jim Brown, Ernie Davis, and Floyd Little were immortalized with statues at the 44 Plaza near the Ensley indoor practice facility. © Syracuse University. Photo by Stephen Sartori.

nomination for Best Supporting Actress in the 2009 film *Up in the Air* and an Emmy nomination for Outstanding Lead Actress in a Drama Series for *Bates Motel* four years later. Farmiga has appeared in more than forty movies, including *The Conjuring*, *The Departed*, *Safe House*, and *Godzilla: King of the Monsters*.

US Army Lieutenant Colonel Tara Carr gained national attention as a contestant during CBS-TV's 2017 *The Amazing Race* when she and TV partner Tony Covino of the Boston Police finished second overall. The next year, the 2001 Syracuse alumna proceeded to make the finals for the 2018 Ms. Veteran America competition in Hollywood, California. As part of Carr's involvement with the pageant, the Afghanistan war veteran actively fundraised for Final Salute, a charitable organization dedicated to helping homeless female veterans and their children.

In 2008, Molly Corbett Broad, a Phi Beta Kappa Syracuse graduate, was named the first female president of the American Council on Education (which had been established ninety years earlier in 1918). For the next nine years, Broad pushed America's college presidents to embrace innovative and technological changes such as massive open online courses, or MOOCs. In 1997, she became the first woman to serve as president of America's oldest public university, the University of North Carolina's seventeen-campus system. From 1985 to 1992 she held several positions in Arizona's three-campus university system, including that of CEO, and from 1992 to 1997 she held several executive positions within the California State University system. Her academic career started as an SU student and fourteen-year administrator at her alma mater, where she earned an economics degree from Maxwell in 1962.

When Patricia Battin received the 1999 National Humanities Medal from President Bill Clinton and First Lady Hillary Rodham Clinton, she had good reason to celebrate. Battin, who earned her master's degree in library science from SU in 1967, was honored for leading the Commission on Preservation and Access, a national program designed to protect America's written-word heritage. Battin played a key role in the Council on Library Resources' 1987 commitment to "develop ways to preserve millions of volumes of decaying, archived materials in university and college libraries." Her 1988 Congressional testimony led to a twenty-year funding program provided by the National Endowment for the Humanities.

Professor Zhen Ma's lab in the Syracuse Biomaterials Institute in Bowne Hall is a special place—a place where he and his team of scientists are attempting to grow human hearts from real heart cells in petri dishes. These cardiomyocytes, engineered from human stem cells, are finicky. But Ma, whose biophotonics PhD dissertation at Clemson University focused on heart physiology and stem cell biology, has long believed he could build and then use "optics instruments to study biological questions." The majority of Ma's SU research takes place in the System Tissue Engineering & Morphogenesis Lab, which has been set up to better understand congenital heart disease in developing fetuses. Heart disease affects more than forty thousand infants annually and represents the most common birth defect in the United States. The engineering and biochemical challenge is getting model heart cells to grow so Ma's team can study genetic mutations and heart malfunctions. Ma clearly is committed to fixing broken hearts.

The Syracuse University Board of Trustees unanimously established a precedent in November 2018 when they appointed 1973 alumna Kathleen Walters as SU's first woman chair elect. An executive vice president of Georgia-Pacific and president of the company's consumer products group, Walters succeeded Steve W. Barnes as chair in May 2019. Walters previously held leadership positions in Europe and North America for Scott Paper, Kimberly-Clark, and SAPPI Fine Paper North America. She is married to Orange classmate Stan Walters, who played professional football for the Cincinnati Bengals and Philadelphia Eagles from 1972 to 1983, and appeared in Super Bowl XV.

In the mid-1980s, SU alumnus Richard Seth Hayden oversaw the restoration of the Statue of Liberty. And nearly four decades later, four other alumni were involved in the building of a museum on Liberty Island in New York Harbor. The museum, which includes the statue's original torch, was designed by Bruce Fowle and built by the Phelps Construction Group, which was founded by 1981 SU graduates Douglas Phelps and Frank Salerno and 1997 graduate Jeffrey Rainforth. "This landmark project is just another place a few proud Orangemen have dug their heels into the grounds of history," Rainforth told the Daily Orange.

Dirt for dollars. Syracuse's Brandon Steiner once sold Yankee Stadium basepath dirt as one of the offerings available from his multimillion-dollar sports memorabilia company, Steiner Sports. Steiner's acumen for autographs and authenticated sports items (helmets, jerseys, pucks, and lockers) made him what Newsday called "one of the most innovative, influential figures in the history of sports memorabilia." For more than thirty years, Steiner, a 1981 graduate of SU's Whitman School, has maintained relationships with big-name teams plus thousands of athletes, bringing them and their avid fans together via signed collectibles.

Moviegoers of varying ages and generations are likely familiar with the 1941 Walt Disney animated movie Dumbo or Disney's 2019 live-action feature film featuring Michael Keaton and Danny DeVito. Perhaps they read Disney's Little Golden Book version of Dumbo that featured a flying elephant with massive ears. What they may not have known was that Helen Aberson, a 1929 graduate of Syracuse's School of Speech had collaborated with future husband Harold Pearl to write the famous children's story. Or that Aberson wasn't the only SU grad involved with the original cartoon pachyderm. Artist Helen Durney, a 1927 SU alumna, drew the first images of Dumbo for Aberson and Pearl's book. While the two Syracuse women made virtually nothing from their creativity, Disney biographers have suggested Dumbo's success saved Disney, then a "small struggling company from financial ruin."

Major General Peggy Combs began her distinguished military career at Syracuse University as a cadet in the Army ROTC Stalwart Battalion. Upon graduation in 1985, the biology major was commissioned as a second lieutenant and built a notable career, eventually becoming the first female commanding general of Fort Knox and only the eleventh commanding general of the US Army Cadet Command. She has earned the Distinguished Service Medal, the Army's Legion of Merit, a Bronze Star, the Iraq Campaign Medal, the Parachutist Badge, and the Air Assault Badge. She also overhauled and relaunched a Prevention of Sexual Harassment training program throughout the entire Cadet Command and pioneered the first Sexual Assault Review Board in Fort Knox's history. That effort served as a model for the entire US Army.

Supercalifragilisticexpealidocious, the funny-sounding, nonsensical word popularized in the 1964 film Mary Poppins, has Orange origins. Although the Disney movie's songwriters, Richard and Robert Sherman, are credited with concocting the fourteen-syllable word, which means "extremely good and wonderful," the Oxford English Dictionary traces its birth to a March 10, 1931, column by Helen Herman in the student newspaper then known as the Syracuse Daily Orange. In a story, headlined "A-muse-ings," Herman created a similar-sounding word spelled supercaliflawjalisticexpialadoshus. According to the dictionary's editors, this is the earliest known written record of the word. It would become part of the pop culture lexicon shortly after it was first sung on screen by Julie Andrews and Dick Van Dyke, but its etymology can be traced to an SU student having some fun with the language during the Great Depression.

13 SU and the Salt City

A Long and Special Bond

From the top of the SU campus, one can see the City of Syracuse skyline and Onondaga Lake beyond. © Syracuse University. Photo by Stephen Sartori.

In 1868, two years before the founding of Syracuse University, author Charles Dickens visited the Salt City to give a reading of two of his most famous works—*A Christmas Carol* and *The Pickwick Papers*. After having experienced cosmopolitan cities such as London, Boston, New York, and Philadelphia, the British literary giant wrote that Syracuse was "the most wonderful, out-of-the-world place, which looks like it had begun to be built yesterday and (was) going to be imperfectly knocked together with a nail or two the day after tomorrow."

Dickens's observations were spot-on because the post-Civil War era Syracuse he observed was a bustling boomtown of 43,000 undergoing a dramatic growth spurt that would see its population increase fivefold during the next eighty years. It was, if you will, a city of great expectations.

Nestled smack-dab in the center of New York State, it had established itself as a manufacturing and transportation hub, benefiting not only from the construction of the Erie Canal a half century earlier but also from the proliferation of railroads, which had greatly reduced the time required to transport people and goods. As a result, numerous industries sprouted there, including manufacturers of items as diverse as traffic lights and typewriters.

But despite this burgeoning prosperity at the time of Dickens's visit, Syracusans yearned for something more. "What gives to Oxford and Cambridge, England, to Edinburgh, Scotland, to New Haven, Connecticut, their most lustrous names abroad?" a local newspaper scribe pondered in print. "Their Universities. Syracuse has all the advantages: business, social and religious—let her add the educational and she adds to her reputation, her desirability."

The "educational" would be added in 1870, when the Methodist Episcopal Church and Syracuse joined forces to build a university on the Hill. It would prove a marvelous, though sometimes contentious, partnership. Their histories would become inextricably intertwined, as SU became the engine that drove the region's economy, and hundreds of thousands of students would come to regard the city as their home-away-from-home.

Many of them, particularly those from more temperate climes, would falsely believe that the Salt City nickname was given to Syracuse because of the copious amounts of sodium chloride needed to melt the ice and snow on roads and sidewalks during the region's infamous winters. In reality, the moniker owes its origins to the natural salt springs near Onondaga Lake, discovered first by members of the Onondaga Nation and later by French priest Simon Le Moyne while on a Jesuit mission in Central New York in 1654. The colonists saw a gold mine because salt was used to preserve food during prerefrigeration days. The mineral would be a major contributor to the Syracuse economy through the late nineteenth century.

Long before they were forced to negotiate treaties with European settlers—treaties that robbed them of much of their ancestral land—the Onondaga people inhabited the area now occupied by Syracuse and its surrounding communities. Known as the people of the Longhouse and the people of the hills, the Onondagas became part of the six-nation Haudenosaunee (or Iroquois) Confederacy. Hiawatha, or Ayawentha, was the chief credited with bringing about the "Great Peace" among the Onondagas, Oneidas, Senecas, Tuscaroras, Mohawks, and Cayugas long before Le Moyne's arrival.

It wouldn't be until 1825—nearly a half century after the United States declared its independence from Great Britain—that the Central New York village would become known as Syracuse. The name would derive from the ancient Greek city of Siracusa, which was founded in 734 BC on the Mediterranean island of Sicily and was later conquered by the Romans. During the United States' first decades, it was common for cities to take on names from the Greek and Roman empires. Salt City officials originally had applied for the name Corinth but were turned down because another New York State community had claimed that name. Local postmaster John Wilkinson then suggested Syracuse because, like the Sicilian city of the same name, the Onondaga community was hilly and faced water.

Given that few metropolitan areas in the United States pile up more snow than Syracuse, perhaps a name from a city closer to the arctic circle might have made more sense. Because of its location, Syracuse has to deal with the nasty combination of lake effect snow from Lake Ontario to the northwest, and nor'easters off the Atlantic Ocean. The result is an annual average snowfall of 124 inches, with the granddaddy of all Syracuse winter storms occurring in 1993, when a blizzard dumped 42.9 inches in just forty-eight hours.

The relationship between the university and its host city can be traced to rented downtown office space in the Myers Block building. Three years after its founding there, SU students, faculty, and administrators would move into the Hall of Languages—a building in a hayfield on a bluff overlooking the city. Over time, the campus would sprawl northward, down the Hill, and into the Marshall Street and South Crouse Avenue area, which remains a favorite hangout of students and locals alike.

Syracuse eventually would establish itself as a home to big-time collegiate sports, and the majority of the spectators attending contests at Archbold Stadium and Gymnasium, Manley Field House, and the Carrier Dome were residents of the community who viewed the Orange as their own.

The Salt City also became home to world-famous businesses, including the Franklin Automobile Company, Smith-Corona (typewriters), the Carrier Corporation (air conditioners), and Gustav Stickley's handmade furniture. General Electric located its main television manufacturing plant there, General Motors and Chrysler built cars there, and Crouse-Hinds became known for making traffic lights there. Because of its central location and its proximity to numerous farms, orchards, and vineyards, Syracuse was chosen as the permanent home to the New York State Fair in 1890. The two-week fair is among the biggest in the country, drawing more than one million people annually to partake of food, concerts, and exhibits.

Actors Tom Cruise and Richard Gere were born in Syracuse, as were Twilight Zone creator Rod Serling and Robert De Niro, an accomplished artist who became better known as the father of the Academy Award-winning actor of the same name. Future president Grover Cleveland spent his formative years in a Syracuse suburb and later became a member of SU's board of trustees. *Wizard of Oz* author L. Frank Baum grew up in nearby Chittenango.

The City of Syracuse's population peaked at 220,583 in 1950, but—like many Northeast and Midwest manufacturing cities—it experienced a decline in subsequent decades as major industries moved overseas. A 2015 census estimate put the city's population at 144,142. However, the four-county metropolitan area experienced growth of 1.4 percent, reaching an all-time high of 742,603 residents according to 2010 census figures, a testament to the high quality of living, natural beauty, and affordability of Central New York.

Today, Syracuse University remains the indisputable economic, educational, cultural, and sports hub of the region. And in the past two decades it has returned to its downtown roots, establishing academic buildings near Armory Square, a vibrant area of shops and restaurants in repurposed factories and historic warehouses—an area that now attracts young professionals as residents. Buses take SU students to and from downtown Syracuse along the Connective Corridor, as well as to and from Destiny USA, one of the nation's largest malls, less than four miles north of campus. In partnership with SU, the city has become a "living laboratory" for urban revitalization. And Orange fans from the Salt City continue to flock to the Dome, where they live and die by the fates of their beloved teams.

Syracuse may be different today from the bustling burg Dickens described in 1868. But in many respects, this snowy metropolis remains a place of great expectations, and nowhere is this more evident than at the great university that shares its name.

Afterword

My game plan was all set. I was going to take General Douglas MacArthur up on his offer to attend the United States Military Academy at West Point. Instead of bleeding Orange, I was going to become part of the long, gray line, and maybe even beat Colin Powell to the punch and become the first African American general to lead the Joint Chiefs of Staff.

But then I got a phone call that mid-May day in 1963 from my mom telling me that my hero, Ernie Davis, had just died. And like a shifty running back encountering a tackler he wasn't expecting, I decided to zig rather than zag. I adjusted on the fly, and changed the course of my life.

I immediately thought back to how Ernie and Syracuse football coach Ben Schwartzwalder had plowed their way through a blizzard to visit me in New Haven, Connecticut, a few weeks after I had dinner with General MacArthur. And how I told Ernie that I would attend Syracuse—not because I really meant it at the time, but because the first African American Heisman Trophy winner had talked my ear off for forty-five minutes in the restroom of the swank restaurant he and Ben had taken me to, and I couldn't wait to get back to our table and sink my teeth into surf and turf for the first time in my life. "You convinced me, Ernie," I told him. "I'm going to attend Syracuse. Now, let's go eat that steak and lobster before it gets cold."

The reality, though, is that I had, in fact, given Ernie my word that night. And what integrity does a man have if he's not true to his word? So when I learned of his death, I didn't hesitate picking up the phone and telling Ben I was coming to Syracuse.

Wound up being one of the best decisions of my life.

I showed up on campus in the summer of 1963, and although I would leave four years later to pursue careers as a Pro Football Hall of Fame running back for the Denver Broncos and as the owner of several West Coast automobile dealerships, Syracuse University never left me.

Like I tell people, I reside in Las Vegas, but SU is my home. SU is family. Thanks to the education I received and the people I met there, a hopeless kid from New Haven, Connecticut, was able to

Floyd Little. © Syracuse University. Photo by Stephen Sartori.

realize his dreams—and then some. I often think back fondly to the coaches, professors, classmates, and teammates who helped me become a better student, a better football player, a better person.

The older I get, the more I understand and appreciate just what an impact that place had on me.

And, to think, there was a point toward the end of my senior football season in 1966 that I was ready to quit and throw everything away. I had hurt my ankle late in the season, and it was frustrating because I just wasn't able to perform to the lofty standards I had set for myself. My numbers dropped off a bit as a result, and I was hearing some boos and taking some heat in the press. I became really frustrated and emotional. It reached a boiling point where I couldn't take it anymore, so I went to see Ben the Monday before our regular-season finale and told him I was going to quit. I expected him to read me the riot act, thought for sure he'd be yelling and screaming and telling me: "You can't quit. You're the captain of this team. What kind of leader are you?"

To my surprise, Ben remained calm, just heard me out, looked at me over his glasses, which he always wore about halfway down his nose. After I had spoken my piece, he reached into his desk drawer and pulled out the wings he had earned from parachuting behind enemy lines during the D-Day invasion in World War II.

"I want you to have these," he said. "I know all about tough times, and I understand what you're feeling. You have every right to feel the way you do. I just want you to do me a favor. I promised your mother that you would graduate, so I don't want you to quit. You don't have to come to practice. You don't have to come to any more games. You've earned that right because you've done as much for this program as any player I've ever had. But please don't quit school. Please don't break that promise I made to your mom."

I was stunned. His reaction caught me totally off guard. I shook Ben's hand, and when I walked out of that office, I was in tears. Tuesday came, and I still wasn't in a state of mind to play football, so I didn't show up. Same thing on Wednesday and Thursday and Friday. That Saturday—game day—I walked into the locker room at Archbold Stadium fully expecting I wouldn't be allowed to play because I hadn't practiced. Ben didn't say a word. He just pointed to the jersey in my locker. I put on my pads, cleats, and helmet, and when I ran onto the field with my teammates, I noticed the guys from my dorm had sewn together several sheets and made a big banner. It featured a drawing of me in my football uniform with the words: "Booth 3 Thanks Floyd."

I ran wild that day—scored four touchdowns—as we beat up on Florida State in my final game at old Archie.

The moral of that story is that even during one of my lowest moments everybody from my coach to my teammates to my dorm mates had stuck by me. That's what families do. They stick by you. And, like I said, SU is family to me.

In 2011, several years after I had sold off my car dealerships, I received a phone call from athletics director Daryl Gross asking me to come back as his assistant. He wanted me to mentor student-athletes. I couldn't say yes fast enough. A smart man once said you can't go home again. Well, I'm here to tell you that man was wrong.

Forty-four years—isn't that appropriate?—after I graduated from Syracuse University, I was back on campus, trying to give a little part of me to these young people the way so many had once given me a part of themselves. I filled my office at Manley Field House with photographs and memorabilia from my life, including pictures of me with prominent SU alumni, such as Vice President Joe Biden, famed running backs Jim Brown and Larry Csonka, and sportscasting legend Mike Tirico. I wanted the student-athletes who visited me to be inspired, to realize how my dreams came true, and how theirs could, too. I also put up a large sign in my office that read: "Success is a journey, not a destination." It was so cool that my journey had brought my life full circle.

Although I retired in 2016, I still receive texts from students I mentored. They usually simply say, "Thank you, Floyd. You were right. Syracuse University is a place where greatness is nurtured, where dreams come true." I can't tell you how good that makes me feel. That's part of the Syracuse tradition, too. Giving back some of what you were given.

A few years ago, Chancellor Kent Syverud called to tell me the university was going to reward me with an honorary doctorate. The news completely blindsided me. I was speechless, and oh-so grateful. This was every bit as rewarding, maybe even more so, than the many football accolades I received. After thanking him from the bottom of my heart and soul, I hung up the phone and began to cry. A person who once was told he was too dumb to attend college was going to receive a doctorate. Imagine that?

When I decided way back when to make good on my promise to Ernie Davis, I vowed I would try to live an exemplary life and not squander the opportunities he never was afforded because he had died so young. I thought about him every time I put on the Number 44 jersey that he and Jim Brown had made famous. During my freshman year, Ernie's mom, Marie Fleming, came to Archbold Stadium, where she donated her son's Heisman Trophy to the university during halftime of the Penn State game. Ben and athletics director Les Dye asked me to take part in the ceremony. It was such a humbling experience, such a thrill. One forty-four's legacy being passed on to the next.

It was another reminder that I was at the place I was meant to be. And although I may no longer reside there, it remains home. Like the hundreds of thousands who've attended Syracuse University, I will be Forever Orange.

—FLOYD LITTLE
Class of 1967

Acknowledgments

It took a campus, rather than a village, to make this book a reality, and the authors wish to gratefully acknowledge the numerous people who contributed. We couldn't have completed this massive undertaking without them. A tip of the cap to:

- Syracuse University chancellor and president Kent Syverud for believing in our concept from the start, and entrusting us with the awesome responsibility of researching and writing this history of our alma mater;
- University librarian and dean David Seaman, who provided archival support and office space, and spared no expense in procuring the compelling images that grace these pages;
- Pioneering astronaut Eileen Collins and football Hall of Famer Floyd Little for graciously taking the time to write the foreword and afterword, respectively;
- Senior SU vice president Matthew Ter Molen and associate vice president Lynn Vanderhoek for their support, trust, and sage suggestions;
- Indefatigable Syracuse University Archives librarian Nicole Westerdahl, who played an integral role in our research and served as the point person in tracking down hundreds of images;
- SU Press director Alice Randel Pfeiffer and editor-in-chief Suzanne Guiod, who, along with staffers Kelly Balenske, Meghan Cafarelli, Mona Hamlin, Kay Steinmetz, Fred Wellner, and Lynn Wilcox, and copy editors Elizabeth Myers and Sandi Mulconry, helped make sense of our words and images and brought order and life to our abundant manuscript;
- SU Photo and Imaging Center manager Steve Sartori, whose dynamic photographs (including the compelling cover shot of campus at twilight) greatly enhanced our ability to tell this multifaceted story;
- Falk College and Sport Management administrative assistant Margie Chetney, who truly was the glue that held everything together, coordinating chaotic schedules and resolving problems, big and small;
- And our wives, Barbara Burton and Beth Pitoniak, who served as sounding boards and provided unconditional support, particularly during the harried moments that inevitably occur during a years-long project such as this.

Others who helped make this book possible include Joan L. Adler, Mary Jo Alaimo, Marv Albert, Joseph Alfieri, Lonnie Allgood, Robert Andrews, Susan Ballard, Michael Barletta, Libby Barlow, Hadley Barrett, Michele Barrett, Scott Barrett, Fergus Barrie, Terri Battisto, Chari Bayanker, Laura Beck, Thomas C. Benzel, Lou Berends, Dave Bett, John Boccacino, Ed Bogucz, Craig Boise, Jon Booth, Mehrzad Boroujerdi, Lorraine Branham, Eboni Britt, Bill Brod, Duncan Brown, Monique Brown, Tom Brutsaert, Brett Burke, Andrew Burton, DeAnn Buss, Rocco Carbone, Lauren Carr, Melissa Collier, Rob Conrad, Dana L. Cooke, Souher Cosselman, Bob Costas, Jay Cox, Valerie Cramer, the Daily Orange, Pam Davis, Daylight Blue Media Group, Ellen de Graffenreid, Michaele DeHart, Bill DeLapp, John Desko, Alexa Diaz, Francis DiClemente, Emily K. Dittman, Nicolette Dobrowolski, Mike Dooling, Baylee Douglass, Sue Edson, Robert M. Enslin, Dolan Evanovich, Mary Alice Evans.

Kyle Fetterly, Thom Filicia, Jodi Finnegan, Michael Fisher, Jan Fleckenstein, Elisabeth Ford, Dan French, Ed Galvin, Getty Images, Cathy Goddard, Bea Gonzalez, Ed Gorham, Mike Grannis, Gabrielle Green, Oliver Grigg, Daryl Gross, Kathleen Haley, Geoff Hansen, Kate Hanson, J. Michael Haynie, Joe Heath, Bob Hill, Michelle Holme, Mark Holtzman, Jim Hopkins, Marcia Hough, Abby Houston, Cara Howe, Julie Hughes, Kim Infanti, Candace Campbell Jackson, Bob Jacobs, Eileen Jevis, John F. Kennedy Presidential Library and Museum, Chris Johnson, Cynthia Jones, Ken Kane, Kim Keenan-Kirkpatrick, Mary Kelly, Warren and Kimble, Dale King, Sean Kirst, Ross Oscar Knight, Carol Ko, Keith Kobland, Brian Konkol, Marie Kulikowsky, Dennis Kulis, Steve Kuusisto, Elise Lagerweij, Bob Lemke, Mary Ann Lemke, Jeffrey Levitt, Renee Gearhart Levy, Greg Linn, Stu Lisson, Alex Livadas, John Lobon, Joe Lore, Melinda Lothes, Wendy Loughlin, Simon Luethi, Meg Lynch, Oren Lyons.

Scott MacFarlane, Major League Baseball, Bob Mankoff, Amy Manley, Lawrence Mason Jr., Meg Mason, Elizabeth Mattes, Justin Mattingly, Janis Mayes, Larry McCallister, Isabel McCullough, Pamela Whiteley McLaughlin, Donovan McNabb, Don McPherson, Susie Mehringer, Eric Meola, Stephanie Burton Moldan, Connie Moore, Pete Moore, Chuck Morris, Joe Morris, Mike Morrison, Lucy Mulroney, Diane Lyden Murphy, Shannon Myers, Diana Napolitano, NASA, Larry Nayman, NBC Sports, NBC/Universal, New York Yankees, Lisa Nicholas, Denis Nolan, Ron Novack, Gabriel Nugent, Mary Ellen Nunes, Mary O'Brien, T. S. O'Connell, Jim O'Connor, Sam Ogozalek, Sean O'Keefe, Dylan Otts, Julia Oxman, Paramount Pictures, Jolynn Parker, Kelley Parker, Steve Parker, PARS International, Cathy Pescatore, Jason Poles, Bud Poliquin, Maren Guse Powell, Christine Praino, David Lake Prince, Lauren Pyland, John Quigley, Kevin Quinn, David Rezak, Liza Rochelson, Mick Rock, Mick Rock Studios, Holly Rodricks, J. D. Ross, Dara Royer, Jeffrey Rubin, Carlos Ruiz, Jennifer Russo, Elizabeth Ryan.

Peter Sala, Stephanie Salanger, Angela Sabetta, George Saunders, Sarah Scalese, Sari Schneider, Michael Scott, Julie Sharkey, Ed Shaw, Tadodaho Leon Shenandoah, Toby Silver, Roy Simmons III, Sony Music, Michael Speaks, Amy Speech, Sports Illustrated, Pat and Cathy Stark, Vanessa St. Oegger-Menn, Joseph Stoll, Syracuse.com, Syracuse 8 LLC, Syracuse New Times, Syracuse Post-Standard, Tracy Tajbl, Michael Tick, Mike Tirico, Ray Toenniessen, Nicole Topich, Topps Inc., Alexa Torrens, Megan Turner Travis, Lee S. Trimm, Gregg Tripoli, Kathryn Tunkel, Bert Ulrich, David Van Slyke, Chris Velardi, Elaine Wackerow, Don Waful, Tim Wasserman, Michael Wasylenko, Heather Allison Waters, Mike Waters, Laura Wellner, Barry L. Wells, John Western, Michele Wheatly, Matt Wheeler, Angela Williams, Ryan Williams, Charles Willie, Sarah Willie-LeBreton, John and Amy Wildhack, Jon Wolf, Taylor Wood, Glenn Wright, and Katherine Young.

Appendix

Syracuse Alumnae in the National Women's Hall of Fame

2011	Kathrine Switzer
2009	Karen DeCrow
1995	Eileen Collins
1994	Reverend Betty Bone Schiess
1993	Ruth Johnson Colvin
1990	Helen Barben
1983	Belva Lockwood

Commencement Speakers

2019	Mary C. Daly, head of Federal Reserve of San Francisco
2018	Kathrine Switzer, marathoner/activist
2017	Vernon E. Jordan Jr., civil rights activist
2016	Donald Newhouse, newspaper/magazine magnate
2015	Mary Karr, best-selling author
2014	David Remnick, editor of the *New Yorker*
2013	Nicholas Kristof, *New York Times* columnist
2012	Aaron Sorkin, award-winning screenwriter, producer, playwright
2011	J. Craig Venter, world-renowned scientist
2010	Jamie Dimon, chairman and CEO of JPMorgan Chase
2009	Joseph Biden, forty-seventh vice president of the United States
2008	Bob Woodruff, ABC News journalist
2007	Frank McCourt, author and Pulitzer Prize winner
2006	Billy Joel, singer/songwriter
2005	Jane Goodall, English primatologist and anthropologist
2004	Phylicia Rashad, American actress
2003	Bill Clinton, former president of the United States
2002	Rudolph Giuliani, former mayor of New York City
2001	Eileen Collins, NASA astronaut
2000	Ted Koppel, anchor of ABC News *Nightline*
1999	Charles E. Schumer, US senator from New York
1998	Robert Fulghum, author and philosopher
1997	Robert Coles, professor of social ethics, Harvard University
1996	Steve Kroft, *60 Minutes* correspondent and editor

1995	Donna Shalala, secretary of health and human services	1956	Joseph William Martin Jr., minority leader of the House of Representatives; Sam Rayburn, speaker of the House of Representatives
1994	Kurt Vonnegut, American novelist, short story writer, and literary critic		
1993	Oren R. Lyons, member of Onondaga Nation Council of Chiefs of the Six Nations of the Iroquois Confederacy	1955	William Averell Harriman, governor of New York
		1954	Harold Edward Stassen, director of the US Foreign Operations Administration
1992	Wendy Kopp, founder and president, Teach for America		
1991	John Naisbitt, futurist and author	1953	Robert Ten Broeck Stevens, secretary, Department of the Army
1990	William Safire, *New York Times* columnist	1952	Margaret Chase Smith, US senator from Maine (January); Frank Abrams, chairman of Standard Oil (May)
1989	Daniel Patrick Moynihan, US senator from New York		
1988	Malcolm Stevenson Forbes, chairman, CEO, and editor-in-chief, *Forbes* magazine	1951	Warren Robinson Austin, chief US delegate to the United Nations (June); Sir Gladwyn Jebb, permanent representative of the United Kingdom Delegation to the United Nations (January); Frank Pace Jr., secretary, Department of the Army (June)
1987	Thomas H. Kean, governor of New Jersey		
1986	Mario M. Cuomo, governor of New York		
1985	Stefan Lorant, photojournalist and author; Pearl Bailey, singer/songwriter		
1984	Dan Rather, anchor and managing editor of the *CBS Evening News*	1950	Eugene Garrett Bewkes, president of St. Lawrence University (January); James Edwin Webb, undersecretary of the US Department of State (June)
1983	Daniel J. Boorstin, director of the Library of Congress		
1982	Ted Koppel, anchor of ABC News *Nightline*	1949	Lester Bowles Pearson, secretary of state for External Affairs, Canada (June); Irving McNeil Ives, US senator from New York (January)
1981	Alexander M. Haig, secretary of state of the United States		
1980	Bill Moyers, PBS journalist and former White House press secretary		
1979	Rev. Timothy Healy, president of Georgetown University; Tom Brokaw, NBC *Today* coanchor	1948	William Pearson Tolley, chancellor of Syracuse University (February); James William Fulbright, US senator from Arkansas (June)
1978	William Safire, *New York Times* columnist	1947	Norman John Oswald Makin, ambassador to the United States from Australia (June); William Pearson Tolley, chancellor of Syracuse University (January); Carter Davidson, president of Union College (September)
1977	Hugh Carey, governor of New York; John C. Sawhill, president of New York University		
1976	Claiborne Pell, US senator from Rhode Island		
1975	Edward Brooke, US senator from Massachusetts	1946	Joseph Hurst Ball, US senator from Minnesota (April); Admiral Chester William Nimitz, US Navy (August)
1974	Soia Mentschikoff, dean of the University of Miami School of Law		
1973	Edward M. Kennedy, US senator from Massachusetts	1945	Charles Franklin Kettering, vice president and director of General Motors Corporation (April); William Pearson Tolley, chancellor of Syracuse University (August); James Phinney Baxter III, president of Williams College (December)
1972	Sol M. Linowitz, president of the National Urban League		
1971	Ramsey Clark, lawyer and political activist		
1970	Julian Bond, Georgia legislator; U Thant, United Nations secretary general		
1969	William F. Buckley Jr., American conservative author	1944	Samuel Paul Capen, chancellor of University of Buffalo (May); William Pearson Tolley, chancellor of Syracuse University (December)
1968	Walter Cronkite, *CBS Evening News* anchor		
1967	Barbara Ward, British economist	1943	Robert H. Jackson, justice of the US Supreme Court (May); Dixon Ryan Fox, president of Union College (August); Everett Needham Case, president of Colgate University (December)
1966	Nelson A. Rockefeller, governor of New York		
1965	Hubert H. Humphrey, thirty-eighth vice president of the United States		
1964	Terrence Edward Cawthorne, British surgeon and scientist	1942	Lord Halifax, British ambassador to the United States
1963	Sir Charles Percy Snow, British novelist and physicist; Adlai Ewing Stevenson, US representative to the United Nations	1941	Leonard Walter Brockington, executive secretary to the prime minister of Canada
		1940	Owen D. Young, founder of Radio Corporation of America
1962	William Pearson Tolley, chancellor of Syracuse University	1939	Arthur Hendrick Vandenberg, US senator from Michigan
1961	Stewart Lee Udall, US secretary of the interior	1938	Herbert Henry Lehman, governor of New York
1960	Gilbert Highet, professor of Latin language and literature, Columbia University	1937	Dorothy Thompson Lewis, American journalist and activist
		1936	Harold Glenn Moulton, president of the Brookings Institution
1959	Finla Goff Crawford, vice chancellor of Syracuse University	1935	Sir Josiah Stamp, director of the Bank of England and chairman of the London Midland and Scottish Railway
1958	Sir Leslie Knox Munro, president of the United Nations and New Zealand ambassador to the United States		
		1934	Harvey Cushing, professor at Yale University, School of Medicine
1957	John F. Kennedy, US senator from Massachusetts		
		1933	William Hartman Woodin, secretary of the treasury of the United States

1932	R. B. Bennett, premier of Canada
1931	George Woodward Wickersham, attorney general of the United States
1930	Frank Pierrepont Graves, president of the State University of New York; Franklin Delano Roosevelt, governor of New York
1929	Alanson B. Houghton, ambassador at the Court of St. James; Friedrich Wilhelm von Prittwitz und Gaffron, ambassador to the United States from Germany
1928	Harlan F. Stone, justice of the US Supreme Court
1927	Rev. Charles Clayton Morrison, liberal Christian activist (February); Henry Lewis Stimson, secretary of war, secretary of state of the United States (June); James Brown Scott, American lawyer and authority on international law (June)
1926	Sir Henry Worth Thornton, president of Canadian National Railways
1925	Rev. Frederick Franklin Shannon (February); Adna Wright Leonard, Methodist bishop of Buffalo (June)
1924	Frank Orren Lowden, former governor of Illinois (February); Julius Howland Barnes, president of the US Chamber of Commerce (June)
1923	Royal S. Copeland, US senator from New York
1922	Louis Marshall, corporate and constitutional lawyer, conservationist
1921	Elbert H. Gary, cofounder of US Steel
1920	John H. Finley, president of the University of the State of New York
1919	Col. George Harvey, editor of Harper's Weekly
1918	Rev. Dr. Charles Henry Parkhurst, clergyman and social reformer
1917	Rev. Bishop Edwin Holt Hughes, bishop in the Methodist Episcopal Church
1916	Rev. Bishop W. S. Lewis, bishop in China
1915	James Alexander Macdonald, editor of the Toronto Globe

1914	Rev. George Peck Eckman, religious author
1913	Rev. George Peck Eckman, religious author
1912	Rev. Bishop James Whitfield Bashford, bishop in the Methodist Episcopal Church
1911	William Renwick Riddell, justice of the Supreme Court of Canada
1910	Rev. Dr. Charles Carroll Albertson, American religious author
1909	George Edwin MacLean, president of the State University of Iowa
1908	Hamilton Wright Mabie, American essayist, editor, and critic
1907	Andrew Sloan Draper, US commissioner of education
1906	Rev. Samuel Parkes Cadman, founder of Federation Council of Churches in America
1905	Rev. James Monroe Buckley, editor of the New York Christian Advocate
1904	Rev. Robert Stuart McArthur, Baptist clergyman and orator
1903	Gen. O. O. Howard, commissioner of the Freedmen's Bureau, founder of Howard University
1902	Martin A. Knapp, chairman of the Interstate Commerce Commission
1901	William De Witt Hyde, president of Bowdoin College
1900	Bradford P. Raymond, president of Wesleyan University
1899	Henry King Carroll, professor of theology, Free Church College
1898	Henry Wade Rogers, president of Northwestern University
1897	Borden P. Bowne, professor at Boston University
1896	Rev. Charles J. Little, professor at Syracuse University
1895	Rev. Bishop Charles H. Fowler, Episcopal bishop from Minnesota
1894	Rev. James M. Buckley, editor of the New York Christian Advocate
1893	Stewart L. Woodford, US ambassador to Spain

Arents Award Winners

2018

Kevin Bell '74, H'16
Dr. Sharon Brangman '77
Emme '85
Joseph Strasser '53, G'58
Abdallah Yabroudi '78, G'79

2017

Thomas R. Coughlin '68, G'69
Daniel A. D'Aniello '68
Diane Nelson '89
Mary Spio '98

2016

Jim Brown '57
Ambassador James Cunningham '74

Robert Jarvik, MD '68, H'83
Arielle Tepper Madover '94

2015

Erica Branch-Ridley '87
Eric Mower '66, G'68
Donna Shalala G'70, H'87
Brandon Steiner '81

2014

Richard M. Jones '92, G'95, L'95
Angela Y. Robinson '78
Donald Schupak '64, L'66

2013

Taye Diggs '93
Carole Swid Eisner '58
Henry E. Grethel '54

Sid Lerner '53
George Saunders G'88

2012

Dennis P. Crowley '98
Thom Filicia '93
James Arthur Monk Sr. '80
Jane Werner Present '56

2011

Joann F. Alper '72
S. Richard Fedrizzi G'87
Oren R. Lyons '58, H'93
Sean C. O'Keefe G'78

2010

Suzanne C. de Passe '68
Brian P. McLane '69

Bill Viola '73, H'95
Karen B. Winnick '68

2009

Karen L. DeCrow L'72
Samuel V. Goekjian '52
Frank A. Langella '59
Donald G. McPherson '87
Joyce Carol Oates '60, H'00

2008

Shirley Jackson '40
Edwin London '49
Andrea Davis Pinkney '85
Daniel Present '55
William Ronan '34

2007

Lou Reed '64

2006

Gerald B. Cramer '52
David M. Crane G'80
Ali Khalif Galaydh G'69, G'72
Richard J. Gluckman '70, G'71
Ned Rifkin '72
Kathrine V. Switzer '68, G'72, H'18

2005

Joseph R. Biden Jr. L'68, H'09
Nicholas M. Donofrio G'71
Joyce Hergenhan '63
Ted Koppel '60, H'82
Albert Maysles '49
Michael T. Tirico '88

2004

Rev. Joseph C. Ehrmann Jr. '73
Carole Wolfe Korngold '57
Chancellor Emeritus Kenneth A. Shaw H'04
Mary Ann Shaw H'04
Kenneth R. Sparks '56, G'61, G'64
Martin J. Whitman '49, H'08

2003

Gil Cates '55, G'65
Nina V. Fedoroff '66
Ralph Ketcham G'56, H'99
Joseph O. Lampe '53, L'55, H'05

2002

Roger S. Berkowitz '74
Walter H. Diamond '34
Warren L. Kimble '57
Roberta Chamberlain Schofield '57, G'77
Marilyn Smith Tennity '42

2001

Lansing G. Baker G'64, G'72
Walter D. Broadnax G'75
Robert Q. Costas '74
Bruce S. Fowle '60
Elsa Reichmanis '72, G'75
Aaron Sorkin '83

2000

James A. Boeheim '66, G'73
Renée Schine Crown '50, H'84
Robert Fagenson '70
Antje B. Lemke G'56
Charles V. Willie G'57, H'92

1999

Lynn Ahrens '70
Bradley J. Anderson '51
Molly Corbett Broad '62, H'09
Bernard J. Wohl '51

1998

M. Elizabeth Carnegie G'52, H'98
David Falk '72
Marty Glickman '39
Alan Rafkin '50

1997

Irma Kalish '44
F. Story Musgrave '58, G'85
Arthur Rock '48
William L. Safire '51, H'78

1996

Eileen M. Collins '78, H'01
Ruth J. Colvin '59, H'84
Marshall Gelfand '50
Vanessa L. Williams '85

1995

Richard W. Clark '51

1994

Martin N. Bandier '62
David Bing '66, H'06
JoAnn Heffernan Heisen '72

1993

George W. Campbell Jr. G'77, H'03
Mary Schmidt Campbell G'73, G'80, G'82
John A. Couri '63, H'08
Marvin K. Lender '63

1992

Stephen F. Kroft '67
Susan C. Penny '70
Robert S. Rigolosi '57
Anthony Y. C. Yeh '49

1991

L. Ross Love '68
Joan Lines Oates '50
J. Robert Tomlinson '41

1990

Diane Camper '68
Theresa Howard-Carter '50
Eleanor Ludwig '43, G'45
Albert Murray '30
Richard C. Pietrafesa '50

1989

H. Peter Guber '64
Luise Meyers Kaish '46, G'51
John L. Martin '59, L'62

1988

Candace Bahouth '68
Douglas D. Danforth '47, H'99
Robert S. Phillips '60, G'63
Peter W. Yenawine '69

1987

George H. Babikian '53
Robin R. Burns-McNeill '74
Anthony C. Chevins '47
William J. Smith '50

1986

Robert A. Beck '50

Vincent H. Cohen '57, L'60
Michael O. Sawyer '41, G'47, G'52

1985

Alfonse D'Amato '59, L'61
Richard S. Hayden '60
Betsey Johnson '64
Richard Stockton '64

1984

H. Douglas Barclay L'61, H'98
Mel Elfin '51
Robert Pietrafesa '47
Maxine D. Singer '33

1983

Stella Biercuk Blum '38
William J. Brodsky '65, L'68
Sidney L. Krawitz '33
Tarky J. Lombardi '51, L'54, H'87

1982

P. Gordon Gould '27
Eva Holmes Lee '41
George A. Sisson '42, G'45
Lewis Slingerland '27

1981

Mark A. Clements '36
Carlisle S. Floyd Jr. '46, G'49, H'97
Athena C. Kouray '41
Christian X. Kouray '41, G'43

1980

James A. Britton '25
Lora S. Flanagan '50
Robert B. Menschel '51, H'91
Chester Soling '54

1979

Louis F. Bantle '51, H'94
Charles E. Boddie '33
Gerald Stiller '50

1978

Robert W. Cornell '28
Seymour M. Leslie '45
L. Douglas Meredith '26, G'27

Dorothy E. Rowe '38

1977

Susan Reid Greene '62
Gerald J. Leider '53
Harry A. Devlin '39
Dorothy Wende Devlin '40

1976

Floyd D. Little '67
Nancy Harvey Steorts '59
Lee J. Topp '51

1975

Horace J. Landry '34, G'36
Rosemary S. Nesbitt '47
Lawrence R. White '48

1974

Phyllis Hickman Demong '40
Robert T. Schuler '52
Demetria Taylor '24

1973

Arthur J. Barry '32, G'36
Marjorie Reeve Elliot '15
Howard F. Miller '42

1972

Elizabeth Barstow Alton '29
Albert W. Brown '49, G'52
Kenneth E. Buhrmaster '37

1971

Shirley Martine Burdick Clayton '50
John D. MacDonald '38
Bernard M. Singer '27

1970

Louis R. Bruce '30
Julia Chase Fuller '43
John A. Olver '39, G'42

1969

Franklyn S. Barry '31, G'41, G'56
Donald S. MacNaughton '39, L'48, H'78
Cornelia T. Snell '19

1968

Robert W. Cutler '28
Delmont K. Pfeffer '23
Madeline J. Thornton '23

1967

Jean DuBois Galkin '48
Sheldon Leonard '29
Joseph H. Murphy '37, G'39, L'40

1966

James F. Bunting '27
Helen R. Hagan '33, G'36
Millard G. Roberts '39

1965

Donald J. Grout '23
J.G. Fred Hiss '15, G'17

1964

Frances Clark Dietzold '20
Samuel Rosen '21

1963

Lewis P. Andreas '21
Mary C. Egan '44
Frederick G. Vosburgh '25

1962

Margaret Long Arnold '34
Norris O. Johnson '27
Eric W. Will '18

1961

William G. Atwell '86
Harvey O. Banks '30
Marion Clayton Link '29

1960

Donald Q. Faragher '30
J. Burch McMorran '22
Eloise Andrews Woolever '09

1959

Vernon L. deTar '27
Eric H. Faigle '28, G'30, H'68

Clare Brown Williams '31

1958

Darius A. Davis '07
Elizabeth Sweeney Herbert '42, G'45
Lester O. Schriver '17

1957

Walter S. Bourlier '05
Pyo Wook Han '42
Agnes E. Law '15

1956

Florence Kerins Murray '38
D. Kenneth Sargent '27
Clarence L. Van Schaick '29

1955

Leslie A. Bryan '24, G'24, L'39
June Buchanan '13
Malcolm P. Ferguson '18, H'55

1954

Gertrude Skerritt Brooks '13
Edward C. Reifenstein '04
Chancellor Emeritus William Pearson Tolley '22, G'24, H'69

1953

Mary Ames Becker '28
Martha Keefe Phillips '94
Carlton F. Sharpe '26

1952

Evelyn Millis Duvall '27
Edgar B. Ingraham '12
William D. Lewis '92

1951

T. Frank Dolan Jr. L'16
Helene W. Hartley '20
Gordon D. Hoople '15, G'19, H'67

1950

Harry J. Carman '09
Clara Bannister Congdon '75
Florence Bailey Crouse '99

1949

Hilda Grossman Taylor '12
Harry E. Weston '21
Nelia Gardner White '15

1948

LeGrande A. Diller '23
Welthy Honsinger Fisher '00, H'65
Drew Middleton '41, H'63

1947

T. Aaron Levy '95
Harry L. Upperman '22, G'28

1946

J. Roscoe Drummond '24, H'55
Winifred Fisher '15

1945

Neal Brewster '02
Ernest H. Hawkins '07
Katharine Sibley '36

1944

J. Winifred Hughes '14, H'58
Edmund H. Lewis '09, H'37

1943

Carl L. Bausch '09, H'56
DeWitt T. MacKenzie '07
Marguerite W. Wriston '18, G'28

1942

Cora Dodson Graham '94
William P. Graham '93

1941

Lurelle Van Arsdale Guild '20
Cecilia B. Martin '26
J. Robert Rubin '04

1940

Frank J. O'Neill '04
Anna V. Rice '04
Herman G. Weiskotten '06, G'09, H'51

1939

William M. Smallwood '96
Dorothy C. Thompson '14
John Shaw Young '24

Buildings of Syracuse University

2020	Institute for Veterans and Military Families
2019	Barnes Center at the Arch
2015	Ensley Athletic Center
2014	Dineen Hall
2013	Outdoor Education Center and Challenge Course
2012	Syracuse University Libraries Facility
2010	2331 South Salina Street
2010	1320 and 1330 Jamesville Ave
2009	SyracuseCoE (Syracuse Center of Excellence)
2009	Green Data Center
2009	Ernie Davis Hall
2009	Carmelo K. Anthony Basketball Center
2008	Life Sciences Complex
2007	Newhouse Communications Center III
2007	808 Nottingham Rd
2006	810 Nottingham Rd
2006	2610 South Salina St
2005	Nancy Cantor Warehouse
2005	Management Building, Whitman School of Management
2005	900 Block East Genesee St
2003	Winnick Hillel Center for Jewish Life
2000	Tennity Ice Skating Pavilion
1999	Menschel Media Center
1998	MacNaughton Hall
1997	Walnut Hall
1997	Joseph and Shawn Lampe Athletics Complex
1995	Roy D. Simmons Sr. Coaches Center
1993	Melvin A. Eggers Hall
1991	Pole Barn
1991	Iocolano-Petty Football Wing

1990	Dorothea Ilgen Shaffer Art Building		1959	Vincent Apartments
1990	Ann and Alfred Goldstein Student Center		1959	Skyhall I
1989	Minnowbrook Conference Center, Blue Mountain Lake		1959	Nuclear Reactor
1989	Lora and Alfred Flanagan Gymnasium		1959	M-17 Skytop
1988	Paul Greenberg House, Washington, DC		1959	Hospital of the Good Shepherd Rehabilitation Center (804 University Avenue)
1988	Institute for Sensory Research			
1988	Center for Science and Technology		1959	Continental Can
1985	Sheraton Syracuse University Hotel and Conference Center		1958	Regent Theatre
1985	Hildegarde and J. Myer Schine Student Center		1958	Mount Olympus: Day Hall Dormitory for Women and Graham Dining Center
1983	Crouse-Hinds Hall			
1982	Hawkins Building		1957	Chapel House
1982	Comstock Art Facility		1956	Mount Olympus: Flint Hall Dormitory for Women
1982	Belfer Audio Laboratory and Archive		1956	Lubin Hall
1981	Marshall Square Mall		1955	William Lawyer Hinds Hall, Engineering Building 1
1980	John D. Archbold Theater		1955	Sherbrooke Apartments
1980	Carrier Dome		1955	Morris and Fannie Haft Co-operative Dormitory for Women
1977	Skybarn		1955	Crouse House
1974	Slocum Heights Apartments		1954	Watson Hall, Dormitory for Men
1974	Skytop Housing Complex Phase II		1954	Sagamore Conference Center, Raquette Lake
1974	International Living Center, now Oren Lyons Hall		1954	Minnowbrook Lodge, Blue Mountain Lake
1974	Faculty Center, now Goldstein Alumni and Faculty Center		1954	Marion Hall, Dormitory for Men
1973	Skytop Administrative Services Building		1954	Ernest I. White Hall
1973	Newhouse Communications Center II		1954	Engineering Building 2, basement and sub-basement
1973	Marshall Apartments		1953	Women's Building
1972	William B. Heroy Geology Laboratory		1953	Hoople Special Education Building
1972	Skytop Housing Complex Phase I		1952	Robert Shaw Dormitory for Women, Shaw Living/Learning Center
1972	Ruth Van Arsdale Henry Center and Health Services Building			
1972	Nursing School Building (until 2006), now 426 Ostrom Avenue		1952	Nursing School Building (until 1972)
			1952	Joe and Emily Lowe Art Center
1972	Ernest S. Bird Library		1950	New Steam Plant
1970	Slutzker Center		1949	Remington Rand
1970	Link Hall		1948	Ski Lodge, now Inn Complete
1969	Drumlins Country Club		1948	Pinebrook Conference Center, Upper Saranac Lake
1968	Brewster, Boland, Brockway Complex		1948	Physical Plant
1968	621 Skytop Rd		1947	Thompson Road campus
1967	Physics Building		1947	Quonseteria
1967	Merrill Hall		1946	University College
1966	Grant Auditorium		1946	M-0 and M-1 / Child Care Center
1966	Commissary		1946	Colonial Building (Triple Cities College in Endicott, New York)
1965	Lawrinson Dormitory for Men			
1965	Film Rental Center		1946	Bauhaus / Sculpture Studio
1964	Samuel I. Newhouse Communications Center I		1945	Nursing School Building (until 1952)
1964	Lubin House, New York		1944	Orange Publishing Company Building
1964	Haven Hall Dormitory for Women		1943	Washington Arms
1963	Syracuse University Florence		1943	Brewster House
1963	Booth Men's Dormitory		1937	SU College of Medicine (until 1950), now Weiskotten Hall
1963	Biological Research Building		1937	Maxwell Hall
1962	Kimmel Men's Dormitory		1937	James A. Ten Eyck Boat House, Onondaga Lake
1961	Huntington Beard Crouse Hall		1930	Recreation Hall for Nurses
1961	George Leroy Manley Field House		1930	Hendricks Chapel
1961	DellPlain Men's Dormitory		1927	Steam Plant
1961	Ambassador and Roosevelt Apartments purchased		1927	Lehman Hall
1960	Sadler Hall, Dormitory for Men		1926	Infirmary and Student Health Service (109, 111, and 113 Waverly Avenue)

1926	Hackett Hall
1919	Joseph Slocum College of Agriculture
1918	Greenhouse
1915	SU Hospital of the Good Shepherd, now Huntington Hall
1915	Chancellor's House
1914	Syracuse Dispensary, named Reid Hall in 1958
1914	Carriage House
1913	Photography Building
1912	University Bookstore
1910	University Farm
1908	Archbold Gymnasium
1907	Sims Hall, Dormitory for Men
1907	Machinery Hall
1907	Lyman Hall of Natural History
1907	Carnegie Library
1907	Bowne Hall of Chemistry
1907	Archbold Stadium
1905	Renwick Castle, Yates Castle
1904	Haven Hall, Dormitory for Women
1904	Crouse Mansion
1902	Lyman C. Smith College of Applied Sciences
1902	Chancellor Day's Residence (604 University Ave)
1900	Winchell Hall, Dormitory for Women
1898	University Block
1898	Esther Baker Steele Hall of Physics
1896	SU College of Medicine (until 1937), dedicated as Peck Hall in 1958
1895	Bastable Block
1892	Gymnasium (Old Gym, Women's Gymnasium)
1889	Von Ranke Library, now Tolley Humanities Building
1889	SU College of Medicine (until 1896)
1889	John Crouse College of Fine Arts
1887	Old Oval
1887	Holden Observatory
1873	Hall of Languages, College of Liberal Arts
1871	Myers Block

Significant Campus Spaces

2016	University Place Promenade, now Einhorn Family Walk
2010	Kenneth A. Shaw Quadrangle
2003	Orange Grove
1990	Place of Remembrance

Carrier Dome Concerts

Date	Show	Attendance
Sep. 23, 2017	Paul McCartney	36,200
Apr. 28, 2017	Travis Scott	9,777
Nov. 4, 2016	The 1975	4,025
Apr. 29, 2016	Chainsmokers	11,445

Date	Show	Attendance
Apr. 9, 2016	Luke Bryan	36,141
Apr. 24, 2015	50 Cent	8,820
Mar. 20, 2015	Billy Joel	36,594
Apr. 25, 2014	Zedd	7,439
Mar. 21, 2014	J. Cole	5,841
Nov. 11, 2013	Macklemore	9,354
Apr. 26, 2013	Kesha	7,680
Nov. 16, 2012	Zac Brown Band	23,987
Oct. 9, 2012	One World	22,366
Apr. 27, 2012	Kaskade	5,341
Feb. 2, 2012	Ludacris	6,963
Apr. 29, 2011	Kid Cudi	15,027
Apr. 30, 2010	Drake	9,065
Apr. 26, 2009	Ben Folds	3,285
Apr. 22, 2008	Fergie	3,620
Apr. 22, 2007	Ciara	1,993
Apr. 30, 2006	Kanye West	8,108
Mar. 25, 2006	Billy Joel	38,723
May 1, 2005	Snoop Dogg	4,407
Apr. 27, 2003	George Clinton/P-Funk	2,904
May 5, 2001	Billy Joel/Elton John	38,653
Dec. 11, 1998	Billy Joel	29,415
Apr. 17, 1998	Rolling Stones	27,220
Apr. 26, 1997	Garth Brooks	27,094
Apr. 25, 1997	Garth Brooks	26,511
Sep. 21, 1996	Neil Diamond	28,851
Dec. 8, 1994	Rolling Stones	36,730
Jun. 6, 1994	Pink Floyd	38,951
Nov. 13, 1993	Billy Joel	32,823
Nov. 12, 1993	Billy Joel	37,292
Jun. 19, 1993	Neil Diamond	30,492
Nov. 13, 1992	Bruce Springsteen	29,411
Sep. 26, 1992	Elton John	39,082
Jun. 7, 1992	Genesis	25,386
Jun. 2, 1992	Genesis	37,462
Sep. 28, 1991	Rod Stewart, Santana	23,785
Feb. 9, 1991	ZZ Top, Black Crowes	19,741
Nov. 24, 1990	New Kids on the Block	37,997
Apr. 7, 1990	Eric Clapton	35,548
Feb. 3, 1990	Billy Joel	36,168
Feb. 2, 1990	Billy Joel	35,871
Sep. 22, 1989	Rolling Stones	38,848
Sep. 21, 1989	Rolling Stones	35,723
Mar. 3, 1989	Bon Jovi, Skid Row	30,754
Nov. 26, 1988	Kenny Rogers, Dolly Parton, Oak Ridge Boys	13,414
Oct. 15, 1988	Van Halen	19,094
Oct. 9, 1987	U2, Los Lobos, Little Stephen	39,248
Oct. 3, 1987	Pink Floyd	34,710
Mar. 30, 1985	Prince	30,715

Date	Show	Attendance
Jan. 27, 1985	Bruce Springsteen	39,548
Jan. 26, 1985	Bruce Springsteen	39,667
Oct. 20, 1984	Grateful Dead	31,056
Mar. 3, 1984	Duran-Duran	12,930
Feb. 4, 1984	Police	42,058
Dec. 2, 1983	Genesis	40,681
Nov. 25, 1983	Kenny Rogers	18,936
Nov. 1, 1983	Bob Hope Show	11,466
Oct. 22, 1983	Grateful Dead	32,312
Sep. 6, 1993	David Bowie	28,820
Jul. 2, 1983	Willie Nelson	24,241
Apr. 2, 1983	Rush	19,470
Dec. 10, 1982	Who	45,000
Nov. 26, 1982	Kenny Rogers	21,681
Oct. 9, 1982	Van Halen	29,852
Sep. 24, 1982	Grateful Dead	21,938
Apr. 6, 1982	Police	32,396
Apr. 3, 1982	Foreigner	31,661
Feb. 12, 1982	Waylon Jennings	9,293
Dec. 11, 1981	Genesis	32,539
Nov. 28, 1981	Rolling Stones	43,051
Nov. 27, 1981	Rolling Stones	42,761
Oct. 9, 1981	Journey	28,963
Jul. 30, 1981	Styx	20,258
Apr. 25, 1981	Santana	15,213
Oct. 22, 1980	Republican Fund Raiser (Frank Sinatra)	11,350

Orangemen in the College Football Hall of Fame

2012	Art Monk
2009	Dick MacPherson
2008	Don McPherson
2001	Tim Green
1995	Jim Brown
1989	Larry Csonka
1984	Hugh "Duffy" Daugherty
1983	Floyd Little
1982	Ben Schwartzwalder
1979	Ernie Davis
1973	Vic Hanson
1969	Bud Wilkinson
1966	Lynn "Pappy" Waldorf
1959	Clarence "Biggie" Munn
1958	Tad Jones
1954	Joe Alexander
1951	Howard Jones
1951	Frank "Buck" O'Neill

Syracuse Football Retired Numbers and Jerseys

2019	Tim Green (72)
2018	Joe Morris (47)
2013	Donovan McNabb (5)
2013	Don McPherson (9)
2007	Larry Csonka (39)
2007	John Mackey (88)
2005	Number 44 (25 players)

Syracuse Basketball Retired Numbers and Jerseys

2018	Lawrence Moten (21)
2018	Dennis DuVal (22)
2015	Roosevelt Bouie (50)
2015	Louis Orr (55)
2013	Carmelo Anthony (15)
2009	Billy Gabor (17)
2008	Billy Owens (30)
2007	Rony Seikaly (4)
2006	Derrick Coleman (44)
2005	Wilmeth Sidat-Singh (19)
2003	Sherman Douglas (20)
1996	Pearl Washington (31)
1981	Vic Hanson (8)
1981	Dave Bing (22)

Syracuse Football Bowl Games

Date	Bowl	Location	Result
Dec. 28, 2018	Camping World Bowl	Orlando, FL	Syracuse 34, West Virginia 18
Dec. 27, 2013	Texas Bowl	Houston, TX	Syracuse 21, Minnesota 17
Dec. 29, 2012	Pinstripe Bowl	Bronx, NY	Syracuse 38, West Virginia 14
Dec. 30, 2010	Pinstripe Bowl	Bronx, NY	Syracuse 36, Kansas State 34
Dec. 21, 2004	Champs Sports Bowl	Orlando, FL	Georgia Tech 51, Syracuse 14
Dec. 29, 2001	Insight.com Bowl	Phoenix, AZ	Syracuse 26, Kansas State 3
Dec. 29, 1999	Music City Bowl	Nashville, TN	Syracuse 20, Kentucky 13
Jan. 2, 1999	Orange Bowl	Miami, FL	Florida 31, Syracuse 10

Syracuse Football Bowl Games (cont.)

Date	Bowl	Location	Result
Dec. 31, 1997	Fiesta Bowl	Tempe, AZ	Kansas State 35, Syracuse 18
Dec. 27, 1996	Liberty Bowl	Memphis, TN	Syracuse 30, Houston 17
Jan. 1, 1996	Gator Bowl	Jacksonville, FL	Syracuse 41, Clemson 0
Jan 1, 1993	Fiesta Bowl	Tempe, AZ	Syracuse 26, Colorado 22
Jan. 1, 1992	Hall of Fame Bowl	Tampa, FL	Syracuse 24, Ohio State 17
Dec. 25, 1990	Aloha Bowl	Honolulu, HI	Syracuse 28, Arizona 0
Dec. 30, 1989	Peach Bowl	Atlanta, GA	Syracuse 19, Georgia 18
Jan. 2, 1989	Hall of Fame Bowl	Tampa, FL	Syracuse 23, LSU 10
Jan. 1, 1988	Sugar Bowl	New Orleans, LA	Syracuse 16, Auburn 16
Dec. 21, 1985	Cherry Bowl	Pontiac, MI	Maryland 35, Syracuse 18
Dec. 15, 1979	Independence Bowl	Shreveport, LA	Syracuse 31, McNeese State 7
Dec. 31, 1966	Gator Bowl	Jacksonville, FL	Tennessee 18, Syracuse 12
Jan. 1, 1965	Sugar Bowl	New Orleans, LA	LSU 13, Syracuse 10
Dec. 16, 1961	Liberty Bowl	Philadelphia, PA	Syracuse 15, Miami (FL) 14
Jan. 1, 1960	Cotton Bowl	Dallas, TX	Syracuse 23, Texas 14
Jan. 1, 1959	Orange Bowl	Miami, FL	Oklahoma 21, Syracuse 6
Jan. 1, 1957	Cotton Bowl	Dallas, TX	TCU 28, Syracuse 27
Jan. 1, 1953	Orange Bowl	Miami, FL	Alabama 61, Syracuse 6

Bibliography

Newspapers and News Sources

Associated Press
Bird Library
Boston Globe
Central New York Sports Magazine
Chicago Tribune
Daily Orange
Essence
Finger Lakes Times
Getty Images
Hartford Current
Los Angeles Times
MLB.com
Modern Times
National Aeronautics and Space Administration
National Collegiate Athletic Association
National Women's Hall of Fame
New York Daily News
New Yorker
New York Times
Newsday
Newsweek
O, *The Oprah Magazine*
Onondaga Historical Association
Parade
People
Philadelphia Daily News
Rochester Business Journal
Rochester Democrat and Chronicle
Rochester Times-Union
Sport
Sports Illustrated
Star
Syracuse.com
Syracuse Herald-American
Syracuse Herald-Journal
Syracuse Post-Standard

Syracuse University Alumni News

Syracuse University Archives

Syracuse University basketball media guides, game day programs, and yearbooks

Syracuse University football media guides, game day programs, and yearbooks

Syracuse University Magazine

Syracuse University News

Time

United Press International

Upstate

U.S. News & World Report

USA Today

Utica Daily Press

Utica Observer-Dispatch

Washingtonian

Washington Post

www.syracuseuniversity.edu

Books

Collins, Allyson, Ashleigh Graf, and Courtney Rile. 2003. *100 Years of The Daily Orange's Best Stories (1903-2003)*. Syracuse, NY: Daily Orange Corp.

Falk, Peter. 2006. *Just One More Thing: Stories from My Life*. New York: Carroll & Graf Publishers.

Galpin, William Freeman. 1952. *Syracuse University, Volume I: The Pioneer Days*. Syracuse, NY: Syracuse Univ. Press.

———. 1960. *Syracuse University, Volume II: The Growing Years*. Syracuse, NY: Syracuse Univ. Press.

Galvin, Edward L., Margaret A. Mason, and Mary M. O'Brien, eds. 2013. *Syracuse University*. Charleston, SC: Arcadia Books.

Glickman, Marty, with Stan Isaacs. 1999. *Fastest Kid on the Block: The Marty Glickman Story*. Syracuse, NY: Syracuse Univ. Press.

Gorney, Jeffrey. 2006. *Syracuse University: An Architectural Guide*. Syracuse, NY: Syracuse Univ. Press.

Greene, John Robert. 1998. *Syracuse University: The Eggers Years*. Syracuse, NY: Syracuse Univ. Press.

———. 2000. *The Hill: An Illustrated Biography of Syracuse University, 1870-Present*. Syracuse, NY: Syracuse Univ. Press.

Greene, John Robert, with Karrie A. Baron. 1996. *Syracuse University: The Tolley Years (1942-1969)*. Syracuse, NY: Syracuse Univ. Press.

Keeley, Sean. 2013. *How to Grow An Orange: The Right Way to Brainwash Your Child Into Becoming a Syracuse Fan*. Bloomington, IN: Wordclay.

Kirst, Sean. 2016. *The Soul of Central New York: Syracuse Stories*. Syracuse, NY: Syracuse Univ. Press.

Leonard, Sheldon. 1995. *And the Show Goes On: Broadway and Hollywood Adventures*. New York: Limelight Edition, Proscenium Inc.

Marc, David. 2015. *Leveling the Playing Field: The Story of the Syracuse 8*. Syracuse, NY: Syracuse Univ. Press.

Mullins, Michael, and Michael Holdridge. 1989. *Syracuse University Football: A Centennial Celebration*. Norfolk, VA: Donning Co.

Norgren, Jill. 2008. *Belva Lockwood: The Woman Who Would Be President*. New York: New York Univ. Press.

Pitoniak, Scott. 1997. *Playing Write Field: Selected Works of Scott Pitoniak*. Rochester, NY: CASS Publishing.

———. 2003. *Syracuse University Football*. Charleston, SC: Arcadia Books.

———. 2011. *Color Him Orange: The Jim Boeheim Story*. Chicago: Triumph Books.

———. 2014. *100 Things Syracuse Fans Should Know and Do Before They Die*. Chicago: Triumph Books.

Pitoniak, Scott, and Sal Maiorana. 2005. *Slices of Orange: Great Games and Performers in Syracuse University Sports History*. Syracuse, NY: Syracuse Univ. Press.

Syracuse University. 1890-present. *Onondagan Yearbook*.

Tobin, David T. 2018. *Syracuse University: The Shaw Years*. Syracuse, NY: Syracuse Univ. Press.

Waters, Mike. 2003. *The Orangemen: Syracuse University Men's Basketball*. Charleston, SC: Arcadia Books.

Williams, Vanessa, and Helen Williams. 2012. *You Have No Idea: A Famous Daughter, Her No-nonsense Mother, and How They Survived Pageants, Hollywood, Love, Loss (and Each Other)*. New York: Gotham/Penguin Press.

Index

Courtesy of Beth Pitoniak.

Courtesy of Andrew Burton.

SCOTT PITONIAK is a nationally honored journalist and best-selling author of more than twenty books. The Rome, New York, native and 1977 magna cum laude graduate of Syracuse's S.I. Newhouse School of Public Communications has worked as a sports columnist for the *Rochester Democrat & Chronicle* and Gannett News Service, and has been a frequent contributor to *USA Today* and other national publications and websites. He also has been a correspondent for CBS television affiliates and has cohosted an ESPN radio talk show. Scott is the recipient of more than one hundred national and regional journalism awards and is a member of five halls of fame. The Associated Press Sports Editors and Professional Football Writers of America have recognized him as one of the nation's top columnists several times. A former adjunct journalism professor at St. John Fisher College, Pitoniak lives with his wife, Beth, in Penfield, New York.

RICK BURTON is the David B. Falk Distinguished Professor of Sport Management in the David B. Falk College of Sport and Human Dynamics. A 1980 graduate of Syracuse's S.I. Newhouse School of Public Communications, Burton's forty-plus-year career in sports marketing and management took him from Syracuse to Sydney (as commissioner of the Australian National Basketball League) and from Beijing, China (as chief marketing officer of the US Olympic Committee for the 2008 Beijing Summer Olympic Games) back to Syracuse. He is the coauthor of numerous books, including *20 Secrets to Success for NCAA Student-Athletes Who Won't Go Pro* and *Sports Business Unplugged*. He serves as Syracuse's faculty athletics representative to the Atlantic Coast Conference and National Collegiate Athletic Association. He lives with his wife, Barbara, in Skaneateles, New York.

(Following 3 spreads)

Map of SU. Syracuse University Cartographic Laboratory.

Mortar board tossing on the Quad is an SU commencement tradition.
@ Syracuse University. Photo by Stephen Sartori.

(Following spread) The SU campus looks resplendent on this sunny day.
@ Syracuse University. Photo by Stephen Sartori.

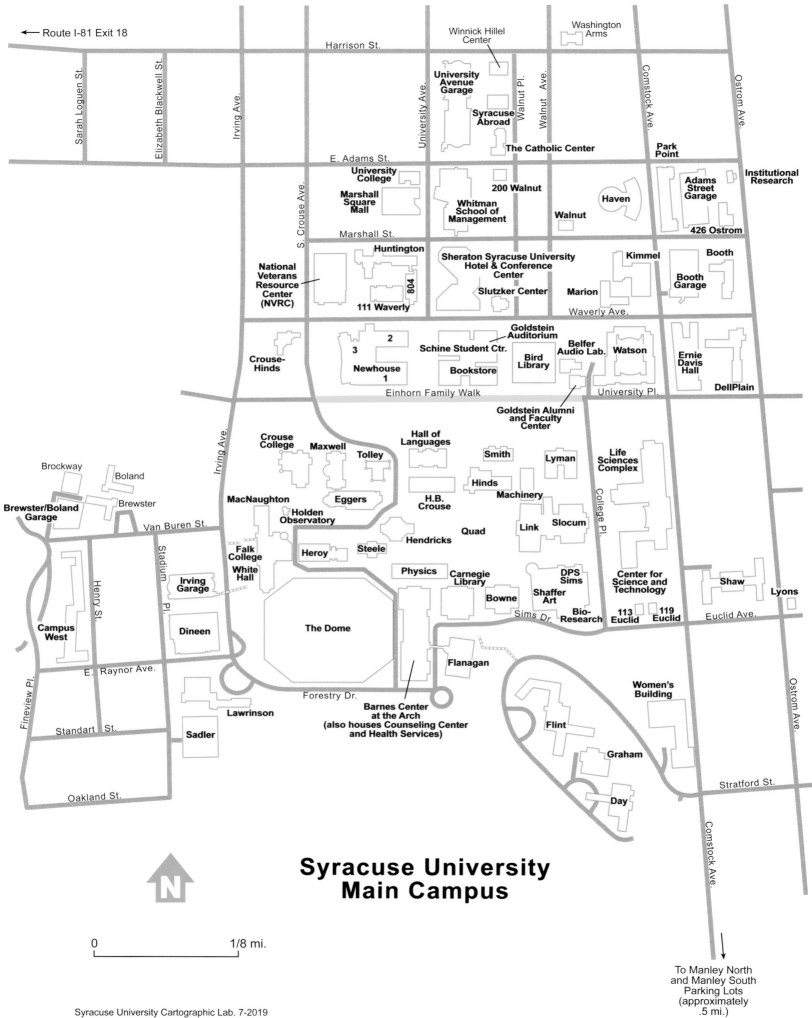

← Route I-81 Exit 18

Harrison St.

Sarah Loguen St.

Elizabeth Blackwell St.

Irving Ave.

University Ave.

Walnut Pl.

Walnut Ave.

Comstock Ave.

Ostrom Ave.

Winnick Hillel Center

Washington Arms

University Avenue Garage

Syracuse Abroad

The Catholic Center

Park Point

E. Adams St.

S. Crouse Ave.

University College

Marshall Square Mall

200 Walnut

Whitman School of Management

Walnut

Haven

Adams Street Garage

Institutional Research

426 Ostrom

Marshall St.

National Veterans Resource Center (NVRC)

Huntington

804

111 Waverly

Sheraton Syracuse University Hotel & Conference Center

Slutzker Center

Marion

Kimmel

Booth

Booth Garage

Waverly Ave.

Crouse-Hinds

3

2

Newhouse 1

Schine Student Ctr.

Goldstein Auditorium

Bookstore

Bird Library

Belfer Audio Lab.

Watson

Ernie Davis Hall

DellPlain

Einhorn Family Walk

University Pl.

Goldstein Alumni and Faculty Center

Brockway

Boland

Brewster

Brewster/Boland Garage

Crouse College

Maxwell

Tolley

Hall of Languages

Smith

Lyman

Life Sciences Complex

MacNaughton

Eggers

Holden Observatory

H.B. Crouse

Hinds

Machinery

College Pl.

Van Buren St.

Stadium Pl.

Henry St.

Falk College

White Hall

Heroy

Steele

Hendricks

Quad

Link

Slocum

Irving Garage

Physics

Carnegie Library

Bowne

DPS Sims

Shaffer Art

Center for Science and Technology

Shaw

Lyons

Campus West

Dineen

The Dome

Sims Dr.

Bio-Research

113 Euclid

119 Euclid

Euclid Ave.

Ostrom Ave.

E. Raynor Ave.

Fineview Pl.

Forestry Dr.

Flanagan

Women's Building

Lawrinson

Barnes Center at the Arch (also houses Counseling Center and Health Services)

Flint

Standart St.

Sadler

Graham

Stratford St.

Day

Oakland St.

Comstock Ave.

N

Syracuse University
Main Campus

0   1/8 mi.

To Manley North and Manley South Parking Lots (approximately .5 mi.)

Syracuse University Cartographic Lab. 7-2019

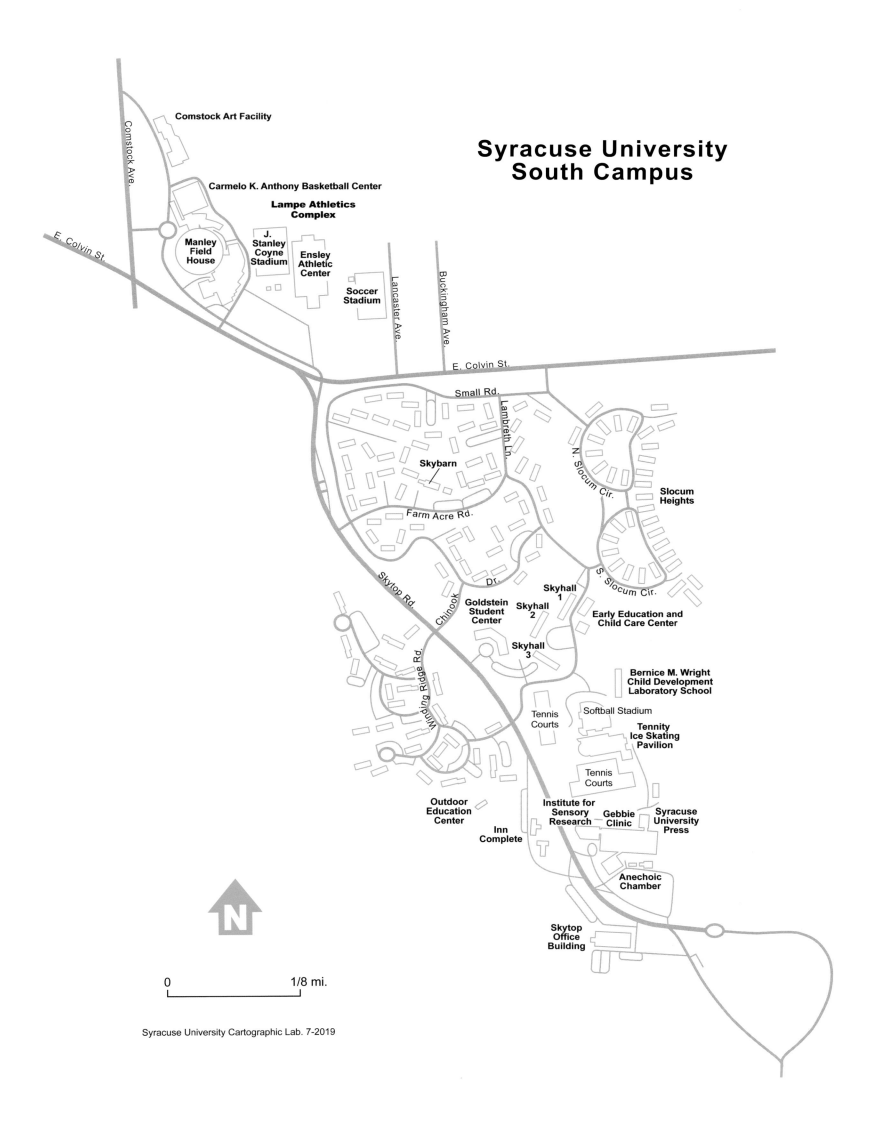

Syracuse University South Campus

Comstock Art Facility

Carmelo K. Anthony Basketball Center

Lampe Athletics Complex

Comstock Ave.

E. Colvin St.

Manley Field House

J. Stanley Coyne Stadium

Ensley Athletic Center

Soccer Stadium

Lancaster Ave.

Buckingham Ave.

E. Colvin St.

Small Rd.

Lambreth Ln.

Skybarn

N. Slocum Cir.

Slocum Heights

Farm Acre Rd.

Skytop Rd

Dr.

Chinook

S. Slocum Cir.

Skyhall 1

Goldstein Student Center

Skyhall 2

Early Education and Child Care Center

Skyhall 3

Bernice M. Wright Child Development Laboratory School

Winding Ridge Rd.

Tennis Courts

Softball Stadium

Tennity Ice Skating Pavilion

Tennis Courts

Outdoor Education Center

Inn Complete

Institute for Sensory Research

Gebbie Clinic

Syracuse University Press

Anechoic Chamber

Skytop Office Building

N

0   1/8 mi.

Syracuse University Cartographic Lab. 7-2019